Understanding the Global Economy

Howard Richards

Peace Education Books

First published in January 2000
Second Edition January 2004

Typeset and published by
Peace Education Books
P. O. Box 6214 Santa Barbara, CA 93160
http://global-economy.info

100% recycled paper ○ chemical free process

Publishers-Cataloging-in-Publication Data

Richards, Howard
Understanding the Global Economy—Second Edition
Santa Barbara, CA 2004

XVI, 311 P
Includes bibliographical references, index, review questions
ISBN: 0-9748961-0-1 LCCN# 2004100710

1. International Economic Relations
2. Globalization
3. Comparative Economic Theory
4. Feminist Economics
5. Economic Development
6. Ethical aspects of Economic Development

Library of Congress card catalogue
HF 1359R542004
dc # 371.1

Foreword

A more apt title for the foreword of this book is—welcome; for me that is what the book evokes. As a troubled world citizen and a struggling peace educator, I welcome Richards' work as a ray of hope in a foreboding time. Now a deep divide splits our humanity due to the gross economic disparities and resulting ecological devastation that blight our planet.

It seems an auspicious time for this volume to arrive. Questions, challenges, and crises are emerging in greater numbers and stridency from what Richards calls the "neoliberal juggernaut wreaking havoc worldwide." Now we turn from the century of great cultural significance, which formed the mentality that Richards chooses as well. And it is the beginning the International Year and Decade for a Culture of Peace and Nonviolence. This book offers profound insight and a likely cure to the underlying juggernaut with analysis and strategy toward resolving what is the major impasse of our time. In order to facilitate this, he examines the major relevant economic theories and provides a basis for the changes vital to alleviate the consequences and reverse the course of the collapse.

This time cries out for innovative approaches that go to the root of global problems and use the best reasoning to plan solutions. Richards' book does that, while it presents an antidote to the plodding pontifications of the mainstream economists and their critics. He shares his views of the metaphysics and the ethical flaws of what he argues to be the global market established by culture. He engages us in an approach that speaks—with us—rather than at or to us in the conventional academic style. He speaks with us about the most relevant and useful theories for understanding the present crisis. He communicates the nature and political power of culture in clear and complex terms that should easily instruct those who would propose theories and strategies to bring forth a culture of peace. That task, I would argue, calls us to understand a core assertion of this work: the global market economy is, in fact, culture. This unprecedented assertion provides more possibilities for change and cause for hope than most other analyses of the world's economic woes.

As a peace educator, I find *Understanding the Global Economy* to be, above all, an instructive model of modes of scholarship, argument, and exposition that should be added to the curricula of peace studies. The author advocates and defines holism as an essential component of his proposed problem solving method. He practices holism in his expositions, which explore multiple theories from various disciplines. He integrates those elements into a unified and comprehensive view of the global economy and the thinking that conceived and developed it.

Richards proves that scientific analysis can indeed be consistent with normative evaluation. He reintegrates ethics and values into economic discourse, as he helps us to understand that we face problems that call for philosophical rather than technical resolutions. The work contrasts the *instrumentalist thinking* that is the standard view imposed upon students of the global economy.

The narrative, in which he uses the works and theories of others to illuminate his own theories and prescriptions, will also represent an alternative to the standard adversarial argument that characterizes so much of academic discourse. You will find no absolutist pronouncements, nor shocking refutations, but rather sources that inform this work with a refreshing direct appreciation of what he finds to be the positive and helpful aspects. His style of discourse is one that peace educators seek to nurture in their classes. This book is useful as an exemplar of that style, apart from whether or not the syllabus includes the global economy.

His use of the concepts of transformation and ecology instruct precisely the rethinking that peace education seeks to cultivate; likewise, Richards proposes an alternative means to analyze globalization and thus a fresh analysis of it. If we are to escape the tyranny of technology that enthralls us as other forms of magic did our ancestors, we need to learn, as Richards advocates, thinking in terms of living systems rather than mechanical constructs. Such thinking may help us to understand that while the power of culture to form our world views and control our beliefs is far greater than we recognize, culture itself is evolving into other forms. If we can transform our thinking, we can transform our culture. We can achieve the purpose that lives in the goals comprehended in a culture built upon peace; paramount among those goals is a just global economy.

As well argued in this book, when we understand the global economy we can transform, humanize, and give strength to it. I welcome with vigor, the inspiration and the instruction offered by *Understanding the Global Economy* and welcome other readers to the confident learning it offers.

August, 1999

Betty Reardon • Peace Studies • Columbia University

Preface

This book began as a way to help my friends with their homework. (I have been helping friends with homework since fourth grade.) Now, as a member of the middle-aged professional class in California—when I am not teaching Peace Studies at Earlham College, Indiana—I have friends who see themselves, with reason, as victims of the global economy. They are engineers who have lost high-paying jobs as corporations have downsized or moved operations offshore. Other friends suffer in other ways, while still others are not suffering— yet. All of them—it is my destined honor to have socially conscious friends—are active within orgs that protest the global economy and seek to reform it. We all sense that the global economy has power over us and does not love us.

I wrote this book because I believed that my friends had not done their homework; they did not have time; they had no training in philosophy. I had the preconception that economics could not be understood, much less transformed, without philosophy. I think I always knew in the back of my mind that I had a thesis to prove. My initial plan was to review all of the scientific efforts undertaken to understand the global economy, without declaring any conclusions in advance. Thus, I wanted:

- ❑ outlines of the new and enhanced understandings of the global economy, outlines that would include and go beyond the knowledge and insight of all the extant theories
- ❑ my conclusions to state and prove themselves by the weight of the evidence alone
- ❑ the reader to see—guided by my survey—that there is a better way to understand the economic dilemma, which humanity now faces, thus to see the way to solve it.

My initial plan was vague, so I use this preface to state what I will try to prove and how I propose to prove it. Ultimately, even if the conclusions do not affirm themselves, I will have supplied a vocabulary for formulating them. I will be able to write my thesis in my terms and those borrowed from authors (such as Wittgenstein). I merely surmise about what concepts and terms are familiar to most readers; although, I do define some of the knotty ones, context often suffices. I state my thesis using the common terms: culture, cause and effect, and needs. **My thesis: the solutions to global economic problems are, in the end, cultural rather than economic**. Otherwise stated: the lines of reasoning by which economists explain international trade are, in the end, descriptions of how certain basic cultural norms work out in practice on a global scale.

Hence, social changes intended to alter the present disastrous course of events must—if they are going to solve humanity's fundamental problems—change culture. By contrast, traditional societies not fully incorporated into the basic normative structures that govern the global economy, in most cases, will find better solutions to their problems if, as a rule, their cultures do not change.

We should ask the question, "How can we construct a culture of of peace, justice, and ecological balance?" That question should precede and set the framework for more specific questions about what sets of economic policies to pursue. The process of making cultural change without which economics is powerless to solve the problems it addresses has two apt names: *cultural action* coined by Paulo Freire,[1] and *moral and intellectual reform* by Antonio Gramsci.[2]

The thesis that culture is the primary reality and that economic institutions and theories are forms of culture is explained by cause and effect. If we ask how and why the global economy became the way it is, then we are asking what mechanisms produced it and what mechanisms it uses to produce its effects. The short answer is: the market. I will argue that the market is best understood as a form of culture and that the cause is market culture of which the global economy is an effect.

As I review each major theory that claims to accurately explain the global economy, I will discuss, case by case: 1.) each theory's *normative basis*, which is its answer to the question, "What should we do?" and 2.) each theory's *epistemological basis*, which is its answer to the question, "How do we know?" The resulting theoretical matrix, which combines knowledge about the global economy with explicit or implicit norms to guide action, I will call a *metaphysic*.

The norm to guide our action, which has support from many precedents (which I endorse) is: invent and employ cultural forms that meet the needs of humans and regard the human family as a part of Earth's living systems. In effect, it is the love (care) ethic combined with the Earth ethic. Thus, I join the common term *needs* with *culture* and *cause and effect* to articulate my thesis.

In bringing to the fore the cultural basis of economic phenomena, I do not deny the validity of the explanations economists give. What economists predict often happens, in part, because their cultural assumptions mirror a culture that exists. Likewise, I approve of most all the critiques that progressive economists have made of the neoliberal juggernaut, which is wreaking havoc worldwide.

In Part 8, I comment on the twenty-six guidelines for political action formulated by Professor Jane Kelsey, a progressive economist from New Zealand. Although I agree with most of her guidelines, I also propose to modify and extend her action program. In Part 8, I outline a philosophy of culture, which views economics as a part of culture and adds important new contributions to implementing transformation, while it supports the conclusions reached by intelligent economists committed to the cause of social justice.

Readers may wonder why I do not refer to or cite popular books on the globalization of the economy. In short, I have limited my topic to scientific explanations of it. I discuss only books that claim to explain step-by-step why economic events occur. Scientific books have, or at least claim to have, a practical advantage that popular books lack: the principle of causal explanation, which is subjected to the rigors of empirical testing by confrontation with historical facts gathered and analyzed systematically. Arraying the historical facts under one or more explanatory principles enables the scientist to advocate future policy on the basis that the same causes will produce the same effects.

A classic example is Adam Smith's *Inquiry into the Nature and Causes of the Wealth of Nations*.[3] Taking the tendency of human nature to barter, exchanging one thing for another as an explanatory principle, Smith deploys an extensive array of historical facts to argue that the relative prosperity of Great Britain and The Netherlands in the 18th century is due to giving that tendency free reign in free markets. Smith's normative recommendation, a prudent and moderate policy of *laisser faire*, drew strength from the premise that the same causal factors that had operated in the past would continue to operate in the future.

A popular book, such as Jerry Mander's excellent work, *The Case against the Global Economy: and for the Return to the Local*[4] appears to have a logical disadvantage. Lacking a systematic explanation of why the world is the way it is, the popular book thus lacks a principle to justify the inference that the measures advocated will produce the preferred results.

Popular books, nevertheless, are helpful and important; in some instances, popular books that do not test scientific theories, nonetheless do have facts that will mobilize public opinion and change history. Certain popular books may even have better explanations than scientific books. Scientific theories propose generally applicable models to explain human conduct and institutions. In contrast, the events of history are often due to particular human actions unexplainable (or hard to explain) by general theories. For example, violence, lies, coincidences, surprise, passion, pride, illusions, and stupidity are powerful in the real world, yet hard to explain by general theories. Popular books—long on facts and short on theory—are likely to provide better explanations of current events and better insights into the particular human motives that produce particular actions. Attempts to achieve a scientific comprehension are most relevant to the steady persistent factors, which, in the end, shape the structures within which human action takes place.

Having limited my scope to theories that propose scientific explanations, I do not attempt to review all of them. Instead, I attempt to review all of the types of explanation they employ. First, I discuss what I find to be the logic relating causes to effects in a type of explanation of international trade, (such as comparative advantage theory or Marxist theory). I then desist from discussing all of the theories of that type because if my thesis is true of a general type of explanation, then it is must be true of any instance of that general type. In some instances, however, I may have failed to regard one or more of the extant scientific explanations of the global economy because either I was not aware of it, or erred by regarding it as a species of a genus previously considered. Thus readers: please bring to my attention scientific explanations of the global economy that contrast those described and analyzed in this book so that I can discuss it in a later edition.*

The Commission on Global Political Economy discussed the earlier edition of *Understanding the Global Economy* at the meetings of the International Peace Research Association in Durban, South Africa, in June of 1998.

Acknowledgment

For helpful comments on earlier drafts, or parts of them, thank you: Professors Jonathan Diskin and Gilbert Klose, Department of Economics at Earlham College • Professor Osvaldo Croci, Department of Political Science, Laurentian University, Canada • Dr. Catherine Hoppers, Social Sciences Research Council, Republic of South Africa • Professor John Newman, Departments of Philosophy and Religion, Earlham College • Richard Spahn first proofread • Roger Hand researched the footnotes. In this second edition, I thank the editors of Peace Education Books: David Faubion and Jeanene Clark.

New in the second edition: Part 10: • A Vision of a World Free of Poverty and Economic Insecurity; it unifies my previous research and analysis with insights and awareness from M. L. King, Gandhi, and five current social critics. • Part 11: A Logical Plan for Peace, which confirms the link between war and economic domination. Part 11 consolidates my view as a Professor of Peace Studies: working for peace is working for economic justice, which means economic security for all. Part 11 develops the conclusion of my book: the path to economic justice and security for all needs reevaluation by asking: 1) What is economic security? 2) How will we attain the universal economic security needed for peace? 3) How is economic security maintained?

New, as well, in this edition are review questions for Parts 1 through 11, except Part 8. The editors of Peace Education Books compiled the questions; I screened them. They did try to find the important and the concealed questions; nevertheless, the questions do reflect the editor's values and awareness. Please address your questions about the review questions to the editors at the web site listed below (with telephone access) or via postal correspondence found herein. Additionally, the editors will publish an expanded version of the review questions in a workbook format to be anounced at: *http://global-economy.info for updates the evolving topics of the global economy, which includes reader's input. The list serve: utge@lists.riseup.net is our interactive discussion of the peace and justice issues within the global economy and the related causal factors.

Howard Richards

Notes

1. Paulo Freire, "The Adult Literacy Process as Cultural Action for Freedom," *Harvard Educational Review*: 40, 2. May, 1970.

2. Tomas Valdivia, *Gramsci y la Cultura, Mensaje*. Santiago de Chile: 28, 285 December 1979.

3. Adam Smith, *An Inquiry into the Nature and Causes of the Wealth of Nations.* Modern Library Edition. New York: Random House, 1937. p. 13.

4. Jerry Mander, *The Case against the Global Economy, and for the return to the Local*. San Francisco: Sierra Club Books, 1996.

Contents

Foreword ..... **iii**
Preface ..... **vi**
Acknowledgment x
Notes x
Introduction ..... **xvi**
Notes xviii
1, Comparative Advantage **1**
1a. Comparative Advantage as Explanation 2
1b. Comparative Advantage as Prescription 5
The Natural is Good 5
Utilitarianism and its Successors 7
Deontic Ethics 9
1c. Comparative Advantage as Metaphysic 10
Notes 14
1a. Explanation 14
1b. Prescription 15
1c. Metaphysics 17
Review Questions 18
2. The Globalization of Production **20**
2a. The Globalization of Production as Explanation 20
International Division of Labor as Explanation 25
2b. The Globalization of Production as Prescription 26
2c. The Globalization of Production as Metaphysic 30
Notes 34
2a. Explanation 34
2b. Prescription 34
2c. Metaphysics 36
Review Questions 38
3. Theories about Choices of Technology **40**
3a. Technology as Explanation 41
3b. Technology as Prescription 44
3c. Technology as Metaphysic 48
Notes 52
3a. Explanation 52
3b. Prescription 52
3c. Metaphysic 54
Review Questions 56
4. Circular and Cumulative Causation: Trade Practices of Firms and Nations **58**
4a. Kaldor's Explanations 59
4b. Kaldor's Prescriptions 64
4c. Kaldor's Metaphysic 69
Notes 76
4a. Explanation 76
4b. Prescriptions 78
4c. Metaphysics 79
Review Questions 81

5. Theories of Historical Discontinuity 85
5a. Historical Discontinuity as Explanation 85
5b. Historical Discontinuity as Prescription 90
5c. Historical Discontinuity as Metaphysic 92
Notes 96
5a. Explanation 97
5b. Prescription 97
5c. Metaphysic 97
Review questions 98
6. Marxist Theories and the Feminist Theory of Maria Mies ... 100
6a. Marxist Explanation 101
6b. Mies's and Marx's Prescriptions 110
6c. About Metaphysics 112
Notes 114
6a. Explanation 114
6b. Prescriptions 118
6c. About Metaphysics 119
Review Questions 120
7. Post-Marxist and Post-Structuralist Theories 122
7a. The Disintegration of Social Science 123
7b. Escobar's Ethics 128
7c. Gibson-Graham's Metaphysic 138
Notes 150
7a. The Disintegration of Social Science 151
7b. Escobar's Ethics 153
Review Questions 155
8. How to Work for Justice in the Global Economy 158
1. Be skeptical about fiscal and other so-called crises: 158
2. Do not cling to a party that becomes neoliberal: 159
3. Take economics seriously: 160
4. Expose the weaknesses of their theory: 161
5. Challenge hypocrisy: 161
6. Expose the masterminds: 162
7. Maximize every obstacle: 163
8. Strive to maintain solidarity: 163
9. Do not compromise the labor movement: 165
10. Maintain the concept of an efficient public service: 166
11. Encourage local leaders to speak against the injustice: 169
12. Avoid anti-intellectualism: 171
13. Establish a think-tank: 172
14. Invest in the future: 172
15. Support those who speak out against the injustice: 173
16. Promote ethical investment: 173
17. Think globally, act locally: 173
18. Think locally, act globally: 174
19. Develop alternative news media: 174

20. Raise the level of popular economic literacy: 175
21. Resist market-speak: 175
22. Be realistic: 175
23. Be proactive: 176
24. Challenge TINA, (there is no alternative) claim: 176
25. Promote participatory democracy: 177
26. Hold the line: 178
Notes: 179
9. Scientific Conclusions 180
II 186
III 190
IV 194
V 197
Notes 205
Review Questions 211
10. A Vision of a World Free of Poverty and Economic Insecurity 213
Paul Volcker: 221
George Soros: 222
Jeff Faux and Larry Mishel: 224
Vandana Shiva: 226
Notes 228
Review Questions 230
11. A Logical Plan for Peace 233
Peace 233
Truth 238
Structure 243
Capital Flight 245
The Race to the Bottom 247
The Growth Imperative 249
The Holocaust 251
Transforming Rules, Relationships, and Practices 255
Summary 269
Notes 269
Review Questions 275
Index 282

Illustrations

Quasi-mechanical Market Forces 41
Technology Choices 45
Circular and Cumulative Causation 82
Market Growth 85
Positive Alternatives 200
Security Community 237
The Growth Imperative 278
Treadmill of Growth 280
Global Trends through History 280

Introduction

Citizens who seek to understand the global economy face a confusing array of scientific theories. The proponents of the theories claim to have the one that explains the global economy accurately.[1] That confusion adds distress to realizing the grim results of the global economy, for example:

❑ the decrease of union jobs with benefits in, e.g., New York, due to competition with low-wage labor in countries such as Indonesia and Mexico

❑ the loss of high-tech jobs in Massachusetts due to high-tech imports from Japan

❑ the stagnation of economies such as Haiti and the Dominican Republic with unemployment at fifty percent.

The effects on global politics are profound; they include the rise of the power of China and Southeast Asia and the corresponding decline of the power of the West.[2] The indirect effects, to which global trading patterns contribute as causal factors, are even more profound, such as:

❑ the destruction of the rain forests worldwide

❑ the breakdown of the social order in Somalia, the West African coast, Latin America, Indonesia, and other regions

❑ the instability of families and increased rates of: violence, drug use, and mental depression

❑ the penetration of US culture replacing traditional cultures worldwide, met with religious fundamentalism by people resisting the materialistic individualism.[3]

Today, a growing number of people throughout the world are aware of these economic realities:

❑ their daily bread depends on something called the economy

❑ they are vulnerable because the economy is vulnerable

❑ their local economies are somehow inserted into the international trading patterns

❑ what happens to them personally in their daily lives is affected by the distant commerce.

In spite of the broad and growing awareness, the effect of the global market on society is often underestimated; this has a conceptual basis, which will be diagnosed and treated herein.

Statistics show that about 8% of goods consumed in the US are imports. Statistics of this kind, for the US and other nations do, however, not show the full effect of living in an international market. A market is a place where goods are displayed and offered for sale. The buyers and sellers in a market decide what sales to transact and at what prices, by choosing among the alternatives that the market offers. Hence, the full effect of being in a large marketplace—the whole world—is not evident from physical facts such as goods crossing docks in cargo containers. The full effect includes the result of prices being influenced by the potential availability of alternatives not, (so far) in fact, chosen. Ferdinand de Saussure, the founder of modern linguistics, relied on that conceptual point when he explained *synchronic* meaning by analogy with the relative values of goods for sale in a market. The values of words, like the values of coins, depend on what they serve to exchange (trade) and compare (define).[4]

In light of the world's unrealized possibilities for trade, it is likely that a person can live in the global economy and never see a foreigner or foreign goods. For example, a worker earning low wages in a factory may never meet a foreign factory worker. In spite of that, one of the causal factors that determine the amount of one's take home pay is the millions of able workers elsewhere willing to do the same work for even lower wages.[5]

Besides emphasizing the broad influence of the global marketplace in contemporary life, the concept of a language as a market implies a corollary: a market as a language. This suggests that the scientific explanation of economic phenomena, including international trade, might proceed by comprehending a market as a system of meanings. For now, let us defer that idea until Part 9 and consider some of the scientific explanations of global economic phenomena, which students of international trade have offered.

Seven theories of international trade, some of which overlap one or more of the other seven, will be examined:

1. *neoclassical trade theory*, which is as much to say, the theory of *comparative advantage*

2. the *globalization of production* and, within it, the *new international division of labor*

3. theories regarding choices of what kind of technology to use as the creators of the global economy

4. Kaldor's account of *circular and cumulative causation* as an explanatory principle for the strategic trade practices of firms and nations, most notably Japan and his neo-Keynesian explanations

and prescriptions

5. theories of *historical discontinuity* as explanations of the genesis and nature of the global economy

6. Marxist theories and the feminist theory of Maria Mies

7. post-Marxist and *post-structuralist* theories

Roughly speaking, the scientific process of the theories is their efforts to test and demonstrate explanations of phenomena, which link causes to effects. When causes and effects are linked by a true explanation, the way is open to make policy proposals, which promise to achieve desired effects, through action that will cause them. I preface this paragraph with the caveat —roughly speaking— because the concept *scientific* is a contested concept. Herein all the scientific concepts or concepts explained in scientific terms I contest as well.

Notes

1. See the discussion of alternative theoretical frameworks for understanding the world economy in Helzi Noponen, "Trading Industries, Trading Regions" within the journal *International Trade. American Industry, and Regional Economic Development*. New York: Guilford Press, 1993. Julie Graham, Ann Markusen (eds.)

2. Samuel P. Huntington, *The Fading of the West: Power, Culture, and Indigenization*. "The Clash of Civilizations and the Remaking of World Order." New York: Simon and Schuster, 1996.

3. Daniel Goleman, *Emotional Intelligence*. New York: Bantam, 1995. pp. 234, 240.

> This [instability of family life] is not just an US phenomenon, but a global one, with worldwide competition to drive down labor costs creating economic forces that press on the family. These times produce:
> ❑ debt besieged families in which both parents work long hours, so that children are left to their own devices or the TV as baby-sitter
> ❑ the highest rates ever of children in poverty
> ❑ higher rates of single-parent families
> ❑ more infants and toddlers in substandard day care (virtual neglect).
> Thus, even parents who want the best for their kids see the rapid erosion of the nourishing exchanges with their child that build emotional competence. International data show what seems to be an epidemic of depression, which escalates juxtaposed with the adoption, throughout the world, of modern ways. Troup [a school] is in a decaying working-class neighborhood that, in the 1950s, had twenty thousand people

employed in nearby factories, from Olin Brass Mills to Winchester Arms. Today, that job base has shrunk to under three thousand, shrinking with it the economic horizons of families who live there. New Haven, like so many other New England manufacturing cities, has sunk into a pit of poverty, drugs, and violence.

4. Robert D. Kaplan, *The Ends of the Earth: a Journey to the Dawn of the 21st Century.* New York: Random House, 1996.

5. Ferdinand de Saussure, *Course in General Linguistics*. London: P. Owen, 1974. p. 115, cf. p. 79. (First edition in French, 1915).

6. Evelyn Iritani, "Global Glut Bringing Asian Chaos to Stable Economies: How Crisis Spread" in the *Los Angeles Times,* Sunday, October 25, 1998.

Marcus Noland, senior fellow at the Washington-based Institute for International Economics explained:

> It's difficult to judge the disciplining pressure that world trade places on national economies. The logs don't have to leave Norway. If everyone knows that the logs sit there, they can affect prices here in the US.

1

Comparative Advantage

Neoclassical trade theory is an application of *neoclassical economics* to the field of international trade. It argues that the optimal economic strategy for a nation is to exploit its *comparative advantages* with the most efficient means possible, through the free operation of production and product markets and open competition among companies. Extended to the global economy, neoclassical theory implies that:

- ❑ free mobility of products and factors of production across national boundaries will maximize efficiency [1]
- ❑ all economic factors are specialized in what they do best within a nation and between nations
- ❑ all resources will be allocated toward the industry or investment that will produce the highest rate of return, which results in optimal allocation of resources
- ❑ once the optimal allocation of resources is achieved, no one can become richer through further exchange without making someone else poorer [2]

Productive efficiency is also achieved through the exploitation of comparative advantages as companies are forced by competition in the market to use the most efficient production techniques available. Because—the wider the market, the greater the possibilities for specialization—it follows that the most efficient market is a global market.

An intergalactic market would be even more efficient than a global market, if beings to trade with were discovered in other galaxies, or if Earthlings were to colonize the planets of other suns.

Comparative advantage is conferred to a nation by its natural endowment of factors of production. A nation with abundant labor relative to capital will specialize in the production of labor-intensive goods. A nation with high savings rates, which make capital abundant relative to labor, will specialize in the production of *capital-intensive* goods. A nation endowed with natural resources will produce natural resource-intensive goods.

In 1817 David Ricardo wrote the classic case for the theory of comparative advantage. He used the concept of comparative advantage to explain why Portugal exported wine, while England exported cloth:

> To produce the wine in Portugal might take only the labor of eighty men for one year; however, to produce the cloth in the same country might take the labor of ninety men for the same time. It would, therefore, be advantageous for her to export wine in exchange for cloth.[3]

1a. Comparative Advantage as Explanation

The *explananda*, those things that are to be explained, are the facts of trade; central among those facts are facts about which nations export what products.

Although the facts about—which nations export what products— arguably are the most basic type of facts to be explained, other types of facts often commingle: facts about who succeeds in achieving export-led economic growth. That latter type of fact can be sorted by: regions, nations, industries, or companies. The facts to be explained include, for example, why:

- ❑ growth in Europe was slow in the 1990s
- ❑ Japanese economic growth was fast in the 1970s
- ❑ Germany is successful in chemical exports
- ❑ Merck grew to be a leading pharmaceutical firm

For these facts, neoclassical theory gives a name to the *explanans*, that which explains: comparative advantage. Because it has one or more comparative advantages:

- ❒ Portugal still exports wine
- ❒ England, in the early19th century exported cloth
- ❒ Europe's exports grow slowly: it lacks comparative advantage
- ❒ Japan had comparative advantage in many markets in the 1970s
- ❒ Germany still has a comparative advantage in chemicals
- ❒ Merck has a comparative advantage in several pharmaceuticals[1]

As with other well-known theories, the theory of comparative advantage is in danger of becoming true by definition, a tautology: a verbal formula compatible with facts that have been and may yet be discovered telling us nothing about the real world. The risk is that the concept becomes empty as the valid name for whatever happens. It is similar to the risk run by positive reinforcement: if people do what they do because they find it a positive reinforcement, then that motivates even the masochist who gains it through pain. Comparative advantage also runs the risk of being compatible with any evidence that is true whatever happens.

In Ricardo's original examples, comparative advantage was saved from being true by definition because Ricardo referred to certain physical facts: the soil and climate of Portugal, which is suited to growing the kinds of grapes that make good wine; thus, Portugal exports wine. These facts refine further by listing the molecular and crystalline structures distinct in Portuguese soil and temperatures at which the desirable chemical reactions inside growing grape cells most rapidly occur. The phrase comparative advantage then takes form in Ricardo's original context as a name for certain physical facts that may or may not be true at any given time and place, which would make their being true in the early 19th century in Portugal a significant fact.

Facts about the physical characteristics of the factors of production that belong to, fall upon, or are earned by nations and firms, thus, define a comparative advantage. The concept can then be construed in narrow or broad terms depending on how many factors causing trade to flow as it does, enter the example. We can explain why which nations export what products by observing the main comparative advantages of:

- ❑ cheaper labor costs
- ❑ superior technology
- ❑ cheaper compliance with environmental regulations
- ❑ government subsidizes exports
- ❑ reputation for reliable and high quality products
- ❑ superior marketing organization
- ❑ facilitation via bribes or intimidation of the buyer
- ❑ the seller owns the buyer as a foreign subsidiary or colony

In the limiting case, one may have no clue why nation X exports product Y successfully. One can, nevertheless, assert that the explanation of its success is that X has a comparative advantage; whatever the reason for the fact to be explained may be, its name is comparative advantage.

A scientific explanation (causal explanation), however, requires more than an *explanandum* to be explained and an explanans proposed to explain it. Disregarding for now some weaker senses of the term *cause*, let us take the term in two of its standard strong senses and postulate that to say that X causes Y is to say: 1) the existence of X is a sufficient condition for the existence of Y; thus, if X exists Y must exist and 2) X produces Y. When we put comparative advantage in the place of X, the explanans, (that which is supposed to do the explaining) and the facts of trade in place of Y, the explanandum, (that which is supposed to be explained) we get: 1) the existence of comparative advantage is a sufficient condition for the existence of the facts of trade and 2) comparative advantage produces the facts of trade.

Now we have a choice, suggested by the discussion above, concerning what kind of meaning to give to comparative advantage as either:

❒ a concept
❒ an economic theory
❒ a name for the facts, in the most apparent case, physical facts said to explain the facts of trade whatever the facts may be in any given case.

If we choose meaning 1), then the theory in question is open to the objection that it offers a more-or-less plausible story claiming to explain the facts observed. Once the facts to be explained are known, it is possible to spin any number of theories from which they can be deduced or predicted. For example, we know that Detroit has become a rust belt city characterized by poverty, crime, and vice; therefore, we can form a theory about the comparative advantage of Japanese automakers, a theory about the breakdown of US family values, and other theories, for which the observed facts serve as confirmation because the theory will predict the facts observed. The generality of a conceptual theory like comparative advantage makes it vulnerable to the charge that manipulation can make it true whatever the facts may be.[2]

If we choose meaning 2) we then give specific content to comparative advantage. Then it becomes clear that the facts that it explains are incomplete. Even in a simple case such as Ricardo's Portuguese wine, it is clear that, in addition to the soil and climate of Portugal, other factors must be present before wine barrels ship from Lisbon. Thus the comparative advantage specified is not a sufficient condition for wine export; a country could not produce a wine export by relying only on the factors of production Ricardo lists that give Portugal a comparative advantage.[3]

The inverse point is valid too: just as the existence of a natural comparative advantage is not sufficient to cause international trade, the existence of the international trade does not necessarily reflect a natural comparative advantage. An example among many is:

> The large quantity of grain that Poland exports every year would give the impression that the country is one of the most fertile in Europe.*

Those familiar with Poland and its people, however, know that even if Poland has fertile regions there are more fertile, better cultivated regions elsewhere, which do not export grain. The truth is that the nobles own the land in Poland, hold the peasants as slaves (90% of the population), taking their products and, thus, leaving them to eat barley and oats. While other Europeans eat most of their best grains, the Poles retain a small part of their wheat and rye; so, one might think the Poles only harvest their grain for foreign lands.[4] * From a dictionary of commerce in 1797

Regarded thus as an explanation of the observed facts of international trade, comparative advantage is either too broad, too narrow, or somewhere in between. When it is too broad it is a superfluous comment on whatever happens; when it is too narrow it is not a causal explanation; when it is somewhere in between it lacks substance to the extent that it is a broad theoretical construct without explanatory power to the extent that it is specific.

1b. Comparative Advantage as Prescription

Neoclassical prescriptions for international trade appeal to at least three types of ethical principles:

- ❑ natural law: what is natural is good [1]
- ❑ utilitarian: right is whatever brings the greatest happiness to the greatest number of people
- ❑ *deontic*/Kantian: respect for liberty is required by the moral imperative: respect for persons

Thus, one might object that I am reading history backwards and argue that capitalism formed first and then produced these ideologies to justify it:

- ❒ neoclassical economics
- ❒ the relevant versions of the natural law principles
- ❒ utilitarianism and its successors
- ❒ Kantian ethics. I will, for now, ignore that objection and treat arguments that advocate following the principle of comparative advantage in international trade as grounded in ethical principles; I prefer that to treating modern ethical principles as an essential part of the ideology of our commercial civilization.

The Natural is Good

To review: the physical facts like soil and climate define a comparative advantage as an *explanatory principle*. Other factors followed that explain trade flows, which may work with the principle. One of them was that nation X exports commodity Y because the government of X subsidizes the export of Y; that suggestion should stand out as an odd item on the list.

That an export subsidy would be a comparative advantage is unusual: subsidies typically interfere with the natural play of comparative advantages. *Government intervention* in the market may distort the market, thus, creating artificial prices. It is true that the concept comparative advantage can include a competitive advantage created by a government subsidy; however, it is more commonly true to narrow the concept in order to say that the subsidy violates the natural principles of trade. Such allusions to nature (explicit or implicit) illustrate the tendency of neoclassical economics to make a critical distinction between certain practices and institutions viewed as natural or not based on their relationship to capitalism. Those viewed as natural include:

❒ private property
❒ the market
❒ freedom of contract
❒ trading shares in stock markets
❒ taking security for loans.

All of these are disguised behind the positive moral "halo." In contrast, practices and institutions viewed as unnatural include:

❑ public ownership of a production means
❑ tariffs
❑ subsidies
❑ labor unions
❑ rent control
❑ cancellation of debt.

All of these are supposed to portray the negative moral "shadow."

Neoclassical prescriptions for policy, however, often draw strength not from the view that what is natural is good, but the view that human nature is bad; thus, it backs the argument that the decisions made by the market are better than those made by governments, which consist of fallible people. Competitive markets are not comprised of people in the same way that governments are. Competitive markets are impersonal and impose a discipline that is said to make humans behave better than they would otherwise behave; overall, markets manage to harness *selfishness* and make it work for human welfare. Given that human nature is bad, any deliberate policies designed to improve society by interfering with market mechanisms are flawed by power politics, corruption, dishonesty, influence-peddling, prejudice, and the like. Similarly, any appeals to higher motives will be less effective than the appeal to lower motives brought by market competition.[2]

Utilitarianism and its Successors

Neoclassical economics revises and restates the propositions of classical economics, which were expressed in late 18th and early 19th century England and France. In those optimistic days, leading thinkers expected freedom and the advancement of science to lead to happiness for all humanity. It was the task of the science of political economy to show that a free economy would lead to happiness. It was the task of the philosophy of utilitarianism to justify the expected outcome of free markets and free trade by showing that happiness is the goal for humans to pursue.[3]

One optimistic thinker, Jeremy Bentham, defined happiness as pleasure.[4] Bentham advocated evaluating legislation (in order to decide whether to enact it or to repeal it) by measuring how much pleasure it produced. Rousseau suggested a way to measure happiness even cruder than Bentham's schemes for measuring the quantity of pleasure produced by any given law. Rousseau measured happiness by counting the population.[5] Under unhappy conditions of extreme misery, most infants do not survive. Whether children survive, hence whether the population grows was, thus, for Rousseau, a measure of happiness.

At first mainstream economics allied itself with utilitarianism in maintaining the greatest happiness for the greatest number. They touted the specialization of labor guided by the law of supply and demand; they exaggerated its global corollary: free trade guided by the principle of comparative advantage. John Stuart Mill refined the concept of happiness so that educated tastes and perhaps even spiritual regeneration would count among the desirable outcomes the wonderful economic quasi-machine promised.[6]

Mainstream economics, however, withdrew the *happiness principle* because the free markets, in many ways, did not always lead to happiness. That was clear, for example, in the proposition of welfare economics that an extra dollar for a poor person buys more happiness than the same extra dollar would buy for a rich person,[7] which implied that sharing the wealth, rather than free markets, would maximize happiness. Mainstream academics discovered that happiness was a vague and unscientific concept and therefore, economics should omit it. Instead of taking happiness as the aim, one could rewrite, for example, the law of supply and demand with lists of people's *revealed choices*: made known whenever people walked into markets and took one product off the shelf instead of another, with an economist standing by to observe the facts of choice and count them.

The move from the happiness principle to the *choices code* made economics more exact and insulated it from criticism.[8] Having given up utilitarianism happiness, mainstream economics retained utilitarianism's premise: an optimum is always a maximum or a minimum. It continued to borrow tools from physics and pure mathematics for calculating the *maxima* and *minima* in general; the optimum prescribed was to maximize *preferred choices* (benefits) and to minimize costs. That the code of comparative advantage ought to be followed became a precision tautology.

A society in which everyone reveals all their choices will be one in which a maximum of preferences are revealed. Likewise, the traders in an international transaction reveal that they prefer what they buy to what they sell. The conclusion—the more trade the better—does not require a premise once the definition of *better* becomes established by choices because trade is mainly the name for the bargains that people, companies, or nations choose to make.

In the practice of economic research, the magnitude of the preferences revealed is measured by how much money changes hands; thus, it follows from X = X: the more that people buy the more they buy. Measures of welfare such as *gross domestic product per capita* are established mainly by counting how many dollars worth of goods and services are produced, which in turn depends on how much people are willing to pay for what they buy. An oft noted paradox resulted: where traditional cultures are being monetized, people become impoverished by: 1) detachment from their means of production and 2) dependence on unstable opportunities for wage labor for their subsistence. At the same time, the traditional peoples begin to suffer from what sociologist, Emile Durkheim called *anomie*: social instability resulting from a breakdown of standards and values because of the dissolution of the traditional social structures. For these two reasons, among the others, those people become more miserable. The standard statistical tools of mainstream economics (e.g., per capita income in dollars per year), nevertheless, report that *human welfare* (not *entitlement welfare*) is increasing.

Critics of neoclassical economics have called for the measuring of economic performance based in the physical reality. Hazel Henderson, for example, favors measuring:

- ❒ longevity
- ❒ air quality
- ❒ nutritional adequacy
- ❒ water purity
- ❒ sustainability.[9]

In a sense, she proposes to restore the division of tasks between the science of political economy and the utilitarian philosophers. The successors to the political economists are, thus, the Hendersonian social scientists, whose role is to study:

- ❑ combinations of markets and planning
- ❑ distributions and forms of property
- ❑ institutions for organizing work
- ❑ processes of international exchange of each element and as the permutations and combinations to produce a particular outcome.

The successors to the utilitarian philosophers are the Hendersonian evaluators and social critics, who provide the rationales for the measurements used to assess the outcomes. In such a framework, questions about the merits of using the principle of comparative advantage, however broadly the concept might be construed, would become empirical questions; it would be relevant to offer physical and psychological facts as evidence to answer them.

Deontic Ethics

The advocates of free trade no longer try to prove that a nation specializing within its comparative advantages brings prosperity to its people. They still claim that consumers are better off with greater access to inexpensive foreign goods though they have quit claiming that it makes consumers happy. Now it is enough to say that they get what they want. The moral case in favor of free trade, thus, relies less on a theory about what is good for people; it relies more on an appeal to freedom per se, regardless of its consequences.

The appeal to free consumer choice, therefore the case for free international trade guided by comparative advantage, finds support in those theories of ethics, such as Kant's, that make right and wrong independent of the results of actions. Such theories typically enshrine freedom as an overriding value that ought to be respected, come what may.[10]

The same overriding value is applied to the distribution of wealth within the principle known as *Pareto optimality*. It asserts that the distribution of goods in society is optimal when all willing trades have been made and there are no longer any two parties willing to exchange what one has for what the other has even if the disparity of wealth worsens; the option that the distribution of the world's goods could be improved by compelling someone to give something unwillingly is excluded as ethically unacceptable.[11]

1c. Comparative Advantage as Metaphysic

The theory of comparative advantage can be regarded as the application of neoclassical economics to international trade. In turn, neoclassical economics can be regarded as the application to a particular social science of the *metaphysic* of economic society. The general assumptions of economic society form the background from which the implicit and explicit premises of neoclassical economics are derived.[1]

My use of the term *metaphysic* instead of the more familiar terms *ideology* or *worldview* has more than one motive; moreover, it has my optimistic confidence. The system of metaphysics is the traditional activity of philosophers, which has contributed to the construction of Western ideas in general and of economic ideas in particular. Here I emphasize the extent to which *social reality* is a deceptive construct by design and I encourage efforts to reconstruct it. I share the romantic optimism of the early nineteenth century because I expect the right combination of ethical philosophy and advancing social science to lead to happiness for all humanity. Classifying the presuppositions of neoclassical economics as a metaphysical model is, among other things, a way of saying that economics can be improved and even superseded by the design and growth of a better social reality.

What I choose to call *the metaphysic of economic society* Louis Dumont calls an *economic ideology*.[1] Dumont compares the ideology (the metaphysic) of modern economic civilization to the ideologies of other great civilizations. He sees similarities between the central concept of his work, economic ideology, and a number of well-known concepts and theories in social science:

> We verge here on the forceful demonstration by Karl Polanyi in *The Great Transformation* of how exceptional the modern era is in the history of mankind in regard to the separation of the economic aspects and the sacred role of the market and its cohorts in the liberalism that dominated the 19th and early 20th centuries. I propose a wider view, while at the same time building on an old sociological tradition. The holism and individualism contrast as it has developed from my study without any conscious imitation is in line with Maine's Status and Contract and with Tonnies *gemeinschaft* and *gesellschaft*.[2]

It is well known that neoclassical economic theory begins with and presupposes the market and its cohorts of:

- ❑ private property
- ❑ rational economic actors
- ❑ competition

This fresh novel approach places the institutional structure of modern society and its ideological reflection—economic theory—into the context of:

- ❒ scientific explanation
- ❒ ethics
- ❒ the tradition of metaphysics

A *metaphysical shift* will challenge some ways of thinking of scientific explanation and promote others. In his seminal essay, *Interpretation and the Sciences of Man*, Charles Taylor proposes what I call the metaphysical shift. He argues that social science is now in a position to improve the quality of its explanations by taking a more perceptive view of the regularities observed in social behavior.[3] After Ludwig Wittgenstein, social science can improve its accounts of social phenomena by acknowledging and exploiting the relationship of human action to language shown by Wittgenstein in his later works. He thought of human action as governed by the *constitutive rules* of language-games (*sprachspielen*) in which discourse and practice are inseparable.[4]

A great deal of social science, in contrast, and in particular neoclassical economics, has taken the mechanism instead of the language-game as its implicit and sometimes explicit metaphysic.[5] Much of the vocabulary of economics, thus, is borrowed from the science of mechanics: equilibrium, stability, elasticity, expansion, inflation, contraction, flow, force, pressure, resistance, reaction, movement, and friction. Human behavior is, thus, simplified in order to analyze it in terms of mechanical metaphors.

Wittgenstein realized that thinking of reality in terms of machines, presupposes, what is often not the case, that it is made of parts which function consistently in standard ways. So, to dismiss metaphysics in general and in particular mechanistic metaphysics (ones by which he was most tempted), Wittgenstein wrote:

> If we know the machine, it seems that every movement it will make, is exactly predetermined. We speak as if the parts could only move in a certain way, as if they could not do anything else. Why do we forget that they might bend, break, melt, and so forth?[6]

Wittgenstein's theory fails to produce the usual product (output) from the usual factors (inputs); thus, it shows that the mainstream neoclassical economic theories fail to provide accurate predictions of economic behavior when the parts do not function as expected. Samuel Huntington provides an example:

> The easy assumption by Western economists in the 1980s that devaluing the dollar would reduce the Japanese trade surplus proved to be false. As the yen appreciated to nearly one hundred yen to the dollar, the Japanese trade surplus remained high and even increased. The Japanese were, thus, able to sustain both a strong currency and a trade surplus. Western economic thinking tends to posit a negative trade off between unemployment and inflation with an unemployment rate much less than five percent thought to trigger inflationary pressures. Nevertheless, for years Japan had an unemployment rate averaging less than three percent and inflation averaging half that. Japan's low level of manufactured imports, one careful study concluded, cannot be explained through standard economic factors. The Japanese economy does not follow Western logic.[7]

The unstable parts that falsify explanations and predictions offered by social theories rooted in the image of the machine are Homo sapiens, whose adaptation to its ecological niche is culture. Because economic culture is only one form of culture, the kind of culture whose metaphysic is that of economic society, the social change projects that are conceived and planned as exercises in economics do not fit traditional cultures. Larry Naylor's report on *Operasi Koteka,* a major development project undertaken in Indonesia illustrates:

> Operasi Koteka provided for the introduction of new agricultural practices, cash crops, and the wearing of clothing. Without a market-exchange system, wage-labor jobs, and knowledge of money, these changes had little chance of being implemented. The mandate that the local people wear new styles of clothing was clearly out of step with economic reality. It simply did not fit with local conditions let alone traditional culture. The purchase of clothing and its care required money. Although the Dutch had brought the concept of money, Indonesian money was just as strange as clothing to the Dani. As their traditional culture had neither markets nor money, the Dani had little understanding of money, little of it, and even fewer opportunities to acquire it.[8]

I noted in the context of Ricardo's classic example of comparative advantage, the export of Portuguese wine, that when comparative advantage is not a *tautology* it is an incomplete causal explanation. The sun shone on Portugal, and microbes beneficial for viticulture thrived in its soil, for many years before a single keg of porter crossed a Lisbon dock bound for England. This type of metaphysic—an institutional structure reflected and articulated as a logical ideology—brings about some of the additional conditions needed to complete the causal explanation of the wine trade. The requisite elements for the trade were:

- ❑ a market
- ❑ money
- ❑ rational economic actors
- ❑ accumulated capital devoted to business for profit
- ❑ a government disposed to encourage and protect trade.

It follows that a metaphysic has causal powers; thus, where a different metaphysic prevails, different human behaviors result.

A metaphysic: the system of basic concepts that frames an outlook and basis for both *epistemology* and ethics. In such a framework, epistemology and ethics support each other. I have argued elsewhere that such was the character and social function of the first book to bear the name: *The Metaphysics of Aristotle*.[9]

The market and its cohorts provide a common root and mutual support for a certain version of scientific knowledge and for a certain version of ethics. That is another reason for thinking of the theory of comparative advantage as embedded in a metaphysic. Thus, the market produces a result that is ethically unacceptable, when, as Frances Moore Lappé wrote, "The peasants of El Salvador who have no money are left voiceless at the dinner table." [10]

Neoclassical science rescues the market from ethical indictment. The answer to the indictment reads: that is just the reality because there is no *effective demand* for rice and beans in rural El Salvador, which, thus, has a comparative advantage in the production of cotton to manufacture clothing for export; so, naturally the land grows textiles to feed the insatiable export, while the satiable people go hungry. The scientific theory of the market as used here explains how the world works, whether we like it or not.

Then again, ethics does at times rescue science by: 1) permitting the preferred conclusion to be drawn and 2) denying that the facts as they are must simply be accepted. When Japan, for example, declines to import TV sets from the US, the facts do fail in terms that rely for their connotations on ethical criteria. The Japanese market for television sets is therefore distorted with artificial prices and government intervention into its free operation. Here the market reappears again, though this time, not as a brute (inescapable) fact, but instead as a normative ideal, which has been violated. The market and its cohorts, thus, bridge the is/ought divide in a most remarkable way—one that provides conceptual foundations both for statements of fact and for value judgments. This is another reason to think of neoclassical economics as a metaphysic.

Notes

1. Candace Howes, "Constructing Comparative Advantage: Lessons from the U.S. Auto Industry," in *Noponen* and others. op. cit. pp. 48 ff.; Candace Howes and Ann Markusen, "Trade, Industry, and Economic Development," in *Noponen* et al. op. cit. pp. 12 ff.

2. This is the Pareto criterion for optimality. William J. Baumol, in *Economic Theory and Operations Analysis* discusses it. Englewood Cliffs, New Jersey: Prentice-Hall, 1965, chapter 16, especially p. 376.

3. David Ricardo, *The Principles of Political Economy and Taxation*. London: J. M. Dent, 1911 (first published, 1817), p. 82.

1a. Explanation

1. Helzi Noponen, "Scale and Regulation in an Innovative Sector: Jockeying for Position in the World Pharmaceuticals Industry," in *Noponen* et al. *op. cit.* pp. 175-211.

2. The introduction to a UN statistical report on the world economy shows that when analyzing comparative advantage, the economists at first focused upon a country's relative factor endowments, such as labor and capital. Later, economists realized that much more needed to be considered as well: education, research and development, technology transfer, the availability of raw materials and feedstock, cross-border mobility, political constraints on (or incentives for) restructuring, and other realities:

> The interaction between the determinants of comparative advantage is more complex than they had first thought. Comparative advantage is a constantly changing concept. [p. 5.] In the end, comparative advantage refers to whatever determines costs.

Page 6, United Nations Industrial Development Organization (UNIDO), *Changing Patterns of Trade in World Industry: an Empirical Study on Revealed Comparative Advantage.* New York: United Nations, 1982. pp. 4-6. Instead of describing an explanandum, which explains why prices and trade flows are as they are, comparative advantage becomes a name for whatever the explanations may be.

3. Jacob Viner, after an extensive review of the attempts of 19th and early 20th century economists to quantify the consumer surplus or gain from trade produced by the operation of the principle of comparative advantage in international trade, thus, concluded:

> The theory of international trade, at its best, can provide only presumptions, not demonstrations, as to the benefit or injury to be expected from a particular disturbance in foreign trade; it deliberately abstracts from some of the considerations which can rationally be taken into account

> in the appraisal of policy; it never takes into account all the variables which it recognizes as significant and within its scope, either because they are out of reach or because to take them all into account would make the problem far too complex for a neat solution.

Jacob Viner, *Studies in the Theory of International Trade.* New York and London: Harper, 1937. p. 593.

4. Fernand Braudel, *The Structures of Everyday Life: the Limits of the Possible*. New York: Harper and Row, 1981. pp. 125-26.

1b. Prescription

1. The notion that the market (and therefore comparative advantage as a principle that guides international trade) is good because it is natural, seems to have been advanced first by the French physiocrats in their doctrine of natural order. Adam Smith later adopted it. See Sir Eric Roll, *A History of Economic Thought*. London: Faber and Faber, 1973, pp. 135-37, pp. 144 ff.

2. Sometimes reliance on higher motives spells disaster. Karl Popper, criticizing the application of a love ethic to politics and economics, thus, writes, "The attempt to make heaven on Earth invariably produces hell." Karl Popper, *The Open Society and its Enemies*. Princeton University Press, 1950. p. 422. Sometimes the problem with higher motives is that they are less reliable than self-interest. Adam Smith wrote:

> It is not from the benevolence of the butcher, the brewer, or the baker that we expect our dinner, but from their regard to their own interest.

Adam Smith, *The Wealth of Nations*: *1,* 2. various editions, first published 1776)

3. See Elie Halevy, *The Growth of Philosophic Radicalism*. New York: Macmillan, 1928.

4. Jeremy Bentham was a classical proponent of the view that because: 1) the purpose of life is pleasure and 2) each person has both the necessary expertise and motivation to pursue pleasure well: the market rather than the government ought to be society's principal ruling institution. Bentham wrote, for example:

> What the legislator and the minister of the interior have it in their power to do towards increase either of wealth or population, is as nothing in comparison with what is done of course, and without thinking of it, by the judge and his assistant, the minister of police. With the view of causing an increase to take place in the mass of national wealth, or with a view to increase of the means of either subsistence or enjoyment, without some special reason, the general rule is that nothing ought to be done or attempted by government. The motto, or watchword of government, on these occasions, ought to be —Be quiet. Jeremy Bentham, *Manual of Political Economy in Works*

of Jeremy Bentham: III. Edinburgh: William Tait, 1843., p. 33.

5. Jean-Jacques Rousseau, *The Social Contract*. various editions, first published in France 1762. Book III, Part 9. As with all the thinkers associated with the rise of economics, Rousseau was in conscious rebellion against ancient and medieval philosophy. He wrote:

> No people have ever been made into a nation of philosophers; but it is possible to make a people happy.

Jean-Jacques Rousseau, *Discourse on Political Economy*. (published first in France as an article in the *Encyclopedie* edited by Denis Diderot, 1755) in *Great Books of the Western World*. Chicago: Encyclopedia Britannica, 1994: 35, p. 374

6. John Stuart Mill, *Utilitarianism*. London: Longmans, 1879.

7. A. C. Pigou in *The Economics of Welfare*. London: Macmillan, 4th edition 1932.

> Utility is increased, with all other factors staying the same, by transferring wealth from the rich to the poor.

8. William Baumol describes how economics became more scientific by avoiding basing its analyses on an introspective utility. "Towards Observeability: Revealed Preferences and Expenditure and Cost Functions," Chapter 14 of his *Economic Theory and Operations Analysis.* Englewood Cliffs, New Jersey: Prentice Hall, fourth edition, 1977. The general idea was that economists should separate positive and empirical research from utilitarianism, the labor theory of value, and any other ethical framework. With respect to the study of comparative advantages in international trade, Eli Heckscher and Bertil Ohlin pursued that general idea, among others. See Bertil Ohlin, *Interregional and International Trade*. Cambridge: Harvard University Press, 1935.

9. Hazel Henderson, *Paradigms in Progress: Life Beyond Economics*. San Francisco: Bennett-Koehler, 1995. Hazel Henderson, *The Politics of the Solar Age: Alternatives to Economics*. Garden City, New York: Anchor Press/Doubleday, 1981. Hazel Henderson, *Creating Alternative Futures: The End of Economics*. New York: G. P. Putnam, 1980.

10. Ludwig von Mises sees a great merit of the market in that it requires no consensus on ethics.

> The market economy makes peaceful cooperation among people possible in spite of the fact that they disagree with regard to their value judgments.

Ludwig von Mises, *Human Action: a Treatise on Economics*. New Haven Yale University Press, 1949 p. 689. Von Mises holds that, in addition to its practical defects, socialism has the ethic defect that it does not respect the rights of individuals to make their choices.

11. Regarding Pareto optimality, see note 2, Part 1.

1c. Metaphysics

1. Louis Dumont, From *Mandeville to Marx: The Genesis and Triumph of Economic Ideology* Chicago: University of Chicago Press, 1977. See also, Louis Dumont, *Essays on Individualism: Modern Ideology in Anthropological Perspective*. Chicago: University of Chicago Press, 1986.

2. Dumont, *From Mandeville to Marx*. op. cit. p. 6. Some of the works to which Dumont refers are: Karl Polanyi, *The Great Transformation*. Boston: Beacon Press, 1944. Maine, Sir Henry, *Ancient Law: Its Connection with the Early History of Society and its Relation to Modern Ideas*. London: Murray, 1897. Tonnies, Ferdinand, *Community and Association*. a translation of his *Gemeinschaft und Gesellschaft*. London: Routledge and Kegan Paul, 1955.

3. Charles Taylor, "Interpretation and the Sciences of Man" in the *Review of Metaphysics: XXV*, pp. 3-51, September, 1971. The essay is reprinted in several anthologies.

4. Ludwig Wittgenstein, *Philosophical Investigations*. Oxford: Blackwell, 1956. 20th century Austrian born philosopher/linguist

5. Irving Fisher, *Mathematical Investigations in the Theory of Value and Prices*. New Haven: Yale University Press, 1925. (first as a doctoral dissertation, 1892, reprinted in the *Reprints of Economic Classics*. New York: August M. Kelley, 1965).

> Most writers on economics make some comparison between economics and mechanics. One speaks of a rough correspondence between the play of economic forces and mechanical equilibrium. Another compares uniformity of price to the level seeking of water. Another (Jevons) compares his law of exchange to that of the lever. Another (Edgeworth) figures his economic system as that of connected lakes of various levels. Another compares society to a plastic mass such that a pressure in one region dissipates in all directions. Thus, economists borrow much of his vocabulary from mechanics.

6. Ludwig Wittgenstein, *op. cit*. paragraph 193.

7. Samuel Huntington, *op. cit*. in note 2, Introduction., pp. 225-26.

8. Larry Naylor, *Culture and Change*. Westport, CT: Bergin and Garvey, 1996. p. 116.

9. Howard Richards, *Letters from Quebec: A Philosophy for Peace and Justice*. San Francisco and London: International Scholars Press, 1993. Letter 16.

10. Frances Moore Lappe and Joseph Collins, *Food First: Beyond the Myth of Scarcity*. Boston: Houghton-Mifflin, 1977.

Review Questions

1. What are the implications of comparative advantage that makes it an argument in favor of the global economy?

2. What makes a utilitarian premise such as: ethical is what brings the most happiness to the most people, an argument in favor of global economy? P 6

b. If you see it, explain how this utilitarian premise argues against the global economy.

c. How is the break from the utilitarian—revealed choice—more conducive to the global economy? P 7

3. Discuss the value of the role of the economist measuring of people's revealed choices.

b. Do you consider the monitoring of your purchases via supermarket cards or credit purchases a privacy intrusion or a necessary economic function?

c. Discuss the pros and cons of the mechanism and it overall effects.

4. Why is an intergalactic market (larger market) more efficient than a global market? P 1-3

b. For further consideration, what is the criterion of efficiency as it relates to global capitalism?

c. Discuss efficiency in terms of all the economic actors involved with the mega-economies: is a global or galactic economy more efficient for workers, consumers, ecosystems, resources, Earth, as well as producers?

d. In terms of what objective or objectives is efficiency defined?

5. What risk do society and individuals face in allowing an economic theory, which is a tautology (true whatever the facts) to prevail? P 12

6. How is the 16th century Poland's grain export a classic example of the deceptive use of comparative advantage as a rationale for global economy?

b. How does it compare to the textile exports in El Salvador today? P 4

7. What is the basic contrast between the neoclassical measure of economic performance and the Hazel Henderson realist approach? P 8

8. How is Kant's deontic ethic—that which is a moral obligation—used to prolong the argument in favor of free trade? P 9

b. How does Pareto optimality use the deontic ethic to justify the disparity in the distribution of wealth?

9. How does the improved quality of explanation in the social sciences, especially sociology help us to understand the economic metaphysic of society? p 10-11
b. How does Dumont express the economic metaphysic? p 10
c. How might the terms *metaphysic* and *worldview* be more apropos than Dumont's usage for a comprehensive system?
10. What is the obstacle inherent in the neoclassical economics' to acknowledging an economic metaphysic?
b. Would you consider this obstacle an aspect of an unknowledged neoclassical economic metaphysic?
11. Think of some common euphemisms, proverbs, adages, and clichés e.g., "make believe," which describe the process of a metaphysic creation?
12. "The Japanese economy does not follow Western logic," Japanese economic behavior might be taken to illustrate a number of facts about economic metaphysics. What are some of the facts as seen in the economics of Japan? p 11
13. "The advocates of free trade no longer try to prove that a nation specializing within its comparative advantages brings prosperity to all its people. " Do you see that as confessing the failure of free trade?
b. If so, how would you exploit the open confession toward reform of the global economy?" p 9
14. "They still claim that consumers are better off with greater access to inexpensive foreign goods though they have quit claiming that it makes consumers happy." What, in your view, does this suggest? p 9
b. Do you sense the quality of global goods declining more than their prices in relation to domestic goods?

2

The Globalization of Production

Since the late 1970s, a group of theorists have developed a focus on the new international division of labor and the globalization of production. It is a logical extension of the theory of comparative advantage, though with different results. According to the theorists, conditions in the late 20th century have made it possible to realize production on a global scale. It is mainly through both the age-old laws of property rights and the more recent trade agreements that:

❒ corporations now have carte blanche to transfer advanced technology to countries with low labor costs, while they:

❒ exploit the advantages of cheap capital in capital-rich countries

❒ relative production costs determine global patterns of trade, as it does within the theory of comparative advantage.[1]

Because of enhanced global mobility, a new capitalist world economy has emerged. Its main feature is a massive migration of capital from the industrialized countries to low-cost production sites in the third world. Because of *capital mobility,* capital-rich countries have no economic rationale for producing where the capital is; it is more logical to produce where the well disciplined, inexpensive labor resides.

2a. The Globalization of Production as Explanation

Central among the *explananda,* which the globalization of production theorists seek to explain, is a set of interrelated and concurrent phenomena, summarized as the:

❑ deindustrialization of the first world manufacturing areas: plant closings and other capital disinvestment

❑ moving production to third world countries with low labor costs,

❑ marketing products in the first world and, indeed,

❑ expanding markets to create a global market/global factory.

In a study titled, *Capital and Communities: the Causes and Consequences of Private Disinvestment,* two leading exponents of this type of theory, Barry Bluestone and Bennett Harrison, outline an explanandum that explains why these phenomena happen.

Under capitalism, private ownership, for the most part, controls the means of production; that includes the necessary machinery and equipment in order for society to produce more than the minimal subsistence for its members. To some extent, the ability to produce depends on the: 1) skills of employees and 2) capital: the tools and the money used to purchase the tools. When the products are sold, the revenue is divided between people who earn wages and salaries (workers) and the owners. The owners have, as Bluestone and Harrison say, every incentive to keep employee compensation down.

Their point survives the objection: it is often possible to make high profits by paying high wages, which attract skilled employees who are loyal and enthusiastic. Such possibilities, however, are not the rule because if it were possible to buy the same: • skill • loyalty • enthusiasm—while paying lower wages—then profits would be even higher. Bluestone and Harrison write:

> Employers must keep their costs of production down, which compels them to coax as much productivity from their employees as the existing technology will allow.[2]

Managers representing the owners use a variety of means to reduce labor costs in their companies because they are in constant competition with other companies. Workers use a variety of tactics to increase wages, notably action through labor unions and by the ballot box in Europe and the US in recent decades. Via the ballot box, workers can force owners to pay a portion of revenue as taxes to support social programs. Besides higher wages and overtime pay, labor victories include:

❑ unemployment insurance benefits
❑ pension rights
❑ public assistance
❑ disability insurance
❑ minimum wage laws
❑ health and safety regulations
❑ seniority rights
❑ some degree of job security, thus
❑ a *living wage,* narrowly so-called with benefits to augment.

Necessity as well as ambition drives owners in the never-ending battle to counter the efforts of workers to increase wages. The basic structure of the economic system forces them to keep the costs of production down. Markets have their ebbs and flows, technology changes are expensive to keep up with, and aggressive competitors are tireless in their efforts to sell a better product at a lower price. Every crisis drives many employers out of business, especially the smaller and weaker ones. Among the survivors is an intense and increasingly global competition.

The ceaseless battle to lower production costs is one that owners must wage in order to survive; those who win expand commercial empires and amass wealth; those who lose go out of business. The resources of the workers include:

❒ organizing drives
❒ strikes
❒ the right to vote en masse for pro-labor candidates—the owners still have greater resources as Bluestone and Harrison show:

> Against those resources, the employers have the legal right to:
>
> ❑ move their property from one place to another
> ❑ open and close stores, factories and offices
> ❑ seek friendlier governments and cheaper labor: a tool to be used against both workers and other competitors. Trade unionists are particularly concerned with how companies use capital mobility to:
>
> ❒ keep labor off guard
> ❒ play off workers in one region against those in another and
> ❒ weaken labor's ability to resist corporate attacks on the living wage.[3]

Thus, Bluestone and Harrison outline an explanandum, which discovers and therefore explains the phenomena observed:

❑ a socially constructed quasi-mechanism as explanandum
❑ an opportunity for profit is the input to the *quasi-mechanism*, which leads to relocation to low wage production sites
❑ the causal mechanism producing the result is the market force that drives companies to relocate their production to low-cost sites
❑ the enabling condition is property ownership, which gives the companies the legal right to move.

Nothing new of substance stands out in the Bluestone and Harrison account. Ricardo stated its main elements in 1817, as did Adam Smith in 1776. Bluestone and Harrison extend the classical logic of comparative advantage to the contemporary international division of labor.

Ever since economics began as an organized academic study almost three centuries ago, philosophers have compared its quasi-mechanisms to the mechanisms, properly so-called, of physics. Galileo's law of freely falling bodies (s = 1/2 gt2) is analogous to Bluestone and Harrison's explanation of industry relocation. Galileo's driving force is gravity; its analogy to economic *market forces* is clear. Thus—the enabling condition as the free space within which the body falls—is a metaphor of private property. The values of just a few variables permit Galileo to calculate the location of a body freely falling in space at any given time. In Bluestone and Harrison's quasi-mechanism, the values of more variables enter into the calculation, nevertheless, the result is similar: knowledge about the where and when of the back and forth movement industries. Perhaps most importantly, the economic quasi-mechanism and one of the mechanisms Galileo discovered are alike in that they are scientifically valid even though from a superficial viewpoint they sometimes contradict experience. If you hold a feather and let it fall, its trajectory, as seen from a superficial viewpoint, will not conform to Galileo's law, which, nevertheless, is still valid. When you correct for friction, wind, and air pressure you will have explained the trajectory of the feather. Moreover, without Galileo's law you will not be able to explain its trajectory.

Likewise, by 1817 Ricardo had realized that the classical economic description of market forces implies that capital will move wherever higher profits are to be made. Ricardo recognized that greater profits could be achieved by reducing production costs exclusively, he thought, by lowering wages. He was aware that the economic mechanisms he was analyzing implied that capital would pursue profit around the globe; thus, he asked why the phenomena predicted by the theory did not (in his day) occur more often. He answered:

> Experience shows that the insecurity of capital, when not under the direct control of its owner, with the reluctance that everyone has to quit their country of birth and ties and entrust, with all habits fixed, to a strange government and new laws, curbs the emigration of capital. These feelings, which I should be sorry to see weakened, induce most men of property to be satisfied with a low rate of profits in their country, rather than seek a greater return on their wealth in foreign nations.[4]

The explanandum for Ricardo, for Bluestone and Harrison, and for Galileo threatens to prove too much. It is reduced by postulating a cause with simple and uniform results, which contradicts the complexity of the fact observed. To be true to reality, the causal quasi-mechanisms discovered must be supplemented by accounts of the various kinds of friction that modify the effects that the causes produce.

For Ricardo, the major source of friction that impedes the globalization of production was the capitalist's fear for his security and property. Bluestone and Harrison agree via this corollary:

> When the world becomes better policed so that investors everywhere can feel assured that their property will not be stolen anywhere, the inherent tendency of market forces to bring about the globalization of production will come to the fore and assert itself.

Describing the first great wave of globalization: the expansion of US industry overseas after WW II, Bluestone and Harrison recount the political and military policies of that era, which contributed to making the world safe for US capital and, ultimately, for anyone's capital. In retrospect, the many third world civil wars of the era in which right-wing regular armies put down left-wing rebels, appear as a pacification paving the way for investment. The rebels, even when they had Soviet support, tended to promote traditional and ethnic values; it was the regular army, with US and, at times, European support, which was held the revolutionary values. The army was preparing the way for the massive social change, which in fact happened—the "MacDonaldized" world. About this era, Bluestone and Harrison write:

> US military policy and US foreign aid were vital in extending the global reach of US industry. Whatever their manifest military purposes, US troops, military advisors, offshore cruising naval vessels, strategic long-range bombers, and, finally, long-range ballistic missiles, all helped, at least indirectly, to protect and extend US business abroad. During these years, the US government made commitments to a whole network of antidemocratic dictatorships, whose leaders seemed dedicated to, along with keeping themselves in power, promoting the entry of US business into their economies. In this context, many of the new US third world allies—South Korea, Taiwan, Brazil, and Argentina—courted US corporations with temptations, such as low wages and prohibitions of free union activity.[5]

Bluestone and Harrison distinguish between a cause and reinforcement: a cause, like Galileo's gravity, is a fundamental operating factor; however, a cause can be mitigated or reinforced, slowed or speeded, as the force of gravity slows by friction or speeds by a downward push. Thus, they find that US tax laws after WW II accelerated globalization because they favored big business, which was in the process of becoming multinational. Likewise, technical improvements in communication and transportation were important reinforcements of the trend toward globalization—though not important enough to make them causal. Bluestone and Harrison wrote:

> As with the new technologies of production, transportation, and communication, it is not the case that the preferential tax and tariff treatment of foreign investment caused US corporate managers to shift their capital abroad. Instead, these public policies reinforced corporate decisions that were based on factors that are more important: markets, labor costs, and political security. [6]

International Division of Labor as Explanation

About half of all international trade occurs among multinational corporations, as different subsidiaries and divisions of the same corporation ship goods back and forth to each other. The international division of labor explains this trade by the principles of minimizing costs and maximizing profits. Consider this simple example:

Country A has low wages, high taxes, and, thus, it has impoverished consumers.

Country B has slightly higher wages, low taxes, and slightly less impoverished consumers.

Country C has high wages, high taxes, and rich consumers.

Widget International Inc. therefore, will, do its basic manufacturing in Country A. Its subsidiary in Country A will then sell the nearly finished product to the subsidiary of Widget Inc. in Country B at a low price. Widget will pay low wages because wages in A are low. It will pay low or zero taxes because, even though the tax rate in A is high, its Country A subsidiary will sell its goods at a price just high enough to cover costs; therefore, the Country A subsidiary will make little or no profit. The Widget subsidiary in Country B will then put a few final changes on the product and sell it at a high price to the Widget subsidiary in Country C. The cost of wages will be low because not much labor will be done in Country B. The cost of tax will be low because tax rates in 'B are low. The profits from—buying cheap and selling dear—may be piled up in B. More likely, the profits made in B will move back and forth among bank accounts in countries D, E, and F, which are selected because they are, at a given moment, the favorable places to keep cash. The Widget subsidiary in C then sells the finished product to the rich consumers in Country C. The wage cost is low because Widget Inc. runs only a sales operation in C. The tax cost will be low because the Country C subsidiary makes very little profit, because of the high cost of goods purchased from the Country B subsidiary.

The international division of labor uses similar principles to explain transfers within corporations much more complex than this simple example.

2b. The Globalization of Production as Prescription

Those who praise globalization attribute ethical merit to it. It is said to:

❑ proceed according to sound moral principles
❑ maximize that which ought to be maximized
❑ spread modern ideals of liberation and inclusion worldwide.

Beyond the positive value judgments grounded on principle, praise for the new international division of labor appears not to rely on a principle; except, that is, to express a sense of satisfaction or triumph so that globalization basks in the glow of a favorable light; thus, Rehman Sobhan, for example, advocates that labor services be treated as any other commodity.[1] He writes:

> South Asia remains the main source of international trade in labor. The colonial practice of labor export only showed the way to the post-colonial generation, with their limited opportunities for employment at home. In response to their greater opportunities open to enterprising young men willing to work long hours at low wages in the hostile terrains, sustained a flow in even greater numbers throughout the 1950s and 1960s, as improved communications contracted the global village.[2]

The scholars from Malaysia and Taiwan proudly set forth statistics showing the growth of their nation's economies. As well, Sobhan celebrates a global labor market that creates new opportunities for the most impoverished; thus, it gives a new status to nations and regions previously neglected, which investors now prefer because of their abundant willing labor.

The principled justification of globalization begins with the ethical underpinnings of the quasi-mechanism that causes it. Market forces and property rights are the essential elements of Bluestone and Harrison's scientific explanation of the phenomena observed. Freedom is the ethical ideal embodied in the market. The classics of modern ethical philosophy—Rousseau, Locke, Spinoza, Bentham, Mill, and Kant—are alike in establishing principled moral foundations for economic society, i.e. for freedom and for property.[3] The logical apparatus used to derive the conclusions differ by author, yet these same fundamental conclusions remain:

❑ the basis of moral legitimacy is free consent
❑ respect for property rights is a: • moral imperative and • *categorical*

imperative in Kant's version: a moral command valid for all rational beings and akin to:

- ❑ respect for other people's freedom
- ❑ keeping promises and contracts.

As long as the market forces and property rights elements of the quasi-mechanism driving globalization are intact, it will move forward; as long as modern liberal ethics define the moral rules, globalization can move forward as a legitimate entity; which is not to say that globalization always moves forward lawfully. As a rule, history consists of lies and violence; the history of the globalization of labor and capital markets is no exception.[4]

Suffice it to say that a great deal of ink and a great deal of breath is wasted in printing and shouting matches attempting to establish whether: 1) the partisans of grassroots local self-sufficiency or 2) the partisans of free trade and 1b) the left wing dictators or 2b) the right wing dictators—have lied more, tortured more, and massacred more.

Globalization on its best behavior is a faithful student of "Ethics 101" as it is taught in Western and Western-influenced universities around the world.[5] When, for example, assembly factories move from the US to the *maquiladoras* in Mexico, they justify themselves by appealing to the standard ethical principles. For example, the young Mexican women hired to assemble television sets freely consent to their employment, wages, and working conditions. Moreover, the property rights of the factory owners authorize them to move their assembly plant wherever they choose to relocate them.

Capitalism as a Western institution has become a global institution; wherever it goes it carries Western values. When assimilation into the global economy means that work for wages replaces household work or feudal forms of labor, the result liberates the wage earner as the: wife, young woman, young man, landless sharecropper peasant. For that reason, the globalization of production may get credit for liberating the oppressed and, thus, improving the morality of traditional societies. Nevertheless, at other times and concurrently, globalization spreads materialism and the values of US individualism. Always, the global or local capitalists use sweatshops and other patriarchal forms of production that combine the worst of the old and the new.

In the same way, any increase in the use of money to govern human relationships and practices may point to an increase in tolerance. Money is:

- ❑ a cipher, a neutral medium, and a pure abstraction consisting of quantity with no qualities

❑ the same whether it comes from a Jew, a black, a woman, a man, a Muslim, a Japanese, Catholic, or Protestant

❑ indifferent to the personal qualities of the people who use it to enter into commercial transactions with each other; thus, it:

❑ brings together people of diverse ethnic backgrounds and cultures. The globalization of production, therefore, with the free flow of capital and labor across national boundaries, guided only by the principle of profit seeking that is—money—appears to be the fulfillment of the ideal of tolerance. No one with money faces discrimination or rarely, whatever the person's other qualities may be. The globalization of production in theory, thus, appears to have an affinity with the best modern ideals:

❑ freedom
❑ personal autonomy
❑ independence
❑ tolerance
❑ cultural diversity
❑ equality, though only in some respects. Many, even scholars, consider free trade to be a corollary of the ideals of the Enlightenment. Therefore, constructive alternatives to globalization have the drawback that critics may perceive them as opposed to the moral progress of the last three centuries.

In technical terms, mainstream economists justify globalization as more efficient. William Baumol prescribes a criterion of efficiency:

> Never take resources out of a use where they bring in say, 9 % in order to utilize them in a manner that yields 6 %! [6]

Thus, maximizing the rate of return is clothed with a moral imperative derived from society's need to ensure the efficient use of resources.

Progressive economists criticize the mainstream's efficiency criteria with examples such as: Ford Inc., which gradually lets a plant in Michigan become obsolete, closes it, and builds a plant in Brazil. The move is efficient according to Baumol because the yield on investment goes up from 6% to 9%. It is a profitable move for Brazilian workers, who now make two dollars per hour instead of one. It is unprofitable for US workers, who suffer from psychic depression, move their kids to new schools in new towns, and on average, make ten dollars per hour instead of twenty. Moreover:

❒ communities are torn apart
❒ buildings are at least temporarily abandoned
❒ real estate values fall
❒ the tax base falls
❒ social services are cut back.

When all the gains and loses total, the net result is that the move was socially inefficient, even though from the point of view of the few Ford shareholders it was efficient, at least in the short-term. Thus, if Ford had internalized all the external costs it was imposing on others by its decision, it would have made a different decision.[7]

I believe that the economists on both sides of such debates have the best of intentions; however, I suggest that Hazel Henderson's approach is a better ethical framework for evaluating global corporations, trade institutions, and policies. The term *efficient* is meaningless without a specific pursued objective. Efficient therefore describes achieving the quantity objective at the least cost, or a higher quality at the same cost.[8] In the Ford example, I would agree with Buckminster Fuller that the manufacture of most automobiles is not an ethically defensible objective; so whether they manufacture in Brazil or Michigan ought to be a moot point. The point is that we should be making light rail and bicycles.[9]

The term *efficient* seems meaningful to economists because they treat the consumer's revealed choices, which become sales transactions and, thus, revenues in dollars, as an indication that something worthwhile was achieved. They excuse themselves from asking what or why. Seen in this light, the claim that globalization is efficient has no meaning. Allocating resources by market criteria is a form of ethical skepticism. Not knowing what good means and, thus, not being able to define a good objective, the economists settle for calculating how to allocate resources to maximize profits. An economist would hope that profits reflect a market, which has persuaded people (with enough money) to buy products. This then justifies that the economist consider profits as: an indication of how efficiently allocated the resources are overall. In an indirect way, this ought to reflect how much welfare was derived from the resources consumed; whereas, in turn, ethical skeptics define welfare as: people getting whatever they appear to want.

Henderson's approach: ecology and the wisdom of the world's great spiritual traditions (the approach to ethics that I advocate and develop in detail in another book[10]) shows ways to make a concept like efficient meaningful. Efficiency is a concept that if it has any prescriptive force, logically requires justifying the pursued goals.

Even with legitimate Hendersonian objectives specified, the concept of *efficiency* is still defective because it generally implies that there is one best way to do something (subject to any given set of constraints), and that the one best way can be calculated as a maximum or a minimum.[11] Nature, Aristotle, and the traditional wisdom of the East and West agree that *good* is characterized by redundancy rather than committing all resources to a single best way; thus, the good is characterized by moderation, not by extremes.

Apart from its association with the enlightened morality of modern times and its specious claim to be efficient, the globalization of production is advocated upon the premise that its opponents have no better alternative. Nonetheless:

❑ would you compel capital to stay forever where it is?
❑ how would you enforce a law against capital flight?
❑ should all international trade be state trading?
❑ if we want government to manage trade by slowing the rate of capital mobility, what criteria will determine an effective policy?
❑ how then will it enforce its policies without driving capital into hidden Swiss bank accounts?
❑ should the state compel landless peasants to stop producing cash crops for export, returning to producing for use?
❑ should each nation produce for itself prohibiting all imports?
❑ is it feasible for labor unions to organize worldwide to counteract the multinational corporations?
❑ how could Japan survive with less trade?
❑ should we go back to:

- barter trade
- the *potlatch:* Chinook Native American celebration: a contest of giving, morphed into *potluck* replacing trade with gift giving
- self-sufficient medieval manors?

❑ would it be possible for all companies to become nonprofit; even so, would it do any good?

For those of us who complain about the global economy, such questions challenge us to find or create a better way.

2c. The Globalization of Production as Metaphysic

Metaphysics has not become a less controversial term since I suspended my discussion of it at the end of Part 1c. Metaphysics is, for many people, synonymous with meaningless words without content and or context. For others, metaphysics denotes an abstract form of religion, a withdrawal from the world to contemplate ultimate reality; its concerns are so distant from the joys and sorrows of life that they could not be relevant to the price of bread, or to any other practical issue.

Oddly though, while it is the consensus of many 20th century minds that metaphysics is an irrelevant nothing, this century a number of philosophers have built their careers on attacking metaphysics, as if it were a ghost that needed constant burial. Some of these anti-metaphysicians, such as Rudolf Carnap and Sir Alfred Ayer,[1] are willing to grant that a metaphysic may express the subjective attitude of the person who believes it, provided that it is understood that metaphysics has no cognitive content. For others, such as Jacques Derrida and Ludwig Wittgenstein, metaphysics is a harmful error that humans can hardly avoid; we are tempted to it by language, as we are tempted to lust by our bodies.[2]

Two decades ago, the general educated public found a use for the word *metaphysics* when critics of the Vietnam war attributed to advocates of the war a *military metaphysic*. Because of their military metaphysic, they could not see the reality of the suffering in Southeast Asia. Their perceptions filtered through the lenses of a general way of viewing the world, such that military terms interpreted everything. Similarly, I argue that people today do not (can not) see the reality of the suffering in Southeast Asia, or anywhere else, because of an *economic metaphysic*.

Here, I will resume my discussion of metaphysics and make two points: 1) the globalization of production is the consequence of the metaphysic of economic society and 2) it is useful in practice to regard mainstream economics as a metaphysic. The cause of the globalization of production revealed itself as market forces and property rights, which are metaphysical concepts for the reason noted. They are fundamental ideas from a matrix, which generates both explanation and prescription.[3] In answer to the question, "Why?" both mainstream economists and progressive economists such as Bluestone and Harrison say:

> It is because of market forces. In answer to the questions, "With what right?" and "By what authority?" the classical philosophers and jurists of economic society answer, "By the authority of contracts freely entered into and by the consent of the parties."

Then those contracts freely entered into—sales, leases, hiring, currency exchange transactions, and investments—turn out to be just the phenomena the behavior of which economists describe in terms of market forces. The same is true of the fact of property, which serves as a basis for Bluestone and Harrison's explanation of global capital mobility. Property is also a value according to John Locke:

> Property is the value for the protection of which humans first entered into social contracts, to thus form political societies.

According to John Stuart Mill:

> The moral rules defining property rights are so fundamental to society that they are the moral principles to which the word *justice* primarily refers and violation of which is properly punished by imprisonment.

The quasi-mechanism producing the globalization of production is metaphysical for another reason: it preexists as presupposed rather than as a discovery. Employing the term used by Aristotle and Kant, market forces and property rights are categories, i.e. concepts in terms of which whatever is experienced is understood. The economist does not set out to discover whether markets and or forces exist. That reality, understood as a play of forces, factors, and variables, is not a discovery of economic science; instead, it exists as part of a worldview built into the mathematical tools and statistical methods that economists use.

The economics professor's hypotheses were quantified as propositions about the impact of a particular X on a Y, so X and Y were always on the blackboard. If one were of a mind to quibble about a minor inefficiency, one might complain that chalk and human energy were wasted every evening when the janitor erased the X-axis and the Y-axis, because right after 9 o'clock the next morning, the professor would always draw them again.[5]

Likewise, whether there is such a thing at any given time and place as a market or property, which are the normative entities, is a question an anthropologist might ask a historian such as Polanyi or Braudel. Inside the worldview of economic society and mainstream economic science, markets and property are concepts in which experience is understood. They give form to economics, though their existence or nonexistence is not data that economists seek.[6]

Nevertheless, the normative entities as 1) markets and 2) property rights move capital and labor around the world in search of profits and jobs. Therefore, the normative entities are presupposed by an economic metaphysic that forms the quasi-mechanism formed of social practices and the rules governing them. Thus, it is useful to be aware:

❑ of the metaphysical basis for the causes of the globalization of production. For the sake of all life, we want the quasi-machine to stop operating like a machine. It helps to know that, so far, it is only a quasi-machine

❑ that to reconstruct the global economy for the sake of peace and social justice, it is necessary to change both what the mainstream economics considers and what it presupposes that:

❑ by changing norms, we can cause facts to change

As Rom Harre defined it, "By reinterpreting social institutions, we change their causal powers"

- ❑ the explanations given by economic science depend on the existence of a metaphysical framework that has a history. Its categories and the institutions they describe, which is its language-games,[8] did have a beginning; thus, the categories and institutions may have an end as well. Humanity may graduate to a more adequate economic metaphysic.

Even at the practical level, it is useful to understand the metaphysical basis of society's dominant guiding worldview. Because, when we evaluate it, we realize that we cannot transform the basic structure of global society all at once. Perhaps known to many and likely to professionals in peace studies and research—we cannot build positive peace without transforming the basic structure of global society. Meanwhile, we take on small projects that we believe will contribute to transformation such as:

- ❑ planning a curriculum
- ❑ supporting alternative approaches to community organizing
- ❑ leading a work camp
- ❑ organizing cooperatives
- ❑ presenting conflict-resolution workshops for prisoners in jails.

When we evaluate it, we wonder, "Are we taking the right course to, in fact, reform society or just easing a particular result of its dysfunctional structure?" It is useful, therefore, to bring into our evaluation questions that concern the root causes of poverty; therefore, it is useful to rewrite the metaphysical categories of mainstream economic science; thus, how do we:

- ❑ build a world governed more by the spirit of cooperation and less by the machine mind of market forces?
- ❑ encourage sharing?
- ❑ encourage the socially responsible use of property?
- ❑ demonstrate that the righteous alternatives to the profit-driven global factory exist and do work?
- ❑ empower people at the grassroots to infuse friction slowing the operation of the global quasi-machine, thus gain time to reorient and then transform it?
- ❑ take a step toward transforming the global economy?

Notes

1. Folker Froebel, Jurgen Heinrichs, and Otto Kreye, *The New International Division of Labor: Structural Unemployment in Industrialized Countries and Industrialization in Developing Countries*. London: Cambridge University Press, 1980 (first published in Deutsch 1977).

> For the first time in human history, anything can be made anywhere and sold everywhere.

Lester Thurow, *The Future of Capitalism*. New York: W. Morrow, 1996 p. 115.

> The globalization topic arises from a cluster of empirical data, which shows that, in many areas of activity, a small number of relevant corporations operate without national boundaries to competition. In sectors such as finance, telecommunications, aerospace, high-tech, etc., worldwide competition, thus, exists among a diminishing number of corporations.

Jose Molero (ed.), *Technological Innovation, Multinational Corporations, and New International Competitiveness*. Singapore: Harwood Academic Publishers, 1995, p. 7.

> The changing patterns of international competitive advantage integrate production operations across national boundaries. Such a globalization of industry is based on the complementary matching of the factors of production in developing and developed countries, with unskilled assembly in low wage areas.

Joseph Grunwald and Kenneth Flamm, *The Global Factory*. Washington, DC: Brookings Institution, 1985 p. 1.

2a. Explanation

1. Barry Bluestone and Bennett Harrison, *Capital and Communities: Causes and Consequences of Private Disinvestment*. Washington, D.C.: Progressive Alliance, 1980. p. 3.

2. *Id.*

3. *Ibid.* p. 7

4. Ricardo, *Principles*. cited in Part 1, p. 83.

5. Barry Bluestone, Bennett Harrison, *The Deindustrialization of America*. New York: Basic Books, 1982. pp. 129-30.

6. *Ibid.* p. 130.

2b. Prescription

1. Rehman Sobhan, in Mihaly Simai (ed.), *Global Employment: An International Investigation into the Future of Work*. Tokyo: United Nations University Press, 1995. p. 116.

2. *Ibid.* p. 119

3. Jean-Jacques Rousseau, *The Social Contract: I Part 9.* (various editions and translations):

> Far from despoiling individuals, the social contract assures them legitimate possession and changes usurpation into a true right and enjoyment into proprietorship. The great and chief end of men uniting into commonwealth, and putting themselves under government, is, therefore, the preservation of their property.

John Locke, *Concerning Civil Government: Second Essay* (various editions) *XI, pr. 124*. Spinoza's version is close to the Rousseau version. *Ethics* (various editions) *pt. IV Of Human Bondage - 37.2.* For Bentham the main moral justification for freedom and property is that their protection is conducive to security, which is conducive to industry.

> Who has renewed the surface of the Earth? Who has given to man the domain over nature—over nature embellished, fertilized, and perfected? That beneficent genius is security.

Jeremy Bentham, *The Theory of Legislation*. London: Routledge and Kegan Paul, 1950. p. 119 (first published 1802) For Mill too respect for freedom and property is obligatory because:

> The interest involved is that of security, to everyone's feelings the most vital of all interests.

John Stuart Mill, *Utilitarianism*. London: Longman's, 1879. pp. 80-81. For Kant, the categorical imperative:

> It leaps to the eye best when we bring in examples of attempts on the freedom and property of others.

(Paton translation) Immanuel Kant, *Foundations of the Metaphysics of Morals* (various editions) Chapter 2, review of four previous examples, example 2.

4. For contemporary accounts of globalization, which stress the false and misleading ideas used to justify it, see, e.g., Hans-Peter Martin and Harald Schumann, *The Global Trap*. London: Zed Books, 1997; Steven Solomon, *The Confidence Game: How Unelected Central Bankers are Governing the Changed World Economy*. New York: Simon and Schuster, 1995. The difference between my approach and theirs is subtle. My emphasis is upon:

- the basic structural quasi-mechanisms at work
- the worldview or metaphysics
- the ethical basis, which make legitimate those basic structural quasi-mechanisms. Martin and Schumann recommend, in the end, a series of policy measures, such as (p. 242) a European Union Tobin tax upon foreign currency transactions, which would not lead to

changes in the basic metaphysical or ethical structures of modern Western (now global) civilization.

5. Karl Marx penned the classic account of how the precepts of modern Western ethics justify the circulation of commodities and the exploitation of labor according.

> This sphere that we are deserting within the boundaries of which the sale and purchase of labor power occurs, in fact, is a very Eden of the innate rights of man. There alone rule freedom, equality, property, and Bentham. Freedom: because both buyer and seller of a commodity say of labor power, are constrained only by their own free will. They contract as free agents, and the agreement they come to is merely the form in which they give legal expression to their common will. Equality: because each enters into relation with the other, as with a simple owner of commodities, and they exchange equivalent for equivalent. Property: because each disposes only of what is his own. And Bentham: because each looks only to himself.

Karl Marx, *Capital: 1, Part 2*.

6. William J. Baumol, "On the Appropriate Discount Rate for Evaluation of Public Projects" in Harley Hinrichs and Graeme Taylor (eds.) *Program Budgeting and Cost-benefit Analysis.* Pacific Palisades CA: Goodyear Publishing Co., 1969 p. 203

7. Peter Bohm, *Social Efficiency* New York: John Wiley and Sons, 1973. p. xiv.

> Social efficiency involves an attempt to take into account all individuals' evaluations of all consequences of economic acts.

8. See my discussion of the concept of efficiency in Howard Richards, *The Evaluation of Cultural Action*. London: Macmillan, 1985 Chapter 4.

9. See R. Buckminster Fuller, *Operating Manual for Spaceship Earth.* New York: Simon and Schuster, 1969.

10. Howard Richards, *Letters from Quebec: a Philosophy for Peace and Justice*. San Francisco and London: International Scholars Press, 1995.

11. Boulding and Spivey remark that,

> Economic optimization is always a matter of maximizing or minimizing some mathematical function.

See the introduction to Kenneth Boulding and W. Allen Spivey, *Linear Programming and the Theory of the Firm*. New York: Macmillan, 1960.

2c. Metaphysics

1. Thus, for the young Carnap:

> A metaphysic is theory without theoretical content, expressing attitudes that should have been expressed through artistic media or in the

practical conduct of life.

Rudolf Carnap, *The Logical Structure of the World.* Berkeley and Los Angeles: University of California Press, 1967 (first version in Deutsch 1922-25). Later however, Carnap came to understand philosophy as a normative discipline involved with making pragmatic choices among alternative conceptual frameworks. Thus he left discussion open to regarding a metaphysic as a chosen cosmology or worldview. See the discussion of Carnap's later views in the title essay of A. J. Ayer's *Metaphysics and Common Sense*. London: Macmillan, 1969.

2. Jacques Derrida's enigmatic and illuminating *Spurs/Eperons*. Chicago: University of Chicago Press, bilingual edition, 1978, subtitled: *Nietzsche's Styles/ Les Styles de Nietzsche*. It is, by design, the response to Heidegger's critique of Nietzsche (see *Spurs*, pp. 122-23). Heidegger had argued that although Nietzsche claimed to be destroying the Western metaphysical tradition, his *Will to Power (Wille zur Macht)* was, in fact, the culmination of the metaphysical heritage bequeathed to the West by Plato. M. Heidegger, *Nietzsche.* San Francisco: Harper and Row, 1979. (Stuttgart: Neske Verlag, 1961). *Spurs* may, in fact, claim that Nietzsche escaped the fate of those who, condemned by language, inadvertently erect another metaphysic—when their intent is to disprove all of metaphysics. Nietzsche escaped writing another metaphysic because of his style: "There is no totality in Nietzsche's text, not even one that is fragment or aphorism. "*Spurs*, pp. 134-35. Nietzsche concludes, according to Derrida, not with a statement, but rather with a peal of laughter. *Id.*

3. The word metaphysics began with and always refers to the work by Aristotle, which was the first to bear the title *Metaphysics*. It is a book about key terms like *ousia* (substance, existence), *archai* (beginnings, principles, rulers, ultimate underlying substances) and *energeia* (functioning, activity, act), which, as *market*, are fundamental ideas from a matrix, which generates both explanations and prescriptions. See Howard Richards, *Letters from Quebec*, Letter 16.

4. See note 3 to section 2b.

5. *Letters from Quebec*, cited Letter 8.

6. In Carnap's terminology, the questions economists ask are internal questions within a conceptual framework, rather than external questions about the choice of framework (worldview or paradigm). See Ayer's discussion referred to in note 1 above. Certain economists move from one conceptual framework to another and offer alternative economic models, whose methods might be incompatible with comparative advantage; their categories might

come from Buddhism, deep ecology, or from some other innovative source. I prefer to think of such writers as not economists, but as post-economists, who have freed themselves from the metaphysical limitations that are an essential part of the history of the discipline.

7. Rom Harre, *Social Being: a Theory for Social Psychology*. Oxford: Blackwell, 1974, p. 237.

8. Language-game *(Sprachspiel)* is a concept introduced by Ludwig Wittgenstein in paragraph 21 of his *Philosophical Investigations*. Oxford: Blackwell, 1953.

> Imagine a language-game in which A asks and B reports the number of slabs or blocks in a pile, or the colors and shapes of the building-stones that are stacked in such-and-such a place. Such a report might run: Five slabs. Now what is the difference between the report or statement Five slabs and the order? Five slabs! Well, it is the part for which uttering these words plays in the language-game.

Earlier (paragraph 2) Wittgenstein had suggested that a practice in which: • each building material has its name • the builder calls the names to his assistant • the assistant then brings the appropriate material to the builder. That process might be considered a complete primitive language. I use Wittgenstein's idea of language-game because it emphasizes that language interconnects, for example: the terminology of economics and actions, such as buying and selling made possible by the institutional facts that are formalized in contract and property law.

9. For more about the project evaluation that gauges what the contribution a project makes toward social transformation, see *Evaluation for Constructive Development*, the second of my Nehru Lectures presented at Baroda University in India.

Review Questions

1. What political and economic conditions since the 1970s have facilitated the upsurge of the globalization of production? P 19

b. What specific trends in the corporate world have worked toward global production?

c. What preexisting ethics paved the way for the mostly unchecked global production? P 25-26

2. Describe the term *well disciplined, inexpensive labor* in your own words to explain who does what and why they do it. P 19

b. What are the historical roots of that well-disciplined labor mechanism from its birth in the global economic revolution in the 16th century?

c. What do you think are the ancient roots? Does it have a remnant that exists today?

3. Advocates of the global economy argue that shifting production and employment overseas will level the playing field and, thus, raise all boats. Describe the exaggeration within this superficial view using the factual results of globalization. If the wealth to poverty disparity were the barometer that gauged the positive effectiveness of economic policy what direction has globalization sent the barometer? (Low pressure is the positive.) p 22-23

4. Choose one or more questions on page 29 that you would like to research in depth. Do you have answers, for all the questions with which you are confident?

5. What is the twofold quasi-mechanism that drives the globalization of production? What comprises the market forces aspect of the quasi-mechanism? p 25

6. What is the criterion that makes globalization a faithful student of "Ethics 101?" p 26

7. Given that globalization results in sweatshops nearly everywhere (the US, too), what is the direct cause of it—the owner motivation and the legal basis—and what, in your view, are the possible solutions? p 25-26, 281

8. How is the mainstream economic science expressed as an economic metaphysic? What is your sense of which one is "the chicken and the egg"? Does it matter; are the roles interchangeable p 30 - 31

9. How does a metaphysic compare and contrast to an: ethic, ideology, a doctrine, a policy, a philosophy, a worldview, a paradigm, a mentality, or a mind-set?

b. What is the advantage of identifying the economic ideas underlying the theories, principles, and practices of a functioning economic system as a metaphysic? p 9 - 10, 36

10. The economic metaphysic that forms the quasi-mechanism —the market force that drives the global economy—presupposes certain normative entities. What are the normative entities in this instance? p 31 - 32

11. If a change to the metaphysic of economics starts by asking the questions about principles that are ignored by the current metaphysic, then what other questions do you think might be included with the ones on page 32?

3

Theories about Choices of Technology

I dedicate this chapter to my brother, who wrote the screenplays for the film *Powaqatsi* (sequel to *Koyanisqatsi*) and for the HBO production *Earth and the American Dream*. In addition, I dedicate this to my friends, who support R. Buckminster Fuller's concept of *design revolution*. Fuller, knowing politics as useless, devoted his life to serving humanity through his inventions: the *livingry* technology, which enables us to do more with less.[1]

Neither the ecological films that raise consciousness like my brother's, nor Fuller's theories and inventions are theories of international trade. Their relevance to my topic is that if you believe in them, as I do, then you might think that you do not need a theory of international trade.

Green films such as: *Ecological Design* (a tribute to Fuller[2]) and Norberg-Hodge's *Ancient Futures: Learning from the Ladakh,*[3] contrast the modern energy/resource-intensive, inhumane technology with the pre-modern and postmodern *soft-energy paths*. The difference is palpable. Modern cities, like Dante's hell, are made up of ugly sights, unnerving noises, noxious smells. Images such as fields cultivated by peasants with centuries-old sustainable technologies, a *permaculture* site, or a community woven into nature such as Findhorn, remind us that, "We are nearer to God's heart in a garden than anywhere on Earth."

The documentary points out that we chose the wrong technology: the wrong way of life; thus, we should choose the right technology: the right way of life. The factor that determines our choice of technology is the money not shown on the screen; purely numeric, it is less visible. Financial statements project no images, as they are pure monetary abstractions.

Planet Neighborhood[4] (a three-hour PBS TV special underwritten by Bank of America) goes a step further with its theme: green is profitable; the sustainable way to make money is to use eco-friendly technologies; the way to organize communities is to cultivate a mentality that is at once greener and more entrepreneurial. The video shows the innovative biological system to purify the polluted Lake Champlain designed by a leading *bioneer* in the Fuller tradition, John Todd.

It is unclear from the film whether Todd believes that:

❑ market forces and private property can or will rectify humans with Earth

❑ the new engine of civilization will be green tech, which, once invented, institutions and motivation will insure its adoption.

❑ green-tech, once adopted, will create lifestyles in which poverty and violence are rare

Not everyone who claims that mass production technology built the global economy, rather than the inverse, is a filmmaker. Instead of considering the views of the extreme technological determinists, I will examine the work of two authors who present a sophisticated and moderate argument that assigns a causal role to technology choice in history. Their moderate argument is more credible and likely true. Michael Piore and Charles Sabel argue in their book, *The Second Industrial Divide: Possibilities for Prosperity,*[5] that the quasi-mechanical market forces (described by Bluestone and Harrison, and others) do not provide an adequate account of how the global economy developed. Piore and Sabel project their interpretation of history in order to argue that wise choices of technology improve all life.

I will assess how technology and markets influence each other via my analysis of Piore and Sabel's study and as the analysis relates to my evaluation of the premise: it is mainly our technology choices that make the global economy.

3a. Technology as Explanation

Piore and Sabel do not employ the linear concept of causality in which an *explanans* (cause) produces an *explanandum* (effect). Instead, they design a method for explaining the economic history:

> A world in which technology can develop in various ways is a world that would have turned out differently from the way it did; thus, it is a world with a history of abandoned though viable alternatives.[1]

Suppose that at some future date and state of knowledge in the natural sciences and the practical arts, technology will offer multiple paths of possible development: which path we follow is a matter of choice: our choice depends mainly on political and economic power. The adopted technology will be one that corporate power believes will serve its interests and ideals.

An example of an ideal that influenced technology choice is the patriotism of the Japanese elites, who after the *Meiji* restoration decided that Japan needed to adopt Western-style mass production

After a new technology becomes accepted and entrenched, a corporation will:

- ❒ sell off, disregard, or mothball other possible technologies
- ❒ invest capital outlay into the technology chosen
- ❒ problem-solve the details of technology application
- ❒ make market strategies to finance investment repayment
- ❒ cease funds allocation for start-up investment into new tech.

During such an *industrial divide,* the path technology and, thus, industry and society will take is uncertain. The mass production technologies—steel, automobiles, meatpacking, consumer durable goods, and chemicals—might have developed with different methods; in general, mass production might not have happened, though it did. The decision to adopt mass production techniques was a national political decision made by powerful elites, though not in the US. Once having chosen mass production, each nation had to follow through; thus, what had not been possible a few years earlier in the 19th century became a necessity overnight.

The central economic aspect of mass-production is that it requires long production runs; a firm has to produce and sell many units in order to recoup the costs required to start production; it is expensive to stop and start. Frequent shutting-down and starting-up assembly lines, in order to respond to fluctuations in market demand, destroys the low cost per unit of a product and the raison d'etre of mass-production. Furthermore, a firm that stops production when the market falls and surplus peaks will, thus, lack the supply to take advantage of the next surge in the market *demand;* the firm will be undersold by competitors who, during the downswing, prepared themselves to manufacture more units at less cost per unit.

The story of mass-production is one of *chronic excess capacity,* coupled with obstacles to fine tuning capacity to match demand. The principles can be illustrated by this simple hypothetical case: Japan, Brazil, South Korea, Australia, Germany, and Canada decide to mass-produce refrigerators: the result is a world with more fridges than buyers of them. If fridge factories run at 25% of capacity, then costs exceed revenues and nobody makes money. Then suppose that one of the countries, say Japan, decides to reduce capacity in the light of reduced demand. Then, (simplifying the hypothetical by assuming free-trade) instead of selling fewer fridges, Japan may sell none at all because if say South Korea goes ahead and expands capacity in spite of slack demand it will have longer production runs and, therefore, lower unit costs. The stakes are high: those who win conquer the mass markets; those who lose end up with closed factories because they cannot profit.

Investors do not want to or cannot endure instability and high risks such as those in the hypothetical fridge example. The advent of mass production technology, therefore, brings with it the need to manage the market and to stabilize demand. These are the historical explanations of the:

❑ origin of the modern giant corporation, as typified in the meatpacking and petroleum industries: among the first to merge in order to form corporations large enough to:

- monopolize the market
- subdue labor
- shape policy; thus, the ability to achieve economies of scale coincided with the ability to manage demand

❑ rise of Keynesian economics, through which the government shores up aggregate demand

❑ rise of radio and, then, TV as advertisers creating mass desire and appeal for the products of mass production

❑ *pattern bargaining* between big labor and big business, which pegged wages to productivity, for example, in the US, the pattern set by negotiations between GM and the UAW rippled throughout the economy, thus:

- regulating the technology of mass production, which meant
- reducing work stoppages
- increasing consumer power.

Thus, Piore and Sabel reverse the causal analyses of comparative advantage and globalization of production theories. Instead of the market forces determining the technology that will prevail, the new technology dictates how the market must be molded to fit the new requirements.

The classic age of steady demand for mass produced goods was the age that the US dominated the world economy after WW II. In the 1970s, however, the regulation of the world economy broke down; disorder has reigned since. The defeat of big labor symbolized the regulatory breakdown by ending: 1) the practice of pegging wage increases to productivity gains and 2) the advent of free-floating exchange rates among the world's currencies, which took away the privileged status held by the US dollar. The causes of the breakdown are thought to be a series of shocks rocking the international trading system as evident in the:

- ❐ broad, widespread social protests of 1968
- ❐ huge increase in the price of oil by way of OPEC
- ❐ failure of the Soviet harvest, which drove up grain prices
- ❐ other oil shocks, which were produced by the Iranian revolution.

On a deeper level, the cause of the breakdown was inherent in the tendencies of mass production technology.

The most far-reaching and long-term postwar development was the saturation of the consumer goods market in the industrial countries and the consequent penetration through trade among the industrialized economies. Because of the saturation, it became difficult to increase economies of mass production through the expansion of domestic markets alone. Further development along the trajectory of mass production brought the major industrial economies into direct competition for one another's markets and for those of the developing world. It [saturation of goods markets] also exposed the limits of the postwar regulatory system.[2]

Piore and Sabel see two possible paths for the global economy:

1. regulate mass production technology by reviving and extending to the global level the market management mechanisms formerly in place in the US and in several other countries. That would require these international standards:
   - ❐ Keynesian economic policies
   - ❐ market-sharing agreements
   - ❐ labor standards with collective bargaining, or
2. a different economy based on different technologies.

3b. Technology as Prescription

Assume that technology choice: 1) is driven by more than blind forces beyond human control and 2) once made, has far-reaching consequences. Piore and Sabel illustrate those facts by tracing the history and outcomes of mass production technologies. It is reasonable to generalize that the adoption of any technology has far-reaching costs and benefits, including the likely cost-risk that the technology will have to be regulated. Another assumption we can make is: 3) humans need to adopt sustainable technologies.[1] If one interprets sustainable to mean conducive to sustaining life, as distinct from meaning that the particular technology employed is one that could or should be used forever, then assumption (3) must be true. By definition, it would be desirable to adopt only technologies that make human life on this planet unsustainable if it were desirable to end the existence of the human species. Point #3 is more than a truism, however; it is an essential indictment, which alleges that the technological course we follow is unsustainable. It implies, among other things, that establishing *Keynesian economics* on a global scale in order to rescue modern energy/resource-intensive mass production would not be desirable even if it were possible; it would be disastrous.

Those who downplay or overlook the radical implications of point 3 do not argue that we should use unsustainable technologies. What they argue is that the transition from current technology will not require major institutional shifts, because either: 1) the market itself will guide us to wise choices, or 2) the problems are mainly technical ones, which will resolve at the technical level.[2]

John Todd, designer of sustainable biotechnologies wrote:

> Mass production has created the potential for destroying everything humans desire.

If, as Aristotle and a long tradition held, "The good is that toward which human desire aims" then Todd affirms that mass production is leading us away from the good.

Fuller calculated that *resource constraints* are such that the designs for living that prevail in the industrial societies spread around the globe would meet the needs of 44% of the world's people. He concluded:

> A design revolution, which does more with less, is a moral imperative because the alternative is to condemn more than half the world's people to misery.

A utilitarian ethic defines the good as: the greatest happiness of the greatest number. The care ethic sees the moral life as attention to human rights, which are the needs of others. The latter would imply that, if Fuller's facts are correct, it is true that—doing more with less—is a moral imperative, as is the ingenuity, which the architect Paolo Soleri equates with preserving Earth while meeting everyone's needs.

He projects a world population of eight billion and then calculates

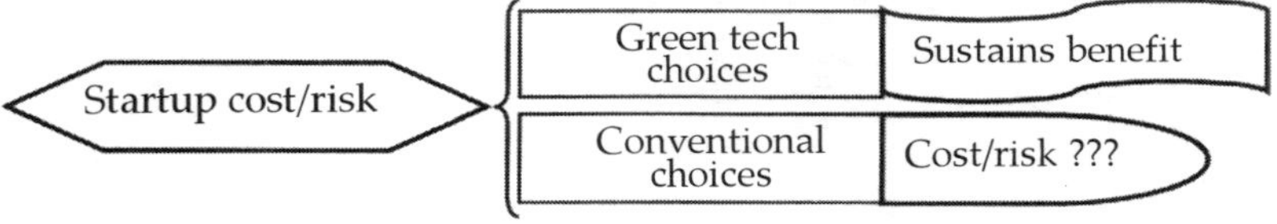

the resources needed to provide a single family dwelling for each family. One conclusion he reaches is that the end sought is unattainable; the other is that attempting to reach it would spell disaster for Earth; the difference between the two conclusions is minor.

Amory Lovins proclaims that sustainable technology is a moral imperative for another reason. It is unjust to future generations to bequeath them a planet with fossil fuels exhausted, biodiversity reduced, and the atmosphere poisoned. Even if it is true, as optimists assert, that techno-genius is boundless and will devise solutions to problems as they arise, it is not fair to put our descendants in a circumstance where they and Earth mother survive only if the speculation that is techno-optimism proves to be true.[3]

Advocates of sustainability assert that a human-centered ethic is too narrow; instead of using the preferred choices of consumers as the standard of value, they urge that we think of living systems as wholes and use the welfare of the whole as the standard of value. Humans should be partners with nature, as Bill Mollison concludes: "Our ethic should be the care of Earth, not just the care of our own species."

E. F. Schumacher, echoing Gandhi, argued in *Small is Beautiful* that the appropriate scale technology could and should be used to generate work in the countryside and, thus, (among other benefits) to stem the tide of migration to India's overcrowded cities. Among other considerations he thought relevant to technology choice were whether it:

- ❒ is conducive to enjoying work
- ❒ gives scope to creativity
- ❒ is consistent with what the Buddhist knows as *right livelihood*.

Though Schumacher held no special brief for Buddhism, he did say:

> Economics could be improved by a *meta-economics* taken from the spiritual teachings of any of the world's great religions.[4]

Anthropologist Mary Bateson and other green writers suggest deriving norms for sustainable living by studying the ethics of so-called primitive peoples; they continue to use ancient, nevertheless, sophisticated techniques for sustaining communities and relationships with the soil and wildlife. Our challenge, however, is greater than theirs; adopting the success of the original people is not enough because the human populations we need to sustain are now much larger.[5]

A principle often suggested for a technology at peace with nature is that humans should live within the Earth's energy budget. Every year a certain amount of new energy arrives from the sun. Instead of drawing down on Earth's stored energy year after year, humans need to learn to give back as much as they take and to leave Earth no poorer at the end of the year than it was at the beginning. This principle is an example of the more general idea that we have to reform our human economics into subsystems of the larger systems that function to make the biosphere habitable for all life.

Compared to the ethical arguments for green technology, the ethical basis for neoliberalism and comparative advantage theory are formal. In contrast, the green arguments are substantive. For example, when economic indicators that depend on the revealed choices of consumers to measure prosperity or welfare, the procedure is formal because the writer merely counts data and does not make value judgments or critical analysis.

Ethical skepticism is an integral part of the market liberalism tools. Without needing to know right from wrong, good from bad, or without presuming to have an opinion about such questions that would be valid for anyone but oneself, one can, nevertheless, derive an ethic by asserting everybody's right to make choices. Consent is the source of legitimacy. The economic theory of the market and the ethical theory of self-determination are two means toward the same end: one affirms the other. If consumers decide to buy coal-fired power-plants and hamburgers, then that is their preference; how many of them they buy will be counted in measuring welfare, in calculating the gross domestic product, and in evaluating the success of economic policies.[6]

Green thinking, by contrast, makes substantive value judgments. Greens have studied what it would take to move Homo sapiens off the endangered species list and they assert that what is necessary for the survival of the species ought to be done. The free choices of consumers have been overrated as the basis for policy decisions, which ought to insure our sustainable economic well-being. Thus, Schumacher realizes:

> In a sense, the market is the institutionalization of individualism and non-responsibility. Neither the buyer nor the seller is held accountable for anything but himself. Humans ought to regard themselves as responsible participants in living systems, instead of licensed to pursue their short-term self-interest.[7]

Amory Lovins criticizes the market as a decision-making mechanism for the sole reason that it rests on the ethical legitimacy of the purchases consumers make. Lovins points out that the market will discount the importance of the Earth's long-term significance to zero in just a few years—over a minute period of geologic time. The market interest rate (the mirror image of the discount rate) is a measure of consumers' preference for satisfaction in the short-term. The moral interest rate that is imperative is the inverse: save Earth's living systems for the future.[8]

Piore and Sabel show that the need to advertise to create desires that match the outputs of mass production may well be a *reductio ad adsurdum* of the ethics of freedom. If the ethical basis of the system is consumer choice, then the basis crumbles when it is necessary to manufacture consumer choice in order to stabilize the system. Likewise, Bluestone and Harrison's account of the defeat of labor by the power of capital to move elsewhere undermines the argument that wages are fair because they are set by free agreements. Thus, it is tempting to:

❑ refute charges that the ethic of self-determination has been violated by criticizing only its distortion and not its principle

❑ say that if advertising were truthful then consumers could, in fact, make free choices; and then market demand would be the accurate guide to technology choice

❑ say that if labor unions were strong, then real collective bargaining and the free agreements of contracting parties would form the basis for wage rates.

At its core, however, the green argument goes beyond correcting the current economic distortions, which deny sustainable choice to the economic actors: consumers, producers, advertisers, and Earth. The greens present an economy based on sustainable choices in which all economic actors are secure and stable. The green warning is that if we do not choose the prescribed green tech, the result will be the demise of nearly all species, including ours.[9]

3c. Technology as Metaphysic

Fuller warned that the challenge before the human species was to "graduate" before it is too late:

> Our graduation time will occur when we learn to organize our interaction with the planet in a way compatible with the physical reality; it compels us to think in terms of whole systems; and more importantly, it compels us to act in terms of whole systems.[1]

One might be tempted to regard the philosophy of the design revolution as the metaphysic of humanity's graduation. It might seem to be an adequate worldview, because its focus is based on life: Earth's systems. Only half of the reform needed to reign-in the current economic metaphysic needs to focus upon technology, however; the other half concerns social relationship. To clarify, I will sketch a way of looking at the history of metaphysics.

It is useful to think of humans within the context of Earth's living process in terms of two related structures:

1. the *technostructure,* which governs:
   - the relationship of humans to the environment
   - the tools that comprise the physical world
   - the science that makes it work
2. the *command-structure* governing culture, which includes political and social relationships.

Homo sapiens is the species that the anthropologist Clifford Geertz defines as: the animal for whom culture is its adaptation to its ecological niche. From the earliest anthropological records, we see humans inventing various technical and command-structures. Human interaction with the earliest technologies was organized and directed by mythology, as is shown, for example, in Hesiod's *Works and Days*. The time for plowing, planting, harvest, celebration, and all the roles that individuals played in those activities had meaning and guidance from religion. Indeed, the origin of language—the communication and guidance quasi-mechanism that is characteristic of our species—is inseparable from the earliest stories (myths) that humans told one another.

Philosophy and later its "daughters" the sciences, arose in ancient Greece, China, India, Mesoamerica, Peru, and other cultures with technostructures, command-structures, and languages. The original intention of Western philosophy, from which science later grew, was to use the expertise achieved in the technostructure to reform the command-structure. Plato advocates the idea that:

> There is no law higher than the *episteme,* [craft-knowledge] of the different specialized *technai, techne* [the root of technology].

Metaphysics is known as first philosophy; it became the subset of philosophy that unified discourse in the West, with parallel developments in other civilizations; it provided, as the mythical cultural cosmology had provided, a common foundation and context for the main uses of language; it became the conscious articulation of the worldview that defined human beings, societal roles, and our place in nature.

The coming of modern society was the coming of an economic society. As the historian Karl Polanyi puts it, in general, economic relations became removed from social relations; the economy took on a life of its own. Instead of being, as its etymology implies: household management, the economy became the overall international context, which provided the necessities of life and defined the social institutions and the worldviews for increasingly more of the world's people. A new command structure emerged, a democratic one in the sense that according to its ideology, each person had sovereignty. Money emerged as: 1) the medium of exchange and account and 2) the store of value. Thus, money governed:

- human relations
- defined rights and duties
- provided the logic for managing human activity: deciding who would do what and when it would be done.[6]

Philosophers invented modern philosophy, which was regarded as the anti-metaphysics; it began as polemics against the metaphysics of academia. Philosophy carried on the social function of traditional metaphysics by providing society with a unifying discourse and logical foundations that justified its principal institutions. Central to the new philosophy was:

1) an ethics of freedom and property rights, which gave authority to markets and market forces and

2) the empiricist and rationalist theories of knowledge, which suppressed reactionary tendencies to revert to the ancient cultural cosmology, which might have thwarted progress. The ethics of freedom made sacred the democratic command-structure, which was consistent with using: 1) consumer choices and 2) the market as the justification for modern industry.

Within the code and execution of the new command structure, the technostructure was to have constant revision by institutionalized science, which used the critical scientific method. The job of science was (still largely is) to research and develop never-ending upgrades in technology. In practice, what philosophy had made as a matter of principle was what had to happen, because entrepreneurs needed (still do) constant technology upgrades in order to stay ahead of their competitors. The new metaphysics known as the anti-metaphysics, thus, carried on the traditional social function: providing a common discourse; it was equipped with the intellectual tools to unify the technostructure with the command-structure. Putting the evolution of the technostructure in the context of their interaction with the command-structures shows why it is a mistake to make technology a metaphysic. That is to say, it is a mistake to see all problems and all solutions as technical. The design revolution is only half the revolution. So, if Fuller is correct, that with the current technology, it is doable to meet the needs of only 44% of the world's people, it follows that:

❑ meeting everyone's needs requires that we learn how to do more with less

• however, it does not follow that if sustainable technologies were adopted then everybody's needs would be met

❑ all needs could be met

• still, it does not follow that they would be met

❑ technology has a certain force of its own, so that it is as much a cause as it is a effect of historical events

• and it does follow that market forces, property laws, and other culture, at times, influence history as well

❑ however, it does not follow that if we make the right technology choices we can ignore the issues that divide investors from workers and divide both from the unemployed.

In regards to social issues, the inventors of green technology want Homo sapiens to:

❑ graduate to a sustainable species while preserving the democratic ideals of modernity

❑ choose equality, democracy, and self-sufficiency by designing cheap and simple tools that ordinary people can control

❑ gain full employment: everyone in pleasant, meaningful work

❑ choose humane habitats that strengthen community

❑ gain the skill to do more with less: conservation and ingenuity to bring within our reach meeting everyone's needs.

Markets, laws, and mentalities need to change so that the good intentions that are built into human and eco-friendly technologies will manifest. All that, however, depends mainly on whether humans can, if we will, relate in a more humane and ethical way to one another. The search for resources that build better human relations needs to include: 1) anthropology as the history of culture and 2) the histories of religion and of the philosophy within it. Through the study of how cultures have been constructed, we will learn to use the tools and skills that construct culture. With the tools and skills to build community, we can bring forth the mosaic of diverse lifestyles compatible with living together on the earth, our common mother, Earth.[7]

Notes

1. In general, see Fuller, R. Buckminister, *The Buckminister Fuller Reader*. Harmondsworth: Penguin, 1972.

> Ninety-nine percent of humanity does not know that we have the option of economic security on Earth. It can only be accomplished, however, through a design science initiative and technological revolution.

R. Buckminster Fuller, *Critical Path*. New York: St. Martin's Press, 1981. p. xviii.

2. *Ecological Design: Inventing the Future.* film directed by Brian Danitz, written by Phil Cousineau in Brooklyn, NY: Ecological Design Project, 1994.

3. *Ancient Futures: Learning from Ladaka.* a film co-directed by Helena Norberg-Hodge based on her book of the same name. Oakland, CA: Video Project, 1993. *Ancient Futures: Learning from Ladaka*. San Francisco: Sierra Club Books, 1991.

4. *Planet Neighborhood.* a film. Washington, DC: WETA-TV and National Academy of Engineering, 1997

5. Michael Piore and Charles Sabel, *The Second Industrial Divide*. New York: Basic Books, 1984.

3a. Explanation

1. Piore and Sabel, cited just before, page 38.

2. Piore and Sabel, page 184.

3b. Prescription

1. Generalizing a premise taken from Piore and Sabel, I arrive at a principle typical of the green thinking: given the premise that technology choice has a far-reaching cost/benefit, we should choose sustainable technologies; thus, we should choose technologies conducive to building the world we want to see. Here I characterize as green those who, like Buckminster Fuller tend to: 1) explain the world we know as determined by energy/resource-intensive technologies and 2) advocate improving our world by choosing renewable energy resources and resource recycling technologies.

The green movement is a holistic macro-cultural movement, which embraces important ethical principles that seem, at first, only indirectly linked to the issue choice of technology and green technologies. The green cause for Paul Ekins is:

> Whether the free market is desirable depends on whether; 1) the distribution of property is fair and 2) whether externalities have been internalized into the market, which is: decisions-makers paying for the consequences of their decisions. When this is not so, the state has cause to

> intervene in the name of social justice and economic efficiency on behalf of those against whom the market is discriminating.

Paul Ekins, *The Gaia Atlas of Green Economics* New York: Doubleday, 1992. p. 34. As well, Ekins praises the enabling state of Kerala, India. p. 79. One can believe, as Paul Ekins does, in internalizing costs, redistributing property, and the enabling state of Kerala; thus, one can be assured that following these principles will, as well, favor solar and wind energy, small organic farms, and bicycle paths. The two are of the same vision. I omitted, however, from Part 3 those aspects of the green thinking that seem peripheral to the choice of technology, only to keep the focus upon technology.

2. "Nobody argues in favor of unsustainable technology. Everyone agrees that sustainability is good," wrote T. F. Allen and T. W. Hoekstra in, "Toward a Definition of Sustainability," Covington and Lebano (eds) *Sustainable Ecological Systems.* Fort Collins, CO: USDA Rocky Mountain Forest and Range Experiment Station, 1993. p. 98.

> One of the significant political achievements of our time is the international adoption of principles of sustainable development as a philosophy for global, national, and local economies.

Peter Miller, "Canada's Model Forest Program: the Manitoba Experience," in *Lemons,* Westra, Goodland (eds.), *Ecological Sustainability and Integrity: Concepts and Approaches*. Dordrecht: Kluwer, 1998., p. 135. Then again, academic departments, policy research centers, and professional journals exist devoted to treating the achievement of sustainability as a technical problem for scientific and economic analysis, which does not require reconsideration of the rational bases of science and ethics, i.e. of a metaphysic. See, for example, the proceedings of the First International Conference on Ecosystems and Sustainable Development published by Uso, Brebbia, and Power (eds.) *Ecosystems and Sustainable Development*. Southampton, NY: Computational Mechanics Publications, 1998. For a sustained argument showing that market rationality and other rationality employed in public policy analysis do need to be reconsidered, see John Dryzek, *Rational Ecology: Environment and Political Economy*. Oxford: Blackwell, 1987.

3. The views of Todd, Soleri, Lovins, and Bateson herein are recorded in the *Ecological Design.* a film cited above. See also, John Todd, *Re-inhabiting Cities and Towns.* San Francisco: Planet Drum Foundation, 1981. Paolo Soleri, *Arcology*. Cambridge, MA: MIT Press, 1967. Amory Lovins, *Soft Energy Paths.* Cambridge, MA: Ballinger, 1977.

4. E. F. Schumacher, *Small is Beautiful: Economics as if People Mattered*. New York: Harper and Row, 1973.

> Those old-fashioned enough to believe that the chief sources of gratification are to be found in intimate relationships and the sense of participating in a community cannot view the advance of an all-embracing technology without misgivings.

E. J. Mishan, *21 Popular Economic Fallacies.* New York: Praeger, 1970, p. 245.

5. Lanham, MD: Rowman and Littlefield, 1998. p. 357. The reference to Sagoff is to Mark Sagoff, *Values and Preferences, Ethics*: 96 (1986) p. 301.

> While most economists find the ethical standing of preference obvious, philosophers and other social scientists (e.g., Sagoff 1986) generally find the concept of revealed choices unconvincing as a standard of welfare, much less as an overall theory of the good.

Tyler Cowen, "The Scope and Limits of Preference Sovereignty, Economics and Philosophy": 9, no. 2 (1993), p. 253, reprinted in Charles K. Wilber (ed.), *Economics, Ethics, and Public Policy*.

6. Schumacher, *Small is Beautiful*. cited in note 4, p. 46.

7. Lovins in *Ecological Design*

8. Free choices are not always the choices conducive to sustainability: a logical consequence of the green premises that green thinkers sometimes overlook. It is easy to overlook it where it makes no difference to the conclusion, i.e. where the outcome criticized is both unsustainable and the result of binding choices, for example, needing to drive a car to work because energy-efficient transportation is unavailable.

3c. Metaphysic

1. R. Buckminister Fuller, *Critical Path. p. xxvii.*

> All that science has discovered is that the Universe consists of the most exquisitely inter-reciprocating technology.

2. Howard Richards, *Letters from Quebec*, Letter 3. and others.

3. The allusion to Clifford Geertz is to his essays, *The Interpretation of Cultures*. New York: Basic Books, 1973. Apart from the idea that culture is the human species' adaptation to its ecological niche, the ideas in these paragraphs are mine from *Letters from Quebec (passim).*

4. David Korten finds that the traditional worldviews of non-Westerners are still more conducive to sustainability than the liberal

scientific metaphysics of the modern West, from which economics emerged. He finds that a metaphysical monism shaped traditional Asian cultures. David Korten, *When Corporations Rule the World*. San Francisco: Berrett-Koehler Publishers, 1995. See also, P. A. Payutto (Phra Ratworamuni), *Buddhist Economics*. Bangkok, Thailand: Buddhadhamma Foundation, 1994. See Schumacher's chapter, *Buddhist Economics, in Small is Beautiful.* cited in Part 3b, note 4.

5. Plato, *Laws.* discussed in *Letters from Quebec*, Letter 14. Plato opens with a reference to the common idea that the gods have instituted the laws of the city, but he then goes on, as in *The Republic*, to develop rational criteria for instituting laws.

6. Polanyi in his book *The Great Transformation*. (cited in note 2 to section 1c above) wrote about—the extracting of economic relations from social relations. He refers to the historical genesis of the institutional structures that is the world market and its concomitants, which produced modernity. It is not that modernity existed first and then produced the global economy; on the contrary, the extension of markets worldwide was a major causal factor in the genesis of modernity. In contrast, the Chilean green economist Manfred Max-Neef writes:

> It is necessary to counter a logic of economics, which permeates modern culture, with an ethics of well-being.

Manfred A. Max-Neef, *Human Scale Development: Conception, Application, and Further Reflections p. 64.* New York and London: Apex Press, 1991. Max-Neef calls for a metaphysical shift reversing the shift Polanyi describes, a shift that reinstates economic relations in social relations. Max-Neef does not, however, endorse just any social relation; instead, he proposes a conceptual framework for social relations as governed by an ethics of care, one that organizes life to meet needs. Charles K. Wilber and Kenneth P. Jameson at the end of *An Inquiry into the Poverty of Economics* advanced the idea of re-embedding economics in society. Notre Dame, IN: Notre Dame University Press, 1983. See also, by the same authors, *Beyond Reaganomics: a Further Inquiry into the Poverty of Economics*. Notre Dame, IN: Notre Dame Press, 1990.

7. Ideas that are as well within *Letters from Quebec*, cited in 9 section 1c

Review Questions

1. Based on your experience and facts that you know, can you give examples of technology and market forces having an effect on the global economy?

b. Which of the two categories of influence do you think has a more important effect upon the global economy? In a column for both, add to them as it pertains, your observations of the facts about trends in these categories: trade, consumption, economic institutions, and the geopolitical trends of unemployment, poverty, war, crime, illiteracy, eco-degradation, etc. p 41

c. How do the global economy and its driver—market forces—affect technology choice?

2. Chronic excess capacity names the "global chapter" of the mass-production story. What are the consequences of such a lack of foresight and positive goal? p 41

b. What credibility issue does the imbalance between supply and demand pose vis-a-vis the contrast between the warehouses of unsold stuff and the masses of people living homeless? p 45

3. Consider the current issues of society, which include: population, pollution, poverty, and the increasingly wealthy, though shrinking owner-of-production class. Based upon those factors, speculate on paths that the global economy might take:

- ❑ global regulation of mass-production
- ❑ a different economy based upon different technology
- ❑ the owners will choose a mix of better tech and regulation
- ❑ it will not change for the obvious reasons p. 43

4. Consider the ethic of self-determination—freedom without responsibility—in the following contexts: driving, sex, parenting, voting, purchases, health care choices, relocation to another nation, and so forth? Can you correlate some common global corporate practices with the negative outcomes of the activities as carried out by individuals, partners, families, and other small groups? p 49

5. Mass production has an added mechanistic aspect, which is caused by the principle of *competition* as a subset of accumulation as a market force of capitalism. What is this major cause of chronic excess capacity?

6. By implication, what questions about the application of green technology justifies and even requires the diagnosis and treatment of the metaphysical basis (or lack) of it in the global economy and its associated structures? p 53

7. What would it take to make the choices of all new technology appropriate and sustainable?

b. Do you think that the all-green-new-tech choice would take a metaphysical shift and, if so, would the shift need to be only the deliberate action of consumers so to lead the corporate world, instead of the inverse, as usual? Base the answer on your experience as a consumer and your observation of consumers in general.

c. What is the most significant strategy or tool for overcoming the built-in and imposed suppression of right choices?

8. New products and technologies will always boost consumer confidence and spending. What then are the obstacles that prevent the major corporations from retrofitting to produce sustainable technologies and Earth-friendly goods and service related practices?

9. To say and or believe that technology will resolve problems, crises, and even avert calamity leads consumers to the rationale: "why me worry," which is a form of apathy (Gk: pathos). Technology choices are, at least, the outward cause of our current predicament. Thus, by risking our future and shared environment with such an attitude, the consumer is either: • gambling • paralyzed by horror and denial • ill informed, or • all of these. What strategies might you try to remedy these forms of alienation and apathy?

b. What are the best strategies that you practice or of which you are aware to alleviate this pervasive ignorance and ill at ease?

c. What word did Marx use in his writing and practice to remedy apathy and, thus, alienation?

4

Circular and Cumulative Causation: Trade Practices of Firms and Nations

An essay by Candace Howe and Ann Markusen within the collective volume *Trading Industries, Trading Regions* dissects an $84 billion US manufacturing trade deficit in 1990. Some $53 billion of the trade deficit is explained by the globalization of production due to the comparative advantages of low wage areas: The essay pinpoints the cause of the deficit further:

> A chunk of the trade deficit, $40 billion with Asia and $13 billion with Latin America can be explained by neoclassical trade theory, or its modern version, the ethic of *the new international division of labor theory*.
>
> The US had imported low-wage consumer goods and labor-intensive electronics assemblies from Southeast Asia. Much of the trade between the US and Mexico is automotive products and electronics sent to Mexico for assembly and fabrication and then shipped back to the US. Consumer goods imports from Southeast Asia came about due to a native peoples development effort. The electronics and auto parts imports followed the corporate search for low-wage havens of blue-collar assembly.[1]

To say that the phenomena observed are explained by low wages is, to recall a point made above, to use explanation, or cause, in a *weak sense*. The low wage scale abroad is not a sufficient explanation (cause) of the US trade deficit. It might be the case, though, that the US would stop all trade with low wage areas and, thus, make zero deficit. A complete list of the conditions that need to be met before the observed phenomenon, a $53 billion trade deficit, will be produced and would, therefore, include all the institutions, decisions, and physical (brute)[2] facts that led to or allowed such trade. A complete causal explanation would also have to explain why in 1960 the deficit did not occur, even though the US traded in those regions and used low-wage labor.

The main conclusion Howe and Markusen want to draw in the passage quoted is that a theory of globalization like that of Bluestone and Harrison sketches some main features of a plausible causal explanation of $53 billion of the 1990 US manufacturing trade deficit. Nevertheless, as Howe and Markusen make clear in the sequel with regard to the remaining $29 billion, such a theory cannot possibly explain that remaining chunk of the deficit because that part of the deficit was in trade with high wage areas. The implication is that some other causes must be at work besides low wages. The suggestion is that we may need theories of a different type to understand international trade.

Toward this goal, Part 4 will engage the economic ideas and processes such as *circular and cumulative causation* as applied by the late Nicholas Kaldor, a prominent 20th century economist whose major breakthroughs were to:

❑ distance himself from neoclassical economics by

• endorsing and proposing explanatory principles different than the neoclassical principles and

❑ prescribing a series of *neo-Keynesian* remedies for the ills of international trade.

4a. Kaldor's Explanations

At least two types of causal explanation are characteristic of Kaldor's work; his two main explanan are inseparable. One is the principle of *circular and cumulative causation,* which Kaldor adopted from Gunnar Myrdal;[1] it emphasizes that within international competition for markets: success tends to lead to more success, whereas failure tends to lead to more failure. The other inseparable twin explanan of Kaldor's theoretical basis is of a type that may be useful to call *accounting causality*: central in the work of the 20th century economist, John Maynard Keynes. Unlike the neoclassical economists who tend to approach economics as a social physics, economists in the Keynesian tradition, such as Kaldor, tend to conduct economics as a *social accounting.*[2]

Kaldor does not deny that technology has played a causal role in history; instead, he sees technology and economics in constant interaction, so that it is impossible to know how much historical change is due to one or the other.

Kaldor notes that Ricardo's theory of comparative advantage, as improved by Mill, Hecksher, Ohlin, and Samuelson, is the mainstream international trade theory today. It implies that:

❒ every nation gains from free trade

❒ due to trade, the poorer countries will gain most, while

❒ the richer countries gain least

❒ as trade increases real income per person will tend to be the same in all countries.

> In the last two hundred years, international trade has increased excessively in relation to the total world income; however, the trends in income per capita for have been the inverse. Disparities between wealthy countries and poor countries have widened much, which is the inverse of what the theory predicts.[3]

Kaldor's explanation of the growth of the difference between wealthy countries and poor countries is that business in the poor countries is inefficient in almost every way. Thus, integration into the global economy means that farmers are driven out of business by, for example:

- ❑ cheap imported wheat
- ❑ local spinners lose to cheap imported textiles (the issue of Gandhi's movement against free trade)
- ❑ native artisans are unable to compete with less expensive goods from foreign factories.

> Pre-developed countries are less efficient in production, which means that they require greater inputs per unit of output; that is not just in terms of one factor, but all factors.[4]

Because free trade eliminates local producers, it condemns the poorer countries to specialize in the production of raw materials and minerals. Sadly, the specialty production is capable of employing only a small fraction of the labor force.

> The countries depending on the exports of primary products, thus, remained poor by comparison. The poverty was a consequence, not of low production by labor in their export sectors; instead it is the limited employment capacity of their profitable industries.[5]

The inverse of the pre-developed people's cumulative failure is that the success of free trade is cumulative. About ninety percent of the funds invested to expand manufacturing capacity come from *retained earnings*. Those who have earnings to reinvest in technical upgrades and greater economies of scale reap even greater earnings and create a cycle of greater efficiency. Thus, the wealth to poverty disparity escalates, largely unchecked, worldwide.

An example, though not mentioned by Kaldor, of cumulative success in the global market is the pharmaceutical industry in the US. Companies like Merck and Lilly have attained commanding leads in an industry that take:

- ❒ enormous capital investment
- ❒ great scientific expertise
- ❒ long lead times for research and development.

So far, at least, the low wage countries have been unable to challenge the US (and to some extent, European) *technology lead* in drugs.[6] The process of circular and cumulative causation has, thus, polarized wealth and poverty within nations as well as between nations. In Italy, for example:

> The economic unification of Italy is a well known example of polarization. The unification occurred when the industries of the north of Italy had developed more than those of the South did. Though the difference was small, industrial productivity was near twenty percent higher in the north than in the South. The difference was sufficient to allow the free and guaranteed access by the northern industries to the southern markets; and that inhibited the development of the South at the same time as it accelerated the industrial development of the North.[7]

With the polarization produced by free trade as prescribed by neoclassical economics, the world has seen a balancing trend: the spread of industrialization from one country to another. After Britain, which was the first country to industrialize, every other country starting with France, Germany, and the US has industrialized by violating the prescriptions of neoclassical economics.

> All nations that industrialized (except Britain) did so with the aid of protective tariffs, which were high enough to give home-produced goods the comparative advantage over imports.[8]

An effect of the causal processes at work in the world economy is that high wage countries wishing to remain as such need to focus upon export market leadership by developing products with that in mind.

> The proper division of international trade in manufactures is not so much the traditional division between capital-intensive and labor-intensive trade, but rather between low-wage and technology lead trade. The high wage industrial countries need to export goods in which they have a technology lead over others; that lead is either the design and marketing of new products (such as high-tech and electronics) or because of advanced manufacturing processes, which yield comparatively high productivity.[9]

Japan designed the best trade strategy to create technology leads; it succeeded in field after field. The success of that model has spurred the call for an industrial policy in the US, which likewise would make product development and the conquest of export markets a concerted national effort. Japan's industrialization was motivated via military defense as it was for most nations that industrialized by design and with protective import restrictions. Without modern industry, Japan would be too weak to resist foreign domination. "Export or die!" was the slogan coined by Kaldor's friends in post-WW II Britain; it might well have been the motto of Japan.

Arguments for investment in growth industries derive strength from: 1) the explanatory principle of circular and cumulative causation 2) *social accounting*.

An accounting identity important for Keynes is that as money circulates as a medium of exchange, the total of revenues must equal the total of expenditures. What is, from one person's point of view, a purchase is from another person's point of view a sale; one person's *outlay* is someone else's income. Every time money changes hands, the account of the spender is debited, as the account of the merchant is credited; thus, debits equal credits. Disregarding subtleties, the overall result for society, upon adding up all domestic transactions, is that society has the same amount of money as it had before; money merely changed hands.

At its best, the exchange process is a part of the technostructure in which society gains via produced and distributed goods and services. In theory, if money continues to circulate as the medium of exchange, an unimpeded flow of goods, services, and joy follows.[10] People, however, often keep accounts where they define success as ending up with more money than they started with; for this and other reasons, people are often inclined to treat money as a store of value by saving it instead of spending it. Keynes writes:

> The psychology of the community is such that when aggregate real income is increased, aggregate consumption is increased, though not by so much as income. Hence, employers would make a loss if the total increased employment were devoted to satisfying the increased demand for immediate consumption. To justify any given amount of employment, there then must be an amount of current investment sufficient to absorb the excess of total output over what the community chooses to consume when employment is at the given level.[11]

For society as a whole, total revenue for time period X is greater than the total available for expenditures in time period X + 1, because some part of the revenue is saved instead of spent. Sales lag, for lack of effective demand, i.e. for lack of purchasing power coupled with the desire to spend. When sales lag all else lags because, as a rule, we produce goods and services to sell them. All would be well if each cent we saved we invested, because investments are, from the investor's point of view, purchases of raw materials and labor and so forth; therefore, investments are, from someone's point of view sales and, thus, income.

The Keynesian explanation justifies saying that government policy can cause, in Kaldor's terms: *growth* or *stagnation*. If the government takes those measures that result in the purchasing power being in the hands of those who want to spend it or to invest it, then its policy will cause growth. It will make society's books balance by compensating for people's tendency to save without investing. Kaldor wrote:

> In the years 1980-82, Britain's policies caused a deepening recession in Europe. I hold Britain mostly responsible for that recession because of the coincidence of North Sea oil and Mrs. Thatcher coming on stream more or less at the same time. Because of the North Sea oil, the balance of payments on current account had a turnaround of nearly nine billion dollars (from -1.4 to +7.5 billion) between 1979 and 1980, rising by 5.5 billion to 13.2 billion in 1981 The deflationary policies of the monetarist government of Mrs. Thatcher caused a turnaround of total real domestic demand by 6% of the gross domestic product, (+3 % in 1979 to -3 % in 1981) which caused a rise in unemployment of almost two million.[12]

The North Sea oil, thus, was an opportunity that Britain missed:

> The new source of income from oil should have been combined with a bold policy of expansion of both public and private investment. Instead, Britain's gain from oil was wholly offset by the 15% fall in her manufacturing output.[13]

Mrs. Thatcher's policies caused growth to decline through a series of measures that restricted access to money, including higher interest rates. The lack of money caused demand to fall, which in turn caused employment to decline. In contrast, the policies Kaldor proposed would have made money available to finance public and private investment. I call this an accounting causality because it operates by keeping track of the national accounts and then adjusting them through government or concerted private action. The accounts are adjusted at the *macro-level* in several ways. The intended result of policies advocated by Kaldor and others makes it easier for people to access money in their bank accounts to pay for consumer purchases and for investments. Having money in the bank is the power to perform certain actions; thus, a favorable adjustment to one's account coupled with a desire to spend or invest will generate purchases/sales, which produce employment and growth. In contrast, the Thatcher policies caused unemployment, stagnation, and a loss of consumer confidence in most economic sectors in Britain and Europe.

By Kaldor's account of it, Mrs. Thatcher's deflation resounded throughout Europe because a deflated British economy was not a good customer for the goods that her continental trading partners would have otherwise exported to her; thus Europe's sales fell, so then its entire economy fell.

In a Kaldor world, accounting causality tends to support the need to attain and keep technology leads. A nation's policy should stimulate investments just to balance the national books, i.e. to keep money flowing. Given that investments in general ought to be stimulated, what better choice of investment could there be than one which:

❒ develops new products for export
❒ exploits and expands the nation's technology leads
❒ captures new export markets with its superior technologies.

4b. Kaldor's Prescriptions

The ethical basis of Keynesian economics differs little from those of neoclassical economics. The two schools advocate competing means to the same end: maximizing the satisfaction of the preferences of buyers, while respecting the freedom of the individual. However, the Keynesians:

❒ are free of most bias in favor of decisions made by the market, casting suspicion on the ethic of government market intervention
❒ rarely let the premise: what is natural is good filter into economic theory casting unethical overtones on government programs designed to achieve objectives, in contrast with Rousseau and Locke
❒ reject the notion that the market is a fact of nature and that government is artificial with its actions as distortions of market prices resulting in imperfections in the market mechanisms.

Kaldor is among the unabashed activists who attack the neoclassical theorists not because they have wrong values, but because they have absurd theories. Backed by a better theory, Kaldor prescribes a different route to prosperity and freedom. He was a lifelong scholar and an activist who made many proposals for reshaping the global economy. Toward the end of his life, he proposed a four-point program for restructuring the associated economies of the Western powers; it is similar to his proposals for the global economy and the Keynesian option within Piore and Sabel's design. Kaldor's four-point prescription summarizes as follows:[1]

1. full employment budgets coordinated with lower taxes and increased expenditure [2]
2. lower interest rates coordinated internationally
3. international price supports for basic *commodities* that suffer price slumps due to their competitive markets, coordinated through a system of buffer stocks. An international agency would buy

commodities when their prices were low to increase their prices using an international reserve currency created for the purpose.

4. Kaldor concedes that the first three points would leave one important problem unresolved, one that Keynes left unresolved, too: the tendency to chronic inflation during full employment conditions.[3] He views the control of inflation a matter of curbing wages as well as fiscal and monetary policy; in this respect, he advocates that we: devise a system of consultation between the social partners —workers, management, and government—in order to arrive at a social consensus concerning the distribution of the national income, which is considered fair and consistent with the maintenance of economic growth, near full employment, and monetary stability. We might then presume the coordination of an international process in an effort toward a national wage consensus.[4]

The weight of academic and political opinion has turned against the Keynesian prescriptions such as the ones Kaldor presents. *Expansionist* prescriptions have led to increasing debt burdens, which is one reason for the advance of neoliberalism and the decline of the social democratic mandarins who managed capitalism to make it achieve social goals. Keynes' original idea of *counter-cyclical* government budgets proved to be a fantasy: ⇨ deficit spending when business is down and then ⇨ repaying the debt via higher taxes when business thrives inspired negative confidence at home and abroad.

The legacy of Keynesian policies is continuous deficit spending; thus, Kaldor attributes the postwar boom from 1949 to 1971 to the US deficit spending. After WW II, the US created purchasing power in the world economy by running up huge public and private debts. It could afford to do this because until 1971 the dollar was the international currency. Foreign governments were content to hold reserves in the form of dollars. The US credit was golden because it could print whatever amount of money it needed to pay its debts. When Europeans began demanding gold and *deutschmarks* instead of dollars, the US currency ceased to be the world's reserve; its ability to generate purchasing power on a world scale ended and with it, the postwar boom.

Neoclassical economists and others, thus, often oppose Kaldor's prescriptions as unworkable in the long-term. Even though as Ross Perot said, "It is imperative to balance the budget and start paying the debt" [6] and even if fiscal decisions are, in fact, more effective in the private sector, we still may not have: 1) a viable alternative to Keynes' proposal to offset the tendency of capitalism toward stagnation by counter-cyclical spending; therefore, the conclusion from the premise that Keynes was wrong may simply be that capitalism is chronically unstable or 2) a better means to Kaldor's objective of growth than his means: the concerted national support of product development for export. Thus, one might support Kaldor's analysis of what needs to be done, though propose a different, perhaps better means toward it.

Even if one agrees with a neoliberal critique of Keynes, thus, rejecting Kaldor's prescriptions for expanding economic activity, we still have two more dimensions of the analysis to consider. So, we decide whether or not:

1. we should (if possible) reject the goal of economic growth and launch a *steady state economics* that does not require growth,[7] or
2. Kaldor believed that the present anti-Keynesian trend has as its main motive its wish to strengthen management and weaken labor by taking the unfair wages issue off the national agenda.

Rejecting government macro-management of the economy invites the passive aggression of *laisser faire*; thus, it denies voters the opportunity to vote for wages and rights beyond those imposed by free market forces and property rights. To remove the government from the economy is to get the poor hand out of the rich pocket. Making the same point from the opposite direction, Jurgen Habermas argues in *The Legitimation Crisis*, that Keynesian management of the economy proves that the allotment of revenue between property and wages is a political contrivance, determined by political power, not a natural fact.[8]

Similarly, advocates of industrial policy combine the advocacy of measures to increase national competitiveness with measures to increase social peace. Consensus on social issues among the social partners is good PR for the export trade. Well-distributed subsidies ensure that both the rich and the poor get some. Some sort of consensus-producing social bargaining is required for the smooth and uninterrupted functioning of the economy, once the people of the state decide that a democratic (elected) government will manage it. Thus, another ethical dimension of Kaldor's proposals is whether an activist industrial policy is viable as a way to put social issues onto a government's agenda.[9]

Kaldor's four-part program for economic recovery may not make it clear that his prescriptions were in principle global and permanent. He recognized that in today's world managing the economy through social accounting, if it is going to work, must function at the

international level. In terms of related ideas he ascribed to Kaldor:
❑ was confident that all nations could enjoy export-led growth by exporting to each other
❑ found shortcomings in Harrod's theory that a warranted rate of growth is sustainable, but he amended it to repair the shortcomings; thus, he was able to argue in a critique of Marx, delivered in Peking in 1956, that, "There can be no presumption of crisis based on a falling rate of profit." [10]
❑ made major contributions to the theory and practice of taxation: he was confident about his approach to adjusting the heavy tax to be compatible with growth and the sustainable welfare of all.

I critique the main features of Kaldor's prescriptions by assessing the concept of growth, which:
❑ balances the social books by making savings equal to investment, and supply equal to demand
❑ brings about, theoretical, progress and prosperity
❑ is the vital remedy for its alternative, the fate of which Kaldor cares to teach the world how to avoid: stagnation.

It is the promise of growth that cements an anticipated social consensus in which the government's action to achieve social justice had a majority support or a consensus from bankers, investors, and entrepreneurs. Growth as an ideal may survive when Kaldor's prescriptions for pursuing growth are discredited as inflationary, inefficient, and or leading to unsustainable debt. Pursued by other means, growth may survive as an ideal.

The most obvious objection to the growth ideal is that it destroys the environment. It is impossible to continue indefinitely the present destruction of habitat by *Homo sapiens* it is a crime against posterity to attempt it.

The objection to the ideal of growth by green economists meets with valid criticism from Kaldor's close associate, Joan Robinson: "Those who protest growth should instead redefine it." The greens should define growth so that the undesirable outcomes, such as—it pollutes, exterminates species, warms the atmosphere—are given a name other than growth, e.g., anti-growth or toxic growth. Thus, true growth—the green growth—would consist of desirable outcomes: activist governments would pursue it instead of anti-growth.[11]

Redefining and renaming growth, however, does not solve the problems for which Kaldor offers growth as a solution. Product development has to occur in order to maintain technology leads, which is never easy. To keep a lead in the market of exclusive green growth products would, thus, not always meet the outcome that product development has to achieve: sale of the product. To solve capitalism's problem, new products have to sell on a massive scale, and thereby reap the super-profits, which would counteract what would otherwise be a falling rate of profit. Super-profits from the exports of new technology justify the super-investments needed to balance the social books. Kaldor wrote:

> Technical progress is a continuous process, which takes the form of development and marketing new products, which provide a new and preferable way of satisfying a need or want. Such new products, if successful, replace existing products, which serve the same needs. Because of marketing, the heightened increase in demand for the new product is disproportionate to the normal increase in demand resulting from economic growth.[12]

The development of new products for which demand is disproportionate to normal demand will not stop, even if it is anti-growth that breaches ecological norms. Nor will it cease to be necessary to balance society's books. The *new products process* will persist as necessary if "islands" of high wages are to be preserved in a global "sea" of low wages, which is essential to the status quo. Thus, high effective demand and consumers who like to shop with their credit cards, will still be necessary to keep employment at acceptable levels. Therefore:

❑ the most obvious objection to growth is a valid one

❑ redefining and remaining growth does nothing to create the institutions and culture needed to guide us toward green growth.

Kaldor's prescriptions, workable or not, display the treadmill that ensnares humanity; it is necessary to go forward faster just to stay in place. The potential demand worldwide for new products determines the direction of movement. Meanwhile, we defer truth, beauty, justice, compassion, partnership with nature, and other ideals. We may honor ideals, although merely as conditional and imposed by what we need to do to stave off economic collapse. Keynes wrote:

> For at least another century, we must pretend that fair is foul and foul is fair; for foul is useful and fair is not. Avarice, usury, and precaution must be our goals for a bit longer, still. For only these can lead us from the tunnel of economic necessity, into daylight.[13]

Thus it is, that caring and aware humans everywhere are asking the questions, "Why did we get on this treadmill?" and moreover, "How can we get off of it?" (graphic on page 280)

4c. Kaldor's Metaphysic

Kaldor was a part of a generation for who the word *metaphysical* was a synonym for unverifiable. In his polemics against his neoclassical opponents, he delighted in castigating their theories as at best a branch of metaphysics.[1] Yet, Kaldor's world takes its form via the metaphysic of economic society described in section 1c, 2c, and 3c.

The term *metaphysic* delineates the basic categories of a civilization by embracing its cosmology, ethics, epistemology (understanding: path to knowledge: science), and its view of human nature defining a worldview; it is what Plato, Aristotle, St. Aquinas, and Kant [2] attempted. Kaldor is an adherent of modern philosophy; he has kind words for Karl Popper's philosophy of science. Modern philosophy does articulate the metaphysic of economic society. It is not so much, however, his explicit sympathy for a *falsificationist* philosophy of science and for modern ideas, as it is the implicit basis of his economics that makes Kaldor a participant in a world shaped and justified by metaphysical ideas.

First, I will extract the metaphysical assumptions latent in the explanations Kaldor gives of economic phenomena. The bases of his explanations are the basis of his prescriptions as well. Modern practices and discourses are at the core of Kaldor's thought; they are that for which philosophers have composed rationales, which serve the functions of traditional metaphysics (even when they describe their work as anti-metaphysical). I do not believe Kaldor disagrees as he wrote:

> The study of economics is concerned with the problem of how, in a decentralized and undirected market economy, do scarce resources become allocated in proportions that give the highest satisfaction to consumers as a body; this is to say, in Pareto's sense, that no one could become richer with any alternative allocation, without making someone else poorer. [3]

In such passages, Kaldor appears to acknowledge that economics is, so to speak, a local science, which applies to recent centuries and to those parts of the world where the institutions that it takes for granted exist.

Next, I will compare and contrast the traditional economic metaphysic with the modern metaphysic, by using the conceptual distinctions that are inherent between:

- ❑ Max Weber's traditional *value rationality* v
- ❒ modern *instrumental rationality* (*zweckrationalitat*)
- ❑ Christopher Hill's the *ancients* v

• the *moderns*, who replaced them in the universities the early modern era

❑ *final causes* v

• *efficient causes*.

Kaldor describes how a technology lead and, thus, the country's *export lead* proves that international trade cannot be explained by comparative advantages due to low wages:

> The successful exporters are able to increase penetration both in foreign markets and in home markets because their products replace existing products; which is because they provide a new and preferable way of satisfying some existing want.[4] That explanation works with the assumption that the new products are sold in markets conceived, as Schumacher put it, populated by bargain-hunters with money: people who will buy a new, cheaper, and better product when they find them.[5]

People do not always act as bargain-hunters, however, or are markets always open. In the 19th century, Japan declined to open its markets to European and US exports; it took Admiral Perry's naval artillery to compel Japan to behave in a way consistent with economic theory. In general, the history of the expansion of markets for European exports is a history of conquest. A contemporary observer, John Locke described a process of circular and cumulative causation from a different view than did Myrdal and Kaldor. Locke wrote:

> With the money gained from foreign trade, England armed ships and paid soldiers and, thus, obtained the power to gain more money, which in turn it used to buy more power to acquire more money.[7]

The mines of South Africa provide another case in point:

> Because the Africans had no monetary system, the British could not induce them to work in the mines for pay until the government imposed a tax on them, which had to be paid in money. The government, in collaboration with the mine owners, rounded them up and set them to work in the mines for wages so they could earn money to pay the tax. Thus, the British conscripted Africans into the market.[8]

Then again, traditional peoples have, at times, allowed their ways of life to be seduced out of existence by cheap manufactured goods and wage labor. Cheap goods, *colonialism*, and other factors of human weakness have all played roles in modernization. I reaffirm, however, that nothing natural or inevitable describes market behavior.

A logic of market behavior, nevertheless, does exist: the logic of the bargain-hunter. Moreover, a metaphysic of the market exists, which is the early modern Western philosophy: empiricism and rationalism, culminating in the philosophy of Kant, and later, romanticism, Marxism, and other philosophical movements; it rebelled against the metaphysic of the market. A similar point applies to the causal explanations derived from social accounting as Keynes wrote:

> The psychology of the community is such that when aggregate real income increases, consumption increases too, though not as much as income.[9]

In addition, Keynes assumes and or accepts that:

❑ we are talking about a cultural structure where people meet their basic needs by exchanging money for products;

❑ workers work for wages, while investors invest for profits

❑ (revealed in what he does not say and the questions he does not ask) that what people do with their money is their matter alone, which the social scientist observes and explains.

For Keynes, the just price theory of Aristotle and St. Aquinas have been dead four hundred years and forgotten for two hundred. The question, "What ought to happen when incomes rise?" is not a question an economist is entitled to ask, or one that deserves an answer. Thus, Keynes reports, "When aggregate real income increases," as if he were an astronomer reporting on the gravitational attraction of a moon for its planet. Likewise, when Kaldor, interpreting Keynes, writes:

> A private enterprise economy requires such an excess (revenue exceeding costs): the receipts obtained from the sale of output must exceed the entrepreneurs' outlay on production. Hence, it is the external component of demand, which will determine what the level of output in the aggregate will be.[10]

Kaldor is telling a story about the need for new external demands because the wages and profits paid in the aggregate will not yield enough to buy the products in the aggregate. The story includes words such as *must* and *determine,* which appear in mathematical theorems and in laws of natural science. This language tends to regard socially constructed realities as if they were natural realities.

This is not to say that to regard its socially constructed reality as if it were natural is rare: every culture does it. It does say that a comprehensive intellectual system that does it is a metaphysic. What is unusual about the recent Western metaphysics is the recognition of a sphere of social activity to which moral rules prescribing solidarity do not apply. That is what marks the thought of Kaldor, Keynes, and other economists as participating in a metaphysic generally distinct from those of all the world's other great civilizations and most of the smaller entities known as cultures.

I do not exaggerate the extent to which the institutions and norms of recent Western civilization, which, by expansion, have defined the rules of the global economy, are constant historically and socially. Certain generalities are, nevertheless, plausible, and without exception, each of these generalizations links to the recent Western civilization's definitive institution: the disembodied market. One such generality is Max Weber's concept of *zweckrationalitat*. Weber held that social action, by which he meant action with a meaningful relationship to the behavior of others, could be oriented in four often-overlapping ways:

1. instrumental rationality
2. *value-rationality*: determined by values
3. *affective rationality*: emotional
4. *traditional rationality*.

The first zweckrationalitat typifies modern society, which could not have come into being and would not function without a certain amount of it. Weber defines instrumentally rational social action:

> It is determined by expectations as to the behavior of objects in the environment and of other human beings; these expectations are used as conditions or means for the attainment of the actor's own rationally pursued and calculated ends.[11]

The purest form (although not the only kind) of instrumental rationality is *capital accounting* in which money quantifies the decision-making process.

> From a purely technical point of view, money is the perfect means of economic calculation. That is, it is formally the most rational means of orienting economic activity.[12]

Within non-modern societies, the—value, affective, traditional—orientations predominate. Kaldor's example recognizes that:

> Modern economic life by its very nature has destroyed those other associations [i.e. other than the coercive power of law] which used to be the bearers of law and, thus, of legal guaranties. This has been the result of the development of the market.[13]

The modern demeanor of the instrumental rationality is, thus, an essential feature to modern society's institutional structure. Hence, Weber's zweckrationalitat concept helps to explicate what it means to locate the discourse of an economic theory such as Kaldor's in the broader context of the metaphysic of economic society.

An intellectual sea-change wrought Europe in the 16th and 17th centuries (documented by Hill, Macpherson, and others); it confirms the proposition that economics assumes an economic metaphysic, as

Schumacher defines it, "Economics as a science accepts instructions from meta-economics."[14] The causal mechanisms cited as explanatory principles by neoliberal, globalization of production, and post-Keynesian economists include institutional features of modernity:

- ❑ private property guaranteed by a modern legal system
- ❑ a expectation that people tend to act via calculated self interest
- ❑ certain rights and certain freedoms.

Those features make it possible to speak of market forces and, thus, give a scientific explanation of the social phenomena in which market forces play the role of cause. They are articulated and included in the modern worldview developed first outside the universities, which then began to accept what now is academic orthodoxy. None are endorsed or supported by the traditional Western metaphysic centered on Aristotle, which was academic orthodoxy at least until the middle of the 17th century, and in some places long after that.

Economics did not create an economic metaphysic. If we date modern economics from the publication of Adam Smith's *Wealth of Nations* in 1776, then it arrived nearly 150 years later than the philosophies of Hobbes and Descartes. They helped dismantle the old metaphysic, and form a new one that was supposed to provide a scientific account of human action. In *Leviathan* (1651), Hobbes took Galileo's physics as a model for the social sciences.[15] Equipped with an ideology borrowed from contemporary technology, mechanics, and mathematics, Hobbes constructed a new philosophy using these fundamentals:

- ❒ natural rights
- ❒ private property
- ❒ the market freedom

It excluded the traditional distributive justice: the Judeo-Christian and Greek cultural ethic. The Hobbes philosophy was one that reflected the advancing spirit of the age; it was seminal to, among others, John Locke, who was in turn seminal to, among others, Adam Smith's confidante David Hume.[16] Professor of moral philosophy at Glasgow, Hume did not need to create either the institutional context or the metaphysical context of the political economy; they had been created by 1776 from the evolution of society and by earlier thinkers.

Even if we think of modern economics as beginning before Smith, the sequence of its creation is the: 1) geographical extension of markets 2) ethical philosophy justifying market institutions, and 3) scientific explanation of market phenomena.

The advent of the modern ideas upon which economics depends, met with ferocious resistance in academic halls as well as on battlefields and from pulpits. Century-long battles waged at Oxford, Cambridge, and other centers of learning, as the advocates for the ancient and the modern views fought for intellectual control. When rich merchants endowed new chairs, libraries, and colleges, they did so (with, as a rule, diplomacy) to challenge and replace the reigning metaphysic. For example, Christopher Hill wrote that:

> Sir Thomas Bodley founded his library to promote the struggle against poverty. The Bodleian was a pro-scientific, however, and an anti-Catholic influence in Oxford. The frieze in the Upper Reading Room shocked conservatives by including figures so strange to the university as Copernicus, Brahe, Paracelsus, Vesalius, Mercator, and Ortelius. Thomas James, the first librarian of the Bodleian used the Roman Index for the purpose as he said, "So that we may know what books and editions to buy, their prohibition being a good direction to guide us therein."[17]

The existence of the economic metaphysic, which Kaldor inherited, is, thus, visible through history. It attained the status of being obvious and assumed, which it enjoys today, by its struggle against neo-Aristotelian scholasticism and by defeating it.

The concept of final cause marks a metaphysical chasm separating ancients from moderns. The word *final* here names the word *end* in the sense of an objective or purpose, as in "to what end," (Espaniol *fin* and *finalidad,* Francaise *fin* and *finalité)*. Aristotle had held that:

> The cause or principle (*arche*) of any given thing includes its end, its purpose, and that toward which it aims.

According to the ancients, for humanity, the all-important final cause was humanity's objective: *caritas,* participation in God's love, achieved through the salvation of the soul and good works. The moderns denied that final causes existed in nature. They insisted that a scientific explanation must be confined to what in Aristotelian terms are efficient causes, in other words the forces, factors, or *independent variables* that produce the phenomenon to be explained. The modern paradigm came to be the terrestrial and celestial mechanics of Sir Isaac Newton, whose *Principia Mathematica* (1687) is a story about *vis* (force) from beginning to end, *vis* being the Latin rendering of the Greek *dynamis,* which is the term Aristotle used to name what in English we call an efficient cause.[18]

Failure to understand that the global economy conforms to an ideology that has banished final causes weakens many well-intentioned critiques of it. In the next examples such critiques view the global economy as wrong because it:

❑ rests on the premise that humans have a right to exploit the Earth
❑ pursues the material accumulation of excess for a few instead of meeting the basic needs of all
❑ rests on greed as a value, or because of its "masculinist" rather than feminist values
❑ takes technological progress as an end in itself, or
❑ deifies science in a way that excludes spirituality.

These well-intentioned critiques miss the mark because they fail to understand that **the global economy, regarded as a system of efficient causes studied by economic science, does not have an objective**. It is inadequate to argue that humanity has been pursuing the wrong objective, and that the species could get back on course by pursuing the right objective. **The global economy has a legal structure and an ideology that defends it in such a way that it has no objective at all.**

The possibility of thinking of economics as a science developed in two steps: 1) final causes were banished from nature, which came to be conceived as a great machine, moved by forces and 2) by analogy with nature, so conceived, the market was conceived as a machine, moved by market forces. Modern philosophers synthesized, as Hume had written, "The experimental method of reasoning with the moral sciences"[19] i.e., a science of efficient causes with an ethics of freedom. Thus, they performed the social office of the metaphysician by unifying in a single discourse the languages of the society's technostructure and command-structure.

Theologians contributed to the social construction of the institutions that made economics possible, even before the philosophers. In the 15th and 16th century, at a time when public discourse on social issues had to be conducted in religious terms because there were no other terms, religious reformers contributed to building the scientific and ethical basis of modern accounting and managerial rationality.

The reformers then appealed to scripture to refute the established church, and, in the process, distinguished revelation from natural reasoning. They recognized the independence of the supernatural as the revealed from the natural as the discovered. The natural, having nothing to do with the knowledge required for salvation, could safely be regarded as a system of efficient causes. Thus, natural science obtained a theological legitimacy, and by extension, social science gained the legitimacy to discover the natural causes of prices. Thus, a discursive space opened wherein political economy could occupy part of an area monopolized by the traditional synthesis of reason and revelation, which was conceived in terms of final cause, therefore, in terms of:

- just price
- common good
- the good of the soul
- divine will.

Somewhat later, when terrestrial and celestial mechanics arrived, and when the laws of supply and demand had become recognized as their social homologues, theologians and orators added to the authority of political economy by asserting that God had created it. In 1795, Edmund Burke could write, "The laws of commerce are the laws of nature and, thus, the laws of God." [21]

When Kaldor studied it, economics had long become independent of theology. In the disputes that preoccupied Kaldor and his fellow students at the London School of Economics in the 1920s, an assertion that God had ordained one law of commerce or another would detract from rather than add to its authority. The evolution of religious doctrines, however, did play essential roles in the process of constructing Kaldor's economic metaphysic.[22]

Notes

1. Helzi Noponen, and others (eds.) *Trading Industries, Trading Regions*. New York: Guilford Press, 1993. p. 21.

2. The very idea of –physical or brute facts– deserves criticism in that any observation is theory-laden and dependent on the framework of its interpretation. Among philosophers who have argued that it is, nevertheless, possible and useful to distinguish facts that are relatively brute from those to be regarded as social constructs include: Elizabeth Anscombe *Causation and Determinism, an Inaugural Lecture*. London: Cambridge University Press, 1971. and John R. Searle, *The Construction of Social Reality* New York, Free Press, 1995. p. 190 ff.

4a. Explanation

1. Gunnar Myrdal, Asian Drama, an Inquiry into the Poverty of Nations. New York: Twentieth Century Fund, 1968.

2. That, as Kenneth Boulding asserted, "Keynes's theory depends on accounting identities," can be seen from his basic equations, such as the following which he describes as the essence of his general theory of employment:D1 + D2 = D where D1 is what the community will likely spend on consumption where D2 is the amount will likely spend investment where D is effective demand.

Keynes then goes on to say that:

> D = f (N), i.e. that effective demand is a function of N, [the volume of employment], it follows as an accounting identity that D2 [investment] is determined once each of the other unknowns has an assigned value.

Those identities, set out in Part 2, argue that orthodox economics errs by trying to predict wage levels using the math of the *derivative* (borrowed from mechanics), i.e., the marginal utility of labor and the marginal non-utility of employment. Later, in Chapter 6, Keynes puts some key accounting identities into words:

• Income = value of output = consumption + investment.

• Savings = income - consumption; and, thus, savings = investment.

Keynes, *The General Theory of Employment Interest and Money*. New York: Harcourt Brace, 1936. p. 63.

In spite of what would seem to be an obvious departure from the root metaphors of classical economics, economists have tried to synthesize Keynesian thought, with *marginalism* (from mechanics) and with notions of equilibrium (mechanics, too) that are incompatible with it.

> The General Theory is, however, independent of the concept of equilibrium, in the sense that it is founded methodologically on an analytical philosophy, which is completely alien to the neoclassical notion of equilibrium.

Fausto Vicarelli, in Alain Barrere (ed.), *The Foundations of Keynesian Analysis.* New York: St. Martin's Press, 1988. p. 113.

It is crucial to Keynes' analytic framework that:

> A decision to consume or not lies within the power of the individual; so does a decision to invest or not.

General Theory, op. cit. p. 65. Thus, the classical simplification of human nature: *homo economicus*, the homo who is predictable because he acts to maximize his gain, is made a bit more complex, by acknowledging the freedom of the individual as presupposed and honored by the legal and institutional frameworks of modernity.

3. Kaldor, *Causes of Growth and Stagnation in the World Economy*. Cambridge, UK: Cambridge University Press, 1996. p. 63.

4. *Ibid.*

5. *Id.* Kaldor, *Causes*, p. 65.

6. Helzi Noponen, "Scale and Regulation Shape an Innovative Sector: Jockeying for Position in the World Pharmaceuticals Industry" in Helzi Noponen, and others (editors) *Trading Industries, Trading Regions*, cited above.

7. Kaldor, *Causes*, cited in note 3 above, p. 66.

8. Ibid.

9. Kaldor, *Causes*. cited in note 3 above, p. 70.

10. Karl Marx makes this point in *Capital: 1, Part 2* when he says that selling in order to buy, represented as Commodity-Money-Commodity, C-M-C, where someone exchanges something for money in order to use the money to buy something, is a process aimed at a concrete satisfaction, a use value. Marx cites Aristotle, who called this process natural, and gave it the name economics (*oiko-nomos*), which he discerned from *chrematistics*: the pursuit of money for the sake of money, which Aristotle deemed to be unnatural.

11. Keynes, *General Theory*, cited in note 2 above, p. 27.

12. Kaldor, *Causes*, cited in note 3 above, pp. 83-84.

13. Id.

4b. Prescriptions

1. For another, somewhat similar, set of Keynesian prescriptions for the global economy, see Paul Davidson and Jan Kregel (eds.), *Improving the Global Economy: Keynesianism and the Growth in Output and Employment*. Cheltenham, UK: Edward Elgar, 1997. In this, Brazilian economist Fernanda Lopes de Carvalho accepts the Keynesian growth prescription, though in addition seeks what she calls structural policies to aid the poor. p. 175

> Economic growth alone is necessary, though not enough to solve the problem of the dreadfully poor in Brazil, to improve their living conditions, and to bring them up from below the absolute poverty line.

2. Nicholas Kaldor, *Causes of Growth and Stagnation in the World Economy*. Cambridge UK: Cambridge University Press, 1996. p. 87.

3. Id. Kaldor, *Causes*, p. 88.

4. Kaldor, *Causes*, p. 90.

5. Kaldor, *Causes*, p. 78.

6. Ross Perot spoke the view that: "A nation cannot go on running up debt forever" appears in Tony Chiu (ed.) *Ross Perot in His Own Words*. New York: Warner, 1992.

7. Kaldor, *Causes*, p. 85.

8. Jurgen Habermas, *The Legitimation Crisis. Boston*: Beacon Press, 1975. (translation of *Legitimations Probleme im Spatkapitalismus*. Frankfurt: Suhrkamp, 1973.)

9. See, for example, the testimony of Robert Reich before the US House Subcommittee on Economic Stabilization, *An Industrial Policy for America, is it Needed?* Washington, DC: Government Printing Office, 1983

10. Anthony P. Thirlwall, *Nicholas Kaldor*. Brighton, UK: Wheatsheaf Books: 1987. p. 183.

11. Joan Robinson and John Eatwell, *An Introduction to Modern Economics*. London: McGraw-Hill, 1973.

12. Kaldor, *Causes*. cited in note 2 above. p. 69.

13. John Maynard Keynes, quoted by E. F. Schumacher, *Small is Beautiful*. New York: Harper and Row, 1973. p. 20.

4c. Metaphysics

1. Kaldor, quoted by Thirlwall, cited in note 10 to Part 4b above, p. 186.

2. Howard Richards, *Letters from Quebec*. San Francisco and London: International Scholars Press, 1995.

3. Nicholas Kaldor, *Causes of Growth and Stagnation in the World Economy*. Cambridge, UK: Cambridge University Press,
1996. p. 3.

4. Id. Kaldor, *Causes*, p. 69.

5. Schumacher, *Small is Beautiful*. cited in note 13 to Part 4b above, Part 1.

6. Pat Barr, *The Coming of the Barbarians: the Opening of Japan to the West*. New York: Dutton, 1967.

7. John Locke, MS in Bodleian Library c. 30, f. 18, quoted by MacPherson, *The Political Theory of Possessive Individualism: Hobbes to Locke*. Oxford: Clarendon Press, 1962. p. 107.

> The chief end of trade is riches and power, which beget each other. Riches consists in plenty of movables, which will yield a price to a foreigner, are not like to be consumed at home, and are especially plentiful in gold and silver. Power consists in the number of men, and the ability to maintain them. Trade is conducive to both these by increasing your stock and your people, and they each other.

8. J. S. Crush, *South Africa's Labor Empire: a History of Black Migrant Labor into the Goldmines*. Boulder, CO: Westview Press, 1991.

9. John Maynard Keynes, *The General Theory of Employment Interest and Money*. New York: Harcourt Brace, 1936. p. 27.

10. Kaldor, *Causes*. cited in note 3 above, pp. 32-33.

11. Max Weber, *Economy and Society*. Berkeley: University of California Press, 1978. p. 24. (A translation of *Wirtschaft und Gesellschaft*)

12. Ibid. p. 86.

13. Ibid. p. 337. Kaldor, using terms reminiscent of Weber, once wrote that the real explanation of the failure of many poor countries to develop is to be found in their traditionalism as it contrasts to our rationalism. Thus, he acknowledged that the modern metaphysics in which economics is rooted is one worldview among many, and, indeed, one whose adoption by the poor countries he (when he wrote at least) advocated. See his 1954 paper, *Characteristics of Economic Development in Nicholas Kaldor, Essays on Economic Stability and Growth*. New York: Holmes and Meier, 1960.

14. Schumacher, *Small is Beautiful.* cited in note 13 to Part 4b above, p. 47.

We might say that economics does not "stand on its own feet," or that it is a derived body of thought from meta-economics. As we have seen, economics is a derived science, which accepts instructions from what I call meta-economics. As the instructions change, so changes the content of economics. In Part 5, we shall explore what economic laws and what definitions of the concepts *economic* and *uneconomic* result when the meta-economic basis of Western materialism decomposes, and is replaced by the teaching of Buddhism.

15. *Thomas, Hobbes, Leviathan* (various editions, first edition 1651) Hobbes, following Galileo's physics, calls his method: *resoluto-compositive*.

16. Macpherson, *The Political Theory of Possessive Individualism: Hobbes to Locke.* Oxford: Clarendon Press, 1962.

17. Christopher Hill, *Intellectual Origins of the English Revolution*. Oxford: Clarendon Press, 1966. pp. 24-25.

18. Isaac Newton, *Principia Mathematica* (various editions) (first published 1687). Gideon Freudenthal, *Atom and Individual in the Age of Newton: on the Genesis of the Mechanistic Worldview*. Dordrecht: Kluwer Academic Publishers, 1986. (Deutsch translation)

19. David Hume called his *Treatise of Human Nature* (various editions; earliest version published in 1740) an attempt to apply the experimental method of reasoning to the moral sciences.

20. See Hill, *Intellectual Origins*. cited above note 17, and my *Letters from Quebec.* cited above note 2.

21. *Edmund Burke, Thoughts and Detail on Scarcity* quoted in Peter Stanlis, *Edmund Burke and the Natural Law.* Ann Arbor: University of Michigan Press, 1958. p. 58.

> It is not in breaking the laws of commerce, which are the laws of nature, and, thus, the laws of God, which we hope to soften the divine displeasure to remove any calamities under which we suffer.

22. In his early economics training, Kaldor was preoccupied with the questions that concerned economists in his milieu at the time:

> If we have increasing returns associated with expanding production, what prevents the loss of pure competition? If we have no pure competition,

then how does the "unseen hand" work?

In 1943, he described his ethical views as,

> The ethic I uphold is based on a belief in human equality, which I regard as a postulate more in the nature of a religious belief, than the outcome of a rational philosophy.

Marjorie Turner, *Nicholas Kaldor and the Real World.* Armonk NY: M. E. Sharpe, 1993. p. 10, p. 15.

Review Questions

1. These factors: accounting causality ⇨ capital investment or retained earnings ⇨ research and development ⇨ expanded manufacturing capacity ⇨ technology leads ⇨ comparative advantage are the sequential means toward what end? pp 62, 66

2. By describing both, what is the relationship between accounting causality and the circular theory of cumulative causation? p 58

3. The ethical basis of Keynesian economics differs little from those of neoclassical economics. What is the twofold ethical basis that the two share? p 63

b. What is the primary, though relatively subtle, difference between the two economics? p 66

4. National support of product development for export could replace accounting causality as the means to foster growth. Product export could be more doable than account causality even in the US. What makes this a true or a false statement? p 65

b. What might be the pros and cons of this system?

c. Kaldor's four-point prescription—as with all the expansionist prescriptions—led to increased debt, neoliberalism, and, thus, lost political support. If Kaldor's idea of a national support for a regime of product development is what gave Japan comparative advantage in nearly every product market it touched, then what prevents the US from doing this? p 67

d. What vague (intentionally) national product development strategy is active in the US and other *corporate welfare states*?

5. What are the wildcard human factors that influence market growth in unexpected ways? p 71

6. Kaldor's prescription points to the catch-22 of growth that it is a treadmill, which makes it necessary to go forward faster just to stay put. What are the four market forces as factors that cause this treadmill of growth?

7. Kaldor's points to the bargain hunters who seek the new and improved product as the reason for the success of export driven economies. What are the criteria for "new and improved" that make a global economy more essential? p 69 - 70

8. Although the promise of growth strengthens social consensus for social justice, at the same time, growth destroys the environment. How can we best deal with this paradox? p 72

9. The global economy conforms to an ideology that has banished final causes: How and why did this happen? p 73 – 74

b. What is the significance of this for us today? p 81

10. Modernity is governed by instrumental rationality rather than the traditional value rationality still present with indigenous culture. Based upon this so-called istrumental rationality of modernity, how then does it follow that modernity is unsustainable?

b. Can the basis for modernity—exchange of commodities—be adjusted toward a sustainable form or does must it be transformed into a new form?

c. If so, then how would you begin that process to reform it?

d. Is modernity's lack of a truly ethical basis (basic ethics) the character flaw of its demise?

e. Aside from these two flaws at the metaphysical basis, can you name and describe other arguments against modernity that are more visible to the average person?

f. Can you trace the visible effect back to the metaphysical reasons?

Quasi-mechanical Market Forces

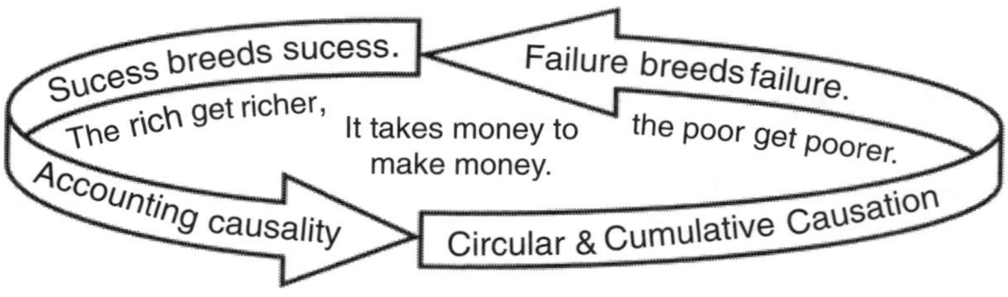

5
Theories of Historical Discontinuity

The treadmill of growth and the drive toward cutting production cost conflicts with other values, such as maintaining a high living wage. This is one of the many problems intrinsic to the basic cultural structures of the modern world. (I use the word *culture* as a broad term, with the word *social* as its subset.) It follows that to ask, "Why did we get on this treadmill?" is to ask, "Why did the modern world come into existence?" Asking this question does not presuppose that pre-modern and non-modern cultures were or are, in general, better than modern society. It does assume, in this context, that modernity brought what Charles Lindblom calls, "the market as prison." Lindblom equates the market to a prison in order to highlight modern society's built-in resistance to making the market conform to humanity and ecology.[1]

Anthony Giddens suggested that the three classic theoretical traditions of sociology initiated by: • Karl Marx • Emile Durkheim • Max Weber map their basic differences in the accounts they give of the origins of sociology's object of study: modern society. Their founders' differing accounts of why modernity arose shape the way their respective followers conceive of society as it is today. After Marx, Durkheim, and Weber, historians have created comprehensive studies of how and why the change from medieval Europe to the modern global economy happened. Much of the literature is known as the studies in *historical discontinuity*: the *Longue Duree,* an archival in France and cited in the US within the work of Immanuel Wallerstein and his school at the State University of New York.

To begin and as a preview of Part 6 and 7, the non-Marxist explanations of why the *modern global economy* began may lie in one of five classes of theories based on:

1. Technology, for example: the industrial revolution as a concept
2. Philosophy as the account of the rise of mathematics, science, and secular ethics
3. Organization of human activity: specialization and supervision within institutions wherein the transition to modernity comes more from the new forms of the deployment of power, rather than new technology.[2]
4. The political theories, for example: the rise and political evolution of the first nation-states: The Netherlands, England, and France

and the accounts of the struggles within them as they interact with the international economic and military strategies that the theories have followed

5. The market accounts of separating the economy from social relations as the extended geographical scope of markets

It may be that all of the explanations of the rise of modernity proposed so far are wrong, and that some other explanation is right. It may be that the theories mentioned are incompatible with each other because in each case, the definition of the phenomenon to be explained is different. For example, the explanation of an energy-intensive mass-production industry finds that the causal factors identified and the dates assigned to them may not be comparable to the causal factors and dates found in, say, an explanation of the decline of empires and the rise of nation-states because the *explananda* are dissimilar. So, the idea of modernity may, in general, be illusory or an idea of opinion rather than fact; thus, no general explanation for its rise may appear.

It seems more likely, however, that the five types of theory mentioned above have partly explained a complex reality, the elements of which form an interrelated set of cultural structures with the useful name: the modern global economy. Perhaps the best explanation would consider and evaluate each element giving due weight to each.

I will outline an argument that leads to the conclusion that the verdict from the studies of historical discontinuity favors my fifth theory. The work of Braudel,[3] Wallerstein,[4] and Polanyi,[5] tends to justify seeing the extension of markets as the leading cause of modernity. I do not assert that they would accept my argument as valid; however, I do assert that it is valid and that the evidence they have compiled supports it. The—technological, philosophical, organizational, and political causes of modernity—can be understood in the context of explanatory narratives shaped by accounts of successive changes in patterns of trade.

Braudel, Wallerstein, Polanyi, and others devote much attention (I do not) to these two questions: 1) Why did the European commercial expansion, which extended markets, come into being? 2) Why was Europe and not China or Islam the center of commercial expansion? Nor will I consider what caused the enlargement of markets. I will, though outline the reasons why it, in turn, caused modernity.

The conceptual pattern of the Part 5 theory:

5a. Historical Discontinuity as Explanation

The explanandum (that which is to be explained) is modernity; the explanans (that which explains) is the enlargement of markets. In one respect, this explanation is true by definition.

One of the central features of modernity is the global economy. Before it became global, the modern economy was what Wallerstein calls the *European world-system*: Europe, the Americas, part of Asia and the East Indies, though not the entire globe. Because one of its essential characteristics is the large market area vs. markets that were mainly local, by definition enlarging markets created an enlarged market; in this respect, the enlargement of markets brought modernity. Wallerstein qualifies such an analysis as follows:

> Trade in luxuries did not produce the historical discontinuity known as the emergence of modernity; the relevant market enlargement consists of regular trade, which includes trade in necessities.

I disagree with him about the luxury trade because, like the necessities trade, it generates profits, moves ships, and creates livelihood. Furthermore, it is hard to draw a line between, for example, the pepper from India as a luxury for the rich and pepper from India to make edible the bad meat of the poor, the early trade of sugar as a luxury, and its later phase when sugar and rum became mass consumer items.

Citing the expansion of trade over larger geographical areas as an explanation is illuminating in that it explains more than trade. To the extent that it is plausible to say that the other important features of modernity were produced by, or at least facilitated by, trade that extended over the globe, it is reasonable to identify market enlargement as the leading cause rather than a contributing factor.

Furthermore, in the case of any given phenomenon in which the proposed explanans is supposed to explain, the plausibility of the explanation is enhanced by an account of: 1.) the sequence of events compatible with the cause producing the effect (*post hoc ergo propter hoc)* is a fallacy; nevertheless, effects do not precede their causes; hence, a proposed explanation has passed a test if it can be shown that the cause preceded the effect and 2.) the quasi-mechanism by which the alleged cause produced its alleged effect.

Market growth caused the 18th century industrial revolution, which occurred then because the economics of society was ready for it. An indication of market growth as causal is the fact that the steam engine, which powered the coalmines and the cotton mills, was invented long before the 18th century. Braudel wrote:

> The steam engine, for example, was invented long before (ancient Egypt had steam engines as toys) it launched the industrial revolution—or before being launched by it.[1]

Another factor indicates that market growth is the lead causal factor. A quasi-mechanism, which in this case is: production on a larger scale for the sake of both exports and an expanded home market and one reason why in the 18th century it became profitable to use steam engines in coal mining and textiles. Enlargement of markets occurred within and between nations, as: 1) local fairs gave way to national systems for selling merchandise and 2) the informal economy of barter gave way to money. The point about steam power could be generalized, although not in a way that denies the facts adduced by writers (such as Piore and Sabel) to demonstrate that technology choices are at times *market-leading* and not always market-led.

The sequence of events also favors counting the growth of the market economy as the cause, rather than the effect, of its ideological justification. The seminal ideas via Descartes, Hobbes, Locke, and Newton were articulated in the 17th century, several centuries after the time when great trade expansion began.

Hobbes made fun of Aristotle's just price theory, which decides what the buyer and seller deserved on the basis that people would not complain if they got more than they deserved from a sale; thus, people should not be heard to complain that they got less than they deserved upon consent to the sale.

Thus it was, that a functioning market economy based on transactions "at arms-length" was extant then in England. When several writers generalized the achievements of technology in a science of mechanics and then articulated the theory of the market as a social analogue of mechanics, an active modern market society existed for their theory.[2]

One can cite mechanisms by which larger markets react back upon and reshape local everyday life and, therefore, explain the world about which writers composed; they reshaped and partly directed it through the art process of writing (given that they wrote about timely ideas and, thus, were read). Such a quasi-mechanism is found in the relationship of the continental wool trade to the enclosure movement as follows.

> Property rights and every aspect of life in English villages changed when it became profitable to devote land to sheep-raising for export; it paid to usurp the common land once used to grow food and fiber for local consumption. Life in the villages of Guinea was forever altered when the slave traders arrived to steal labor; the plantations, in turn, exported sugar to Europe and required from Europe the means of subsistence to support them; this, in turn, meant that agriculture somewhere had to be reorganized to export food to the sugar plantations.

Other examples of the quasi-mechanism abound.

The early factories were organized to support production on a larger scale, which, in turn, was a function of markets; parallel mechanisms apply to the evolution of institutions. 20th century philosopher and historian, Michel Foucault explains the normalizing of human behavior through the new and subtler means of exercising power that is ever more characteristic of modernity; as the reason, he cites economic necessity such as: thievery on the London docks in the late 18th century as threatening to reach intolerable proportions ruining commerce and, thus, initiating the system of modern police and prisons. In the case of the development of many organizational features of modernity, the enlargement of the market came first; the mechanism producing institutional change was the need to establish the institutions that the market economy required to function smoothly. Then again, it may well be the case, as Foucault asserts that:

❑ a vengeful side of human nature exists to delight in the wielding of power (and resistance) even when it serves no useful purpose

❑ bureaucratic and psychological inertia and the self-interest of functionaries produce results and elaborate rationales for those results, which no market imperative needs

❑ power has a life that transcends both individual psychology and collective wisdom.[3]

Similar caveats against exaggerating the importance of the direct and indirect effects of the growth of markets apply to the technological and philosophical theories discussed above. My argument for a theory of historical discontinuity, which treats the enlargement of markets as the leading cause of modernity is not an excuse to ignore the features of modernity, or constants of human nature, that market enlargement does not take into account.

By dating political modernity from the rise of nation-states, it is common to take the Peace of Westphalia in 1648 as a watershed date. That treaty guaranteed the independence of Holland from the Spanish Empire, which dismissed the juridical principle that Christendom was in principle a single temporal and spiritual realm. Holland appears to be the first nation-state, which displayed, in a nascent and transparent form, some characteristics that all the many nation-states since then have had in common.

Before the 1648 Peace of Westphalia, Holland was the name of the loose federation of mostly Dutch speaking states along the North Sea. Holland was also the name of the major state that led the charge to independence from the Spanish/Holy Roman Empire. Thus, Holland became the nation-state as renamed, The Netherlands.

Immanuel Wallerstein's well-documented account of the position of Holland in international trade explains why:
1) nation-state came into existence and
2) the nation-state as an institution emerged in the form it took and at that time and place. Here the word *explains* is the weak sense so to not imply that an unavoidable necessity compelled the nation-state to evolve as it did. Nonetheless, this key fact of political history is explained in the sense that when we understand the position of Holland in international trade, we can see why it would have been reasonable to predict that Holland would:

- ❑ want independence from Spain's tax and regulation
- ❑ have, with allies, the power to gain independence
- ❑ become, upon its independence, a constitutional monarchy dominated by *burghers*: bourgeois capitalists.

The emergence of the first nation-state is not the only event to be explained in a political account of the origins of modernity. It is, nevertheless, one important event; the issues that it illustrates serve to outline this part of an argument for market enlargement as the leading cause of modernity.

The 17th century Dutch merchants became the main distributors of goods in Europe. Although Spain and Portugal had empires rich in silver and gold, they were short of food. In the preceding centuries, the Dutch had improved their fishing and merchant fleets; they were major purchasers of grain from the countries on the shores of the Baltic Sea. The Dutch *Oost Indische Companie* brought spices and fabrics from Asia, which they traded, in part, for Baltic grain. The Netherlands was in a position to supply provisions to the Iberian Peninsula; thus, it acquired the precious metals it used to finance commercial adventures elsewhere. Given The Netherlands wealth and source, again it was predictable that:

❑ the independent state would recognize that,"Commerce has become the pillar of the kingdom"—Lord Mansfield (of the next nation-state, Britain)

❑ it would (as nation-states have since) be a part of an international trading system; its governors would support its merchants with policies designed to help them and, thus, the nation to prosper

❑ as elsewhere, reliance on trading in enlarged markets to supply necessities led to political institutions conducive to trade.

With respect to the origin of the nation-state, the proposition that commercial expansion is the explanans and political modernity the explanandum can, thus, be shown to be in a significant sense true. It cannot be proven in the strongest sense of cause and effect, but neither is the causal connection so weak as to be ineffectual. The sequence of events was that commercial expansion came first, political modernity second. An account of how the one might bring the other provides a quasi-mechanism showing how the alleged cause operates to produce the alleged effect.

It is necessary and to avoid *reductionism* and *determinism*; thus, we need to say that:

1) politics is more than economics

2) once we know 17th century trading patterns and

3) we then still cannot deduce that Holland had to become an independent constitutional monarchy. The weaker, though still significant, claim is sufficient: commerce is the leading causal factor and a background condition operating on other factors.

To complete the argument, it is necessary to show that:

1) the need to find political forms conducive to success in the modern economic world was operative in the case of Holland,

2) the search occurred in the other emerging modern nations, and

3) what is true of the nation-state is true of the other main features of modern politics. The evidence amassed by students of historical discontinuity does show both, even though the weight of the evidence also shows that:

❑ social history is complex

❑ no current can exist without a countercurrent

❑ no generalization can exist without qualifications.

A second set of examples, nevertheless, supports the view for which I argue having used 17th century Holland as the first example. Next, I cite and analyze an account of the French revolution and the form that modern institutions took in the first years of the 19th century from Immanuel Wallerstein's *The Modern World-System Volume III: the Second Era of Great Expansion of the Capitalist World Economy 1730-1840s.*[4]

5b. Historical Discontinuity as Prescription

The enlargement of markets changed the moral status of the "stranger" from an unknown, assumed on contact to be an enemy, at best a lost soul whom a saint might convert to the true faith; the stranger became an essential partner in the business of life, the customer, the source of wealth, even the source of necessities. As local daily life became organized around production for sale in distant markets, the status of the "neighbor" changed too: it became more like a stranger.

The ethics of medieval Europe was, like ethics everywhere, an element of ideal culture, which, although it provided a discourse for criticizing and for guiding practice, did not describe or govern practice. It was, like the ethics of many other civilizations and cultures, an ethics that prescribed self-discipline both for the improvement of one's character and for the good of one another and community. Its ethics were suitable for communities in which survival was always an issue: individuals and families relied on the protection and food provided by neighbors, regardless of class, who paid allegiance to the same lord and prayed to the same God. Medieval Europe garners special attention because, after the medieval period, Europe became the center of the modern system from which today's global economy was born (thus, not because Europe was more important than other pre-modern cultures).[1]

Life was precarious: population grew slowly and in some decades declined. Plagues and poor harvests, the latter often leading to an outbreak of the former, quashed fruitfulness. Medieval settlements in Greenland perished, leaving no survivors. Warfare was endemic: Moors from the south, Tartars from the east, Vikings from the north, as well as feudal lords of Christendom fought each other: villages and farms perished in pillage and war.

The population was more than ninety percent rural. Braudel estimates that even in 1500 A.D. only ten percent of the English and three percent of the Russians lived in towns with more than 400 inhabitants. The main form of production was manual:

- ❐ producing for use more than for exchange
- ❐ for barter more than for cash sale
- ❐ for local fairs more than long trade routes to exotic destinations.

The peasants, who produced food for the knight of the manor as servants in peace, became his infantry in war; the knight protected his people.[2]

Medieval Europe had produced a systematic ethic of conventional solidarity, which was usual within traditional culture with archetypal detail via commentaries in sacred texts. One biblical name for God was *agape*: love. In St. Thomas' summaries of medieval thought, *caritas*, the Latin translation of the Greek agape was central. Many commentators, reflecting current scholastic concerns, find St. Thomas' central thought to be his epistemology: his theory of meaning, or his onto-theological hierarchy. My interpretation of Thomas follows:

Caritas was the basis of moral obligation and was known as the source of joy (*gaudium*) and of peace (*concordia*). The basic duty of the sovereign was to care for the people; everyone's duty was to perform the seven corporal works of mercy, the first of which is to feed the hungry. Law was defined as an ordinance for the common good, made by those charged with caring for the community. Thus, we have the religious basis for aspects of medieval law as outlined below within the context of Aristotle's just price.

The police of medieval Paris supervised the markets partly to assure that food would be plentiful and cheap. In the medieval ethical system, it was the duty of the peasantry to produce and distribute food at low (just) prices: they could be compelled to do so. Merchants who interfered with just prices by committing such crimes as forestalling, which was the purchase of peasants' produce and selling it for a profit risked punishment.[3]

As the medieval period ended, in the commercial expansion of the 15th and 16th centuries, a modern economy was born. When later changes in technology, philosophy, politics (culture) occurred, and trade expanded to become a global economy, the commercial expansion that had taken place conditioned those changes. The historical discontinuity wrought by commerce had to have a corresponding discontinuity in ethics.

Trade had to become possible with people everywhere, while honoring religions and lifestyles, yet imposing universal norms that required compliance with bargains struck in business. As the centers of commerce (towns) grew, the expectation that people would share necessities with indigent neighbors ceased to be a moral and legal duty; still, it might be allowed as a voluntary or self-imposed duty for private religious motives. Some of the moral rules that were repealed included rules:

- ❒ against charging interest on loans
- ❒ forbidding the sale of an item for more than its initial cost
- ❒ allowing the poor to steal when in need.

Expanding markets needed to revive the Roman *jusgentium*, the law of all nations, which was the common law of commerce used in the Roman Empire; with that law of commerce, many cultures gathered to trade in markets. That is what first Europe, then the world, acquired. Revived Roman law became the basis of civil law, which replaced the confessional, canon law, and scripture as the source of moral and legal authority; it occurred in England too, wherein the difference in this respect from the continent is often exaggerated. Less developed areas without civil codes in 1800 had codes imposed on them by Napoleon's armies; when the Napoleonic tide receded, the codes remained. Outside Europe, civil codes came with colonial rule or with modernizing elites such as the Young Turks, or the liberal revolutionaries in Latin America. Europe moved away from what Ferdinand Tonnies called a *gemeinschaft*, G *gemei*: common, a community, whose principle is unity. Europe thus moved toward what Tonnies called a *gesellschaft*, G *gesell*: companion, partner, fellow, brother, and citizen, whose unifying principle is mutual respect for the rights of the individual.[4]

The historical discontinuity of ethics, however, needed a worldview in which the normative principles that governed secular life in the factory and marketplace could remain legitimate. As long as all cosmologies were religious, behavior made sense in religious terms alone. A metaphysic of the historical discontinuity of ethics had to and, thus, did emerge.

5c. Historical Discontinuity as Metaphysic

It is not difficult to establish that international trade theory is derived from economic theory; the latter in its principal versions presupposes the existence of certain institutions and ideas, markets, property, contracts, and so forth that I have characterized as modern. It is more difficult to show how the main concepts underlying international trade theory were part of the metaphysical sea change. Central here is that in the birth of the global economy it was conceptual discontinuity, not simply cumulative advances, that occurred from what Adam Smith called, "the early and rude state of society" toward higher levels of his progress of improvement.[1]

A discontinuity in metaphysics, thus, made international trade theory possible, which I will prove by tracing the evolution of the concept of rent. First, it will help to broaden the context by citing some facts from prehistory and child development, though they are merely of indirect relevance. In *Before Philosophy*, H. A. Frankfort wrote:

> An aphorism that Crawley made is an apt one: "Primitive man has one mode of thought, expression, and part of speech: the personal." He does not mean (as often thought) that primitive man, in order to explain natural phenomena, imparts human characteristics to an inanimate world. For this reason, primitive man does not personify inanimate phenomena.[2]

About the judgment and reasoning of children, Jean Piaget wrote:

> At first, the child puts the whole content of consciousness on the same plane and draws no distinction between the personal I and the external world. Above all, we mean that the constitution of the idea of reality assumes a progressive splitting of this protoplasmic consciousness into two complementary universes—the objective universe and the subjective.[3]

Those allusions to early humans and childhood suggest that the evolution of the mentality in which human symbolic functioning takes place, has a direction. The suggested direction of this evolution is away from undifferentiated thought that is suffused with personal qualities. It moves toward thought that becomes more articulate and objective. The history of the metaphysical basis of rent from the 13th to the beginning of the 19th century is, for our purpose, a fragment in a much larger process of mental evolution.

The discussion of the history of thinking about rent may expand our ability think of rent as a flexible concept (that applies to any historical concept). Then again, it may be that the valuable wisdom of ancient myths, which joined the undifferentiated concept of reality (suffused with personal qualities) got lost along the way. If so, it may be easier to recover the lost wisdom if we remember that economics and the global economy, which are today's dominant discourse and practice, grew from earlier forms.

According to the Oxford English Dictionary the word *rent* was derived from the old French *rente*, derived from the popular Latin *rendita* the classical Latin *reddita:* a form of the verb *redare*, thus *dare*: to give and the prefix *re*: to give back. The O. E. D. suggests a cross-reference from rent to *render*, which has the same Latin source and is sometimes a shorthand synonym for the word *surrender*. In the early common law of England, rent and render were used interchangeably.[4]

> Thus, it was a *render of rent*, which in those days was of corn or other victual. It is frequent in the Domesday Book (a record of survey of English lands and landholdings as ordered by William the Conqueror, circa 1086) after specifying the rent due to the crown, to add likewise the quantity of gold or other renders reserved to the queen. They swore that they would make such renders from the land, as had been done before to any other King.[4]

From this etymology, we deduce that at first the word *rent* was used along with render and terms that refer to the tribute paid by the feudal inferior to the feudal superior. The feudal inferior held land under *socage tenure*: by agricultural service fixed in the amount and *kind* or by money, not by military service, and by which the inferior became the liegeman of a feudal baron. Each had duties to the other in the relationship. The most important duty of the liegeman was to deliver food to his lord. The most important of the lord's duties was the military protection of his vassals. Throughout early history, rent was paid mainly in kind, which is harvest goods or service. With the increasing use of money, however, it became customary to pay a certain sum of money in lieu of surrendering a certain portion of the harvest.

By the time economists came to write about it, rent had become the price paid for the use of land. Awareness existed that the price had its origin in the subjugation of people. Adam Smith wrote:

> As soon as the land of any country has become private property, the landlords, like other men, love to reap where they never sowed, and demand a rent even for its natural produce. The wood of the forest, the grass of the field, and all the natural fruits of the Earth, which, when land was common, cost the laborer only the trouble of gathering them, come to have an additional price fixed upon them. He must then pay the license to gather them and must give up to the landlord a portion of what his labor either collects or produces. This portion, or what comes to the same thing, the price of this portion, constitutes the rent of land.[5]

True to the mechanistic psychology employed by many of the advanced thinkers of his time, Smith declared human nature to be such that landlords would raise rents as high as they could, which was what the market or the tenant would bear. It thus became a fact of nature and a premise to be regarded as a cause when studying its effects: to obtain the use of land it was necessary to pay as much as the tenant could afford to pay. That was the sum for which permission to use the land could be obtained.

> Rent, considered as the price paid for the use of land, is naturally the highest that the tenant can afford to pay in the actual circumstances of the land. In adjusting the terms of the lease, the landlord endeavors to leave

> no greater share of the produce than what is sufficient to keep up the stock from which he furnishes the seed, pays the labor, purchases and maintains cattle, and other instruments of husbandry, together with the ordinary profits of farming stock in the neighborhood.[6]

It thus was easy to conclude that rent was a quality of a physical object, most notably the land. Moral factors were constants that dropped off the equation becoming invisible, two of which were:
1) the institution of land ownership
2) the moral compass guiding the landlord.

Rent attained the metaphysical status of a natural quality of a physical object. With its new metaphysical status, rent attained, from a normative (legal and moral) point of view, the status of a given in a constellation of rent-related institutions. The rent related institutions, which assume that the land yields rent, were:

- ❑ duties of landholding trustees
- ❑ duties of managers as land holding agents for the owners
- ❑ holding land in endowments for educational and charitable foundations
- ❑ landholding by corporations whose directors have fiduciary duties to shareholders
- ❑ lands held burdened with debt for which payments must be made to banks and the payment of property taxes
- ❑ land owned by pension funds and the like.

It became impossible to modify rent as a concept and as an institution, without changing the courses of the other "stars" in the normative "constellation" of which rent is now a part.

David Ricardo, in 1817, articulated and categorized the objective nature of rent as a quality of the land in his theory of rent. Ricardo distinguished rent as a word in ordinary language from rent as a technical term employed in the science of political economy. The latter he defined:

> In technical terms, rent pays for the original and indestructible powers of the soil.[7] When a country is first settled, there is no rent. The time of first settlement is, when land is most abundant and most productive.[8] Then nothing pays for the powers of the soil because the cost of farmland consists only of the labor and capital required to improve it. When the land's powers decay and less yield returns for labor, then a share of the produce of the more fertile portions becomes rent.[9] The rent of a piece of land, the quality of the land, which makes labor on it more productive by pairing it with natural fertility, is measured by the difference in value

> between the crops this piece of land will produce and what can be produced on the worst land then pressed into use with equal labor.[10]
>
> The worst land pressed into use, at any given time, must become cultivated because of the growing demand for food. The worst land does not produce rent; it is marginal. When there is a slight drop in demand, the worst land lays fallow; when the worst land is cultivated, it yields just enough to pay the cost of working it.

Ricardo's theory of rent is often cited as a paradigm to illustrate a law of economic science; it is detailed, quantitative, and passes empirical scrutiny. Once rent becomes a *quality of objects*, economics as a science has a practical use. Analyzing the prices of commodities and the rent necessary to produce them can be studied as one of the causes of the effects observed. Income streams consisting of rent in part or whole can, thus, be treated as objective, natural phenomena; rent income and, by extension of the metaphor, other streams of income can be measured and studied in a manner analogous to the hydraulic study of streams of water.

The transformation of the concept of rent was a part of a metaphysical discontinuity, which was its context. Rent evolved and arose in proportion to the decline in the regard for the value and meaning of personal relationships, in exchange for a higher regard for objective facts. As the world changed, worldviews changed; in terms of human welfare, much was gained; the change represented what Smith called: the progress of improvement; nevertheless, losses occurred too. In *Martin Fierro*, a classic of Argentine literature, the hero laments the fate of the gaucho in words that mock modernity:

Pues todos son sus senores Sin que ninguno lo ampare.[11] Everyone wants you to call them 'Sir,' but no one wants to protect you.

Notes

1. Charles Lindblom, "The Market as Prison" in the *Journal of Politics*. May, 1982.

2. Anthony Giddens, *Capitalism and Modern Social Theory: an Analysis of the Writings of Marx, Durkheim, and Weber*. Cambridge, MA: Cambridge University Press, 1971.

3. Fernand Braudel, *Capitalism and Material Life 1400 - 1800*. New York: Harper and Row, 1973 (translation of *Civilization Materielle et Capitalisme*) See also other works by the same author.

4. Immanuel Wallerstein, *The Modern World-System I: Capitalist Agriculture and Origins of the European World-Economy in the Sixteenth Century*. New York: Academic Press: 1974. This is the first of three volumes on the origins of the modern world-system. See also other

works by the same author.

5. K. Polanyi, *The Great Transformation*. Boston: Beacon Press, 1944.

5a. Explanation

1. Fernand Braudel, *The Structures of Everyday Life: the Limits of the Possible*. New York: Harper and Row, 1981 p. 335. (Francaise translation)

2. These matters are discussed in *Letters from Quebec*, cited in note 9 to Section 1c. above.

3. Michel Foucault, *Discipline and Punish: the Birth of the Prison*. New York: Vintage Books, 1979. (translation of *Surveiller et Punir*)

4. Immanuel Wallerstein, *The Modern World-System: III: the Second era of Great Expansion of the Capitalist World Economy 1730 -1840s*. San Diego, CA: Academic Press, 1989. The facts about The Netherlands are mainly from Wallerstein's *The Modern World System: I*, cited above in note 4 of the Introduction to Part 5.

5b. Prescription

1. Perhaps the best single source for an account of ethical precepts characteristic of medieval Christendom is the second part of the *Summa Theologiae of St. Thomas Aquinas,* where the angelic doctor analyzes the virtues. This is the source of the remarks here on caritas.

2. The facts are taken from Braudel, cited in note 1, Part 5a.

3. John Baldwin, *The Medieval Theories of the Just Price*. Philadelphia: American Philosophical Society, 1959.

4. Ferdinand Tonnies, *Community and Association*. London: Routledge and Kegan Paul, 1955. (translation of *Gemeinschaft und Gesellschaft*)

5c. Metaphysic

1. Adam Smith, *An Inquiry into the Nature and Causes of the Wealth of Nations*. (various editions, first published 1776). The page references below are to the Modern Library edition edited by Edwin Cannan. New York: Random House, 1937. The phrase—early and rude state of society—occurs in Book I, Chapter 6, p. 47. The word *improvement* is within context on the first page and often thereafter.

2. H. and H. A. Frankfort, *Before Philosophy: the Intellectual Adventure of Ancient Man,* an essay on speculative thought in the ancient Near East. Baltimore: Penguin Books, 1961. pp. 5-6.

3. Jean Piaget, *The Child's Conception of Physical Causality*. London: Routledge and Kegan, 1970. p. 242 (translated from Francaise, first published 1930)

4. These are examples given under rent and render in the *Oxford English Dictionary*.

5. Smith, *Wealth of Nations*. cited in note 1 above, p. 49.

6. Smith, *Wealth of Nations*. p. 149.

7. David Ricardo, *On the Principles of Political Economy and Taxation: I*, p. 67 (various editions, first published 1817) in the edition of Ricardo's Works edited by Piero Sraffa. Cambridge, MA: Cambridge University Press, 1951.

8. *Id.* p. 75.

9. *Ibid.*,

10. *Ibid.*

11. Jose Hernandez, *Martin Fierro* Part VIII. (various editions, first published 1872)

Review questions

1. The rise of modernity was the result of the rapid market growth: unbridled, even atypical, without a philosophical justification nor a goal-based outcome. What does this observation of the phenomena tell you about modernity as the direct result of market growth? P 84

2. Starting from the most significant, what are the major features of Europe that gave it the comparative advantage to become the origin, center, and driver of the global economy? P 83

3. Why did the European markets revive the Roman law of all nations? How did that add legitimacy to the markets and the growth of them? P 90

4. The transformation of rent into fixed concept established an economic basis for rent which included:

- it was natural that the rent would be the highest that the tenant could afford
- as a concept, rent became a fixed institution changeable only via the change of other economic institutions
- it was deemed an objective quality of the land itself. What long-term consequence might the transformation of a primary aspect of existence—the right to land—have upon the social mind? Restated in terms of human relations, what was the perhaps unintended, though quite logical consequence of the new paradigm of landlord power? P 93

b. If property rights were as they are today—basic to the quasi-mechanism of the market force ethic—then would the shift in the metaphysic of rent be in the best interest of the owner class?

c. How did that move toward exclusion help the capitalist domination in general?

5. The global economy began in earnest in relative recent history, though it had a loosely defined expression since transcontinental and transoceanic travel began. What other major historical institution coincided with the intense global economy?
b. Which century marked both major historical trends?
c. Compare and contrast the two major structures. Do you now see more difference between the two or less?
d. Could one exist without the other? P 91
6. Markets are the quasi-mechanism for a trio of interwoven structure-like forms of culture; they often act as subsets of the each other depending on the context. What are the three structures still active and with us today, in fact, partly defining us or, at least, our secondary environment?
b. Which structure "paved paradise" for the other two? Recall from the previous question that two structures emerged in earnest at about the same time.
7. "Market growth caused the 18th century industrial revolution, which occurred then because the economics of society was ready for it." Do you think the people of society were ready for industrial revolution because the economics of society was ready for it?
b. Do you think that people normally adjust well to revolutions especially one led by quasi-mechanical structures?
c. How much of a distinction do you think exists between the economic form of society and market growth?
8. Tonnies, *gemeinschaft* and *gesellschaft* (community and association) when applied to the context of the global economy allows us to see one of the Weber rationalities in the extreme form. How does gesellschaft work to facilitate the global economy? P 92
b. Which of Weber's rationalities work with the in concert with gesellschaft?
c. Do you think it possible that the world made small via media and Internet can bring a return of gemeinschaft with its rationalities?
d. Do the corporate and global economy issues simply become part of the spectacle of news entertainment?
e. Does the Internet have more potential for community and its rationalities than the conventional media?
f. Can you describe how this return will, in theory, make the global economy ethically more responsible?

6

Marxist Theories and the Feminist Theory of Maria Mies

The unsettling of traditional ways of life caused by the coming of modernity entered into human discussion as a religious crisis. It took several centuries for the West to frame social issues as debates between the competing secular ideologies.[1] Even then, as now, ghosts of ancient religious ideals hover over the subtexts and the silences of the social sciences, as ghosts of Enlightenment humanism hover over the subtexts and silences of the genealogies as noted by Michel Foucault.[2] When modernity arrived, pre-modern traditions did not depart. The West, like the rest of the world, is an alloy, a "split-level" culture in which the ancient ideals expressed in religious discourse have remained alive as dialogue partners of modernity and as elements in a series of cultural syntheses.

The theories that I consider Marxist are ones, which explain international trade and the global economy through the idea of accumulation explained by Marx as intrinsic to his other key ideas:

- surplus value
- commodity
- the *labor theory of value*
- the private appropriation of the *social product*.

In the same discussion, I include Maria Mies's *Patriarchy and Accumulation on a World Scale: Women in the International Division of Labor* [3] because she often refers to Marxist ideas, either to disagree with them or, as in the case of accumulation, to employ them. The Marxist and Mies theories give important scientific arguments in favor of an egalitarian and communitarian society. Their socialism and the Mies feminism project a future cultural synthesis of the modern ideals of liberty and equality with a holistic sense of society as an interdependent family. In this latter respect, their visions of a better future are the visions of goodwill and sisterhood found in ancient sacred texts.

6a. Marxist Explanation

Marx and Marxists explain international trade and the global economy as: a search for profit: accumulation.[1] In making this generalization I exclude, in addition to the Marxists I do not know about, Louis Althusser, who, although a Marxist, advanced ideas on the causal explanations that are more relevant to the *post-structuralist* theories in Part 7. In order to discuss the global role that Marxists assign to accumulation, it is first necessary to consider the idea of profit.

Much of Marx's *Capital, Volume I* uncovers the secret of profit making. Before Marx, Adam Smith had presented a moral explanation of profit as properly so-called, even though in Smith's work the moral value is disappearing. Smith's explanation is that the entrepreneur would not be willing to invest capital unless he expected to make a profit.[2] If a business venture, thus, appeared not to be profitable the entrepreneur would instead loan his money at interest. Indeed, he would prefer to loan his money for its interest even if he could expect a profit from a business venture: if the expected profit from the business were smaller than the interest he would get from lending. Likewise, the moneylender would not be willing to loan unless the borrower paid interest. [3]

Smith's explanation of profit is one based upon morality because of its reference to the *will* of the entrepreneur. Will is the concept often known as spirit and construed by religion to be in need of salvation.[4] Actions upon deliberated choice continue to be regarded by ethics, including secular ethics, as acts for which the person is responsible.[5] Willful actions merit praise as righteous, or condemnation as wrong because they are acts of an individual's will.

For the explanatory principle that explains profit, Smith uses the will of a stylized individual that is *homo economicus*: an ideal type. Because the will explains, it is necessary to examine Smith's account of profit in the light of appropriate categories for the analysis of actions, such as those proposed by Aristotle and the 20th century philosophies of action by Stuart Hampshire,[6] Stephen Toulmin,[7] Rom Harre,[8] and others. In Aristotelian terms, the conduct of the entrepreneur needs analysis within the categories of the elements of ethics:

- ❑ deliberation
- ❑ choice
- ❑ habit
- ❑ character
- ❑ rule
- ❑ convention.

Smith's account of profit allows room for realism and accuracy because its reference to the will of the entrepreneur allows the option that as an individual, she or he might take some other action. The practices and conventions of the milieu, which guide normal action, might prescribe conduct different than that of the homo economicus Smith supposes. The individual might decide to loan money without charging interest. Indeed, according to canon law and the guidebooks used by confessors even long after the middle ages, making zero interest loans is not merely a logical possibility; it is sometimes the course of conduct required by a moral imperative;[9] it is an action that grace empowers to humans. Upon baptism, caritas enters the human heart, as the mainstream traditional doctrine states, and then becomes the ruling principle of the person's actions.[10]

Smith's reference to will suggests that interest charged or goods sold at a profit assumes that the rate of interest or profit will be at the conventional and customary rate, which is an ethical rate according to the root meaning of the word *ethics* and in the sense of the Deutsch *sittliche*. Allowing for this, is a step toward realism and accuracy, as shown by Cyert and March in *A Behavioral Theory of the Firm* and others who have documented the roles played by custom, ethics, and friendship in the real world of business.[11]

Smith explains profit by reference to what the entrepreneur will or will not do; thus, he invites social psychology or the anthropology of business to study the real life of human beings, which is a moral life embedded in the normative conventions of language and daily practice. Having "invited the guests," he, nevertheless, "refuses their entry" preferring to build a political economy on the basis of his own few and scattered observations serving to confirm his belief that homo economicus is an ideal type, which can be relied on to explain what humans have done, and to predict what they will do next.

Vilfredo Pareto, a 20th century Austrian economist, along with others, prevailed in a debate about the methodology of economic science: *methodenstreit*. They prevailed over those who presumed economics to be a branch of history, which studies the economic norms of any given time and place. Pareto made the validity of Smith's premise about the behavior of his ideal type inaccessible to empirical inquiry via his definition of economic science.[12] Authentic economics according to Pareto is the study and use of the behavior of profit maximizers. Pareto's defense of Smith, in effect, means that economics may well be what others have deemed it to be, as Kaldor wrote: "An arcane academics irrelevant to most of the phenomena observed in the world."

Milton Friedman, a 20th century self-styled positive economist, justifies Smith by claiming that entrepreneurs who do not seek to maximize profit are of no importance to economic science. Friedman wrote:

> A businessman who does not seek in some way to maximize profits will not long be in business. The existence of such people may safely be ignored by social science; their irrational behavior will cause data about them to disappear from all equations.[13]

Thus, Friedman overlooked the:
- ❑ findings of behavioral economics and economic anthropology
- ❑ histories of civilizations in which homo economicus was unknown and which survived for centuries
- ❑ existence of the nonprofit sectors of the economy.

Though one-sided, the claim that nonprofit maximizers will not be in business for long is a statement about the proper methodology for economic research, which is the bearer of some important truths about social structure. It is true that the competitive structure of modern economic life is such that people are often compelled or pushed to act like homo economicus. Friedman's point does not imply that Aristotle was wrong saying "Voluntary human action is the product of deliberation and choice." Friedman's point does underline the fact that what Marxists call—the competition of capitals—does impose severe constraints; it limits the moves that players can make in the complex language-game known as capitalism. Certain moves lead to the forfeit of capital to what Smith called *ruin* in which the player is hence demoted to the working class; even worse, the player is demoted to having no money in a world where all the necessities and conveniences of life have to be purchased with money. In a capitalist society, in terms stated by Braudel, "Those who have no money wander dead among the living."[14]

Marx did not aim to broaden Smith's vision, but instead aimed to exploit the internal *contradictions* of classical economics. Like an insurgency that captures the weapons of government troops, Marx wrote a critique of bourgeois political economy, a powerful ideology for the working class, from the concepts that Smith and others had constructed. Marx mocked economists like Smith for failing to notice that, according to their own premises, exchanging commodities at their values does not yield a *surplus of value (mehrwert).*[15] If the classical theory of the market were correct, making a profit would, therefore, be, as a rule, impossible.

Although Smith's homo economicus may desire a profit and may be unwilling to invest if no profit can be expected, it follows from Smith's postulates that profits happen only in unusual circumstances where the capitalist: 1) succeeds in cheating, or 2) has the good luck to buy at less than market value and sell at more than market value. The exchange process produces no surplus.

> Turn and twist then as we may, the fact remains unaltered. No surplus value results when either equivalents or non-equivalents are exchanged. Circulation: the exchange of commodities causes no value.[16]

Marx's *Capital, Volume I* analyzes this contradiction and solutions to the riddle of profit; thus, profit-making becomes the explanandum; therefore, the labor theory of value, which is the use value of labor power, emerges as the explanans (explanation). By explaining what classical bourgeois economics could not explain, Marx established the scientific superiority of Marxism; he did this by moving the analysis from the superficial level to a deeper level in metaphysical space of society and circulation, in order to encounter the reality that underlies society, which is the level of production. The movement of the argument from surface to depth takes dramatic form in this famous passage:

> The sphere that we are deserting, within whose boundaries the sale and purchase of labor power goes on, is in fact, an Eden of the innate rights of man. There alone rule Freedom, Equality, Property, and Bentham: Freedom, because both buyer and seller of a commodity, say of labor-power, are constrained only by their own free will; Equality, because each enters into relation with the other, as with a simple owner of commodities and they exchange equivalent for equivalent; Property, because each disposes only of what is his; Bentham, because each looks only to himself. The only force that brings them together and puts them in relation to each other is selfishness: the gain and the private interests of each.
>
> On leaving the sphere of simple circulation or of exchange of commodities, which furnishes the *free-trader vulgaris* with his views and ideas and with the standard by which he judges a society based on capital and wages, we think we can perceive a change in the physiognomy of our *dramatis personae*. He, who before was the money-owner, now strides in front as capitalist: the possessor of labor power follows as his laborer. The one with an air of importance, smirking, and intent on business; the other timid, holding back, and like one who is bringing his own hide to market and has nothing to expect but—a hiding.[17]

Between the lines of Marx's explanation of profit, in a silent subtext the ancient ideals of love and justice, chant inaudible *enthymemes* as a mute, invisible chorus. As it turns out, the secret of profit making is the exploitation of labor. The chorus sings: "In as much as ye have done it unto the least of these, so ye have done it unto me."[18]

The capitalist buys labor power at its exchange value, which tends to fall toward—here as elsewhere Marx follows Smith and Ricardo—the cost of buying the means of subsistence necessary to keep the laborer alive. The exchange value of labor-power, like the exchange value of everything else, tends toward its cost of production. The capitalist, having purchased labor power at its fair value, then uses it as a commodity—raw material, resource, and or tool—putting the laborer to work. At the conclusion of the labor process, the capitalist owns the product, which he then sells at its exchange value, with the result that it has *value added*: a surplus of value. Labor power as a source of value is a source of even greater value when applied to a specific use, which produces an exchange value in excess of what the labor cost. The capitalist, thus, makes a profit by appropriating the product of the social effort.

That only begins, what can be called, the *capital syndrome*. Money (value in the form of currency) having been morphed into more money, which is the resulting surplus of money, then returns into the acquisition of more elements of the production process, and the cycle begins again and again. Markets toss surplus value afresh into the production of more surplus value, repeatedly it accumulates; and, it must continue for only the repetition of its self-aggrandizement produces profits and, as by-products, employment, goods, and services. The concept of necessary self-expansion of capital leads Marx and Marxists to think of the global expansion of capitalism as a necessary historical process, an accumulation on a world scale. Whatever the "chorus" may think from a scientific perspective, even the capitalist viewed in historical perspective is no more than the agent of forces that neither he nor anyone else controls:

> From a concrete point of view, accumulation resolves itself into the reproduction of capital at a progressive scale.[19] The social wealth becomes to an increasing degree the property of those in a position to appropriate to themselves repeatedly—the unpaid labor of others.[20] Moreover, the growth of *capitalist production* makes it necessary to keep increasing the capital outlays for any industrial undertaking; and, competition makes the inherent laws of capitalist production to be perceived by each capitalist, as external coercive law. It compels him to extend his capital, though extend it he cannot, except by means of *progressive accumulation*.[21] Accumulate, accumulate! That is Moses and the prophets.[22]

David Harvey integrates the scientific explanations of the global economy offered by contemporary Marxists. Harvey: 1) sees capitalism and accumulation as inseparable and 2) adopts the concept of *regimes of accumulation*, which implies that as long as there is capitalism there is accumulation. The form and method applied to the regime of accumulation, nevertheless, varies through history and location:

> A particular system of accumulation can exist because its schema of reproduction is coherent. The problem, however, is to bring the behavior of all kinds of individuals: capitalists, workers, state employees, financiers, and all manner of other politico-economic agents into a configuration that will keep the regime of accumulation functioning.[23]

Harvey describes the present state of the global economy, circa 1973, as a period of *flexible accumulation*, which is in partial contrast to the previous phases of global capitalism. Its characteristics include:

- ❒ rapid change, flux, uncertainty
- ❒ *flexible labor*: more temp workers, less job security and benefits
- ❒ markets that are more inclusive
- ❒ greater geographical mobility of capital
- ❒ rapid shifts in consumption
- ❒ an entrepreneurial revival
- ❒ neoliberalism
- ❒ postmodern culture
- ❒ the breakup of US economic hegemony
- ❒ new and sometimes exotic financial practices
- ❒ manufacturing decline with service sector rise
- ❒ new industrial ensembles in underdeveloped regions
- ❒ high levels of *structural unemployment*
- ❒ the rollback of labor union power.[24]

The new trends, which characterize this new flexible regime of accumulation, were the consequence of the previous regime's crisis of accumulation, which Harvey broadly characterizes as Fordist/Keynesian, which, for a variety of reasons,[25] was unstable. The pre-1973 Fordist/Keynesian regime of accumulation was unable to keep the accumulation process going; therefore, it had to be replaced.

Harvey finds consistent with Marx's original vision that, in Harvey's words, "Capitalism will produce the conditions of its revolutionary overthrow," today's global economic regime: flexible accumulation is, as its predecessor, unstable and more of a temporary fix than a permanent solution. Harvey wrote:

> Flexible accumulation has to be seen as a particular and perhaps new combination of old and new elements within the overall logic of capital accumulation.[26]

Maria Mies's *Patriarchy and Accumulation on a World Scale* discusses the place of women in the international division of labor; she begins from her observation that:

> A close relationship exists between the exploitation, other oppression of women, and the paradigm of ceaseless accumulation and growth.[27] The confusion in the feminist movement worldwide will continue until we understand the role of women in the context of a global division of labor under the dictates of the capitalist accumulation.[28]

Mies expresses the scientific explanation of the global economy in terms of three phases:

1. the earliest phase is where the main part of her analysis begins, though not without some attention to even earlier times. The explanandum is the oppression of women and, in general, everyone except the dominant males. She conceives that patriarchal control over women is tied to the establishment of class societies. The explanans is violence and coercion.[29]

2. the second phase is what Mies, Marx and others call *primitive accumulation;* it is the period before the capitalist global economy began, which is when the initial capital stock of the wealthy classes of the European core countries began accumulating. It is a phase characterized by commercial expansion and the discovery of the new world, according to Mies and other authors (she cites, e.g., Marx, Wallerstein, Carolyn Merchant, Barbara Ehrenreich, and others). A series of opportunities for capital accumulation occurred, for example: piracy and feeding the working class potatoes instead of grain, which made it possible to reduce their wages. Strong incentives sprang up to amass capital for:

❒ commercial venture
❒ war
❒ government
❒ upper class luxury.

The explanans of how primitive accumulation happened is again violence and coercion, though often under the mask of some moralistic pretext. Mies emphasizes witch-hunts wherein millions of women and some men faced accusations of heresy, were tortured, and burned at the stake; their property was confiscated too.[30]

> The persecution of the witches was a manifestation of the rising modern society and not, as is believed, a remnant of the irrational middle ages. Witch hunts were a mechanism used to subjugate women, quell unorthodox sects, and accumulate capital.[31]

3. the third phase in which the explanandum is the modern global

economy; the explanans is the logic of accumulation. Mies gives parallel accounts of the fate of women in the third world under colonial rule and the fate of women in the first world under what she calls "housewifization." She shows that family structures and gender relations followed the pattern dictated by profit calculations. For example, when it became more profitable to buy new slaves from Africa than to breed them in the Caribbean islands, the slave women lived in forced celibacy. When it became more profitable to treat the African territories as colonies with their own labor forces, to breed slaves in America, then the slave women suffered evangelical brainwashing with pro-family ideologies.[32] For example, until the middle of the 19th century lower classes in Germany and other countries were not expected to marry and have families. An ideology that helped keep wages low did so by discouraging the formation of lower class families, and reserved the concept of family for the upper classes.

In a later phase of capitalism, however, family formation became an important source of consumers. The logic of accumulation led to a different ideology and role for women. The evolution of women's roles in Germany, however, depended on industrial Germany's relationship to the third world, as part of the same global logic of capital accumulation:

> My thesis is: these two processes of colonization and housewifization have a causal link. Without the ongoing exploitation of external colonies, formerly as direct colonies and now as the new international division of labor, the establishment of the nuclear family, which is the internal colony and a woman maintained by a male breadwinner, thus, would not have been possible.[33]

Mies brings her analysis to the present day:

> Asian women in the electronics industry are placed on a global assembly line that reaches from Silicon Valley to Southeast Asia. On this assembly line, the Asian women work at the most monotonous, distressing, and unhealthy jobs. They have to weld together under a microscope the hair-thin wires, which hold the chips together to make an integrated circuit. The US and Japanese corporations have worked out a subtle system of labor control, which combines methods of direct compulsion with methods of psychological manipulation. It is common knowledge that trade unions are banned in the factories. Women in Malaysia lose their jobs when found to be active in trade unions. The corporations employ only young women ages 14 through 25; they lose their jobs if they marry; thus, the corporations avoid the expense of maternity benefits by always having young, inexperienced women, who have to complete 700 chips per day in forced silence and tethered to their work without rest breaks.[34]

Mies's use of—patriarchy and accumulation on a global scale—as an explanans says *au contraire* to the deceived who think that slavery and exploitation happened only in the past. The deceived, however, will cynically say, "Today, advanced societies have put that behind us; what happened in the past is not the fault of anyone living now. So, let's get on with the task of bringing the backward countries up to the standards of the advanced and forget about the bitterness caused by deeds of the past." Mies shows that the same explanatory principles, patriarchy and accumulation, explain capitalism past and present. Whether as exploited factory workers in the third world, or as "shop-a-holics" running up credit card debt in the first world, a woman now is part of a single global economy. It has the same logic now as when some women were slaves in the sugar plantations while other women were pampered favorites in Paris. Hence, it is false to say that the past is behind us; the same causes are still producing similar effects.

Mies's theory is, nevertheless, a delicate balance and a synthesis between: 1) her explanatory principles of coercion and self-interest and 2) the logic of accumulation, (and the additional factors important to explain a phenomenon). The voluntary acts of persons are included in the latter. Mies is troubled by the position taken by Clara Zetkin, a leading 19th century socialist feminist, who spoke in favor of women staying home, dependent on their husband's income. Mies asserts that Zetkin should have taken a different position, which would have made a difference today. Similarly, Marx did not deny that the individual is more than the helpless agent of economic laws:

> I paint the capitalist and the landlord in no sense *couleur de rose*. Here individuals, nevertheless, are dealt with only insofar as they are the personifications of economic categories that is the embodiments of a particular class relations interests.[35]

Marx makes it clear whenever he speaks of what the capitalist will do, that he is referring to a particular person only insofar as that person is regarded as *capital personified*: assumed to act on the basis of economic calculations.

In conclusion, where accumulation is the explanatory principle, deliberate action, subject to moral evaluation, is "twice buried":

1. once by classical economic writers such as Adam Smith who replaced concrete action with a stylized ideal type
2. still deeper when Marx replaced Smith and Ricardo's account of the profit motive with the concept of surplus value ceaselessly augmented through the historical process of capital accumulation.

Deliberate action is, nevertheless, retrievable from its shallow grave. Deliberate decisions can make a difference as Marx concedes, and Mies illustrates even where the logic of accumulation operates. Furthermore, the fact that accumulation operates at all reflects the existence of certain institutions and the performance of certain acts of will.

6b. Mies's and Marx's Prescriptions

Maria Mies believes that deliberate action can make a difference; she proposes a positive future for humanity: the feminist perspective on a new society.[1] The new society would emerge, at least in part, by: 1) embracing better concepts—which she suggests—and 2) taking the steps to enable superior ideas, models, and worldviews.

In her historical account of the global economy, Mies found that people who had wrong moral philosophies often caused negative effects. Mies cites, for example, *A People at School*, by Fielding Hall, who was a political officer in the British administration in Burma in 1887-91. Hall reports that when the British conquered Burma they found a people who practiced gender equity and, thus, enjoyed full women's rights and independence: the Burmese lived in peace via the precepts of Buddhism. Instead of trying to preserve such a happy society, Hall, the militarist and sexist, believed it was the duty of the British to impose his oppression on the Burmese:

> I can imagine nothing that could do the Burmese more good than to have a regiment of their own to distinguish them in our wars. It would open their eyes to new views of life.[2] We must never forget that their civilization is a thousand years behind ours. Men and women have no sufficient differentiation yet in Burma. It is the mark of a young race; ethnology finds that in the earliest peoples, the difference was slight; as a race grows older, the difference increases.[3]

As promoting so-called progress, Hall's policies established male dominance via a new marriage law, which established male succession. At the same time, inexpensive imports from Britain were destroying the local industries that were the basis of the Burmese women's self-reliance.

> The large colonial stores in Rangoon undermine the bazaars where the women used to earn their independent livelihood.[4]

I make this point to dispel the notion that Mies and I believe that deliberate action motivated by good or motivated by bad concepts operates isolated from events in the material world.

The Mies prescription for a positive future begins with

re-conceptualizing work. Disagreeing with Marx and other economists, she proposes to break down the division between work time and leisure time and, thus, promote meaningful activities in which labor and leisure mix. She advocates, in effect, undoing the so-called progress, which has dimmed the joy of activities among peoples who have not yet learned to reckon time as money and to divide it into work time and leisure time.

> If we take as our model of a worker, though not the white male industrial wage earner (irrespective of whether he works under capitalist or socialist conditions), but instead a mother, we can see that her work does not fit into the Marxian concept. For her, work is a burden as well as a source of self-fulfillment and happiness. Children involve much work and issues; nevertheless, it is never alienating or lifeless work. Even when children disappoint their mother, when they leave her, or feel contempt for her, as many do in our society, the pain she suffers is more important than the indifference of the industrial worker or engineer in relation to their products produced or commodities consumed.[5]

By emphasizing the activity, which is the direct production of life and use values—motherhood—Mies distinguishes what is more human from what is less human and speaks of a human essence. She asserts, for example, that men should help with housework and with childcare because that will help men be more sensual, less alienated, and, thus, more human. Men have to start movements opposing the violence against women if they are to preserve their humanity.[6]

Although she differs from Marx on many points, Mies echoes his view that there is an essence of human nature, a *gattungwesen* (human species) and that the human essence is social and sensual. She advocates as a positive goal in her feminist perspective for a new society that humanity create a future where less *alienation* divides women and men and both from nature.

Marx introduced the idea of alienation; Marxists, at times, characterize the achievement of a socialist society as a process of *de-alienation*. Overall, however, Marx refrained from prescriptions. He wanted to separate himself from the utopian socialists[7] by presenting scientific work. In principle, he did not think it wise to write blueprints in advance for a future society yet dimly perceived. Marx, nevertheless, did assign a positive prescriptive force to the concept of use value in addition to asserting the value of humanity free of alienation, which expressed humanity's social and sensual essence.

In the whole sweep of Marx's writings, the key concept: *exchange value* and the related *commodity* appear as unfortunate detours and distortions caused by the present, perhaps transitory, organization of society. Exchange and exploitation interfere with the direct production and distribution of that which ought to be, though under present circumstances is not *la chose qu'on aime pour lui-meme* of use value: *the thing one loves for its own sake* (the Francaise meaning is deeper).

By saying that the whole point of economic activity is to produce use values, Karl Marx does not differ from Adam Smith, although Marx embeds use value in a richer conceptual philosophical context. Going deeper than Smith does, Marx finds that capitalist society is wrong because it often loses sight of, or frustrates the life sustaining and enhancing qualities of use value. Capitalism is a system governed by the exchange value under capitalism and in Marx's words: "The wealth of society presents itself as an immense accumulation of commodities."[8] When defining use value Marx treats it as equivalent to what John Locke called *natural worth*. Locke quoted by Marx:

> The natural worth of anything consists in its fitness to supply the necessities or serve the conveniences of human life.[9]

Marx's prescription is, in a precise sense, a romantic one: society should pursue natural worth. Humanity should leave the outdated era in which the production of necessities tend to be motivated by the pursuit of profit driving production, or else no production occurs.

6c. About Metaphysics

Despite the existence, or former existence, of dialectical materialism (the infamous *diamat*, which bored millions of schoolchildren in the former Soviet Union and in Eastern Europe), I believe that overall the most useful thing to say about the Marxist metaphysic is that it does not exist. The second-most-useful thing to say, I think, is that a Marxist metaphysical bias does exist.

The analysis and critique of the logic of accumulation—my test for distinguishing what is Marxist from what is not—does not imply a positive program. It does not allow the creation of a *comprehensive conceptual system*—a metaphysic—because it lacks: 1) an ethical culture, which has to exist with norms and 2) a social command system merging with the science and technology, in order to create a worldview systematically articulated: a metaphysic in the tradition that Aristotle defined.

To be sure, the logic of accumulation implies an ethical principle: to wit use value ought to be *la chose qu'on aime pour lui-meme.* This is not a controversial principle. Proponents of capitalism agree that enjoyment of goods and services is the goal. They argue that a capitalist market economy is the best means for getting use value produced and delivered. What is controversial and establishes a distinct moral imperative is Marx's further implication: the constraints upon enjoying natural worth ought to be lifted. The constraints exist as imposed by the private appropriation of the social product and by the mechanism of production for exchange.

The Marxist critique, however, does not say what cultural structures, normative principles, and or caring attitudes meshed with practice would achieve the results mandated by this brief sketch of the moral imperative. The confusion of wielding a powerful critique with only a weak sketch of an alternative to offer has been an embarrassment for Marxist revolutionaries, who, though they have seized state power and private assets, have not known what to do next.[1]

Marx's critique of the logic of accumulation, nevertheless, does introduce a metaphysical bias. Because, the critique proceeds by moving downward in metaphysical space (an order, not created by Marxism, but preexisting in the logic of the society Marx critiqued) from the sphere of circulation to the *sphere of production*. This conceptual move, which finds something more real by moving to a deeper level, suggests a series of dualisms, which have been the bane of Marxism since. As circulation is to production, so:

- surface is to depth
- idealism to materialism
- the bourgeoisie to the proletariat
- exchange value to use value
- commodity to natural worth
- alienation to the true human species *(gattungwesen)*
- price to value
- culture to economy
- superstructure to base
- ideology to science.

Marx was the first to denounce simple dualisms; nevertheless, it is hard to resist the conclusion that Marx did mean to say that the sphere of circulation is properly characterized as surface, therefore, less real, less important, more illusory, more deceptive than something else: the sphere of production. Given this premise, it is easy to slip into simple dualisms and hard to avoid them.

The lack of an existing society complete with ethical culture to articulate the structure of it seems to preclude a Marxist metaphysic per se.[2] Moreover, the bias toward seeing the fact of circulation as a surface fact that must be explained by a theoretical apparatus, grounded in processes that are deeper and more real, seems to be an impediment to the improvement of the ethical culture.

A global economy organized to implement the ideals that Marx suggested and implied does not exist; it is doubtful whether a national economy organized as such ever existed. If there were such an economy, it could function only via cultural structures different from those that exist. Hence, no institutional structures for a Marxist metaphysic reflecting the ideology exist.

At best, there are some partly successful experiments, which are nascent communities of solidarity struggling to learn to live more humanly, less alienated. Even those are held back by certain features of the Marxist tradition, such as a tendency to scorn ideals as idealism, which stems from the analogy: circulation is to production as idealism is to materialism.

The task of the would-be Marxist metaphysician is unlike the task of Aristotle, Aquinas, or Kant; the novice would have to articulate, if possible, the fundamental conceptual structures of a culture that is still a dream. Otherwise, the task may be to articulate the basic precepts of a process and a historical movement still seeking the desired outcome toward which it is moving,[3] which, if I am right, will bring the desired outcome it seeks only by transforming culture. It will, however, only transform culture by adopting a conceptual strategy different than Marx's critique of the logic of accumulation.

Marxism remains with us as a project, a pro-ject (Francaise *pro-jet* from *jeter*: to throw, Deutsch *ent-wurf* from *werfen*: to throw.) It is, moreover, a throwing forward into the unknown.

Notes

1. See Christopher Hill, *Reformation to Industrial Revolution: a Social and Economic History of Britain* 1530-1780. London: Weidenfeld and Nicholson, 1968.

2. See Maurizio Passerin d'Entreves, *Critique and Enlightenment: Michel Foucault on 'Was ist Aufklarung'*. Barcelona: Institut de Ciencies Politiques i Socials, 1996.

3. Maria Mies, *Patriarchy, and Accumulation on a World Scale: Women in the International Division of Labor*. London: Zed Books, 1986.

6a. Explanation

1. Among the works which show the key role of accumulation in Marxist explanations of the global economy are: 1) V. I. Lenin,

Imperialism, the Highest Stage of Capitalism in which the need to keep profits increasing (maintain accumulation) was said to require the partition of Africa by the European powers. Imperialism went together with the domination of finance capital—bank ownership of big business—in Europe. Lenin built on the earlier work of Rudolf Hilferding. 2) Likewise, Paul Baran argued in *The Political Economy of Growth* that drawing the poor countries of the world ever more into the capitalist orbit has been a way of subsidizing first world profits by exploiting the third world 3) Rosa Luxembourg makes a similar argument that the accumulation process of capitalism is stabilized through geographical expansion, by incorporating into international markets the natural economies, i.e. the previous non-capitalist areas 4) Maria Mies' *Patriarchy, and Accumulation on a World Scale: Women in the International Division of Labor* names accumulation as central within the narrative history of the origins of today's global economy.

2. Adam Smith, *An Inquiry into the Nature and Causes of Wealth of Nations: I* Chapters 6-7 and *:II*, Chapter 5. (various editions) pages 48, 54-6, 355 of Modern Library edition:

> The profits of stock, it may perhaps be thought, are only a different name for the wages of a particular sort of labor: inspection and direction. They are, however, altogether different being regulated by quite sufficient principles bearing no proportion to the quantity, the hardship, or the ingenuity of the supposed labor of inspection and direction. No country employs its entire annual produce in maintaining its industrious. The idle consume a great part of it; though, in common language, what is called the *prime cost* of any commodity does not comprehend the profit of the person who is to sell it again; nevertheless, if he sells it at a price, which does not allow him the ordinary rate of profit in his neighborhood, he is a loser by the trade, because by employing his stock in some other way he might have made that profit. Unless they yield him the profit, they do not yield him what they may be said to have cost him. Though the price, which leaves him this profit, is not always the lowest at which he is likely to sell them for any considerable time; at least where there is perfect liberty, or where he may change his trade as often as he pleases. The consideration of his private profit, is the sole motive which determines the owner of any capital to employ it either in agriculture, in manufactures, or in a certain branch of the wholesale or retail trade.

3. Adam Smith, *Id.,:II*, Chapter 4 (various editions), p. 333 of the Modern Library edition.

> The stock lent at interest is always considered as capital by the lender. He expects that in due time it is to be restored to him and that, in the mean time, the borrower is to pay him a certain annual rent for the use of it.

4. See, e.g., the near identification of spirit *(animus)* and will *(voluntas)* in St. Ignatius Loyola, *Spiritual Exercises* (various editions).

5. See, e.g., Aristotle's *Nichomachean Ethics: III* (various editions).

6. Stuart Hampshire, *Thought and Action*. London: Chatto and Windus, 1959. pp. 177-78. Echoing Aristotle, he writes:

> A sincere declaration of intentions is the most reliable information about a man's future action, if he is a free agent; this entails that he is not at the mercy of forces that he does not recognize and that are beyondhis control; this is a necessary truth. If the most reliable basis for prediction of his future actions is the record of similar people in similar situations in the past and if his own announced decisions afford no basis at all, then he is not free to guide his own activities; forces beyond his control drive him.

7. Stephen Toulmin, *Knowing and Acting: an Invitation to Philosophy*. p. 305. New York: Macmillan, 1976. Toulmin discusses the human standpoint in a way that characterizes humans as rational creatures who act with reason:

> The least we can demand of a satisfactory philosophy of individual action, at this point, is a clear account of the manner in which we are going to tell these two types of situation apart: 1) acting rationally, vs. 2) being overwhelmed by emotion. How does the individual recognize that a compelling reason exists for acting in this way instead of that? How does the relevance for him of such considerations differ from the influence of those factors upon him that are casually compulsive?

8. Rom Harre and Paul Secord, *The Explanation of Social Behavior*. Totowa, NJ: Rowman and Littlefield, 1973. See also the discussion of the need for a more adequate theory of human action to replace the methodological individualism of orthodox Western economic science in Martin Hollis and Edward Nell, *Rational Economic Man*. Cambridge, MA: Cambridge University Press, 1975.

9. The traditional doctrine concerning the right use of money follows principles summarized by St. Aquinas in the *Summa Theologiae* 2a, 2ae, the part 2 of Part 2, in the treatment of the virtues of charity and justice.

For we should make loans and, indeed, do any good deed not because we expect anything of men, but instead because of what we expect of God.

Id. Question 78, The Sin of Usury, reply to the 4th objection: 38, p. 239 of the Blackfriars Latin-English edition. New York and London: McGraw-Hill and Eyre & Spottiswood, 1975.

10. As Augustine wrote:

> Baptism has the effect that the baptized are incorporated into Christ as his members. The fullness of grace and virtues, however, derives from

> Christ the head to all his members, from his fullness all have received. [*John* I: 16] Thus, it is clear that through baptism a person receives grace and virtues.

St. Aquinas, *Summa Theologiae* 3a, reply in article 5 of Question 69 "Effects of Baptism." p. 135 of *: 57* of the Blackfriars edition.

> Charity *(caritas)* directs the acts of all the other virtues to our end. Thus, it shapes all these acts and to this extent is said to be the form of the virtues, for virtues are so called with reference to formed acts. Charity is likened to a foundation or a root and is known as the mother of the other virtues.

Summa Theologiae 2a, 2ae, answers in Article 8 of Question 23 *The Nature of Charity*: 34, pl 33 of the Blackfriars edition.

11. Richard M. Cyert and James G. March, *A Behavioral Theory of the Firm*. Englewood Cliffs, N.J.: Prentice-Hall, 1963.

The title of this book is somewhat misleading. This is not behaviorism in the sense of treating the mind as a black box, known only by studying its inputs as stimuli and its outputs as responses. The book is behavioral rather in the sense that is an empirical study of what people in business do, as distinct from what economic theories deduced from the behavior of a hypothetical homo economicus suppose they do.

12. Vilfredo Pareto, *The Mind and Society*. New York: Harcourt Brace, 1935. (A translation of the last edition of Pareto's *Trattato di Sociologia Generale,* published in Italy in 1923) Sections 825 and 263. Pareto explains what he repeated many times that human beings perform in order to acquire things satisfying to their tastes. footnote to Section 825. Pareto writes in disapproval of literary economists who compare them to his mathematical economics, even though as he wrote:

> I recognize that my mathematical models have only an approximate relation to the real world; their logical precision is possible merely by definition and that, to a certain extent, arbitrary. *Ibid.*

Pure economics has the advantage of being able to draw its inferences from very few experimental principles; and it makes such a strict use of logic as to be able to state its reasoning in mathematical form—reasoning having the further advantage of dealing with quantities. If the science of political economy has advanced much farther than sociology, then that is chiefly because it deals with logical conduct.

13. Milton Friedman, *Essays in Positive Economics*. Chicago: University of Chicago Press, 1953. p. 22.

14. Cite Braudel "Those without money wander like dead men in the land of the living."

15. Karl Marx, *Capital: I, Part III*. (various editions) Pages 212-213 in the Modern Library edition. New York: Random House 1936. Subsequent page references are also in this edition.

> Our capitalist stares in astonishment. The value of the product is equal to the value of the capital advanced. Our capitalist, who is at home in his vulgar economy, exclaims, "Oh, but I advanced my money for the purpose of making more money." As the way to hell is paved with good intentions, he might just as well have said he intended to make money without producing.

16. Marx, *Capital: I*, pp. 181-182.

17. Marx, *op. cit*. pp. 195-196.

18. *Matthew* 25:40.

19. Marx, *op. cit*. p. 636.

20. Marx, *op. cit*. p. 643.

21. Marx, *op. cit*. p. 649.

22. Marx, *op. cit*. p. 652.

23. David Harvey, *The Condition of Post-modernity*. Oxford: Blackwell, 1990. p. 121.

24. Harvey, *op. cit*. p. 124, p. 147 ff.

25. Harvey, *op. cit*. pp. 141-197.

26. Harvey, *op. cit*. p. 196.

27. Maria Mies, *Patriarchy and Accumulation on a World Scale*. London: Zed Books Ltd., 1986. p. 1.

28. Mies, *op. cit*. p. 2.

29. Mies, *op. cit*. pp. 66-67.

30. Mies, *op. cit*. p. 83.

31. Mies, *op. cit*. pp. 78-88.

32. Mies, *op. cit*. p. 92.

33. Mies, *op. cit*. p. 110.

34. Mies, *op. cit*. p. 136.

35. Marx, *op. cit*. p. 15. Marx made simple assumptions and, as a result, his theoretical framework applies, in part, to the real world; which is stated by Louis Althusser in *Lire, Le Capital*. Paris: Francois Maspero, 1965. English version, *Reading Capital*. London: New Left Books, 1970.

6b. Prescriptions

1. Maria Mies, *Patriarchy and Accumulation on a World Scale*. London: Zed Books, 1986 Chapter 7, p. 205 ff.

2. Mies, *op. cit*. p. 93, quoting p. 264 of Fielding Hall's *A People at*

School.

3. *Ibid.*

4. *Ibid.*

5. Mies, *op. cit.* p. 216.

6. Mies, *op. cit.* p. 222.

7. Friedrich Engels, *Socialism, Utopian and Scientific*. Moscow: Progress Publishers, 1970.

8. Marx, *op. cit.* p. 41.

9. John Locke quoted by Marx, *op. cit.* p. 42. Besides use-value, one might cite the ideal of a society or a socialized humanity from Marx's *Theses on Feurbach,* or the goal of realizing the species of humanity (*gattungwesen)* as a social animal from Marx's early writings. One might cite, as well, the concept of alienation (a word used in English to translate two Deutsch words Marx used, *entfremdung* and *entausserung*) and suggest that the opposite of alienation—engagement—is what Marx prescribed. I advise, however: 1) that the realization of any such Marxist prescriptions would at least overlap and perhaps coincide with producing for use and 2) the conclusion is that Marx proposed only an outline of the character of a better society, not an ethics. See, in these connections, Erich Fromm's, *Marx's Concept of Man*. New York: F. Ungar, 1961; John Torrance, *Estrangement, Alienation, and Exploitation*. New York: Columbia University Press, 1977.

6c. About Metaphysics

1. Among the accounts of the ventures into uncharted territory of those who undertook the arduous tasks involved in the planning of a post-revolutionary economy are Maurice Dobbs,' *Soviet Economic Development since 1917*. New York: International Publishers, 1948; and Arthur MacEwan's *Revolution and Economic Development in Cuba.* New York: St. Martin's Press 1981.

2. Alasdair MacIntyre, *Whose Justice? Which Rationality?* Notre Dame, IN: Notre Dame University Press, 1988, p. 390.

Philosophical theories give organized expression to concepts and theories embedded in forms of practice and types of community.

3. Ernest Mandel, *Marxist Economic Theory*. London: Merlin Press, 1968 (first published in Francaise in 1962) At the end of his two-volume analysis, he agrees with Marx, Rosa Luxembourg, and others that the science of political economy will disappear when the institutions it describes and prescribes disappear. Mandel speculates on a future communist society based on a *positive natural science,* which would be, in effect, a surrogate metaphysic: a comprehensive rational framework articulating the categories in which social life would be recognized and guided. Mandel, *id*. p. 730.

> The survival of the political economy will happen by way of a positive natural science, which will integrate the laws of psychology and health, etc. It is difficult to prophesy what forms will prevail by this positive science. By virtue of the questions it will seek to answer, however, it is clear that it will have little in common with:
> - economic theory,
> - bourgeois political economy, or
> - the Marxist criticism of it.
>
> The Marxist economist can claim the honor of being the first category of people of learning to work consciously toward the abolition of their profession.

Review Questions

1. Smith's interpretation of a market force allows for realism and accuracy in reference to a moral concept. What is the market force, the moral basis, and the other moral basis, which, at the spiritual level brings about action that benefits everyone and Earth? P 100

2. Marx wrote a powerful ideology for the working class from the concepts that the bourgeois had constructed by revealing their contradictions. What contradiction, still active today, defies a basic process of economics? P 101

b. What do you think may have caused Adam Smith to overlook the idea seventy-five years earlier? P 101

3. What idea related to the market force of profit, is a fundamental component of the treadmill of growth? P 103

4. What challenge does capitalism face in its move toward its goal of accumulation, which creates the need to bring the behavior of all individuals into a coordinated configuration?

b. Can you name some of the five or more actor individuals within the coordinated configuration? P 104

5. Marx introduced the idea of alienation, even naming a process of de-alienation as an achievement of a socialist society; for the most part, however, he omits a prescription for alienation. Why?

b. What is the Mies prescription for alienation? P 111, 119

6. Why did Marx not create a comprehensive conceptual system for his economics: a metaphysic? P 110

7. Marx realized that the key to accumulation is also the most flagrant ethical violation of in the global economy. What then is the key to accumulation: profit making? P 110

8. What is the author criterion for his test for distinguishing what is a Marxist concept from what is not? P 110

b. What is the quandary in which the test result faces in terms of being useful toward the goal of reform? p 112
9. What are the impediments and limitations to being the ideal homo economicus within the global economy?
10. Friedman's assertion—nonprofit "maximizers" will not be in business for long—does not invalidate the Aristotle dictum about voluntary human action nor Marx's concession about the fact of a living in capitalist system (or any system). What is the value of both the statements in light of Friedman's? p 100
11. Culture can be transformed only by adopting a conceptual strategy different than Marx's critique of the logic of accumulation. How, in spite of this, might the essential Marxist critique be adapted to make it a starting point for a cultural transformation? p 112
12. Which aspects of Marxism do you see as deconstructing the mainstream economic paradigm? part 6, p 119
b. Do you see the lack of an economic metaphysic in Marxism as: 1) a step toward the abolition of economics as a profession or 2) a return to the etymological meaning of economics?
c. What is the difference between outcome 1) and 2)?
d. If 2) were the result of the Marxist economics, then what effect would it have upon the global economy?

7

Post-Marxist and Post-Structuralist Theories

Post-structuralism is a subset of the *postmodern*, whose adherents share a central conviction: incredulity toward *meta-narratives*.[1] The *meta* in meta-narrative is synonymous with comprehensive; so, postmodern and post-structuralist writers might accept small or local narratives if they accept a narrative at all. They would, however, call it taking a position; they would not call it accepting.

For both the post-structuralist and the postmodern writers, it has been several decades since the social sciences tested hypotheses, models, or theories by assembling data (*the given: data* is derived from the Latin *dare*: to give). The context of incredulity toward meta-narratives assumes an intellectual climate in which discourse is no longer transparent. Had the post-structuralists not embraced the postmodern incredulity they might have "hugged" structuralism. The 20th century Marxist philosophers, Louis Althusser and Michael Foucault largely created the bridge between structuralism and post-structuralism.

The two underlying principles of post-structuralism that form the break with structuralism are:
1. *anti-essentialism*, which is the post-structuralist departure from the classical essentialist paradigm of truth as defined by Aristotle,
2. *over-determination*, which postulates that multiple influences contribute to the observed effects. These two principles are the primary reasons why post-structuralist writers do not explain in the classical essentialist sense.

Structuralism: the analysis of culture using the holistic tenets of the linguistics: Jean Piaget, Noam Chomsky, and especially de Saussure (see pp 186-195). Instead of studying isolated material things, structuralists use signs that are linked via culture to reconstruct relationships.[2]

Within this pivotal discussion, I examine two books: *Encountering Development* by Arturo Escobar,[3] and *The End of Capitalism* by J. K. Gibson-Graham. First, however, using the work of Richard Wolf, I will discuss the broader context of these two books: post-structuralism.[4]

7a. The Disintegration of Social Science

Richard Wolff, author and professor of economics, spoke for many when he wrote:

> The word *explain* is just too implicated in essentialist thought. It connotes fullness, completeness, fixity, closure, and the image of a statement about an object of interest that is not contradictory, particular, and evanescent. It should be displaced in favor of intervention, position, or story.[1]

(Wolff qualifies his position with nuances that I discuss later.)

A few pages earlier in the same article Wolff, interpreting Althusser, gave another reason for eschewing what was the main aim of science: explanation in terms of cause and effect.

> That concept [Althusser's concept of history as a dense network of over-determinations, a process without a subject] holds that every aspect of history—an individual, an event, a social movement, and the like—is constituted by all the other aspects of the social and natural totality within which it occurs. It has its existence and each specific quality of that existence, only insofar as it is over-determined constituted by the relations that bind it to them all. The logic of the over-determined constitutive relations displaces that of causes and their effects.[2]

Wolff lists some motives that inspire anti-essentialism:

> Many of the contributors to anti-essentialism, including Althusser, rejected the sorts of essentialist thinking that they associated with existing social conditions, capitalist and other exploitative class structures, racism, sexism, homophobia, etc. to which they were deeply opposed.[3] The essentialists perceive that:
>
> - ❑ capitalism and the patriarchal family are reinforced by their claim that capitalism alone conforms to human nature
> - ❑ market incentives alone could make the economy work
> - ❑ the patriarchal family alone could produce healthy children

With evils attributed to essentialism and the hopes for the liberation from oppression that anti-essentialism brings, it is no wonder that many social scientists want anti-essentialism to be true. The anti-essentialists are, as are all the economists considered in these pages, well-intentioned.

Essence, that which anti-essentialists refute, is defined in standard dictionaries as: that which makes a thing what it is. It derives from the Latin *esse*: to be. Its current and philosophical meanings traces back to *esse* and to ousia: Gk substance or being, which was the principal term Aristotle sought to define in his *Metaphysics*.[4] Essentialist claims are universalist claims because if there is some essence that a thing has, then it is that essence always and everywhere.

Richard Wolff proposes that social scientists stop using the words —*explain, cause,* and *cause and effect*—because of their close link to essentialism. He lists some of the connotations of the word *essence* that anti-essentialists find false and undesirable:

- fullness
- completeness
- fixity
- closure.

Furthermore, anti-essentialist writers accuse the word *essence* of obscuring what they want to bring to their reader's attention:

• contradiction • particulars • the evanescent.

Whether, in fact, philosophers and scientists err when they employ the term essence and related terms such as substance, reality, cause, explains, and cause and effect, has been debated for over two thousand years. Circa 500 BC, Heraclitus stated the case for anti-essentialism, saying, "All is flux" *(Panta rei).*

It is well-known that, by its nature and structure, language compels humans to speak and write as if the world and their experience were more: complete, fixed, and closed, but less: contradictory, particular, and evanescent than they are. Realists, however, have held up their end of the debate, through the centuries. A realist, as applied here, is one who makes the sorts of conceptual moves that anti-essentialists criticize by calling it essentialism; the lineage of realists extends from Plato and Aristotle through Jung,[5] van Orman Quine,[6] Mies, Jameson,[7] Lacan,[8] Bunge,[9] and Harre.[10] The trend among anti-essentialists, such as Jacques Derrida, author: *Of Grammatology* (a metaphysic of presence), is to attribute to essentialists an implausible view and then deconstruct it.[11] Therefore, people do not, as a rule, call themselves essentialists who: 1) advance philosophies of science where explanation and cause and effect play important roles and 2) even now, talk about nature or the real as something for which the social constructions of culture need to make allowances and adjustments. Their essentialisms are, however, more plausible than those that anti-essentialists identify as their targets. Without adopting the essentialist label as a self-description, they nevertheless, hold views incompatible with radical anti-essentialism. They are more likely to self-identify as:

- ❑ critical realists
- ❑ materialists
- ❑ deep ecologists, or
- ❑ advocates of a naturalized epistemology.

Such more plausible views include:

- ❐ Harre's view that things have causal power
- ❐ Jameson (and others) use of Spinoza's idea of an *absent cause,* which

is at work in history, even though, in the nature of things, human reason cannot fully grasp it

❐ Lacan's philosophy of psychoanalysis in which, in addition to the symbolic and the imaginary, the real exists in its rejection of the symbolic imaginary.

I do not think that Derrida, Foucault, nor any other recent anti-essentialist has an argument proving that, after all these centuries, the heirs of the nominalists and skeptics have won; and the heirs of the ancient and medieval realists have lost. Anti-essentialists have, indeed, shown that there is no truth with a capital 'T', and have shown, in detail, that hidden platonic unities, ideologies, and machinations of power have often deluded people into seeing socially constructed realities as natural realities. The anti-essentialists have, however, no decisive arguments for the proposition that all reality is socially constructed reality. On the contrary, in academic epistemology, critical realism has not lost ground in recent decades; if anything, it has gained ground.[12]

The mechanical Cartesian, Newtonian, or statistical versions of cause and effect reasoning have, nonetheless gained ground, too. Indeed, advocates of realism (include me) are allies of the anti-essentialists when it comes to criticizing the excessive, often devious, use of *mechanical root metaphors*.

Anti-essentialism in the strong form abandons scientific explanation as a goal of social science; thus, it is not a requisite epistemological stance for the contemporary social scientist. The rejection of causal models of any kind is not a rejection imposed by the outcome of debates in which essentialism is refuted, deconstructed, shown as unsupported, and, thus, exposed as an ideological distortion of reality. Radical anti-essentialism is a effective political strategy;[13] the aspects of its merits follow in section 7b and 7c.

The other premise of post-structuralist thought is over-determination: social effects have various causal factors. In *Contradiction and Over-determination,* Louis Althusser uses the idea of over-determination in order to decline to explain historical events using the paradigmatic Enlightenment notion of an explanation that the post-structuralists want to deconstruct. The explanation was the Newtonian X causes Y: the mechanical relationship wherein the impact of force X produces fact Y. Applied to international trade theory and economics in general, this paradigm suggests that the aggregate factors of economic self-interests will produce predictable results. Applied to Marxist economics, this paradigm suggests that accumulation will lead to revolution.

=Over-determination originates with the work of Freud to denote a confluence of subconscious representations, which condense in a single dream image (or neurotic symptom) governed by an emotion. The first use of the term was Freud's analysis of his dream known as "Irma's Injection." Irma appears first as Irma, a patient who had frustrated Freud by refusing to accept his analysis to diagnose the causes of her hysteria. The dream is complex and many faceted: Irma represents a second woman who: • was never Freud's patient • he wanted to analyze • he supposed was more willing to accept his analysis. Irma represents yet a third woman and, as a group, the children at a children's hospital where Freud had worked. In the dream, a Dr. M' was both Freud and a stand-in for several persons Freud knew. The emotion that is *wish fulfillment* (Freud's term), driving the dream was frustration, which Freud felt due to the rejection of his analysis by Irma. An incident the day before the dream had reminded him of the rejection, which triggered his enmity. The synthesis of the dream was that frustration about Irma flowed together with frustration about other failures and resentment about his colleagues regarding him as a quack. Thus, as Freud perceived, it was the confluence and convolution of many elements that made the dream an experience of over-determination.[14]

The historical event examined in Althusser's *Contradiction and Over-determination*[15] is the Russian revolution in 1917. When he borrowed the idea of over-determination from Freud, he declined to explain the revolution in the paradigmatic Newtonian sense of the word *explain*. The economy did not determine the coming of the revolution nor did a quasi-machine analogous to an economy, not even in the last instance. The revolution was over-determined.

It is important, however, to acknowledge that neither Althusser nor anyone else needs the concept of over-determination to make the point that for any social phenomenon many factors contribute to its cause. Mainstream social science research predominate even today, while debates about postmodernism preoccupy the avant-garde, uses statistical regression analysis to quantify the many factors associated with the phenomenon under study. For example, a study of violent acts committed by children might find these variances of explanation: 15% by children seeing violence on television 25% learning violence from parents at home, 5% learning violence from video games 10% learning stereotyped gender roles and machismo 45% error variance not explained yet, although I assume further research would reveal the rest of the explanation.

In reality many factors, variables, and forces are, therefore, at work; advanced scientific tools might be able to organize them. It is not a proposition that requires dissent from the metaphysic of the Enlightenment because complexity alone does not require abandonment of the sorts of explanations that rationalists and empiricists have been refining, amending, affirming, and denying throughout the last several centuries. Freud likely did not intend to abandon the Newtonian paradigm even though, as Jacques Lacan has shown, he did. The Enlightenment metaphysic and, thus, its subset: the economic metaphysic, ought to remain intact: complexity alone should not require deposal of them. What the post-structuralists needed to have deposed was the approval of the role that the capitalist ethical premises play in its economic explanation.

Althusser believed that economics does not determine the course of history. Why then did he not choose the older metaphysical traditions of the West (from Plato, Aristotle, Aquinas, and Hegel), which characterize human action as choice within an ethical context? He chose, instead, to borrow the idea of over-determination from his contemporary, Freud. Althusser answers my question:

> I am not taken by this term over-determination as borrowed from another discipline, though I shall use it in the absence of anything better: 1) as an index and as a problem, and 2) it enables us to see why we are dealing with something quite different than the Hegelian contradiction.[15]

Althusser's essay and his work shows that he wanted to serve the cause of Marxism, therefore of materialism by rejecting idealism. Althusser believed that when Marx praised the rational kernel in Hegel, Marx did not intend to endorse a dialectic in which ideals function as causes in history. Those of us who think that ideals do function as causes in history can, in this light, see why Althusser does not agree with us. We can see why Freud's concept of over-determination served Althusser's purpose; over-determination does not function within:

- ❑ chosen ideals (such as capitalism)
- ❑ the cultivation of agreements
- ❑ cooperative action
- ❑ the ego (the integrating factor of the personality).

Over-determination does function at night in the rapid-eye-movement periods of sleep when the emotions assemble images.

When seen as the indicator of a problem in the social sciences, over-determination (many overlapping causes, no particular cause) reaffirms that we do not know why history happens as it does. However, whatever the course of history, over-determination is the rationale for remaining loyal to materialism, and rejecting the ancient metaphysical hierarchies.

7b. Escobar's Ethics

> The global economy has to be understood as a de-centered system with manifold apparatuses of capture: symbolic, economic, and political. It matters to investigate the particular ways in which each local group participates in this complex machinelike process, and how it can avoid the most exploitative mechanisms of capture by the capitalist mega-machines.[1]

Escobar calls his perspective post-structuralist, which is affirmed throughout his excellent book. It at once progresses within the levels of:

1. the ground or foundation in which Escobar describes particular programs and projects carried out by development professionals in the third-world. He thoroughly documents the anti-hunger programs, the foremost of which is the Integrated Rural Development DRI of his country, Colombia.
2. the global network with programs like DRI that exist within the context of *development discourse*, which came into practice by way of the challenges that the US faced after WW II; development discourse was the creature of a few senior government officials, academics, and bankers; all of whom were white males from the first-world; most all were economists backed by the power of the World Bank and allied institutions; thus, development discourse became a language that the third world had to learn
3. the proactive philosophy in which Escobar treats development discourse as a knowledge that is power and as power that takes the form of knowledge. He calls for a reformed social science in which a reformed post-structuralist anthropology rather than economics would set the tone. The leading role of the new anthropology, however, does not involve creating an alternative theoretical hegemony, which would vie to replace development discourse in particular or economics in general.

> To think about alternatives in the manner of sustainable development, for instance, is to remain within the same model of thought that produced development and kept it in place. One then has to resist the desire to formulate alternatives at an abstract, macro-level; one must resist the idea that the formulation of alternatives will take place in intellectual and academic circles, without meaning by this that academic knowledge has no role in a politics of alternative thinking.[2]

I believe that Escobar's choices at the philosophical level reflect his wish to contribute toward decreasing the vast and endless suffering at the ground level. Escobar's post-economic deconstruction of development is, like postmodernism in general, an epistemology motivated by an ethics.

The earliest of Escobar's ground-level Colombian development stories is about rice. Early in the 20th century, the Colombian elite realized that in order to compete in the international market it would have to exploit, as its comparative advantage, access to cheap labor. The people who would become the cheap labor for whom the entrepreneurial elite and their financial backers would have access, had to move from the countryside to the sites of industry; then the labor needed cheap food, without which they could not survive on low wages. The government subsidized and protected the rice agribusiness because it had the potential to produce a low cost, high-energy food for the workers at low unit cost.[3]

Why are we not surprised? I will answer without paraphrasing Escobar, though in full accord with Escobar and his awareness of the issues:

1. the rice story in Colombia is similar to many stories we have heard. It repeats an oft-told tale with a variant, stated in the early 19th century: Ricardo's argument that the British Corn Laws should be repealed in order to decrease the price of food and, thus, reduce labor costs and increase profits.[4] Colombia's rice tariff was imposed to launch and protect the rice agribusiness; in the British Corn Laws case, a tariff was repealed to serve a similar end. What makes these two cases as variations of the same story is that food policy was a function of the profit imperative and

2. the basic ethical structure of modern society implies that such dealings will repeat given that:

❑ private ownership controls the means of production

❑ the incentive for production is the expectation of profit

❑ profit can only be realized by the sale of the product, which is best facilitated, other things being equal, by bringing the product to market at a price that beats the competition.

Capitalists will therefore seek profits by lowering the costs of production and, other things being equal, by cutting labor costs. Escobar's Colombian rice story bears telling, in some form, many times. The latest of Escobar's ground-level stories from Colombia appears to be the one about the women who pack shrimp in the port city of Tumaco:

> The feminization of the labor force in some industries continues, and it is linked to development schemes; such is the case, for instance, with women in shrimp packaging plants in the port of Tumaco in Colombia. The vast

majority of women working in these plants come from rural families who have lost their lands; they now work under precarious conditions.[5]

We are not surprised because:

1. the feminization of the labor force and the feminization of the labor poverty, are well-known aspects of the trend of global neoliberalism and its mode: *flexible accumulation*.[6] These current trends are similar to what Andre Frank, in the 1960s, called—the development of underdevelopment,[7] which, in turn, is similar to:

❑ accounts of the destruction of African cultures by:

- the slave trade and
- the forced incorporation of Africans into European money economies and speculative markets

❑ the history of driving peasants off the land: "The progressive impoverishment of the English countryside"—Engels

❑ descriptions of the enclosure movement in England given by, among others, Marx in *Capital*

2. the basic cultural structures of modern society set the stage for market behavior, and for the enlargement of markets. Markets, and above all larger markets, imply a drive toward more efficient profit seeking. For this reason, a systemic bias exists in favor of creating classes of easily exploited workers; thus, a systemic bias exists that is opposed to a modicum of security for small farmers and, indeed, anyone else.

The centerpiece of Escobar's ground level series is a pair of Colombian programs, the PAN and DRI. They flourished in the heyday of development discourse: the post-WW II period after the invention and imposition of development discourse and before the recent disillusionment; which has led to a decline of classical development discourse, partly replaced by new forms of power: knowledge and grassroots consensus.

PAN was a program for alleviating hunger, largely by giving away food and other components including nutrition education. It was a structural trap, given the basic cultural and ethical structure of modern society; it was predictable that free food would depress food prices and discourage food production.

The DRI companion program, proposed spending public money provided by the World Bank and allied institutions, with the principal objective of increasing food production. That achievement happened mainly by introducing advanced scientific farming techniques. In the abstract, the increase in production due to DRI might be seen as compensating for the decrease in production due to PAN. In reality, a complex series of political struggles, structural constraints, economic forces, illusions, and errors produced some net winners, net losers, and, overall, no significant alleviation of hunger in Colombia.

Predictably, the absence of a major surge in effective demand for food, i.e. purchasing power, did little to increase the food supply. Furthermore, treating food production as a scientific, physical problem resulted in favoring some farmers while hurting others. It had negative environmental and social side effects. That is what happened, and by the 1990s, DRI had largely ceased to function, which restated the obvious: producing food for sale to people who have no money brings no profit.

I have highlighted Escobar's stories about ground-level development projects in order to clarify the operations of the economic quasi-mechanisms. Escobar however, merely alludes to that explanans because from his perspective explanation in terms of economic quasi-mechanisms is a universalizing, essentialist ploy. His scholarly project is to show that a post-structuralist anthropological approach is more adequate than one that relies on a theory of political economy, and that it is supposed to be applicable worldwide. His achievement consists of making the local constructions visible side-by-side with the analysis of global forces, so that the ground-level facts are seen from a new perspective and in a new light, after having been seen for decades in the light of economics in general and development discourse in particular.

> From the classical political economists to the current neoliberals at the World Bank, economists have monopolized the power of speech.[10]

Now, with Escobar's help, the actions of development agents in remote third world hamlets are revealed as mere dramatic performances scripted by local discourses—in turn shaped by the powerful texts of the development discourse—promoted by the World Bank and its allies. The discourse creates the objects and the actors, who exist by powers they do not understand or, in some cases, do, though, nevertheless, are compelled to pretend not to understand in order to keep their jobs.

Escobar does not offer explanations in the traditional sense: he does not detect cause and effect mechanisms and relationships; however, he does use the word *explain* in the context of discussing why development discourse arose. An example is the famous speech by US president Harry Truman in 1948, wherein he proposed to lift the poor of the world up from poverty by sharing US know-how: sending US technical experts everywhere to teach everyone else how to solve their problems. In retrospect, Truman's Point 4 speech was naive and arrogant. What needs explanation (explanandum) is why the content of his speech made sense to his audience at the time; the explanans (mode to explain) is development discourse. It is a *quasi-explanans,* which quasi-explains why Truman and many others thought as they did. Escobar's explanation of why and how development discourse arose looks more like a genealogy via Foucault, than a particular phenomenon brought under a general causal law, via Newton. Furthermore, it is important for Escobar's argument to insist that the rise of development discourse did not occur predictably. Although it was an understandable response of the first world elite to the challenges of the times, it was not a result destined to happen by factors that caused it. About that, Escobar wrote:

> The free enterprise system was in peril after the WW II. To save such a system, the US faced various imperatives to keep the core nations of the capitalist system together and operable; it required:
>
> ❑ continuous expansion and efforts to avoid the spread of communism
> ❑ ways to invest US surplus capital that accumulated during the war, particularly abroad, where the largest profits could be made
> ❑ finding markets overseas for US goods, given that the productive capacity of US industry had doubled during the war
> ❑ securing control over the sources of raw materials in order to meet world competition
> ❑ establishing of a global network of unchallenged military power as a way to secure access to raw materials, markets, and consumers [11]

In such a context, *development economics* was an idea whose time had come. After WW II, it emerged as a sub-science of economics, building on theories of economic growth written earlier in the century, some of which used the word *development*. It offered a general scientific theory showing how to create a desired world and how to avoid an undesired world. As often advocated in the 1950s, its major prescriptions were:

❑ capital accumulation
❑ deliberate industrialization
❑ development planning
❑ external aid [12]

Development discourse was: • launched, "force-fed and fattened" after WW II by a clique of first world elites comprised of government officials, academics, and bankers • regarded as a normative framework for public policy • supported by development economics as its academic legitimating factor and theoretical backup.

Escobar names names, and gives the dates and places of the meetings where the language of development discourse took form and where institutions that would play key roles in spreading the discourse emerged. Development, as many conceived it, was a companion to the Marshall Plan, which had saved Western Europe from communism by rebuilding its economies; likewise, development would spare the rest of the world from communism.

Created in the first world, the ABCs of development formed a curriculum that the third world had to learn. In every field,—health, education, agriculture, industry, water, electricity, transportation, and women's rights—new programs and projects were touted as the keys to progress, all of which, however, required funding. The principal sources of funding communicated only with people who spoke their language.

Power begat a cosmology that is the development discourse, which oriented the human spirit in space and time, toward objects and ideals. Spatially, the planet split into divisions of developed and underdeveloped regions. The arrow of time pointed from less development to more development; the poor majority of humanity was invited to see its own future high paying union jobs in the US, and in Western Europe's welfare states. The physical objects of the world were objects to be manipulated by engineers applying science to produce. It took about two decades of bitter experience for development, as Truman and the founders of the World Bank conceived it, to lose its charm. By 1970, the World Bank, USAID, and the other funding monopolies, were sponsoring:

- ❐ a basic needs approach
- ❐ growth with equity
- ❐ integral development
- ❐ grassroots development, and later,
- ❐ sustainable development.

To remain credible, development discourse had to be reformed in order to focus upon:

- ❑ extreme poverty
- ❑ environmental degradation
- ❑ loss of cultural identity
- ❑ violence against women, thus,
- ❑ struggle against oppression.

During the 1980s, Latin American countries endured the harshest social and economic conditions since the conquest;[13] African countries weathered nearly the same.[14] Thus, a number of voices, one of which was Escobar's, called for the rejection of the term *development* altogether. They regarded development as a concept fatally flawed from its outset, and irredeemable by its lack of an ethical sense of social justice.

The rise and decline of development discourse illustrates, yet again the absurd tragedy of humans. As Fuller wrote:

> There is no reason why the Earth's resources can`not meet the needs of every member of the human species living in harmony with all living systems.[15]

At this point, however, humanity has not invented the cultural structures and the ecological practices necessary to enjoy Earth's gifts. The gap between our potential and our reality is our tragedy; regardless of whatever consolation one might derive from comparing the relative magnitudes of the sorrows of today to those of yesterday.

It is important to assert the reasons why development has done little to ease human suffering. If Escobar is right in saying that a basic sin of development discourse was that it was essentialist and *universalist*, then the last thing we will want is a post-development era and another essentialist discourse guiding it. Furthermore, if Escobar is right, then we will expect major improvements to flow from the growing influence of post-structuralist perspectives. Yet, what if he is wrong or within the context has made the word *right* irrelevant?

In any case, Escobar is compelled to make judgments about causes and effects. If the widespread adoption of Escobar's post-structuralist position causes life to become harsher, then the results will inflict (not just inscribe) upon bodies. It is unclear whether, all in all, the trend toward post-structuralist scholarship like Escobar's will succeed; it may prove to be—*un engano mas*: another "nail in the coffin" of hope.

The results, I believe, will not be the optimal ones. The two main reasons are: 1) Escobar's post-structuralist approach puts him in an awkward position in regards to non-Western cultures and traditional Western values. Thus, one might expect that a book calling for the empowerment of people in the third world would have included more than passing references to liberation theology, which Escobar mentions in a mere two footnotes, to Islam, and to Gandhi; also, absent is a discussion of progressive Buddhism, for example: the *Sarvodaya* movement in Sri Lanka. Although there are post-structuralists who have written at length on religion, Escobar's neglect of religion is typical and symptomatic of an inherent conflict between the ultramodern philosophy: post-structuralism and traditional societies, which, in their splendid variety are at once: • religious • collectivist • hierarchical • patriarchal, with carefully differentiated gender roles • homophobic • puritanical • xenophobic • superstitious. Those terms are pejorative in the West used to describe others. The people who hold such views describe their views in their terms, and not in terms of the extremism, which, for them, describes the views of others.

Escobar cites, with approval, authors such as, Foucault, Eugene Deleuze, Felix Guattari, Michel Taussig, Garcia Canclini, Dorothy Smith, and others. Their writings and Escobar's show their shared values to be: • secular • individualist in the positive sense of favoring personal autonomy, what Jung called: individuation • democratic • feminist, tending toward gender equality • opposed to mandated heterosexuality • sensual • internationalist • critical.[16]

Post-structuralism is, therefore, in an awkward position, which is not a problem if it just a matter of: 1) criticizing mainstream modernist liberal thought for pretending to be universal and ever rational, or merely 2) listing the attractive examples of which there are many in *Encountering Development,* of small and obscure cultures that have their ways of seeing and doing things, which are more in harmony with nature than the ways of the modern West.[17]

Escobar and post-structuralists, as a rule, do not accept that whatever the oppressed say must be right. The problem, though, is that their approach makes it hard to see the fine-tuning criteria needed for telling the difference between values to be rescued *(valores de rescate*), and themes best left behind *(temas superables*). It is hard to reconcile the following: 1) no one should have a right to define another's reality 2) it is time for the voices of the silenced to speak 3) the freedom to reject many of the things Western and nontraditional people say when they speak. The awkward mixed message is not an incidental feature of postmodernism, which rectifies easily by noting oversights. For example:

> Those intellectuals from the university insist on our right to name our reality as long as we agree with their corrupt, individualistic, materialistic, permissive, and effeminate values.

Another example: Islamic fundamentalists have the right to speak because they share the birthright to it according to a radical *ethics of autonomy*; nevertheless, when fundamentalists speak, those who hear them learn that Islam means submission, not autonomy. Therefore, the fundamentalists Muslims speak to spread the teachings of the *Holy Qu'ran,* not to name their reality.

The *ethic of autonomy* in turn, which is the source of the awkwardness, links right to Foucault and Escobar's central concept: power. Since the 17th century, power has been, and still is, the principal root metaphor with which Western philosophy has erected secular alternatives to the traditional religious worldviews of the West. Autonomy is yours when power does not oppress you. Kant wrote:

> Autonomy is the principle of all genuine morality; heteronomy is the principle of all spurious morality. [Kant's autonomy is similar to what the *isolationist* call sovereignty, i.e. being self-governed, not subject to control by anyone else.]

Escobar's story of the rise of development discourse is a story about power and speech; therefore, it is a story about oppression and silencing; thus, it leads to the conclusion that the oppressed should speak; nevertheless, then they speak in confusion.

The results will not be the optimal, reason 2): taking a post-structuralist philosophical position makes it needlessly tricky to talk about objective physical reality. In principle, there is supposed to be no such thing because the discourse defines the objects. This principle sometimes seems to be a philosophical opinion of no consequence because post-structuralists are able to cope with objective physical reality in life the same as everyone else; nevertheless, sometimes it does have consequences.

It makes a difference when Escobar criticizes Samir Amin who sees no hope for his continent, Africa, without major capital investments in agriculture. For Amin and economists in general, it is obvious that no serious decrease in poverty can occur without capital accumulation. The comfortable people of the first-world enjoy comforts because of the work of people in past generations whose savings and investments made it possible to create advanced technology, install it, and build infrastructure. Whether capital is accumulated by:

❑ the puritan ethic
❑ exploiting colonies
❑ extracting surplus value from workers
❑ forced industrialization under Stalin or Mao: no one emerges from poverty without somebody postponing present consumption for the sake of investing in future productive capacity. Amin has, thus, devoted his time to enlarging proposals for what he calls *auto-centric accumulation*. Given that:

❑ Africa will prosper only after Africa makes capital investments in agriculture and industry
❑ capital-poor Africa has for the last several centuries been to a great

extent at the mercy of capital-rich foreign powers
❑ the capital accumulation processes have, to date, been cruel, destructive, and unjust. He wants to put the accumulation process within the parameters of:
❒ humanity and ecological sensitivity
❒ democratic control for Africans (and all people) of their destinies
❒ using appropriate technologies to achieve shortcuts that will make the tooling-up process less painful than it was in the 19th century
❒ distribute burdens to be shared equitably by all, especially within the imbalances between the urban and rural, and the ethnic, racial, and tribal groups.[19]

Amin's project would appear to be a laudable one; nevertheless, Escobar raises an objection to it in principle:

> It is necessary to emphasize, however, that Amin's prescriptions are written in a universalistic mode and a *realist epistemology*, precisely the kinds of thinking criticized here.[20]

Why does Escobar care so much about the issue of realist epistemology v. post-structuralism that he finds it necessary to criticize Amin's constructive project on philosophical grounds? The likely answer: Escobar has written a two hundred and fifty page book berating development discourse for its bias: realist epistemology.

Foucault showed that prisons have served their real purpose: to extend their power, even though it was clear from the beginning that they would not serve their declared purpose: to rehabilitate criminals.[21] Likewise, Escobar was able to show that development discourse has served its real purpose: extending power, even though it was clear from the beginning that it would not serve its declared purpose: lifting the suffering masses of the third world beyond poverty. Development discourse pulled off the sleight-of-hand trick necessary to disguise its real purpose, and pulled it off in such a way that it was able to de-politicize poverty. What had been a conflict of interest between the exploiters and exploited became a technical problem solvable by experts. All of the problems were allegedly about objective physical reality. A realist epistemology guaranteed the credentials of the development economists and the other technical experts employed to solve, for example, the problem of hunger, as development discourse had defined that problem into existence.

Amin draws Escobar's ire because Amin agrees with his professional colleagues that the need to accumulate capital is indeed an objective physical problem. Accumulation as a concept bifurcates into: 1) another name for exploiting colonies and workers, and for the machinelike global extension of capitalism and 2) the name for the tooling up process which is central to prosperity. In its second identity, it represents a fact of nature. Lack of accumulation is a fact too: a brutal one; it is like the swarms of locusts that God sent to devour the grain of the Egyptians.

None of the priests of Egypt, with all their syntax and semantics, their synchrony and diachrony, their breaks and sutures, story and ritual, texts and subtexts, semiotics, and grammatology, genealogy and deconstruction, could stop the locusts from eating the grain.

In Africa today, the need to bring water to the land, before the seeds will germinate, grow, and produce edible fruit represents the irreducible resistance of Nature against the hegemony of Meaning; it represents the revolt of objects that refuse to allow discourse to define them out of existence. Amin offers an alternative physical solution to a physical problem. His realist epistemology does humanity and him no harm.

Ultimately, Escobar and Amin are kin of the democratic left; Escobar recognizes the merit of Amin's work even though he thinks it must be constantly destabilized.[22] Moreover, Escobar's criticism of Amin's realism overshoots the mark. Showing that mainline development discourse rests on false realist epistemologies does not rule out the possibility that the work of Samir Amin and many others might rest on true realist epistemologies.

I do appreciate and laud the spirit of post-structural approach, while pointing out that result is likely to be less than optimal. The result will:

1) impede distinguishing the better traditions from the worse traditions
2) overemphasize discourse, and
3) de-emphasize facts. I do mean to suggest that the achievements of the post-structural mode do not need approval at the expense of discernment and realism.

7c. Gibson-Graham's Metaphysic

The tradition that takes its name from Aristotle's *Metaphysics* constructs what Aristotle termed *first principles* (*archai*). Its inquiries into the first principles and causes of all things concerned, above all, being or substance (*ousia*).

Explanations of the global economy assume that the global economy has being and exists. Even the best explanation is stultified if the phenomenon that it claims to accurately explain, in fact, does not exist. The criteria for distinguishing being from nonbeing and existence from nonexistence, become crucial when somebody thinks it important to deny the existence of something whose existence somebody else thinks it important to affirm. In the history of metaphysics, the first principles governing the concept of being have been invoked to prove, or to disprove, the existence of God. The present question, however, concerns not whether God exists, but whether the global economy exists. In *The End of Capitalism (as we knew it): a Feminist Critique of Political Economy,* the author argues that the global economy is a fiction:

> Like many political economists, I had theorized the US social formation and the global economy as sites of capitalist dominance located squarely in the social or economic field. Of late, however, a theoretical option emerged that could make a (revolutionary) difference: to depict economic discourse as hegemonic while rendering the socioeconomic world as differentiated and complex.[1]

It is crucial to ask what sorts of reasons would count for or against the theoretical option, that Gibson-Graham embraces—which includes denying (or declining to assert or observe) that global capitalism or the global economy exist. Metaphysics is the standard means to discern whether to attribute being to a concept that is contested, such as: God, capitalism, or the global economy. Aristotle is the source and a representative of the mainstream ancient and medieval metaphysics of the West; thus, a salient divide exists between the traditional metaphysics and the postmodern metaphysic of Gibson-Graham as outlined:

I.) Aristotle tends to attribute being to generalities; Gibson-Graham tends to attribute being to particulars. Aristotle wrote:

> If there is nothing apart from individuals, there will be no object of thought, but all things will be objects of sense; there will be no knowledge of anything, unless we say that sensation is knowledge.[2]

Aristotle often used a characteristic substance, or being as a seed, which has intrinsic to it the plant form or animal it will become, or as a product made by an artisan who had in mind the form before making it, or as a person with a continuing soul self-identical through its passing states (his favorite example is that of Socrates).

> We say the Hermes is in the stone, and the half of the line is in the line, and we say of that, which is not yet ripe that it is corn.[3] Ousia, finally, has two senses: 1) the ultimate substratum, which no longer predicates of anything else, and 2) that, which being a this is also separable—and of this nature is the shape or form of each thing.[4]

Gibson-Graham wrote:

> A capitalist site is an irreducible specificity. We may no more assume that a capitalist firm is interested in maximizing profits or exploitation than we may assume that a woman wants to bear and raise children, or that a US resident is interested in making money. When capitalism gives way to an array of capitalist differences, its non-capitalist other is released from singularity and subjection, potentially visible as a differentiated multiplicity.[5]

Gibson-Graham depicts generalities, such as the global economy, and capitalism as false and oppressive. A discourse that celebrates variety and the proliferation of differences, serves to make visible many things, which ought to have been seen long ago, were it not that the hegemonic discourse about global capitalism has made them invisible.

II.) Aristotle thinks of his inquiries as a quest for truth. Gibson-Graham sees inquiry as invoking the *performative force,* which is *constitutive* of economic representation.[6] Gibson-Graham writes:

> The global economy is an economic representation constituted by other people's performances, the acts in which they performed, and speaking and writing. The global economy was called into being by discourse.

Her performance, the writing of the book *The End of Capitalism,* intends to constitute a different discourse. She writes:

> In the hierarchical relation of capitalism to non-capitalism, lies (entrapped) the possibility of theorizing economic difference, of supplanting the discourse of capitalist hegemony with a plurality and heterogeneity of economic forms. Liberating that possibility is an anti-essentialist project, and perhaps the principal aim of this book.[7]

Gibson-Graham's aim is similar to that of most writers on the topics of capitalism and the global economy: she seeks to understand the way the world works in order to change the way it works. She takes the view, however, that the concepts most often employed, capitalism and the global economy, have backfired. By attributing to the capitalist global economy, an essence—a monolithic nature—they have contributed to its strength. It seems all-powerful because the theories of left political economists tell us it is all-powerful:

> If capitalism's identity is even partly immobile or fixed if it is the site of an inevitability like the logic of profitability or accumulation, then by necessity it will be seen to operate as a constraint or a limit. It becomes that to which other more mutable entities must adapt. We see this today in both mainstream and left discussions of social and economic policy, where we are told that we may have democracy, or a pared-down welfare state, or prosperity, however only in the context of the global capitalist economy and what it will permit.[8]

Gibson-Graham proposes a new anti-capitalist strategy: deconstruct the concept of capitalism, and reject that it exists as we knew it, i.e. as it has been conceived. This theoretical move serves to refocus vision and, thus, make what was invisible visible and what was impossible possible:

> Theorizing capitalism itself as different than itself—as having no essential or coherent identity—multiplies the possibilities of change.[9]

She cites from the writings of other feminists, and from queer theorists, tactics for discourse analysis that deconstruct stereotypes. To refute the existence of capitalism and the global economy, she deploys some philosophical arguments that disprove the idea of the typical woman, and struggle against compulsory heterosexuality by disproving the conventional stereotypes of gays.

Hazel Henderson and others point out that the majority of the work done in the world is either:

1. unpaid household labor and childcare,
2. nonprofit or public sector, or
3. production for direct use (e.g. gardening, do-it-yourself home improvement); only a minority of the world's work is wage or salary labor done for capitalist corporations. Gibson-Graham cites the same facts, and counts self-employment as non- capitalist. The middle level business executive who loses her job to downsizing and ekes out a living as a consultant, and those who sell chewing gum on the streets of third world cities, count as part of the non-capitalist total. The informal sector, which Marx characterized as—the industrial reserve army of the unemployed—is seen in a different light because it produces a series of instances of economic diversity as do the elements of:

• feudal agriculture • household slavery • patriarchal sweatshops, which are found throughout our diverse world. Gibson-Graham is not in favor of that various misery, though she does use it to buttress her case that any general thesis that postulates a world capitalist economy must be wrong.

A considerable part of her book is about the blokes who work in Australian coalmines. Highly mechanized Australian mines are able to deliver coal to the world market at competitive prices; the workers organize in militant unions with left ideologies. The blokes make good money, their wives, who may be nurses or teachers, sometimes make good money too, they may own several houses, and they are likely to fly to Europe for vacations. Gibson-Graham's ethnographic account of bloke-land reinforces her image of the world as a crazy quilt of diverse economic forms; it does not at all resemble the world portrayed by Marx in *Capital* in which capital grew and accumulated through extracting surplus value from workers who were paid an absolute survival wage.

Disclaimer: the following imaginary dialogue with J. K. Gibson-Graham runs the risk that the words that I attribute to her may be different than what she would say.

Critic: Do you mean that capitalism is such a minor component among the variety of economic forms found in the world that if it were to crash again, as it did in the 1930s, that would not be a problem, because humanity with its variety of non-capitalist forms could get along without it?

Gibson-Graham: Of course not.

Critic: So do you recognize that capitalism is an important institution in the world, as it exists today?

Gibson-Graham: If I did not, I would not be writing a book about how to change it.

Critic: You do not mean, either, that the economic policies of the world's governments are mistaken when they seek to:

- ❑ attract investment
- ❑ foster a favorable business climate
- ❑ provide incentives and security for investors
- ❑ build confidence in the economic stability and profit potential of whatever part of the world they govern
- ❑ work to keep up profits so that capitalism will succeed.

Gibson-Graham: I think that profits could be much lower without the dire consequences that even supposed leftist economists threaten will follow if workers and governments do not cave in to all the demands of capital.

Critic: Even so, you do recognize that in order to function capitalism requires some rate of profit?

Gibson-Graham: Yes.

Critic: So, do you recognize that, as a rule, entrepreneurs will seek the highest profits they can get? Do you also recognize that other economic actors, such as workers and bankers seek to maximize their returns?

Gibson-Graham: No.

Critic: Why not?

Gibson-Graham: You do not understand me well. I am writing about political economy as discourse. I am not conducting an inquiry within that discourse about the phenomena of economics and how to explain them. I am not saying that Ricardo, or Marx, or Samuelson, understood the laws of profit wrong. I am analyzing the discourse that constructs profit as a category, defines economic actor as an entity seeking to maximize something, and makes it meaningful to talk about laws of profit.

Critic: So, you think that economists should not even be trying to write general laws, which explain and predict that under X conditions profits will be Y?

Gibson-Graham: It is un-empowering.

Critic: What do you mean by that?

Gibson-Graham: Social reality is constantly being contested and renegotiated. If we think that some supposed scientific laws determine workers pay, and how much profit capital has to get, then we will accept social reality as defined by someone else, instead of participating in creating social reality.

Critic: The laws of economics may be un-empowering; nevertheless, I cannot help thinking that they are to some extent true. Does it help the victims of the system when intellectuals convince them they have power that they, in fact, do not have, so that, like the "rooster Chanticleer" who thought he could make the sun rise by crowing, they think that if they talk tough and go on strike they will get high wages and benefits?

Gibson-Graham: I do not deny that it is to some extent true that capital has power. The question, however, is the extent. If you write economics as if the world economy were a monolithic system governed by inexorable laws of capital accumulation, then you create a myth that capital is all-powerful, the rest of us are powerless.

Critic: It seems, correct me if wrong, that you advance two types of reasons for concluding that capital is less powerful than most people think. First, you attack the concept of a monolithic global economy governed by inexorable laws, saying that the idea of a capitalist global economy makes invisible the world's diversity of economic forms. This is a sort of negative proof of your thesis: you are telling us that believing is seeing. All the evidence we think we see is filtered through the lens of an essentialist discourse, so that if it were true, as you think it is, that the social world is infinitely diverse and constantly under renegotiation and reconstruction, people would not see the truth.

Gibson-Graham: I recognize[10] that in my book I attack a "straw man," although not a straw man I have constructed alone. Probably no one holds that the capitalist global economy is as monolithic and powerful as it is in the image of it that I attack.

Critic: Your straw man, however, resembles the views of Jameson, Harvey, Wallerstein, others, and even your former views in your writing about the global economy.

Gibson-Graham: I simplify my theoretical target in order to make my point; nevertheless, it is relevant to what ordinary people and social scientists actually say and think.

Critic: So, part of your argument is that any theory as general as the straw man you attack must be wrong. You, nevertheless, do not refute a thesis advanced by anyone per se.

Gibson-Graham: I would not put it that way. It is true that I do not refute any of what Jameson, for example, affirms, as if it were a matter of scoring points in macho intellectual combat, or a matter of one mathematician finding an error in another mathematician's proof. I, nevertheless, do elaborate an alternative to a Jameson vision. If you go back and read Jameson again after reading my book, you will find him less persuasive.

Critic: Your work is illuminating: it makes real-live facts visible that could not possibly happen according to the straw man who thinks everything happens according to simple laws of capitalist accumulation. Your straw man's discourse is similar enough to discourses that are employed, indeed are dominant, by helping the reader to see its flaws, you help the reader to see flaws in discourses that exist, like Jameson's.

Gibson-Graham: I would not have put it quite that way, but I won't object either.

Critic: Apart from saying that the straw man must be wrong because in principle essentialism is always wrong, you fill your book with anecdotes.

Gibson-Graham: You mean factual cases.

Critic: Yes, for example, in the 1990s, after a protracted struggle, the USWA (United Steelworkers of America), Local 5668, won a three year contract with Ravenswood Aluminum Company, in spite of the company's use of its bargaining advantage as a multinational company to break the union by locking the workers out. The union's researchers established that the new owner of Ravenswood was a global commodity trader indicted by the US Department of Justice on tax fraud and racketeering. The union's tactic, which you call a nonstandard response, was to portray the company as an international outlaw, damaging its public image and launching investigations by government agencies. "Terrier-like," the USWA pursued the company around the globe yanking and pulling at it until it ceded.[12] This one case refutes the straw man (or perhaps a straw man even simpler than the one you construct), because if labor defeats capital just once, as it did, then it is not true that capital always wins.

Gibson-Graham: This is one of the stories that show the value of my anti-essentialist approach to social theory. If the steelworkers union had believed the myth of the global economy, they might have given up without trying. As it turned out, the workers faced-down internationalism with worker's internationalism, and won.

Critic: You do not, however, attempt to use a significant statistical sample of similar cases. You don't test a hypothesis about how often and for what reasons labor wins. You do not propose a causal mechanism, or a model, to explain the observed facts. You do not design tests that compel your theory to run the risk that it might be shown to be false. You do nothing that mainstream social scientists do to test their theories.

Gibson-Graham: Correct.

Critic: You do not even use descriptive statistics, nor do you tell us how often the sorts of cases you describe occur.

Gibson-Graham: I do think social reality is over-determined, and I do not believe in causal models. Descriptive statistics are less objectionable, although they are often misleading because they mask differences among the cases grouped together. Anyway, quite apart from what I think about what positivist social scientists do or not, what I do is something different. I show how the dominant discourse about the global economy has defined capital as powerful, labor as weak, and, thus, has made invisible many things that happen.

Critic: So, the point of your discourse analysis is not to define a causal mechanism other than the mechanism of accumulation, which can be expected to regularly produce similar results. The point is not to claim that the cases you cite are typical, or even numerous. The point is not to identify the objective conditions under which labor's chances of winning improve. The great advantage of your post-structuralist post-Marxism is that victims of oppression who accept your approach see more possibilities, and have more confidence. Your theory is like a pep talk: Don't just assume that capital can move production wherever it wants! Don't just assume that it is impractical for labor to organize internationally! Look at X! Look at Y! They had courage, fought back, and won!

Gibson-Graham: Pep talk is a shallow way to describe what I do. A better way to describe the process of encouraging people to try what Paulo Freire called the *untested feasibility* is to think in terms of changing scripts. The global economy is not just a false generalization: it is a script, like the script for a play or a motion picture: it defines the roles of the actors. My book attempts to rewrite the script, so that people will transgress the present rules, and act in nonstandard ways, which will lead to new standard ways: new scripts.

Critic: Do the nonstandard transgressions exercise power that people really have, but which the hegemonic script of the capitalist global economy leads them to believe they do not have?

Gibson-Graham: I will answer with an example: I compare the rape script to the global economy script.[11] There is a standard script about men raping women, in which the role of women is defined as passive, powerless: the woman is a victim who allows the rape in order to save her life; by analogy, a similar script governs the rape of the third world by the multinational corporations.

Critic: Before we discuss the analogy, tell me why you know that rape is governed by a rape script. Have you interviewed a significant sample of rapists and rape victims and coded the interview data?

Gibson-Graham: I borrowed the rape script concept from other feminist writers. It is a concept that rings true to me, though not because there is much empirical data verifying its hypotheses; rather it rings an accurate interpretation of meanings that prevail in our culture. I think the rape script concept resonates with my readers for the same reason. We are all participating members of our culture, and we all know that defines man as strong, woman as weak.

Critic: You cite an example of a woman who refused to play the role assigned to her by the rape script. She grabbed the penis of her would-be rapist while he was hitting her head. He lost his erection and ran away.[12]

Gibson-Graham: Similarly, there is a prevailing script, which defines multinational corporations as strong, and third world people as weak.

Critic: Are you implying that if people in the third world, or poor people as a rule, would follow a different script, then they would be powerful?

Gibson-Graham: I don't want to be backed into a position where I am obliged to defend the absurd thesis that all victims are more powerful than they think they are. Some victims are less powerful than they think they are. My point is that certain essentialist scripts define roles in which people are defined as powerless regardless of the facts; the script itself has performative force: it makes people less powerful than they otherwise would be.

The imaginary dialogue above illustrates, that J. K. Gibson-Graham and post-structuralists, in general, have an awkward relationship to the age-old question, "Why do things happen as they do?" Their ill at ease is due to rejecting mainstream and Marxist paradigms of scientific inquiry, without developing new, or reviving old ways to answer the *why* questions. I had stated that the idea of over-determination is, when applied to conscious waking social life, not so much a way to answer the why question as a way to justify not answering it. I suggest now (and will develop later) that ideas like constitutivity, script, and performative performance are more promising. Their diagnoses and prescriptions are unclear, although they do allude to the sources of problems and their grounds for believing that the conceptual reforms and the courses of action they advocate will solve problems.

Aristotle conceived of four main types of principle or *cause archai*, four main ways to respond to the why question:

1. *material cause*, what the thing is made of: a vase made of bronze.
2. *efficient cause*, the source of movement, as the vase- maker who makes the vase, or as love or desire considered as a principle initiating motion.
3. *formal cause*, the form, shape, pattern, definition, or essence, which makes the thing what it is, which causes a shaped bronze to be defined as a vase.
4. *final cause*, that for the sake of which the thing is made, the end the vase-maker serves in making the vase.

By the time Althusser and the post-structuralists took up the critical examination of science, Aristotle had become linked to traditions that were erroneous and undesirable. The idea of final cause was thought to attribute false human purposes to nature. The idea of formal cause was thought (rightly) to give the status of natural facts on social conventions by treating accepted definitions as hallmarks of true being; thus, being-as-form favored aristocracy, divinity, and masculine privilege. Efficient causes were what mechanistic science was all about: the forces, impressions, effects, and variables to which it attributed (efficient) causal efficacy and or explanatory significance. They were not, however, the sorts of sources of which Aristotle had in mind.

Gibson-Graham likely will not, nor can we expect her to, sympathize with Aristotle's treatment of social conventions as if they were natural essences. She might, however, have sympathy in regard to human action as a praxis and as a paradigm for explanation. Aristotle's vase-maker is not making a revolution, though at least he is making something.

> Cause means the form or pattern [and that] from which the change or the resting from change first begins, e.g. the adviser is a cause of the action, and the father a cause of the child, and in general the maker a cause of the thing made, and the change-producing of the changing. *Beginning* means that from which change naturally first begins, as a child comes from its mother and father, and a fight from abusive language that at whose will that which is moved is moved, that which changes do change. For example:
> - magistracies in cities
> - oligarchies
> - monarchies
> - tyrannies
>
> are called *archai*; so too are the arts because all causes are beginnings.[13]

Some 2500 years ago, in his primitive, patriarchal, and naive way, Aristotle expressed some observations about why things happen the way they do; all his citations are in accord with Gibson-Graham's desire to encourage victims to become activists and, thus, not to be misled and discouraged by mechanistic causal models. A number of contemporary approaches to social science are reviving Aristotelian notions of deliberate action as praxis. Once again, a choice is a source of movement that explains an action. Formal causes, the patterns and implicit definitions built into language and accepted by common sense as the framework of action in everyday life have returned, for example as:

- ❐ constitutive rules
- ❐ institutional facts
- ❐ symbolic interaction
- ❐ dramaturgic social analysis
- ❐ emic viewpoints
- ❐ plans
- ❐ performatives
- ❐ phenomenology
- ❐ language-games
- ❐ scripts
- ❐ ethno-methodology
- ❐ act/action structures
- ❐ cognitive structures.

Thus, meanings are causes again.[14]

Gibson-Graham is among the social scientists offering explanations in terms of the causes that Aristotle would have classed as formal. Alternatively, Aristotle might class her explanations as efficient causes in the sense that later centuries deleted from the idea of efficient cause as when one makes a decision to be a source of movement. Examples might be, when a raid triggers a decision to go to war,[15] or in *The End of Capitalism,* a woman's submission to rape is explained by a rape-script, which defines her as powerless. Gibson-Graham is not in dialogue with:

- ❐ contemporary neo-Aristotelians such as Martha Nussbaum, Alasdair MacIntyre

❐ mainstream positivist economists such as Friedman
❐ social scientists influenced by recent mainstream Anglo-American analytic philosophy like Carol Gilligan, Nel Noddings, and Rom Harre. —Gibson-Graham is in dialogue with other feminists, with Althusserians, and with Marxist political economists. She stands in a tradition shaped by Marx, and for that reason encounters a special conceptual impediment standing in the way of accepting a neo-Aristotelian model of human action. Marx begins *Capital* by writing that he is about to analyze: "It is that form of society where wealth appears as a vast collection of commodities."

Commodity, in the original Deutsch is *waren*:[16] the English cognate is the word *wares*, which is things offered for sale. In his first sentence, Marx outlines the structure of his discourse: capitalist common sense is an illusory discourse; wealth only appears as commodities; it appears in what Marx later calls *commodity form*; however, the commodity form is not, for Marx, what Aristotle would have called a formal cause; for Marx commodity form, i.e. exchange, is not the pattern of what truly is and not the source of movement; it is an illusion masking the deeper reality. The essence of the commodity is not on the surface of society; it is the quantity of labor embodied in it and, thus, its value. Marx's analysis asserts that as long as we remain at the formal level, at the level of circulation, we will never understand capitalism. Capitalism occurs beneath the surface at the level of production where business exploits labor and produces surplus value.

For this reason, the anti-essentialist left continues within the Marxist tradition only with great difficulty. Anti-essentialism cannot follow Marx in his moves from: surface to depth, circulation to production, and formal appearance to material essence. If anti-essentialist left intellectuals would take just one more step they could at once undo: 1) the Marx demotion of circulation to the level of mere appearance, and 2) modernity's, for example, Descartes and Locke's demotion of appearance to mere secondary qualities. The anti-essentialist sometimes take this step in practice, e.g. in Gibson-Graham's recognition that the rape script has causal powers. Culture does shape vision, so that one person appears as strong and, thus, is the powerful man; another appears as weak and, thus, is the weak woman; thus, meanings are causes. Perhaps the anti-essentialist would consider recognizing in theory that the commodity form, which is the meanings at work in the ritual of exchange, functions as an explanatory principle: a cause.

It would follow that a capitalist global economy is the operative basis at large today. If you came from a Marxist tradition, likely you define capitalism in terms of the production relationships between owners and workers. The variety of production relationships in the world might lead you to be more impressed by the differences than by the similarities; thus, you might insist that there is no worldwide capitalism, but instead many forms of capitalism alongside many non-capitalist forms. If, however, Aristotle was right by assigning being to forms, then—money, accounts, debts, investments, wares offered for sale, exchange relationships, markets, and all that appears at the level of circulation—is among the things that are. The global market and the worldwide use of money do not constitute a universal truth valid in every circumstance; it does constitute a major feature of the world in which we live. Therefore, it is justifiable to say that the capitalist world economy exists, even if that means capitalism not defined as Marx did.

It does not, however, follow that we are powerless victims of a monolithic system governed by inexorable laws. If by placing Aristotle in agreement with Gibson-Graham, we see forms as social constructions, then it follows that the capitalist global economy is a social construct, which we can socially reconstruct.

Notes

1. Jean Francois Lyotard, *The Postmodern Condition: a Report on Knowledge.* Minneapolis: University of Minnesota Press, 1984 (first published in Francaise in 1979). p. 24.

> Simplifying to the extreme, I define postmodern as incredulity toward meta narratives. The incredulity is no doubt a product of the sciences; however, that progress in turn presupposes it.

2. Jean Piaget, *Structuralism.* New York: Harper Collins 1958. Noam Chomsky, *The Logical Structure of Linguistic Theory.* Chicago: University of Chicago Press, 1985 Claude Levi-Strauss, *Structural Anthropology.* Translated from the Francaise by Claire Jacobson and Brooke Grundfest Schoepf. *Anthropologie Structurale.* [English] New York: Basic Books, 1963

3. Arturo Escobar, *Encountering Development: the Making and Unmaking of the Third World.* Princeton, NJ: Princeton University Press, 1995.

4. J. K. Gibson-Graham, *The End of Capitalism (as we knew it): a Feminist Critique of Political Economy.* Cambridge, MA and Oxford: Blackwell, 1996.

7a. The Disintegration of Social Science

1. Richard Wolff, "Althusser and Hegel: Making Marxist Explanations Anti-Essentialist and Dialectical" in the Antonio Callari and David F. Ruccio (eds.), *Postmodern Materialism and the Future of Marxist Theory.* Hanover and London: Wesleyan University Press, 1996. p. 166.

2. *Id*. p. 153.

3. *Id*. p. 151.

4. Aristotle, *Metaphysics*, especially *Books III and VI-XI* (various editions).

5. Jungians affirm the existence of archetypes in the myths and dreams of the species, which are common across classes and across cultures. Jungian thought is alive, well, and able to hold its own in post-Foucault intellectual life as shown, for example by Andrew Samuels, *The Political Psyche*. London: Routledge, 1993. p. 8.

6. As I read Quine's views, they propose to combine a resolute logic with a firm realism. For example:

> Our talk of external things—our notion of things—is just a conceptual apparatus that helps us foresee and control the triggering of our sensory receptors in the light of previous triggering of our sensory receptors. The triggering, first and last, is all we have to go on. In saying this, I am talking also of external things: people and their nerve endings. What I am saying, thus, applies in a particular to what I am saying; I do not intend it to be skeptical. Nothing exists that we can be more confident of than external things, (some of them anyway) other people, and sticks and stones. Nonetheless, there remains the fact—a fact of science itself—that science is a conceptual bridge of our own making, linking sensory stimulation to sensory stimulation.

Willard van Orman Quine, *Theories and Things.* Cambridge: Harvard University Press, 1981. pp. 1-2.

7. Fredric Jameson, *Postmodernism, or, The Cultural Logic of Late Capitalism*. Durham: Duke University Press, 1991. As with David Harvey, cited in note 23 to Part 6a above, Jameson turns the tables on postmodernism. Instead of admitting that historical materialism is no longer believable because it is a meta-narrative, Jameson (as does Harvey) argues that historical materialism is a meta-narrative capable of explaining the general course of history and the recent cultural phenomena known as postmodernism as well.

8. Jacques Lacan," The Function of Language in Psychoanalysis" Jacques Lacan in *The Language of the Self*. Baltimore: Johns Hopkins Press, 1968 (translation, notes, and commentary by Anthony Wilden)

> Its [the psychoanalytic method's] means are those of the Word, insofar as the Word confers a meaning on the functions of the individual; its domain is that of the concrete discourse, insofar as this is the field of the trans-individual reality of the subject; its operations are those of history, insofar as history constitutes the emergence of Truth in the Real.

9. Mario Bunge, *Causality and Modern Science*. New York: Dover, 1979.

10. Rom Harre, *Causal Powers: a Theory of Natural Necessity*. Totowa, NJ: Rowman and Littlefield, 1978; Jerrold Aronson, Rom Harre, and Eileen Cornell Way, *Realism Rescued: How Scientific Progress is Possible*. Chicago: Open Court, 1995.

11. For example, Derrida attributes to Jean-Jacques Rousseau the view: presence is always the presence of pleasure. The full pleasure *(jouissance)* is a fictive instantaneity compared to which, for Derrida's Rousseau, all articulation is superficial and likely to be deceptive and corrupting, and, therefore, dangerous. "Language is a mere ersatz for the living self-presence" wrote Jacques Derrida in *Of Grammatology,* (corrected edition, translated by Gayatri Chakravorty Spivak). Baltimore: Johns Hopkins University Press, 1997. p. 280. Derrida is correct to find in Rousseau (and in early modern thinkers in general) a tendency to see articulated language as an artificial add-on, not regarded as part of reality per se. The inverse, however, has not been proven: humanity is left with nothing but its own articulated signifiers, and is devoid of nature.

12. See, for example, John R. Searle, *The Construction of Social Reality*. New York: Free Press, 1995, and works there cited.

13. Terry Eagleton, *The Illusions of Postmodernism*. Oxford: Blackwell, 1996. p. 34. Eagleton writes:

> The political differences that matter are not between those who historicize and those who do not; instead it is between different conceptions of history. Some believe that, overall, history is: • a tale of progress • mainly a story of scarcity, struggle, and exploitation • has no plot, like many a postmodern text.

14. Sigmund Freud, *The Interpretation of Dreams: Part 1,* in *The Complete Psychological Works of Sigmund Freud*. London: The Hogarth Press, 1958 : IV, pages 106-121, 292-96, 306-8.

15. Louis Althusser, *Contradiction et Sur Determination in Pour Marx*. Paris: Francois Maspero, 1980. p. 100. From the Francaise, his passage:

> *Je ne tiens pas expressement a ce terme de surdetermination (emprunte a d'autres disciplines), mais je l'emploie faute de mieux a la fois comme un indice et un probleme, et aussi parce qu'il permet assez bien de voir pourquoi nous avons*

affaire de toute autre chose que la contradiction hegelienne.

7b. Escobar's Ethics

1. Arturo Escobar, *Encountering Development.* Princeton, NJ: Princeton University Press, 1995. p. 130.

2. Escobar, *op. cit.* p. 22.

3. Escobar, *op. cit.* pp. 127-9.

4. David Ricardo, *The Principles of Political Economy and Taxation,* Chapter VI, "On Profits" (various editions):

> The whole value of their [the farmer and the manufacturer's] commodities is divided into two portions only: one constitutes the profits of stock, the other the wages of labor. Suppose that corn and manufactured goods always sell at the same price. Profits would be high or low in proportion as wages were low or high. If, however, as is certain, wages rise with rise of corn prices, their profits must fall in all countries and at all times; profits depend on the quantity of labor requisite to produce the commodities of the laborers.

Ricardo makes a further point, though not germane here:

> The rate of profit is determined by the labor needed to produce commodities on the marginal land that produces no rents.

5. Escobar, *op. cit.* p. 175-176.

6. See the collected studies edited by Lourdes Benaria and Shelley Feldman, *Unequal Burden: Economic Crises, Persistent Poverty and Women's Work.* Boulder: Westview Press 1992.

7. Andre Gunder Frank, *Latin America: Underdevelopment or Revolution: Essays on the Development of Underdevelopment.* New York: Monthly Review Press, 1970.

8. A. A. Boahen, *General History of Africa: VII Africa under Colonial Domination.* Berkeley: U. of California Press and UNESCO, 1990.

9. Engels, Friedrich, *The Condition of the Working Class in England.* New York: Macmillan, 1958 (first published in Deutsch: 1854). p. 296.

> We have seen how the growth of large farms forced the peasants off their holdings, turned them into wage-earners and then, in some cases, drove them into the towns. Id. p. 88.

10. Escobar, *op. cit.* p. 100.

11. Escobar, *op. cit.* p. 71.

12. Escobar, *op. cit.* p. 74.

13. Escobar, *op. cit.* p. 217.

14. Catherine A. Odora Hoppers, *Structural Violence as a Constraint on African Policy Formation.* Stockholm: Institute for International Education, 1998. See also Kaplan, *op. cit.* Note 4 to the Introduction.

15. R. Buckminster Fuller, *Utopia or Oblivion.* New York: Bantam

Books 1969. p. 182

> It is eminently feasible to design to triple the mechanical-efficiency level and, thus, care for 100% of humanity. We are committed to the design science revolution by which it is possible, without bloodshed, to raise the standard of living of all humanity to a higher level of physical satisfaction than ever experienced or dreamed.

Id., *Earth Inc*. Garden City, NY: Anchor/Doubleday, 1973. p. 175; Frances Moore Lappe and Joseph Collins, *Food First: Beyond the Myth of Scarcity*. Boston: Houghton-Mifflin, 1977.

16. In support of the claim that postmodernism has values, and that they are, in the end, those of modernity, see Anthony Giddens, *Modernity and Self-Identity: Self and Society in the Late Modern Age.* Stanford CA: Stanford University Press, 1991. Ernesto Laclau and Chantal Mouffe in *Hegemony and Socialist Strategy: toward a Radical Democratic Politics*. (London: Verson, 1985) attempt to articulate a socialist politics synchronized with anti-essentialist postmodern thinking, *inter alia* by utilizing chains of equivalence linking democracy as a political ideal with infusing democracy into: economics, the family, workplace, and so forth. The result is a postmodern ethics constructed by radicalizing the liberal ideals of modernity.

17. Howard Richards, "The Construction of the Metaphysics of Economic Society" Letter 21, *Letters from Quebec*. San Francisco and London: International Scholars Press, 1995.

18. Kant, Immanuel, *Groundwork of the Metaphysics of Morals* (translated by H. J. Paton). New York: Harper and Row, 1964 (first published in Deutsch in 1785) p. 108.

> Autonomy of the Will as the Supreme Principle of Morality: Autonomy of the will is the property the will has of being a law independent of every property belonging to the objects of volition.
>
> Everything in nature works in accordance with laws [e.g., Newton's laws of force and, thus, power]. Only a rational being has the power to act in accordance with his idea of laws that is, in accordance with principles, and, only so, has the being: a will.

Id. p. 80. See also Gideon Freudenthal, note 18 to Part 4c.

19. Amin, Samir, *Maldevelopment: Anatomy of a Global Failure*. Tokyo: United Nations University Press, 1990.

20. Escobar, *op. cit*. p. 100.

21. Michel Foucault, *Discipline and Punish: the Birth of the Prison*. New York: Pantheon Books, 1977. (translated from the Francaise, *Surveiller et Punir)*

22. Escobar, *Ibid*.

Review Questions

1. What underlying deficiency in the metaphysic of the global economy p 74 is supported by the post-structuralist incredulity toward meta-narratives, anti-essentialism, and, to a lesser degree, its preoccupation with over-determination? p 120

2. The observation by Heraclitus that "All is flux" appears, at first glance, to support the anti-essentialist view. What view of the statement makes it, at least, neutral in terms of the essentialist view? The awareness about change (flux) is central to the Greek and, perhaps, every mentality. (The Heraclitus articulation was roughly contemporary with the birth of Aristotle's essentialist thesis.) p 122

3. Why and how did essentialism become the culprit blamed for the evils, which generated from the capitalist system?

4. Arturo Escobar describes the global economy as: "a de-centered system with manifold apparatuses of capture: symbolic, economic, and political." p 126 How does his statement differ in its explanation from the author's thesis that the "global economy conforms to an ideology that has abandoned final causes in favor of a system of efficient causes with a legal structure and ideology that defends it in such a way that the global economy has no objective at all?" p 74

5. Escobar and Samir Amin share largely the same socio-political goals for their respective continents. What, though is the substantive difference in their means toward the goals? p 134

b. Can you name the difference in concise ideological terms?

c. What is the value of the Amin's approach in the short term, and the tacit possibility for the long-term?

6. Gibson-Graham's rejecting the existence of capitalism and, thus, the global economy (as false, oppressive) might be viewed as hyperbole. In addition, her declaration is effort to deconstruct capitalism as it has been conceived. What is the value of her statement, especially in terms of the scripts that she urges us to rewrite, thus, to re-empower our thinking, hence our action? p 137

7. The Henderson study that shows most work to be non-capitalist may or may not support the Gibson-Graham premise that rejects the existence of capitalism. Argue on both sides of it as supporting the rejection of the existence of capitalism. p 139

8. Gibson-Graham's approach to capitalism is that of formal cause. How does it contrast with Marx's understanding of capitalism? p 145

9. Gibson-Graham and Aristotle share an affinity through their expression of praxis toward positive growth. Compare their two varied means to the same end.
b. What is the main difference in the approach to knowledge (epistemology) between Gibson-Graham and Aristotle?
c. How does this difference change everything in terms of the conclusions that the two reach? p 145
10. Gibson-Graham's performative-force is central to her rewriting social scripts prescription. As a project, rewrite a hypothetical common script in our current culture. Contrast the perfomative-force caused by the original script and your revised script. Some themes: • labor to management • tenant and landlord • student and teacher • child and parent • consumer and corporation • patient and health-care provider • displaced worker to downsizing corporation or global colonizer. Examples:
❒ reverse or modify the contractual relationship between: • a tenant and landlord • an auto-dealership and customer • husband as employer-provider and wife as unpaid employee • client and social worker.
❒ act as though you intend to buy a high-price product that is a known product of unethical labor practices in the global economy. Use the Internet or postal service to contact the corporation, e.g. a computer manufacturer, and request information about the workers wages in every stage of production. In addition to worker's rights, insist that the corporation disclose its environmental record. Making contact with the "sales@INC.com" will take the dialog higher in the corporate ranks. Begin by mailing this script: Dear Wink Inc.: I really like the specs and price of you "X system. Before I buy, however, I need to be assured about the following policies for your company: 1) "Do your plants operate as union shops?" 1b) Do you have a gender rights and equity policy?" 2) "Do you *outsource* across our borders?" 2b) "If so, what are your shop standards, and can your policies be verified independently? 2c) What is the gender composition of your outsource labor? 3) "What is your environmental policy?" 3b) Do you allow independent reviews?" 3c) "How much of your paper use is recycled? Do you recycle your paper waste, or do you shred and landfill it?" 4) What is the extent of your political campaign contributions? 5) "Will you allow me to visit the plant where my

system will be assembled?" *

During the UN weapons inspection of Iraq, protestors dressed as inspectors asked and were denied inspection of a US weapons plant in Goleta, CA. Thus, our dissidence was validated by the corporate denial and secrecy.

A corporation may disclose little or no information, which is a statement that, in effect, rewrites the script. Most of these questions have answers that are available from consumer, labor, and environmental advocacy groups. Nevertheless, the power of each citizen acting alone for justice has proportionately much more impact toward the script rewriting. It shows consumers taking individual responsibility for their consumption. It would follow that the corporation will feel more accountable too. Thus, we can use this framework in the context of other institutions: churches, government bureaucracies, schools, and fraternal orgs:

❒ request that a teacher disclose credentials, experience, course

❒ request that your criteria and grading the teacher's course-work be acknowledged by the school administration

❒ through a contract, request that you (or someone you know) gain health-care, including drugs and other meds, on a contingency fee basis

❒ request that your local politicians disclose all campaign finances and legislative voting records to you and your local media. Disclose this request to your media.

❒ advocate on behalf of low-wage nonunion workers in your community: request disclosure of profits in relation to wages and benefits.

❒ seek the disclosure of the profit made by private utilities in your community or another; compare the rates to municipally owned utilities, and then reveal that harmful disparity to the media.

* Appendix A: page 281: A letter of solidarity for workers in the global economy sent to a US corporation manufacturing in China.

8
How to Work for Justice in the Global Economy

Instead of prefacing my advice with a statement of my theory, I will go straight to it. Instead of starting from scratch to answer the practical question, "What shall we do?" I will offer commentary on the excellent guide presented by economics Professor Jane Kelsey of Auckland University in New Zealand. Kelsey has written at length about how multinational corporations—backed by free market economic theory—have undermined the security of her country's people. From her scholarship and activist experiences, she has produced some practical guidelines for resistance and vigilance against the machinelike system. The Canadian Centre has circulated her twenty-six tactics worldwide for the Gandhi Center for Policy Alternatives. With my commentary upon her strategies, we present a path beyond what either could alone.

My aim is to show that in the light of the preceding theoretical efforts to understand the global economy, people can both support and improve practical efforts to change the global economy. Though it may not be apparent on the surface, underlying my comments on Jane Kelsey's guidelines is a search for positive cultural norms suitable for guiding the construction of an ethical global economy. In that search, help comes from four activist thinkers:

❒ Gandhi proposed that those of us who own property regard ourselves as trustees; he viewed his own life as a series of opportunities for service

❒ Dr. King's purpose, as he stated, was to build the beloved community

❒ Carol Gilligan names and defines a care ethic: attending to and responding to needs

❒ Riane Eisler extols partnership.

These are Professor Kelsey's strategies:

1. **Be skeptical about fiscal and other so-called crises**: Examine the real nature of the problem, who defines the crisis, and who stands to gain. Demand to know the range of feasible solutions and the costs/benefits of each and to whom.

Comment—Forty years ago it was easy to believe that the countries of the world were moving in the direction of high wages, social security, and high level social services for all; the Western European social democracies were thought to be models for everyone's eventual future. The reversal of the trends that made such optimism plausible has been marked by a series of crises, such as those characterized by: • oil price-shocks • unpayable debts • sudden currency devaluations. Such crises result from the constant structural problems, however, until a crisis, a government, or other actor will not acknowledge the structural problems, except as distorted by the interests of those who define the crisis. Dependency on oil, especially foreign, is a structural problem. Unpayable debt is a structural problem reflecting an even deeper one: the instability of capitalism. Keynes, typical of those who wrote economic theory for West European social democracies, proposed to remedy capitalism's instability by counter-cyclical spending; however, the cycles nearly always moved downward; and, thus, it became obvious to all that some day the deficit spending to counter the cycles had to stop. Currency devaluations reflect the structural fact that not every nation can win in international economic competition.

The existence of fundamental crises—moments when structural problems can no longer be ignored—creates a climate where it is easy to manufacture bogus crisis. In any crisis—a real one, a bogus one, or a real one made bogus by exaggeration—the decisions made are likely unwise and biased in favor of those who have the most power to influence public opinion. It would be wise to avoid the crises altogether by reforming their deep structural causes beginning with: • dependence on fossil fuel • capitalism • a global economy that is more competitive than cooperative.

2. Do not cling to a party that becomes neoliberal: Struggle to prevent a social democratic party's capture by right-wing zealots is vital. Once a party morphs, though, maintaining solidarity outside it while seeking change within it merely gives them more time. When the spirit of a party dies, leave it by creating the new.

Comment—A political party is rarely in a position to transform society: its primary task is to seek votes. The party normally accepts as given that public opinion and the moneyed and other interests that shape public opinion are as they are. Even if a party advocating socialism or other form of social transformation achieves control of the executive, legislative, and judicial branches of government, it is still not in a position to transform society. The national government is essential to the modern world-system: government protects property as it encourages business and creates conditions for growth of prosperity by helping the capitalist system run well. Each state helps the entrepreneurs of its nation succeed in international economic competition. The first national government—The Netherlands in the 17th century— set the pattern by which most national governments have since conformed. Jane Kelsey is accurate: parties that chime in as neoliberal are not worthy of support; people need political parties that advocate real alternatives. Parties can be educational and can exercise some degree of political influence. We, nevertheless, should not expect much of and rely on political parties or of government; neither will be able to implement workable alternatives without the support of social movements and people leading the way.

3. Take economics seriously:
Neoliberal economic fundamentalism pervades within every aspect of society. No boundary between the economic, social, environmental, or other policies exits. Those who focus on the narrow concerns of sectors and ignore the pervasive economic agenda will lose their own battles and weaken the collective ability to resist. Leaving economics to economists alone is too often fatal.

Comment—Economics is not a science that we can apply universally like chemistry. Economics is not even a general science of human society, such as anthropology, which attempts to study all forms of culture. The data of economics come mainly from accounting and bookkeeping; its models apply mainly in the function of accountants and bookkeepers. Instead of saying that every society has an economic base, we should say that every culture has an ecological context. The general science of humanity's interaction with Earth and other living systems is ecology—*bionomics*, not economics. Culture is the Homo sapiens' overall survival strategy, its ecological niche. Economic society is a special form of culture.

We have to take economics seriously because it is a basic cultural structure of current societies. If, with Wallerstein, we hold that today we have one society, the global, economics is basic because it administers to our shared needs. It determines or is an ideological reflection of the structures that determine: who eats and who does not. Even problems that seem unrelated to economics such as ones motivated by ethnic hatred in the massacres of Bosnia and Rwanda do have an economic aspect. An economic solution is requisite for a viable solution to all social issues, even it the issue seems at first unrelated to economics; ultimately, however, no economic solutions exist; solutions come only from a broader vision, which sees economics as a part of culture, which is a part of ecology. That is why leaving economics to economists alone is folly and often fatal.

4. Expose the weaknesses of their theory:

Neoliberal theories often have dubious assumptions, internal inconsistencies, and lack empirical support. These right wing theories need exposure to reveal them as serving rationalizations that operate in the interests of the elites to whom the policies empower. (The term *neoliberal* is used everywhere else for the ideas known as conservative in the US.)

Comment—Exposing the faulty assumptions and internal inconsistencies of free market economics must go hand in hand with building alternative communities and cooperatives. Mainstream economics is the ideology of mainstream institutions. Though the shelves of university libraries have many books that refute it, economics remains part of the dominant ideology as the standard doctrine taught in most introductory economics courses; although it has, many times, been shown to be false, it is assumed to be true in TV news analyses and in newspaper editorials. Practitioners of neoliberal economics, as a rule, do not take the time to reply to their academic critics; they do not need to because they have power; thus, they spend their time running governments, corporations, media, and the international agencies.

It is vital that we create alternative communities, cooperatives, and nonprofit orgs that function with principles different than those of free market economics. Post-economic living proves in practice what the books on university library shelves prove only in theory.

5. Challenge hypocrisy:

Find out who is promoting a strategy that is in the so-called national interest and who stands to benefit most. Document cases where the so-called public good disguises self-interest.

Comment—Fact: when high taxes force business closures then employees lose their jobs. Inevitable: when the government fixes prices so low that bigger profits occur elsewhere, then production falls and with it employment opportunities. Largely true: business cannot exist without profit; the loss of businesses means the loss of jobs too.

Moneyed interests assert that what is in their interest is in the national interest; their hypocritical assertions are convincing and in part true; however, more than arguments, they are power-laden dictums. A capitalist's investment does produce goods, render services, and create jobs and incomes that governments can tax.

Capital, however, is not above coercive bluffing; its advocates threaten dire consequences if: • wages rise • profits are taxed • safety or environmental regulations are passed and enforced. Although in fact, when the pay raises, tax increases, and enforcements do occur then capital adjusts and the dire consequences usually do not appear, The threat behind the fear that underlies greed does, nevertheless, have some validity: at times the dire consequences do occur.

Therefore, when we challenge hypocrisy, we should also challenge power at the level of the quasi-mechanism through which it operates. The way to disarm economic power is to build alternatives so that: 1) business and jobs, in time, will no longer need profit, and 2) societies will in time, no longer need to offer incentives to investors in order to produce goods, render services, create jobs, and join for the common good.

6. Expose the masterminds:

Name the key corporate players behind the scenes; document their interlocking roles and allegiances; expose the personal and corporate benefits they receive.

Comment—Identifying individuals helps to unmask the true nature and intentions of a movement. For example, in Italy during the 1920s Olivetti was secretly funding Mussolini. Meanwhile, like many opportunists, Mussolini said whatever he thought would please multitudes; he spoke in favor of John Dewey's progressive philosophy of education and once even spoke for feminism. The consequences of Mussolini coming to power could have been predicted by studying whom his backers were rather than by listening to what he said.

Then again, it is generally not true that using a discourse that traces the economic benefits a particular people pursue can solve social problems. The principal causes of poverty and insecurity are deep cultural structures; thus, it is unfair, misleading, and, worse, it contributes to the problem: the faulty assumption that individuals are and always will be vicious automata of egoism. The reality of the human condition is that we are all actors on a stage we did not make; as children we learned to play the roles society prescribed for us. Those of us who are trying to improve society must work to improve society's role definitions and its assumptions about human nature. Behavior in high places will improve when society defines humanity in ways that bring out the best in all people.

The liberation theology of Latin America has an apt way to express the need to hold people accountable for their actions and to call people to act according to higher standards. The *la buena nueva*: the good news encompasses both *denunciar*: denouncing evil, and *anunciar*: announcing the coming of a better world). As the Jewish Yom Kippur liturgy says: "If you do not both praise and revile, then

I have created you in vain, sayeth the Lord."

7. Maximize every obstacle:

Federal systems of government, written constitutions, legal requirements and regulations, supranational institutions like the ILO and the UN, and strong local governments can act as barriers that slow down the pace of the corporate takeover.

Comment—The corporate takeover is a recent version of the relentless pursuit of profit that Adam Smith in *The Wealth of Nations* depicted with a water metaphor—money flows into profitable channels of trade as water flows downhill. Expanding on Smith's hydraulic images, we can make a caricature of the neoliberal global corporate takeover by saying—the pursuit of profit by self-interested individuals is like a never-ending flood. The forces of the market are like rain that never stops. Whatever obstacles stand in the way: • federal and other regulations • written constitutions • legal requirements • ILO standards: are not enough. The water seeps through, soaks, flows around, submerges, and washes away.

According to the metaphysics of neoliberal economics, the market forces are natural, like water, and whatever impedes them is artificial. The barriers that inhibit them from flowing toward profits are like dams. Because the rains never stop, no dam will last.

As we counter-strategize by maximizing every obstacle to slow down the corporate takeover, we can do something more humane as well. We can cooperate at a not-for-profit basis to meet each other's needs. New light dawns, the rain stops, the floodwaters recede.

8. Strive to maintain solidarity:

Avoid the trap of divide and rule. Sect infighting is self-indulgent, and everyone risks losing in the end.

Comment—It is hard to maintain solidarity; people who have everything to gain from solidarity, often dropout and divide over social issues: religion, sexual morality, abortion, homosexuality, generation gaps, race, gender, ethnicity, the unforgiving of past wrongs, language, addictions, and mental illness.

I will explain—addictions and mental illness—because we seldom think of them as issues that divide social movements. It seems impossible to organize a mass movement (at least here in Southern California) without including people who suffer from mental illness: depression, alcoholism, bitter unresolved divorces, odd beliefs, delusions, sexual obsessions, chronic irresponsibility, self-destructive behavior, control obsession, deep anger, and desperate loneliness. A solidarity movement limited to those who are unquestionably sane cannot be a mass movement; it will always be a minority movement.

Mental health issues put solidarity in jeopardy because people with sound mental health, as a rule, do not feel obliged to stay in organizations where they have to cope with the foibles of people afflicted by acute neurosis and borderline psychosis. The crucial aspect as it relates to movement solidarity, is that people who suffer mental illness find it difficult to bond with other people and to work in solidarity with others for a common cause.

Given the standard divisive social issues (religion, etc.) and given the two I have added, I conclude that it is not possible to achieve a high degree of solidarity in heterogeneous groups. It was a theoretical illusion—homo economicus—that created the parallel illusion that a mass solidarity movement could take political power and build socialism. Real people, whatever their economic interests, cannot achieve cohesion without sharing values; the exception proves the rule in communities such as the one I live in, where our love of diversity is a value that we share. It follows that the only way to achieve solidarity on a large scale and across social barriers, is to form coalitions that combine the powers of many grassroots face-to-face groups, each of which meets the need-to-belong of a more-or-less homogeneous type of person.

The role of intellectual leadership, therefore, is essential. To maintain solidarity, people need to step forward to organize their group into broad functional coalitions with people that the group would not like nor agree with if they got to know them well.

Solidarity becomes easier when it is thought of as concentric levels of commitment, or as Nel Noddings puts it—concentric circles of caring. It is futile for one person to try to be in complete solidarity with all humanity and all the animals and plants that share Earth with us. It is, however, a practical possibility for one person to be in complete solidarity with a lover or a family and near complete solidarity with a circle of friends.

Picture a family, then that family within a loving community larger than a family. Step-by-step build upon the elements of solidarity that exist wherever they are and in whatever language they express. Then, after much trial and error, we might be able to achieve the goal announced by the slogan, "Workers of the world, unite!" We can achieve it here, it can happen now because through understanding all is possible.

---

9. Do not compromise the labor movement: Build awareness of the corporate agenda at the union local and workplace levels. Resist concessions that tend to deepen co-optation and weaken the unions' ability to fight back.

Comment—I will:

1. make a general suggestion about how to build a strong union, which is drawn from my experience with Cesar Chavez
2. argue that labor unions alone cannot transform the global economy,
3. state reasons why unions are crucial, though not enough. When asked how he organized the union Cesar Chavez answered:

> First I organized one person, and then another, and another, and another, and then another [a cumulative *critical mass* eventually occurred.

When he and a few others started organizing in the Central Valley of California, they first listened to whatever farm workers wanted to *desahogar* (express from the heart). They found that many were afraid they would die an unknown death: without a funeral and no one to mourn. Chavez, thus, found and used a method from the first working people's associations in Europe; so, the first promise the new union made was to honor each deceased member with a funeral. Though this is just a bit of the profound work of Chavez, I think it is enough to lead up to the general suggestion I want to make: the solidarity needed to solve economic problems will come largely from noneconomic motives.

2. Labor unions alone cannot transform the global economy. Unions do not produce any goods or services (except the services within the union for members). They produce no food, housing, clothing, medical attention, or childcare. Their ultimate tool is the *strike*: the action of refusing to work; still, it is stop-power, not go-power. Therefore, the strike, in principle and for structural reasons, is a weak tool. Refusal to work is always subject to the risk that someone else will be hired, or the risk that the business will close or move. Moreover, even if conditions look as though using the strike might succeed, labor has to use it sparingly. Shutting down business may offend business and government; however, it may alienate the public too, which is the *structural trap* that limits the labor movement. The transformation of the economy requires the transformation of go-power; it will not happen with stop-power alone.

A traditional split of opinion exists in the labor movement between those who favor unions: 1) allied with socialist parties that aim to deliver control of the means of production to the working class and 2) that focus on wages, benefits, and work rules in business enterprises working people will never own or control. In that split, I advocate the former: union action as complementary to political action.

3. I concluded earlier that political parties could not transform the global economy, even if they take power, because national governments (alone or in concert) cannot transform. For that reason, neither unions nor the two in concert can transform the global economy's structure. (Union, and any violence, has the success odds of the proverbial snowball in hell.) The great reform needs a "galvanizing more" toward critical mass of what I call the *culture of solidarity*.

One might ask then, whether labor unions are unnecessary as well as insufficient. If the global economy can reform at all, perhaps it can transform without labor unions. That is impossible, because unions (except the corrupt ones) augment the power of working people. A world where the masses of working people become increasingly powerless would not be a scenario where social transformation could occur. Only the empowerment of the people through many forms, which includes labor unions, will bring about the conditions for transformation.

Collective bargaining is the contract tool in which the workers in mediated process with the owners reach consensus; it is the good-faith, win-win alternative; as such, they are a positive cultural transformation in which the union contract embodies respect, which is not just about wages; it is about human rights in the workplace; it is about replacing arbitrary power with social norms and with grievance procedures for the adjudication and enforcement of the norms. Neither the norms nor the procedures are perfect; improvement is not always possible. Even so, it is a step forward in principle to establish procedures for governing relationships in the workplace (or anywhere else) according to a pattern of standards and an ethic. Both the standards and the ethic seek a policy to consider everyone's needs and rights away from the rule of force and the rule of the quasi-force of the quasi-machine: an economy that creates a world where human beings cooperate to meet needs in mutual respect.

10. Maintain the concept of an efficient public service: Resist attempts to discredit and dismantle the public sector by admitting deficiencies and promoting constructive models for change. Build support among client groups and the public, which stress the need for public services and the risks of cutting or privatizing them.

Comment—Efficient public service needs protection because it is a concept under attack by some who deny the validity of it. They do not criticize government program X or Y for being inefficient; instead, they attack the very notion of efficient public service.

That governments are always and unavoidably inefficient is a metaphysical proposition. It is, however, a proposition that acquired an aura of plausibility through reports of specific case studies. For example, P. T. Bauer, a leading antigovernment, pro-market writer, reports that government programs in India that were supposed to help the poor, in fact, wasted time and favored the middle class. Farmers, for example, spent their time currying favor with government officials and going to political meetings, instead of farming. Those who received the benefits of the programs were not the poorest. They evaded standard *means testing,* even if that existed, because they could:

- ❑ afford to offer bribes and quasi-bribes
- ❑ find time to develop contacts and learn the art of grant writing
- ❑ negotiate through the official procedures required to obtain a share of the government's largesse

Similar horror stories about failures of planning in, e.g., the USSR may even prove that the planning model is always wrong and the market model always right.

The metaphysical proof that efficient public service is a contradiction in terms, advances by defining efficiency in such a way that only free, competitive markets can be efficient. The price fixed by such markets reflects, by definition, an optimal allocation of society's resources. Other criteria for allocating resources are, in principle, inefficient.

From this argument it follows that if modern public institutions are inefficient then humanity's older institutions are too: • family • kinship • religion; thus, the label of *inefficient* includes all the innovative modern institutions, such as: • cooperatives • nonprofit orgs • charitable foundations • volunteer agencies • intentional communities • neighborhood associations • fraternal lodges. All these institutions are inefficient insofar as they operate, by their purpose, according to an ethic that diverges from the norms that govern rational behavior in free competitive markets.

A more convincing metaphysical argument supports the opposite conclusion: public service (and other institutions responsive to ethical criteria that override *market rationality*) may be efficient, however, free competitive markets are never efficient. The argument starts with the standard definition of the term *efficient*: achieving the objective at the least cost or to a higher degree at the same cost. Next, it defines the objective: fulfilling the physical and spiritual needs of humanity within the sustainable parameters of cooperation with Earth's living systems. Based on these plausible definitions, it follows that, in principle, the concept of an efficient free competitive market is mistaken. In such markets, money and the self-interested decisions of economic actors always intervene between the objective and its achievement. The real measure of efficiency in achieving the objective—meeting needs long term—does not necessarily coincide with any of the outcomes that the actors in the market seek, i.e. not with the goal of maximizing money returns for self-interested actors. Efficiency is not a market requirement; in fact, the market does better without efficiency. At least three reasons exist for this conclusion. Markets:

1. are always biased in favor of effective demand: in favor of the demands of people with money. A market, thus, may *Pareto-optimize*; however, it can never (except in the imaginary abstractions of mathematical welfare economics) *Pigou-optimize*: allocate necessities to those who need them the most.
2. never internalize external costs. Two actors who strike a market-rational bargain between them need not consider the consequences of their bargain for other people outside their bargain, or the consequences for Earth.
3. always *discount the value of the long-term future*. A payment to be made 1,000 years from now (a speck in geological time) has a market value of about zero according to any common discount rate.

It follows that public service (or any enterprise or institution that takes meeting real needs as its objective) has a chance, at least, to be efficient; however, the concept of an efficient free competitive market is a contradiction in terms.

What should we say about the historical experiences with inefficient public service, which lend empirical support to the false generalization that government is never efficient? We should say that those experiences are the many reasons to maintain the concept of an efficient public service by admitting its deficiencies and promoting constructive models for change. Of course, we should recognize that the inherent inefficiency of markets does not imply that we should go to the extreme of trying to build a world with no markets at all.

Further inspiration comes from emphasizing the positive. For example, biologists find that the single most important factor explaining the increased longevity in recent centuries is improved public health programs: cleaner water, better treatment of sewage, control of infectious diseases, etc. The physical fact is that people now live longer because of the alliance between science and efficient public service.

11. Encourage local leaders to speak against the injustice: Public criticism from—civic and church leaders, folk heroes, and other prominent names—makes corporate and political leaders uncomfortable while it makes people think. Remind community leaders of their social obligations and the need to preserve their own self-respect.

Comment—When the consequences of globalization violate widely shared humanitarian values, the conscience of the people as expressed by community leaders of various kinds is a viable path of the resistance. An ad hoc protest coalition will, thus, emerge; it might well become part of a global social transformation movement, though only if it is possible to transform the world system through a diverse alliance whose members may not even share a similar ideology.

Community leaders will, however, likely not speak with the voices of those who encourage and urge them, but instead with their own voices:

❐ a priest will reflect some version of the social teachings of his sect, modified by his prayers and reflections

❐ ethnic, tribal, and racial leaders will speak from the matrix of their communal identities

❐ economic interest groups will usually argue for the compatibility of their particular short-term interest with the long-term common good

❐ a woman may speak on behalf of women; or she may express a view about some other dimension of her participation in society.

This point applies to the others, as well, because most people have multiple group affiliations. If an ad hoc protest coalition has no common philosophy, each community leader will speak in a voice that is hers or his and not speak in the consensus voice expressing the goals and the values of a unified global movement, which will transform the bigger culture devoid as it is of substantive solidarity.

For Plato and many others, ancient and modern, Western and non-Western, it was obvious that to transform society, cooperation and, thus, shared values would be requisites. Plato's ideal city created a unity with one shared philosophy. Likewise, Marx perceived as obvious that the working people should unite in practice through sharing in mentality a common socialist ideology.

Liberalism disagrees with the unity of mind approach; instead, it sees a variety of voices in an ad hoc protest-coalition as an asset, not a liability; and liberalism sees as suspect the fact that people speak via community leaders rather than for themselves. It is a sign that there may be too much conformity. According to liberalism, each person should think and act independently.

I believe that Plato and Marx had good reasons for seeking the shared values and a common voice through ideology; then again, liberals also have good reasons to mistrust that and, thus, seek diversity of thought. I hope that it will be possible to transform the global economy through unity-in-diversity.

We can adopt the idea of the classical anthropologists: cultures are largely diverse adaptations to diverse environments. We can think of the global economy as having certain features of modern European culture writ large: a European economics expanded to a global scale. Then we can see global economic transformation as a cultural conversion: it will be our adaptation to one environment: Earth.

A transformation of culture need not, nor does it always, proceed by adopting a single coherent philosophy, belief system, or religion; diverse perceptions can function as equivalents. What people do is more important than what they think and say; thus, a harmony of action need not require a unity of thought. The social conflicts that prevent successful adaptation to the physical environment might resolve although contingent upon: • occasion • place • kinds and classes of people • personalities • languages.

Nonetheless, humanity will benefit from more unity and bonding than it has now. We need community and, beyond that, we need resonance across community boundaries that help us to feel the common human energies that fuel diverse cultural forms; those who work for global transformation need to capture a variety of positive energies; we need to share the vision of a multicultural world.

As we build community, and network with others, we:

❒ celebrate both diversity and homogeneity

❒ treasure the shared values that exist in the world

❒ help the vision grow in the appreciation for diversity

❒ encourage shared values to be ecumenical. This does not mean everyone should be a Buddhist; even so, it is an asset for all humanity that likeminded Buddhists exist who understand each other's spirituality and act in unity. Wherever the following thrive, empowerment thrives as well: • trust • shared norms and beliefs • sacred rites and story • an ethnic identity • solidarity. Wherever empowerment thrives, so too does the capacity for resisting and transforming the global economy.

12. Avoid anti-intellectualism:

A vital resource for the movement are the academics and other intellectuals who can: 1) document and expose the fallacies and failures of the corporate agenda and 2) develop viable alternatives in partnership with community and groups. Our intellectuals need support when attacked and need to hear our disapproval when they fail to speak out, are co-opted, or seduced.

Comment—The people's movement—conceived to make the world work for all humans without ecological damage—should avoid anti-intellectualism because the movement must have the intellectual capacity to enable: **1)** technical expertise: transformation of the economy can occur only with the input of people who know how to make technologies work. In this respect, as information resources, intellectuals have more tangible power than do capitalists because the expertise of intellectuals is a requirement of production, while the rights of owners depend on legal fictions. Against point (1) is the contention that those who wait for technical experts to make common cause with the people will wait in vain because most: A) technical experts are not intellectuals, and B) intellectuals support the status quo. Rebuttal to those contentions follows: (a) technical expertise does lead to a general intellectual culture insofar as it: 1) requires mathematical reasoning and the logical use of language, and 2) leads to greater innovation at the higher levels of technology, which is where creativity, philosophical reflection, and the interplay of disciplines occur (b) an intellectual culture, which is universal, will lead to a committed participation in practices that transform cultural structures as competent thinkers become ever aware of our headlong course toward calamity **2)** humanitarian conceptualization: the intellectual capacity to facilitate the evolution of social norms toward more solidarity and cooperation. If moral evolution is possible and necessary, then the intellectual must facilitate its accomplishment. It will not be easy or automatic; it will require: humanitarian understanding across cultures and faiths, psychological and spiritual study and practice, and artistry.

The need for more cooperation does not mean an end to healthy competition. Even Gandhi played soccer with a team called the Pretoria Passive Resisters; and the Reverend Dr. King Jr. enjoyed pillow fights in the spirit of a shared release from the climate of oppression.

Although I do not object to Jane Kelsey's phrase *corporate agenda*, I would not use it. My emphasis is on the deep structural causes of human problems. Therefore, it may distract us to single out a group as impeding progress in favor of regress.

13. Establish a think-tank:
If one exists in your community, make sure it has adequate funds. Neoliberal think tanks have shown how the well-financed institutes on the right rationalize and legitimize the corporate agenda. The need for one or more well-funded think tanks on the left is obvious. Uncoordinated research by isolated critics will not suffice.

Comment—Because cultural structures need reform, no substitute exists for grassroots action projects in which norms and values transform from an old paradigm to a new one. With that basis known, the vital role of progressive think tanks will reflect it. Having worked within two of them, I see their main limitations to be that: 1.) their survival depends upon funding, which is always precarious 2.) obtaining funds takes much time and energy seeking the favor of moneyed interests 3.) legal restrictions that often prevent close links with political parties, unions, churches, social movements, cooperatives, and self-help groups.

In addition to think tanks, support must emerge for other ways to build the intellectual infrastructure for creating the appropriate global economy. This would include a system of sharing tasks among tenured academics with salaries. Jane Kelsey likely has in mind the systematic dissemination of ideas that would reply directly to the intellectual products of the: • World Bank • IMF • Ministries of Planning • Institutes of Strategic Studies • well-funded neoliberal think tanks.

14. Invest in the future:
Provide financial, human, and moral support to sustain:

❒ alternative analysis publications

❒ think tanks

❒ people's projects that are active in resistance to the corporate agenda and work for progressive change.

Comment—"Help! I do not have any discretionary money; I can barely keep up with paying my bills and my taxes." The philanthropists who give to progressive causes are overwhelmed with valid calls for funding. What can people in my position do? We can: 1) organize productive communities such as Gandhi's ashrams, which generate food, other necessities, and money, thus, depending less upon donations and 2) reduce our personal expenditures, simplify our lives—doing more with less—thus, giving more time and money for the good of humanity.

15. Support those who speak out against the injustice: The harassment and intimidation of the critics of the corporate takeover, works only if those attacked do not have our personal, popular, and institutional support. Our withdrawing from public debate leaves those who remain more exposed.

Comment—Speak your support of other people's good work. Building community requires food, music, and praise. For every protest, we might well bestow at least one award for outstanding service and share our interpersonal gratitude.

16. Promote ethical investment: Support investors whose response to social and ecological problems is proactive; expose the ethic and investors who ignore issues. Boycotts have proven to be a powerful force in environmental, antinuclear and safe product campaigns. Make companies that ignore social and environmental crisis accountable: shame them.

Comment— What needs reform are the cultural structures that are riddled with conventional norms; therefore it does: • little good if workers or government officials take over businesses and operate them with the same conventional norms and corruption • help when people with positions of influence in business use their influence to persuade and reform behavior toward higher ethical standards.

17. Think globally, act locally: Build your comprehension of the global nature of economic power and the forces that drive current trends. Show the links between these global forces and local events. Target the meetings and activities of your local representatives, which feed into the global economic machine.

Comment—I can act close to home for global structural transformation starting with just one act. If I keep one promise: to meet a need for someone not because it is in my self-interest to do so, but instead because I pledged, then I am making (at least) one person a bit more secure because that person can count on a someone else: me. Therefore, I undo the damage done by the global market economy, which, in principle, makes people insecure because people's needs remain unmet without the help of others: no one motivated purely by market incentives will do anything to meet others needs unless their self-interest dictates them to do that.

I can act nearby starting with a connection to just one person. If I can establish solidarity with one person, then the two of us are outside the market. Suppose that we are part of a family or, if you will, a surrogate family: part of a kinship system, tribe, or its equivalent. The process continues with people in different types of alliances: families, unions, cooperatives, towns, nations, etcetera providing different degrees and types of support for one another. Then it becomes clear that what began in the neighborhood was a change of principle that transformed the global economy.

18. Think locally, act globally:

Support international strategies for change, for example:

❒ people's tribunals

❒ NGO forums on codes of conduct

❒ action campaigns against unethical companies and corporate practices. Act on the fact that international action is vital to counter the collaboration of states and corporations, and to empower civil society to take back control.

Comment—With the help of the Internet, progressive organizations are catching up with the domination agenda of the global business. It is easy to subscribe to *list serves* and visit web sites that will keep you current with what you can do to act globally.

19. Develop alternative news media:

Once mainstream media are captured by the mega-corporate right it is difficult for critics to enter the debate and impossible to lead it. Alternative media and innovative strategies must emerge. Effective communication and exchange of information between various groups and activists are essential—despite the time and resources involved.

Comment—To the extent I can, I try to support people who run alternative publications, alternative radio, and public access TV. As well, personal media or mini-media plays an important role and needs support. The *samizdat*, the tiny publications that played such an important role in the fall of the Soviet Union in 1989, includes local church bulletins, which people tend to read and trust because they interact with the authors. The following suggests that messages people read and repeat, at a low cost, will become widespread.

Suppose I send a personal newsletter to one hundred of my friends, communicating a justice message that bears repeating. They, in turn, send a similar message to one hundred of their friends; thus, not counting repeats to the same people I wrote to, that would reach ten thousand people. When the pattern recurs thrice, it reaches one million then a hundred million, then ten billion people, exceeding the human population.

The assumption that each recipient will in turn send one hundred messages to new people, nevertheless, is false. I think this calculation has some tendency to show that if I send out a message that people in general find worth passing on, then the message is likely to become widespread. Therefore, when you send a message, accompany it with a request to circulate it.

20. Raise the level of popular economic literacy:
Familiarize people with the basic themes, assumptions, and goals of economic fundamentalism. Convince them that: • economic policy affects everyone • that everyone has a right to participate • alternatives to the corporate agenda do exist.

Comment—Raising popular economic literacy succeeds apropos to current events. When reporting current events, the mainstream media make the neoliberal assumptions of comparative advantage economics, such as: • whatever price the market fixes is natural and right • that a free market will meet everyone's needs. If, through the alternative media as advocated in guideline #19, it is possible to comment publicly on current events, then alternative interpretations of events can introduce alternative philosophical principles.

21. Resist market-speak:
Maintain control of the language, challenge its capture by the corporate right, and refuse to convert your discourse to theirs. Insist on using specific terms that convey the hard realities of what is occurring.

Comment—Market-speak treats an abstract number—profit—as the bottom line. Real bottom lines have some physical or spiritual substance, for example: a tree that bears fruit, a loaf of good bread, a drink of clean water, and someone who cares about you.

22. Be realistic:
Recognize that the world has changed, to some extent irreversibly, and that the past was far from perfect. Avoid the trap of reacting for and defending the status quo. Defending the past for its intrinsic value adds credibility to the claims of the right and wastes opportunities for real change.

Comment—Several reasons explain the global sea change since 1973, or so, in favor of the neoliberal market economies, and as a stance against: • planning • labor unions • the welfare safety net. This stance is due to the ongoing *market to profit process*: the basic causal mechanisms that have governed the global economy since its inception in the 16th century. The principal method that works for justice in the global economy, therefore, is our concerted effort toward replacing those basic causal mechanisms. The principal method for replacing them is to build alternatives that work: ones which succeed in producing and distributing food, housing the homeless, caring for the sick, and educating the poor equitably.

23. Be proactive:
Rethink visions, strategies, and models of development for the future. Show the workable, preferable alternatives from the start. That will become progressively more difficult the longer you wait to respond to the corporate agenda.

Comment—The only way I can show the reality of the workable, preferable alternative is to join a group. Alone I might be able to read books about alternatives, or even write one; yet, I cannot demonstrate the workable alternative.

If the group's purpose is to prove the veracity of workable, preferable alternatives, then the group needs to be a model of one. Nobody will believe us when we say, "The world could function otherwise" even while we cannot manage our lives otherwise. Lasting leadership is: always leading by example.

24. Challenge TINA, (there is no alternative) claim:
Convince people—as individuals and groups—that the workable alternatives have long been in use, though obscured by the economy that does not work. Present options that combine realism with the prospect of meaningful change. Actively promote these alternatives and have them ready to implement when the corporate agenda fails.

Comment—One scenario wherein it might seem true that there is no alternative, is a national debt crisis: a nation cannot make current payments on its debts. No one accepts payment in the nation's currency; thus, only dollars or hard European money will do. The nation's airports, its port facilities, its gold reserves, and other tangible assets have been mortgaged as security for its debts. It appears that the only course is signing a letter of intent with the International Monetary Fund to receive funds and a reprieve conditioned upon accepting the principles of neoliberal philosophy. In practical terms, this means:

- ❐ reducing public services
- ❐ freezing wages and hiring
- ❐ producing for export
- ❐ making the nation more dependent upon the global market.

Such a situation backs the progressive intellectual into a corner. Does a progressive propose turning the world overnight into a socialist commonwealth that does not use money, and that the nations close their borders and go it alone? Do I have advice for the leader of a third world country whose debt payment cannot be refinanced, which the IMF will soon foreclose? I take cold comfort in treating this TINA scenario as proof of my theory, which I read, "I have long said that if you played by your rules of global capitalism, it would come to this; still, you would not listen. Now will you listen? Now are you ready to play a sustainable game with rules fair for everyone?"

Yet, just what would I say to President Arias of Costa Rica when the New York bankers are knocking on his door, and the IMF sends a rescue mission? I would say, "I do not know what would persuade the bankers and the IMF to give Costa Rica some leeway, though I am sure you will negotiate the best deal you can get under the circumstances." Then, if the President's interest in philosophy were only moderate, I would suggest that he encourage self-reliant community development, permaculture, and the use of sustainable technologies as feasible steps in the direction of reducing the probability of another TINA situation arising in the future. If he seemed at all open to the idea, I would suggest that he threaten bankruptcy and, if necessary, carry it out to invoke the ancient biblical principle of *Jubilee:* cancel debts, reorganize, and begin anew.

25. Promote participatory democracy:
Build a constituency for change through alternative information networks and media. Use community, workplace, women's, church, union, First Nations, and other outlets to encourage people to take back control. Empower them with the knowledge they need so to: 1) understand the right-wing forces affecting them and 2) how they can fight back most effectively.

Comment—Let us call it participatory *social democracy*. My motive for adding the word *social* is to emphasize the creation of what Riane Eisler calls *partnership relationships,* which facilitate cooperative work to meet needs implicit in participation (being part of one another) and democracy (rule by the people). The word *societas* from which the English word social comes is Latin for partnership. My second motive is to build a social safety net for all citizens. Social democracy is the general name for a progressive political trend, which was, within its limitations, in many countries around the world, building the social safety net for all citizens before it was dismantled by the present neoliberal trend.

The practice of participatory social democracy—partnership at grassroots levels—can build political influence at higher levels. Then when the tide of free market ideology crests and begins to recede, and social democracy reasserts itself as the politics of the future, civil society will be greener, stronger, and happier. Social democracy at the national and global levels, therefore, will take hold sooner and work better.

Partnership relationships often take the expression of the ancient pre-capitalist meaning of a word as its real meaning—before market individualism debased it. Thus, we can return to:

❒ a real community (*koinonia*[15] Gk, *communitas* L, *gemeinschaft* G) is one where there is common property, in addition to private property.

❒ a real workplace (*ergon* Gk) is a place to perform vital social functions, such as the work of providing food, or the work of providing medical attention

❒ *mater* L: mother has the roots—*material* and *matrix* (womb) suggesting that the substance and source of life is feminine.

❒ a church, to be a real church, should be an *ecclesia* (Gk and L), a gathering like the house churches in *The Acts of the Apostles* where the members bear one another's burdens.

❒ a union (from *unitas*, oneness, *vereinigung* and *bund* in Deutsch) makes one of many.

❒ the first nations, which often have words reflecting ancient traditions of respect for the land, for animals and plants, and for other people. The Qheswa (Andes Mountains bioregion) expression *ayni ruway*: social relationships as pacts of mutual support: solidarity.

Participatory social democracy can provide solutions to the everyday problems of the participants: • where to find a baby-sitter • how to secure transport of an elder to the hospital • how to find food and lodging for those denied employment. "Love, as the law of our species, as Gandhi said, can grow by our practice of it."

26. Hold the line:
The corporate takeover is not yet complete. Most social programs do remain intact, though often downsized and less effective. Labor unions still have some power, though a fraction of that of previous decades. Not all environmental protections have "fallen to the axe" of corporate hegemony. Enough time remains—through a sustained and coordinated action—to hold the line.

Comment—The forces that are rolling back the gains made by social democracy in the middle decades of the twentieth century have their roots in the basic cultural structures of modernity, i.e. in *market relationships*. Welfare states using Keynesian social accounting to macro-manage the economy were limited in scope and life-span, as they met the limits imposed by the very structure of the global capitalist economy. Those include:

- unpayable debt
- bureaucratic inefficiency
- individualist ethics

• a tendency for the rate growth to falter
• the power of capital to relocate, and so on.

Furthermore, even in the best-case scenario of a New Zealand style social democracy sustained indefinitely and into the rest of the world, it is still physically impossible. Earth cannot bear the resource-intensive standards of living—the cars, freestanding houses, and the glut of consumer goods—attained by the middle masses: the primary beneficiaries of 20th century macro-managed economies.

As we hold the line, we should cut off the forces of neoliberalism at their roots. To use another metaphor, the forces that are rolling back labor gains (and environmental gains) must dissolve through our vigilant green cleansing. We can accomplish this by reviving old ways of life and creating new ways of life governed by ethical principles of solidarity.

More than one future-viable ethic is available to us. Perhaps I should not have chosen *solidarity* as a general name for the ethics of: • caring • love • empowerment • ministry • spiritual enlightenment might have been better. People worldwide have many cooperative practices, ways of talking about them, and celebrating them; likewise, many old and new alternative technologies exist. Together, they make people less dependent on capital, therefore less subservient to it, better able to regulate it, govern it, socialize it, and channel it toward constructive ends.

Notes:

New Zealand, a response to the New Zealand government's paper to the Social Development Summit, Copenhagen, March 1995. Wellington, New Zealand: Association of Nongovernmental Organizations of Aotearoa, *1995*; Jane Kelsey, *The New Zealand Experiment: a World Model for Structural Adjustment?* Auckland, New Zealand: Auckland University Press, 1997.

Gandhi's ideas of trusteeship and service have expression in his own words in the UNESCO compilation of his writings published as M. K. Gandhi, *All Men are Brothers.* New York: Columbia University Press, 1969. For M. L. King's concept of "Beloved Community" see John Ansbro, *Martin Luther King, Jr.: the Making of a Mind.* Maryknoll, New York: Orbis Press, 1982. On Carol Gilligan's findings, see note 33 to section 9 below. For Riane Eisler's idea of partnership see her "Women, Men, and Management: Redesigning our Future," in Pat Barrentine (ed.) *When the Canary Stops Singing: Women's Perspectives on Transforming Business*. San Francisco: Berrett-Koehler Publishers, 1993.

9

Scientific Conclusions

In *Capital, Volume I,* Marx wrote the passage quoted in the following paragraph:

> For the conversion of his money into capital, the owner of money must meet in the market with the free laborer, who is free in the double sense: as a free man he can dispose of his labor power as his commodity, and that on the other hand, he has no other commodity for sale and, thus, is short of everything necessary for the realization of his labor power. The question why this free laborer confronts him in the market has no interest for the owner of money, who regards the labor market as a branch of the general market for commodities. For the present, it interests us just as little. In theory, we cling to the fact as he clings to it for practical reasons. One truth is certain, however: nature does not create on one-side owners of money or commodities, and on the other men possessing nothing but their labor power [*arbeitskraft,* G: the energy force of work]. This relation has no natural basis, and neither is its social basis one that is common to all historical periods. It is the result of a past historical development, the product of many economic revolutions, the cause of the extinction of a whole series of older forms of social production.
>
> So too, the economic categories we discuss bear the stamp of history. Definite historical conditions are necessary so that a product may become a commodity. It must not be produced as the immediate means of subsistence of the producer. Had we gone further to inquire under what circumstances all or even a majority of products take the form of commodities, we should have found that this can only happen with production of a specific kind: capitalist production.[1]

Those words seem optimistic today; the implied message is that earlier periods of social evolution had other forms of social relations and different forms of property; in those times the trade of commodities and labor power either did not exist or was not dominant. Karl Marx sought to restructure the ordinary person's perception of the everyday world of common sense. He wanted us to see the budgets, bills, wages, debts, bank accounts, taxes, and the many economic institutions, which we take for granted as outcomes of a process spanning thousands of years to advance Europe to its 1867 erudition. When we see the everyday world as a temporary configuration of human practices, we can then infer that social evolution is occurring too. If the institutions of the past were, overall, different than, and inferior to the institutions of the present, then it follows that the institutions of the future would be different and improved.

In 1.5 centuries, however, little has changed: the owners of money in the market still confront the masses of so-called free men and women possessing nothing but their labor power. Moreover, the economic categories that Marx articulated in the intervening years have rooted more firmly outside Europe. The masses of Africa no longer live in tribal groups on lands they own: they live in townships and teeming cities. The masses of India and of China are now more fated by commodity production; and they work if they can find jobs for wages.

Since Marx, the rules that govern life in the market economies have remained the same. For a time revolutions inspired by Marx's concepts controlled areas that were home to one third of humanity and seemed likely to conquer the areas inhabited by the remaining two thirds. Instead of expanding, they shrank; thus, today a few isolated governments, such as North Korea and Cuba, fly Marxist banners. The global trend today is that the owner of money meets in the market with the so-called free laborer.

Yet, Marx's analysis—often discredited and refuted in theory and in practice—refuses to go away. Its basis is the analysis of commodity and the exchange of it (in my view the plain meaning of *Capital*, though it is at variance with some eminent scholars). That, along with the labor theory of value as a principle for planning the efficient deployment of human energy, is central to Marx: it does not go away. In addition, Marx showed that the alienation, mass poverty, and instability of modern society are rooted in the basic cultural forms that govern its leading institution: the market. He wrote:

> The simplest form of the circulation of commodities is C-M-C: the transformation of commodities into money, and the change of money back again into commodities: selling in order to buy. Yet, alongside this form we find another form: M-C-M: the transformation of money into commodities, and the change of commodities back again into money: buying in order to sell. Money that circulates in the latter manner is potential capital and, thus, becomes capital.[2]

Marx's work does remain with us, not because he solved the problem—in some ways he was mistaken—but instead because he identified the problem: a deep source of the structural constraints known, in Marxist terminology, as the *contradictions*, which are rooted in the cultural forms defining both everyday life and the global economy. They frustrate even the most well-intentioned efforts to make the world work for every human without ecological injury.

Not by accident, capitalism is still unstable at its basis: the exchange process compelled to pursue its fatal addiction to so-called growth in its desperate effort to stabilize. A root of the problem is that most people remain short of everything necessary for the realization of their labor power; they still face capital in the labor market with no commodity to sell other than their vital energy. Until the achievement of a sustainable steady state economy happens, Marx's analysis of the inherent tendency toward infinite expansion of the exchange process will not go away. Marx quoted Aristotle:

> The circulation of money to produce more money is unnatural because money is in principle infinite and unlimited. There are no bounds to its aims, these aims being absolute wealth .[3]

I have suggested throughout my review of scientific theories that purport to explain the global economy accurately, that the problems of the world economy cannot resolve when they are defined as economic problems. As Fritjof Capra put it, "Poverty is not solvable in the economic terms posed." [4] Marx helps me to make my point as well:

> Poverty is inherent within a global economy where the owner of money meets in the market with the free laborer, free in the double sense: as a free man he can dispose of his labor power as his commodity; on the other hand, he has no other commodity for sale and, thus is short of the realization of his labor power.

Poverty is, thus, inherent whenever the economic categories are those characteristic of historical conditions such that all, or a majority of, products take the form of commodities. It follows that poverty is not a problem economics can solve because the data of economics is prices, sales, investments, loans, rates of interest, wages, etc. That is to say, the facts with which the study of economics makes records to frame explanatory hypotheses presupposes:

❒ that economic categories of commodity production exist

❒ the capitalist as homo economicus going to the market to buy labor power

❒ the worker as homo economicus going to the market to sell labor power.

These basic categories are the ones Marx showed to contain the germs of contradictions that will not go away until the basic categories themselves become restructured. Using economic thinking to frame a solution to the problems of the global economy is like trying to lift yourself by pulling your shoes upward.

The diversity within economics includes thousands of

economists I have never met or read. I will, thus, limit the assertion that economics cannot solve the problem of poverty—because it assumes the use of concepts with a scope in which poverty is inevitable—to those economists who do assume the use of those concepts. Then again, perhaps it would be better to identify the mavericks, radicals, and alternative thinkers as other than economists. In any case, I think that both the socialist planners and capitalist economists have advanced theories that, in principle, cannot solve the problem.

The inverse of that conclusion argues that a capitalist economy is the only viable economy. We know that the worldwide expansion of capitalism is the context in which economics as a science arose and from which it derives its data and its concepts. If we then postulate that economics is in general a valid science, it follows that a capitalist market economy is the only feasible economy. That is the sort of argument Ludwig von Mises and Eugen von Bohm-Bawerk made after the 1917 Russian revolution: the *socialist planning* could not be done. As they conceived the matter, economics requires that goods have prices derived from values. The market sets values, they thought, by the *value preferences* (utilities) of consumers. It follows, therefore, that if: no market ⇨ no values ⇨ no prices ⇨ no economy.[5]

In reply to von Mises, and in an effort to show that socialist planning was doable, the Polish economist, Oskar Lange used the concept of *opportunity cost*: it was not necessary to have private property in the means of production to set prices for goods. The *central planning board* could construct a functional equivalent for a capitalist market mechanism by:

1. setting an initial price
2. ordering managers of state-owned enterprises to produce at quantities based on the assumption that they would sell the product at the initial price, while minimizing the costs of production, and
3. letting consumers spend their incomes as they see fit. When a shortage occurs, the *planners* increase the price; when a surplus occurs, the planners lower the price. Production costs, which the managers are supposed to minimize, could be set in quantitative terms that planners could use by counting as the cost of an input: a number measuring what had to be sacrificed—the alternatives and opportunities—as the opportunity cost. Planning a socialist economy, therefore, is doable; [6] though here Lange might seem to refute, along with Mises and Bohm-Bawerk, my claim that the categories of economics preclude overcoming the contradictions

that Marx analyzed.

Piero Sraffa went even further in his book, *The Production of Commodities by Means of Commodities;* he generalized David Ricardo's corn model in a way that shows that an economy could, in principle, function without people. The idea is that a mono-product economy of producing and consuming needs only a certain quantity of, in this case, corn for seed and energy to do the work of growing corn. Therefore, corn could reproduce corn and use corn to produce corn. Sraffa showed that in an economy with any number of commodities, the necessary inputs could be calculated to produce the necessary outputs, which would in turn be the inputs of the next cycle of production. The quantity of an input needed for a given output is a technical coefficient, which an engineer or agronomist can provide. Neither of the factors—consumers maximizing preferences nor investors maximizing profits—send the signals, which tell the economy what and when to produce.[7]

Both before and after Sraffa, a number of economists have created input/output computer models of the world and national economies. The outputs of some processes are inputs for other processes, which in turn produce more outputs, which become new inputs. If observed ratios continue to hold in the future, models using input/output principles can predict the operation of the present world economy. To assume that past and present ratios and relationships will continue to hold, often amounts to assuming positive feedback loops: a trend will be a stronger trend in the future, like compound interest. The almost uniform result of such future modeling is that the projecting of present trends forward shows that the future of the world economy is one of system collapse, as pollution, resource depletion, and population growth combine to impose disasters. Projections show sustainable scenarios to be feasible only if radical social and environmental changes happen soon.[8]

Lange and Sraffa have shown that a sustainable economics without capitalism is doable. Lange, Sraffa, and others invented ways to build a non-capitalist economic system by organizing production according to principles that depend less on the free consent of the owners of factors of production. Thus, they made great progress in the physical planning of socialism, though not in the human planning of socialism. They showed how to dispense in part with homo economicus, while relying in part on consumer choices and monetary incentives, which presuppose the same homo economicus, as did capitalism. They do not, however, show how to transform homo economicus.[9] Marx, if he were alive today, would likely join those who argue—based on the many horror stories drawn from history—that opportunity cost and input/output planning lend themselves to a net regress: from misery under capitalism toward misery under slavery.

The transformation of basic cultural structures comes from Marx. He revealed the intractable problems built into the formal structure of the social relations that provide both the framework of everyday life and the global economy: the free laborer, the market, the commodities bought and sold. Marx recognized that:

❑ the exchange of commodities was the substance of everyday life throughout the capitalist world

❑ the world economy was a single system

❑ the governments of nation-states were its local administrators, not its lords and masters. Public opinion has vindicated Marx, in recent years, due to the decline of the nation-state power in the wake of the globalization of production.

The flourishing of Western European social democracies encouraged many people after WW II; they underestimated the significance of the temporary features of that historical period and of the privileged role that Western Europe had in the international division of labor. Thus, they perceived Sweden, Denmark, and or The Netherlands to be the image of the ideal future of human society, give or take a glitch or two. If Sweden could have full employment, high wages, and universal health care then, as erred, all other nations could do the same; what is possible for one nation of the world economic system must be possible, as supposed, for all.

The ideas of Marx, considered a pessimist, seem to have failed due to the ability of capitalist nation-states to redistribute income through elected labor governments and strong labor unions. I do think that Marx was too pessimistic in underestimating the possibilities of using political power to shape a national economy. In addition, Anthony Giddens' *A Contemporary Critique of Historical Materialism* gives good reasons for judging Marx's vision wrong in this respect.[10] Overall though, Marx was right as brought home by the present crumbling of Western European welfare states under the relentless pressure of global economic competition; this point is further brought home by the fading dream that some day the poor of Guyana, Botswana, and the USA will achieve the level of security enjoyed by the poor of The Netherlands. I will not repeat here the arguments of Part 2, but will note that the quasi-mechanism identified in Part 2 is the basic cultural structure that is the basis of Marx's analysis: the explanation of the success of global capitalism's end run around labor governments and labor unions

Politics is important: it does matter who is elected and what programs and policies governments implement; however, overall, governments do not rule humanity. A modern government, like any modern institution and much like an individual, has:

- bank accounts
- income
- expenses
- a budget
- the struggle to pay its bills
- interest on its debts.

A government cannot simply rewrite the rules of the system on which its existence hinges. Moreover, humanity's existing economic institutions are not the mere creations of a privileged class of powerful people who made them up and who could make up different ones whenever they might choose, or might find it in their interest to do this. Thus, what we need is not so much insight into who and what does not rule the world, as insight into who and what does.

One would hope that it is possible to: 1) gain a better understanding of who and what rules the global economy, and 2) learn how to contribute more effectively toward solving humanity's and, thus, Earth's problems, if we had a better theory. Thus, I propose that: 1) a fatal flaw in most economic theory is its metaphysical alliance with the natural sciences, borrowing most of its metaphors and mathematical tools from mechanics, and 2) we will do better by treating economics, which is planning, as a human science and as a social science, which would be closer to: • linguistics • philosophy • cultural anthropology , and • sociology.

If cultural forms are, as Marx and others have shown, the root causes of the phenomena to be explained, it would be logical to seek a methodology for explaining them in those sciences devoted to the study of cultural forms.

In the next section, I develop the concept of *a market as a language* (posed in the Introduction). I will expand the theory that the scientific explanation of international trade and other economic phenomena advances by seeing markets as systems of meanings.

II

The two ideas that linguists of the 20th century have found most helpful toward understanding language are: 1) the distinction between the *diachronic* study of language and the *synchronic* study of language and 2) the distinction between the *signifier* and the *signified*

I propose that these same ideas are useful both for scholars seeking to understand the global economy and for activists seeking to change it. I will do this without exaggerating the similarities between economics and linguistics and without pretending that scholars have reached consensus concerning the nature of linguistics.

In his *Course in General Linguistics,* Ferdinand de Saussure used the analogies of markets and prices to introduce and demonstrate his ideas of *diachrony* • *synchrony* • *signifier* • *signified*. Thus, a procedure exists to show the bearing of his key linguistic ideas upon economic institutions: comments are made on Saussure's text, inverting the direction of the analogies, using linguistics to shed light on economics, whereas Saussure used economics to shed light on linguistics. Saussure introduces the distinction between diachronic and synchronic linguistics in the following passage:

> Few linguists doubt that the intervention of the time factor creates special difficulties for linguistics and that it places their science before two routes that are divergent. Most sciences know nothing of such a radical duality; time does not produce any special effects. Astronomy has established that the stars undergo notable changes, but she has not been obliged for that reason to split itself into two disciplines. Geology reasons almost constantly about successive states; however, when it comes to focus upon the fixed states of Earth, it does not make of them the object of a contrasting study. There is a descriptive science of law and a history of law; nobody opposes one to the other. The political history of states moves in time; yet, if a historian describes an epoch, one does not have the impression of making an exit from history. In contrast, the science of political institutions is descriptive, though on occasion, it can deal well with historical questions without disturbing its unity.
>
> **On the contrary, the duality of which we speak imposes an authority upon the economic sciences.** Here, contrary to what happens in the preceding cases, political economy and economic history constitute two disciplines separated in the heart of the same science. The recent books in print on these subjects accentuate that distinction. **Proceeding in this way, one obeys, without an awareness of the fact, an interior necessity; it is a similar necessity, which obliges us to separate linguistics into two parts, each having its own principle. It is the case that there, as in political economy, one confronts the notion of value; in the two sciences, it is a matter of a system of equivalence between two things of different orders: in one: work and salary, in the other: the signified and the signifier.**
>
> To better mark that opposition and crossing between two orders of phenomena relative to the same object, we prefer to speak of *synchronic linguistics*, and *diachronic linguistics*. Synchronic includes: everything that refers to the static aspect of our science. Diachronic refers to: everything that acts within evolutions. In the same way, synchrony: designates a state

of language, and diachrony: names a phase of evolution.[11]

Saussure therefore finds that linguistics and economics are unusual among sciences because part of their subject matter –dia–chronic: exists in the flow of time, while another part –syn–chronic: exists outside of time. The part of linguistics that is synchronic includes what the non-linguist calls *grammar* and *word usage*. A lexicon of linguistics would display how the meanings—values—of all the words in a language are defined in relation to each other without any reference to the temporal and non-temporal processes that caused the meanings to be what they are. Economics would have a list of the prices as the values of all the goods for sale in a market; thus, economics would give the ratios at the right monetary exchange as a report about a given moment of time, without regard to the passage of time.

Perhaps Saussure overestimated what he called: the inner necessity to separate diachronic and synchronic studies as opposites in linguistics and in economics. Perhaps he underestimated the extent to which a similar distinction might apply to other sciences. More important, however, than the accuracy of Saussure's premise is that we see what makes human life give his view plausibility; this then is what led him to say that values are outside the flow of time, while *system change* is immersed in the flow of time. Before we look closer at the synchronic/diachronic distinction, let us observe the other key distinction Saussure uses in the passage quoted: the signifier from the signified.

A common sense model of language regards a language as, largely, a set of words that represent things: *table* is a word representing the thing called a table. Likewise, all or most words represent the things that they name. This common sense model, nevertheless, soon proves inadequate for the scientific study of even one language, not to mention the study of many languages. Linguists have replaced the *word-to-thing distinction* with more accurate technical distinctions, which includes the well known: *signifier to signified.*

Saussure introduces the notion of signifier by identifying it with the *acoustic image*: the signifier is the pattern of sounds, which the speaker speaks and the hearer hears. Thus, the signifier has its identity both as a spoken word and as an identity with other entities that play a similar role. The suffix *'ier* (*'iant* in Francaise) indicates that the signifier is what is active: it acts. It corresponds to the verb: the active part of the sentence and to the will: the active part of the human soul. The spoken word can signify, though something else could signify too, e.g., a footprint, a drumbeat, a kiss, a tassel on a hat, then it would be a signifier.

The active, controlling, responsible side of the notion of the signifier enabled Jacques Lacan, a psychiatrist charged with treating insane prisoners referred by the French justice system, to diagnose paranoid psychosis as a disorder of the signifier. Lacan's diagnosis is apt as well because of its link to the imaginary voices that some who suffer psychosis hear.

Another, related, way to think about signifiers: the question, "What is a signifier?" is "A signifier is not anything." To say that something is, is to say that it is identical with itself. Performing its function, however, constitutes a signifier; its function is to direct the hearer beyond itself to something else. Pointing outward might, so to speak, exhaust the being of the signifier. Once the pointing occurs there is nothing left or, what is equivalent, whatever is left is not a signifier. A corollary of thinking about signifiers in this second way and then thinking of language as a system of signifiers is anti-essentialism. With such a view, the signifiers do not vanish; they remain as free-floating signifiers relating to each other and become what language is all about. What vanishes is the strong sense of the word *is,* which implies that we live in a world of stable essences identical with themselves.

According to Saussure, the signifier does point to something, which is the signified *(signifie).* He at first identifies the signified as the concept. In other words, what the signifier points to is an idea, a meaning, or, as Saussure says, "a value."[13] The spoken word *tree,* functioning as a signifier, does not directly signify a particular solid, real-live tree with some pine needles some fresh and others dusty, roots that curl deep in the ground around pieces of rock, and gum oozing from joints in its trunk.

Saussure maintains that the signifying process is about social values and not directly about brute facts of nature. This not an arbitrary principle that he dreamed up without reason. It is a principle imposed upon linguists, although they do not all use Saussure's terminology in the subject matter of their science. It leads to an important philosophical point: Homo sapiens is not a species in direct contact with reality. As a social and language-using species, we operate in terms of *curtains of meaning* interposed between reality and us.

To return now to the text quoted above, Saussure draws an extended analogy:

❒ Signified is to signifier as

❒ Diachronic is to synchronic as
❒ Work is to salary.

If we change our focus and recast this set of three parallel distinctions as two sets of three, then we have all of the first terms: • Signified • Diachronic • Work have something in common. All the secondary terms: ♦signifier ♦ synchronic ♦ salary, Saussure tells us, have something in common; they are:

❒ all about values
❒ socially defined counters, which can enter into transactions with equivalent counters
❒ exchange for their equivalents; a salary (or a wage), according to the classical economists, thus, represents the exchange value of work.

The first three of each pair: • Signified • Diachronic • Work are, in Elizabeth Anscombe's terminology, *brute* relative to the second three of each pair.[14] Without boasting of any miraculous unsullied contact with nature uncontaminated by a human interpretation of it, they are closer to nature. The orderly systems found in the second three of each pair: ♦ Signifier ♦ Synchronic ♦ Salary are models of *socially constructed reality*.

The first three of each pair: • Signified • Diachronic • Work are social constructs as well, though they play different types of roles in the social construction. They float free of nature to a lesser degree, they are closer to pine needles and roots, to history, and to expenditures of energy, effort, sweat, and toil.

III

Jean Baudrillard illuminates the two passages from Saussure, which I commented upon:

> Saussure offered two perspectives on the exchange of language terms when he compared them to money as follows: a piece of money can be placed in relationship to all the other terms of the monetary system; it can be exchanged against a real good of some value. It was for the former dimension that Saussure increasingly reserved the term *value*; thus: 1) the relativity of all the terms among themselves, which is internal to the general system and composed of distinctive oppositions instead of the other possible definitions of value and 2) the relation of each term to what it designates, of each signifier to its signified, as each monetary unit has a corresponding object as the exchange for it. The first type of relationship corresponds to the structural dimension of language, the second to its functional aspect. The two dimensions are distinct, though articulated, which is to say that they work together and cohere. It is a view that characterizes the classical configuration of the linguistic sign, which can be placed with the *commodity law of value*, where the function of designation

always appears as the goal or finality of the structural operation of language. At this classical stage of signification, there is a complete parallel with the mechanism of value in material production as Marx described:

> Use value functions as the horizon and finality of the system of exchange value.

Thus defined: 1) use value qualifies the concrete operation of the commodity in (the act of) consumption (a moment of the process that is parallel to the sign's moment of designation), and 2) exchange value refers to the interchangeability of all commodities under the law of equivalence (a moment parallel to the structural organization of the sign). Use value and exchange value are organized together as dialectic throughout Marx's analyses and define a rational configuration of production regulated by political economy.[15]

This is just what Adam Smith proposed in the first great work of economic science:

> The whole point of economic activity is to supply the necessities and conveniences of life in ever-greater quantity and quality.

The free market is preferable to the rigid institutions of bygone times and distant places because through exchange among self-interested individuals, powerful motives achieve the common good. Smith noted, with pride, that the high degree of market-driven capital investment applied to improvement of land and stock in his 18th century Britain had produced greater wealth than had been found in the empires of yore, or among peoples that he (with ethnocentric pride) regarded as savages. The market, which is the system of exchange value, was for Smith a social quasi-mechanism, which functioned to produce goods that were, by nature, useful.

The leading progressive thinkers of the 18th century did not doubt that social institutions could reform in order to serve natural functions better. As the 21st century begins, we need to reassess and refine that premise, as well as other founding premises of modern Western civilization that we have inherited from Adam Smith and other great 18th century thinkers. We can see that in some ways the 18th century was a demented one: full of violence and clothed in incoherent ideals. Nature was deemed to be at once savage and the source of so-called true norms; freedom was viewed as at once liberation from the constraints of an ethics of virtue and as the source of the moral legitimacy of contracts. As a better theory, Saussure's distinctions will help us through a difficult process of discernment: deciding which ideals of modern Western civilization we should value and keep. This may well show us that what is best about Western civilization is its common ground with Eastern civilization;

and the best features of modern civilization revise and improve the achievements of ancient civilization.

> Use value functions as the horizon and finality of the system of exchange value.

Further applying Saussure's terminology, we may expand this thought: the purpose of the synchronic structures of language [words, money, and economic exchange (signifier • synchronic • salary triad)] is intended to make life better in the real world (pointed toward by the • signified • diachronic • work triad).

Looking at life in view of this thought, two corollaries about social activism follow:

1. Society cannot transform in the positive sense through violence. It affirms the idea that improving the cultural forms that guide humans, urges us to work with the:

❒ cultural forms
❒ process of negotiating social reality
❒ Signifier • Synchronic • Salary part of Saussure's three distinctions.

The idea that society cannot be transformed by violence is a corollary based on the idea that social life is organized by signifiers, which function in a synchronic world of social ritual and meaning. Some readers may see no logical link between the symbolic character of social reality and the necessity to use nonviolent means to transform it. What will clarify this, however, is to think it through and read Hannah Arendt's *On Violence,* which distinguishes the various forms of power from violence.[7]

2. Society cannot transform by way of superficial action. This is a way of saying that transforming cultural structures to adjust them to physical reality can only be done by working with physical reality, which lies behind the: • signified • diachronic • work part of the Saussure's three distinctions. Ecology (Gk *oikos*: house + logic) is the key to transformation: not economics, which is part of the system of social values that need transformation, rather than the *natural framework* defining the physical context in which social transformation happens. To understand the natural framework, it is necessary to coordinate the findings of physics, chemistry, biology, geology, and astronomy. Thus, we understand the interrelated systems of the biosphere: the *bionetwork* of ecology.

Baudrillard, however, is among those thinkers who are in principle committed to a superficial philosophy. Right after the passage from his works quoted above, he asserts that:

> A 20th century revolution in thinking occurred that has eliminated

production, use-value, and all reference to real things.

He uses the passage quoted above only as a point of departure, in order to describe the modern worldview (in the specific forms it assumed in Marx and Saussure) which postmodernism has now, in his opinion, deconstructed and destroyed.

I will not argue that anything of substance is shown to be true merely because once certain definitions are handy certain logical conclusions follow. It is worth noting, however, that the concepts of Saussure's I defined are not arbitrary definitions, but ones with much support because of their capacity to facilitate the scientific understanding of the phenomena of linguistics, economics, and, in general, as Saussure says, "It is all those areas of culture concerned with values."

It thus follows from the logical conceptual framework, which I have developed, that the (only) solution to humanity's and, thus, Earth's problems is the one I call *nonviolent transformation*. (I have explained why violence does not work.) I have two reasons for joining nonviolence with transformation:

1. transformation means that the forms of human life, the cultural structures must change (*trans* + *form* derived from the Latin: to change form) so, no point exists in trying to change the laws of physics, chemistry, or the other natural sciences; therefore, culture must change
2. the word *transformation* connotes that the changes needed are deep and profound: poverty and other human problems will resolve only by restructuring the basic structures identified by (among others) Karl Marx. Likewise, more than superficial change must happen: change must be practical and physical in relation to the Earth body and the bodies of humans.

The conclusion that nonviolent transformation is possible and desirable can be drawn from various sources. Perhaps most urgently, it is drawn from the practical experience of those who have lived it; nevertheless, it is important to notice that it follows as a corollary from widely accepted principles of anthropology, linguistics, and the human sciences.

Before expanding the theory of nonviolent transformation in the next section, here is an example of the theory in action. In the same city as the IMF and World Bank headquarters is another org, although with a philosophy worlds apart: the Church of the Savior. It meets the physical and human needs of people whom the system has abandoned. Its goals and methods are the oft-shared goals and oft-practiced methods. Thus, a review of the Church of the Savior applies, with slight variation, to thousands of orgs worldwide, many of which I have observed.

The Church of the Savior is a model that offers the community:

❒ bakeries in which homeless learn job search, attitudes, and skills
❒ a system of charitable donations
❒ seeks and uses volunteers
❒ interns as volunteers
❒provides modest stipends
❒ recycles donated items
❒ receives some funding from public and private agencies.

In terms of Saussure's analysis, The Church of the Savior has a clear grounding in the real world, the aim of which is to meet people's needs. In the social world of economic values, the Church of the Savior is eclectic; for example, it does not:

❑ seek to accumulate profits
❑ stop an activity before needs are met for lack of profit, yet
❑ neither does it shrink from running a business. The Church of the Savior organizes whatever pattern of human action it takes to get the job done.[16]

The Church of the Savior is not extraordinary and because of this it represents a practical approach. My theory, in which the Church of the Savior is an illustration, is not extraordinary either; thus, it is more likely to be true. Therefore, an extraordinary outcome may occur when humans follow the practices of the Church of the Savior; the world will have:

❒ freedom from poverty
❒ ecological balance
❒ gender equality
❒ respect for diversity
❒ no war. In the Church of the Savior, as in the base community movement, creative alternatives and empowerment go together. *Positive alternatives* show the way to a positive future; they build the advantage that at once influences and reshapes the system that is now in place.

IV

I base my confidence that the path of the Church of the Savior will solve humanity's problems upon seeing it as one illustration of a principle that works. I am not a member of that church and, thus, do not know the quarrels, quirks, and foibles among the members, which make its everyday life differ from the ideal picture of it that I use for my example. I assume that despite the faults they likely have, they commit to a spirit inspired love ethic, and they dedicate their ethic to a path with heart.

Earlier, I noted that the signifier does not refer directly to things, but instead to signifieds, which, roughly speaking, are concepts. More broadly, the human species does not relate directly to reality. Instead, culture—words and money, images and rituals—is a surrogate that removes most humans from direct continuous interaction with Earth. Certain aspects of culture—the free market, property rights, and the self-interested individual—sustain the global economy. Thus, global trade is in accord with:

❑ comparative advantage
❑ the globalization of production
❑ choosing unsustainable technologies
❑ accumulation
❑ instability
❑ the private appropriation of the social product
❑ the balancing of social accounts that the Keynesians struggle with
❑ the signified • synchronic • salary of Saussure's extended analogy governs the value exchange process.

All these operations proceed according to the regular exchange of equivalent values.

I have assumed that the members of the Savior have bypassed the market. They have achieved a direct insight into the relatively brute nature found in the signified • diachronic • work side of Saussure's extended analogy. They have done that by observing with empathy the homeless people huddled on the streets of Washington, DC, some in the very shadows of the buildings that house the IMF and the World Bank. They observed that the homeless, cold at night and hungry in the morning, need: • medical attention • regularity in their lives s bonding and love • shower facilities • a change of clothes • a safe, clean, warm, and dry place to sleep.

We can assume that the members of the Savior know about global warming, acid rain, holes in the ozone layer, and the exhaustion of fossil fuels. Unlike Adam Smith, who believed that the more use values were produced the better; they realize that the objective reality of our species is that it has to become a responsible family within the larger community of Earth's living systems. Economists have devised complex quantitative methods for choosing the optimum use of scarce resources. In contrast, the Savior has made simple observations that bypass economic calculations as well as the market; they observe that all the needs of some people go unmet. They have asked people to commit to the stewardship of their resources and skills; insofar as they have called forth resources that would otherwise be idle, they have given purpose to resources that otherwise would never act. In the light of their practical demonstration of values in action, the mathematical models used at the World Bank to determine what would be the optimum way to use a scarce resource to meet an unmet need are convicted not so much of erroneous mathematics, but of an erroneous metaphysic. They resolve to operate within a worldview, which assumes that the socially constructed reality of an economic metaphysic is a natural and inevitable reality. Yet, when Elizabeth O'Connor, of the Church of the Savior, urges that, "Servant structures must become the accepted global economic structures" it affirms the value of the opportunities deferred when a resource is put to one use instead of some other use.

Taken on its own, the ability of a group of church members to bypass the circulation of commodities and gain direct insight into objective reality, might lead to practices like those depicted in Solzhenitsyn's *Gulag Archipelago*. The Stalinists in Solzhenitsyn's novel say, "You must obey me because I know the objective truth."

I believe that the members of the Church of the Savior have not made that mistake. They know that a cultural and spiritual reality exists beside the physical. Only eliminating the human species can eliminate the signifier-synchronic-salary side of Saussure's extended analogy; thus, no alternative to transforming it or to treating the means as ends exists. Hence they work as Gandhi did with truth conceived as respect and faithfulness in relationships (*satya* [truth]: openness to another's being, Sanskrit *sat*: being, *ya*: open). Thus, truth is conceived as more than a mere objective scientific fact. If we travel 180° around the world, from the lavish suites/ brutal streets of Washington, DC to the rural villages of Sri Lanka, we will see another movement that illustrates respect for and transformation of the meanings found in local culture. The *Sarvodaya Shramadana* movement works with the twelve-fold path of Buddha's enlightenment. Some of the Singhalese language examples of the path are:

- *karuna:* compassion
- *metta:* loving-kindness
- *muditha:* joy in the joy of others
- *purushodaya:* awakening
- *artachariya:* constructive activity.[18]

IV

My confidence in what the people at the Sarvodaya Shramadana create comes from its leading by example. I see it as an example of meeting objective needs with spiritual inspiration and the way of appropriate culture.

The Church of the Savior and Sarvodaya Shramadana are just two examples of what intelligent people of good will are doing worldwide; they do it with or without pay, drawing resources from wherever they can be found, to meet needs, to save the environment, and to build peace. As the mainstream careens toward oblivion, creative minorities respond to the heartfelt problems in ways that contain the elements of a positive future.

Beyond churches and grassroots movements, the creative minorities act within:

- political parties
- government offices
- labor unions
- international agencies
- foundations
- all professions, which even includes the management of profit driven businesses. Standard forms of economics are not working; so, by trial and error, people who see a need and act to meet it are inventing alternatives that do work. The alternatives that work will, in practice, be alternatives that depart from and modify the metaphysic of economic society, which includes:

- materialism
- private property
- the self-interested individual looking out only for himself
- goods production only if there is profit to be made.

V

My comments on the logical status of two statements that I have made follow:

1. "The alternatives that work depart from and modify the metaphysic of economic society." It might appear to *have the logical status of an empirical generalization*.

Almost every word in my statement,

2. A spiritual and a cultural reality exists alongside the physical reality," would benefit from a clarification of its logical status. I will comment first about the word *spiritual*.

The status of spiritual and cultural, as opposed to physical, is a matter of repeating the distinctions I have drawn from Saussure: the spiritual and cultural is associated with the synchronic side and, thus, with the mental. Spiritual is, however, a controversial term that lends itself to evasions and abuses; thus, the objection might be raised that it would have been wise policy to avoid using it, even though it has a legitimate logical status. The following three reasons may tilt the balance of policy in favor of taking the risk of speaking about spiritual realities:

1. spirit-talk invites communication with the wisdom of ancient, medieval, and non-Western sacred texts and practices, which modern Western secular philosophy has too often decided not to understand
2. spirit-talk acknowledges that the transformation of the global economy must mainly be a transformation of the will. In many languages and contexts, the meaning of the words *will* and *spirit* are so alike as to be synonymous. For example, the *Spiritual Exercises* of St. Ignatius Loyola states that the exercises are designed to purify the will and bring the will into harmony with the divine will
3. speaking about spirit is an acknowledgment that dreams and myths move the world at least as much as concepts.[19]

The alternatives that work depart from and modify the metaphysic of the economic society.

If: 1) we regard this statement as having the logical status of an empirical generalization and 2) social science designed a research methodology to test it, then its meaning would need an explanation in terms that could be measured. Criteria would have to be established to determine which alternatives work by departing from and modifying the metaphysic of the economic society: *transformative*[19.5] *alternatives*. With proper studies in place, using research methods to gather information tied to appropriate criteria, studies would show that the successful policies, programs, and projects are those that transform. Why am I sure of this?

The alternatives that work are at the same time transformative alternatives, by departing from the mainstream Western worldviews. We validate this through the extant study and research. In *Dharma and Development, a Study of Sarvodaya Shramadana,* Joanna Macy shows in detail how the transformative movement is rooted in values distinct from those of the modern Western secular culture in which economic thinking has its context. In my empirical study, *The Evaluation of Cultural Action,* an evaluation report on the Parents and Children Program (PPH) in Chile, I dialogue with an imaginary interlocutor, "The Reasonable Social Scientist." Through it, I show that even procedures that seem to be unbiased and scientific still let the realities of a social movement with a transformative ideology slip through their conceptual nets.[20] In *Cultural Expression and Grassroots Development*, a collection of eleven case studies from Latin America, editor, Charles Kleymeyer, coins the phrase *cultural energy*. It names a power foreign to the explanatory categories of what I have been calling economic metaphysics. Cultural energy revitalizes and empowers communities; however, in order for those seeing it work to believe what they see, it is necessary for them to depart from and modify the existing economic ideology.[21] Yet, it is still misleading to assign the logical status of an empirical generalization to the statement. A serious attempt to test it would then show that it is wrong to think of it as a hypothesis to be tested. After conducting the proper studies using appropriate criteria, I am certain about the truth of that statement. (See the previous page.)

It is a foregone conclusion that any attempt to carry out a comprehensive empirical study designed to test it, would soon become embroiled in controversies over what criteria would make the proper links between the evidence and the concepts. Some would say that the West German post WW II Finance Minister Ludwig Erhard's *social market economy* (*sozialmarktwirtschaft*), which encouraged business and then skimmed taxes off the top of profits to finance a welfare state, was an example of remaining within the framework of the worldview of economic society with success.

In contrast, the genocide by Pol Pot in Cambodia was an example of departing from the concepts of universal human rights, which are essential to the metaphysic of an economic society. Pol Pot did depart from modern Western ideals, albeit on the negative transformative path, not the positive path that transforms.

In contrast, folks like the German Christian Democrat Ludwig Erhard [22] and his British counterpart the Labor Party's Sir Stafford Cripps [23] shaped economics in directions guided by social conscience; thus, the Western European welfare states, which blossomed under their stewardship were, with due regard to their limitations, positive steps toward transforming the human into the humane.

The leading philosopher of Christian democracy was Jacques Maritain. The author identified having the most influence upon the thinking of freshman Labor MPs at the close of WW II was John Ruskin. Both writers shared, as the raison d'etre of their lives and works, a dissent from the metaphysic of economic society.[24]

At some point, some of the members of the panel would begin to suspect (rightly) that the reason I was sure that a study would confirm my statement was that it was not an empirical generalization at all. They would notice that whenever they found evidence proving it false, I would cite reasons for using the same evidence to prove it true.

All the evidence, with a built-in tendency to be true by definition, supports the statement "The alternatives that work depart from and modify the metaphysic of economic society." We see it with a Venn diagram, drawing a circle to represent alternatives that work. Another circle represents the positive departures from the metaphysic of economic society. We draw the two circles to overlap and cross out the parts outside their intersection:

All the alternatives are positive departures; and, alternatives that work are positive. Due to the ease with which evidence that might falsify and, thus, in concept, disqualify the statement, it would be better to regard the statement as a secondary empirical one and regard as primary, the metaphysical shift. It calls us to look at known facts in a new way. We know that some people act in loving, cooperative, intelligent, and enthusiastic ways: they have more interest in solving problems than in making profits or holding onto received ideas. We know that they are implementing alternative solutions while the standard solutions prove unworkable. The logical status of the proposed new way of looking at these known facts (that is, the status it would occupy if the call to look at the world as it proposes were accepted) is similar to that of the central assertions of the great metaphysical systems of the past: • Aristotle • Aquinas • Kant unified the categories and cosmologies of Western civilization at three different periods of its history. Studying their writings shows that once the conceptual framework the philosopher operates within is understood and accepted, the central statements of the metaphysical system become necessary truths.

I suggested in Part 2 that to transform the metaphysic of the global economy, we could benefit by using Wittgenstein's concept of language-games. I then endorsed Charles Taylor's proposal to make the constitutive rules fundamental to research in the social sciences. Now I will develop these ideas further to explain the logical status of:

> The alternatives that work depart from and modify the metaphysic of economic society.

The first language-game Wittgenstein discusses in his *Philosophical Investigations* is a vehicle for criticizing the simple view held by St. Augustine, that the essence of language consists of names for objects. Wittgenstein wrote:

> Imagine a language for which the description given by Augustine is right. The language should serve to communicate between a builder A′ and an assistant B′. A′ builds with building-stones: blocks, pillars, slabs, and beams. B′ delivers the stones in the order in which A′ needs them. For this purpose, they use a language consisting of the words: block, pillar, slab, beam. A′ calls them out; B′ brings the stone which he has learned to bring at a specific call. We conceive that as a complete primitive language.[25]

Even more than Saussure's model, Wittgenstein's model of language sees words as embedded in activities, in social roles, in norms, in the interaction of humans with physical things. The idea of game, presumes rules, a notion Wittgenstein examines at great length. Thinking of human actions in terms of language-games presumes a consciousness-raising idea: the way things are, is not the way things have to be. Unlike Saussure's model, Wittgenstein's model is not based on the exchange of equivalents. In some games equivalents are exchanged, in some games not. From Wittgenstein's analysis, the general pattern of humans interacting with each other and nature is to get some sort of game going; when the game works, it fulfills needs and brings joy.

Adam Smith's account of living by exchange, starting from what he called—the natural tendency to use the barter system—is a more specific account of what humans do, as Newton's theory is a special case of Einstein's. Marx's general formula for capital: buying in order to sell, C-M-C, is one among many basic kinds of language-games people can play, which happens to be the dominant one in capitalist society. What do we make of Keynes' basic observation that the sum of sales must be the sum of purchases because what is a sale (revenue) for the seller is a purchase (expense) for the buyer? Is that just a way of saying X = X, a thing is identical with itself and, thus, not subject to the variation through human creativity implied by the game model? Listen to Wittgenstein: "A thing is identical with itself." No finer example of a useless proposition exists, albeit connected with a certain play of the imagination; as if within imagination we put a thing into its own shape and see that it fits. We might as well say, "Every thing fits into itself," and then, "Every thing fits into its own shape."

> At the same time we look at a thing and imagine a blank left for it, which now is an exact fit.[26]

Thus, we play with identity too, as Keynes did when he played with that self-identical thing, the unit of currency. He suggested, that after the 1917 revolution the Soviets could have inflated away debts by printing lots of money. Governments could then have created employment in Western countries by burying money to make profit in paying people to exhume it.[27]

One might object that the language-game model does not apply to the proletariat. Life might be a game, albeit a serious game, for one who plays the stock market. Life, however, is not a game for the person who has no other commodity for sale, short of the necessities to realize his labor-power, which is sadly, also the necessity to seek a job in order to earn the money to buy the necessities of life. In any case, the value of every word, even game, ends at some point, as Wittgenstein insisted. Another way we have to see the violence inflicted upon the poor by way of the laws of property and contract is: violence masked by the common sense of the victim in the street who has yet to realize that:

> Nature does not produce owners of money or commodities on one side, and workers possessing nothing but their labor power on the other side. This relation has no natural basis; neither is its social basis one that is common to all historical periods.

The process known as *consciousness-raising* helps people become aware, for example, that their oppression is the unnatural consequence of mutable social rules. Consciousness-raising might even be defined as the shifting from a metaphysic of economic society, which, in the classical sense, defines the economy as a *social machine*, to a language-game model: the economy as a game that people play. As Paulo Freire wrote:

> One of the main results of consciousness-raising, is becoming aware of the untested feasibility: all the possible action you can take to change the human world, that you have never tried because your worldview has made you believe that the human world cannot be changed.[28]

Regarded as observed regularities in human behavior, in some given group at some given time, social rules are as the regularities observed in nature: spring, summer, autumn, winter, day follows night, bedtime follows bath-time, the passenger pays the fare then takes a seat on the bus. Regarded as norms, rules have a feature that natural phenomena do not have: breaking rules exposes the rule-breaker to criticism. Rules can be regarded in yet a third way: they have what H. L. A. Hart in his analysis of rules calls:

An internal aspect in which the normal citizen:

- ❑ behaves with a certain degree of predictable regularity
- ❑ joins the general disapproval of those who violate the cultural norms
- ❑ is self-directed, using a conscientious awareness of the accepted rules to monitor and guide the self.[29]

Of particular interest among social rules are those that define the background in which human action takes place. They create social objects and relationships, which would not exist without them and, thus, set the stage upon which social actors act. Those are the constitutive rules that create the social world. John Searle suggests that the general form for a constitutive rule is: X counts as Y in C, where X is some brute or relatively brute fact, Y is an institutional status conferred by the rule, and C is a context.[30] Searle excludes from the category of constitutive rules cases where the Y term just assigns a name or label; so, this sort of object (X) is called a chair (Y) is not constitutive because you could sit in X whether you called X a chair or not.[31] A true constitutive rule has to set up the rules of the game, which (for example, chess used by Saussure, Wittgenstein, Taylor, Searle, and others) would not exist and does not play at all without its constitutive rules. Searle:

> If it has a certain kind of shape, we can use it as a chair regardless of what anyone else thinks. When we say, however, that such and such bits of paper count as money, we have a true constitutive rule because: satisfying the X term such and such bits of paper, is not by itself sufficient for being money; nor does the X term specify causal features that would be sufficient to enable the stuff to function as money at all without human agreement. Hence, the application of the constitutive rule introduces these features: the Y term has to assign a new status that the object does not have just by virtue of satisfying the X term; a collective agreement must exist, or at least acceptance, both in the imposition of that status on the stuff referred to by the X term and about the function that goes with the status.
>
> Our sense of a sleight of hand in the creation of institutional facts out of brute facts derives from the nonphysical, noncausal character of the relations of the X and Y terms in the structure where we simply count X things as Y things. In our toughest metaphysical moods we want to ask, is an X really a Y For example, are these bits of paper really money? Is a piece of land, in truth, somebody's private property? Is making the prescribed noises in a ceremony truly getting married? Is the utterance of certain sounds through

the mouth the actual making a statement or a promise? When you get to the core, those are not facts; rather they are symbols of facts.[32]

A major aim here is to prove that to understand the global economy it is necessary to understand its constitutive rules, the history of those rules, and the effects of them. I do not agree with Searle's analysis that: constitutive rules are noncausal; they do have profound consequences. Without the constitutive rules as institutional facts presupposed by the metaphysic of an economic society, the quasi-mechanisms that explain international trade according to theories of comparative advantage would not exist. Theories of the globalization of production, which explain the exploitation of labor in the third world, along with unemployment and deindustrialization in the first world, rely on the same quasi-mechanisms as their explanatory principles. Theories of technological change contend with only half the problem; the other half is culture. Ecological design solves only half the problem; the other half of the solution is the transformation of cultural forms, above all the transformation of the constitutive rules that govern economic relationships.

In our time, the steady march of social democratic welfare states guided by Keynesian macroeconomic principles has encountered both physical and institutional limits; the latter take the form of unpayable debt, which cannot be overcome without revision of what Marx called the *capitalist economic categories*: without revision of the constitutive rules. Marx pioneered methods for following out the consequences of those constitutive rules of economic society, which produce accumulation, which exacerbates the contradictions if the constitutive rules are not transformed. The historians: Braudel, Wallerstein, and Polanyi have, in exhaustive detail, clarified the story of the processes by which market structures as defined by the constitutive rules of capitalism became, over time, an interlocking set of interrelated quasi-mechanisms, which expanded outward from Europe to become today's global economy. The post-structuralists have deconstructed the guiding and legitimating ideas of socially constructed realities, which include:

- ❑ development
- ❑ global economy
- ❑ capitalism, among others.

They have unmasked the pretensions of mainstream economists who treat poverty as a quasi-physical problem solvable by economists who are quasi-engineers.

Those who do solve social problems are not quasi-engineers

trained to operate conventional quasi-mechanisms. Those who march to the beat of a different drummer solve problems in the traditions of: Gandhi, Jane Addams, Eugene Debs, Dorothy Day, Hazel Henderson, Reverend King, Fuller, Paulo Freire, Mother Teresa , Norberg-Hodge, and millions of famous and unknown, whose lives transform the conventional rules of economic society because: they live according to alternative rules, which, though unconventional now, foretell a bright future.[33]

Notes

1. Karl Marx, *Capital: I*, 2. p. 188 (various editions). Page references are to the Modern Library edition.

2. *Id.* p. 164.

3. *Id.* p. 170.

4. Fritjof Capra, Charlene Spretnak, *Green Politics*—New York: E. P. Dutton, 1984 pp. 82-83.

> After the elections of Reagan, Thatcher, and Kohl, pollsters exposed that in each of their victories, the promise of economic recovery had been the primary factor. While those politicians did receive mandates to solve the economic crisis, they have not delivered except for some fluctuating improvement in a few areas. The reason they and other political leaders —whether left, right, or center—cannot find solutions is that they and their economic experts subscribe to narrow perceptions of the problems.
>
> What economists must do ASAP is reevaluate their entire conceptual foundation and redesign their basic models and their theories accordingly. The current economic crisis will reverse only if economists are willing to participate in the paradigm shift that is now occurring in all fields.

Fritjof Capra, *The Turning Point*. New York: Simon and Schuster, 1982 p. 193.

5. Ludwig von Mises, *Economic Calculation in the Socialist Commonwealth.* F. A. von Hayek (ed.), *Collectivist Economic Planning*. London: Routledge, 1935. According to Bohm-Bawerk:

> The fundamental proposition Marx puts before his readers is that the exchange value of commodities—for his analysis is directed only to this, not to values in use—finds its origin and its measure in the quantity of labor incorporated in the commodities.
>
> Eugen von Bohm-Bawerk, *Karl Marx and the Close of His System*. New York: Augustus M. Kelley, 1949. p. 66. Bohm-Bawerk points out that the fundamental proposition is an erroneous account of prices as set into markets. He adds that after beginning *Capital* with the observation that the wealth of capitalist societies appears as a vast collection of commodities, Marx later narrows the definition of commodity to include: only products capitalists produce for the market by exploiting labor. Bohm-Bawerk finds

that on a correct view the exchange value of commodities (broadly defined) occurs through supply and demand. Further, he finds that the existence of capital, pace Marx, is not the result of exploitation, but rather the result of time. Time-consuming roundabout methods of production yield more. Capital (as the future means of production), therefore, has its price: interest. Because both supply and demand and the need to pay interest on capital are, in Bohm-Bawerk's analysis, rooted in the nature of things, they cannot be avoided by a socialist state, which will be compelled, in effect, although Bohm-Bawerk does not use the phrase: to adopt state capitalism. See *Interest under Socialism*. pp. 339-344 of Eugen von Bohm-Bawerk, *Capital and Interest: 2*. South Holland, IL: Libertarian Press, 1959.

6. Oskar Lange, *On the Economic Theory of Socialism*. Minneapolis: University of Minnesota Press, 1938. For the history of the idea of opportunity cost, see Joseph Schumpeter, *History of Economic Analysis*. New York: Oxford University Press, 1954 p. 917.

7. Piero Sraffa, *Production of Commodities by Means of Commodities*. Cambridge, UK: Cambridge University Press, 1972.

7a. Hannah Arendt argues that power and violence are phenomena and concepts distinct from the other, although mixed in practice. Power is the human ability to act in concert (p. 44). She associates power with consent; violence employs instruments (p. 46). Violence is associated with force, weapons, and the like. It seems that, on Arendt's plausible account, the concerted action that constitutes power requires communication and a meeting of minds. Violence cannot create power, because its instrumental nature excludes communication and a meeting of minds. For the same reasons that Arendt finds violence incapable of producing power, I see it incapable of producing cultural transformation. No doubt, guns and bombs can destroy a people, killing everyone, therefore, destroying the cultural meanings that give their life coherence and make communication and cooperation possible. Violence, however, cannot create a positive cultural transformation. At most, it can create a setting where cultural processes can happen, e.g., people might attend compulsory classes or therapy sessions. Even so, the cultural process itself, the classes or the therapy, has to proceed through communication, not through violence. See Hannah Arendt, *On Violence*. New York: Harper and Row

8. Dennis and Donella Meadows, *The Limits to Growth*. New York: Universe Books, 1974, by the same authors, *Beyond Limits: Confronting Global Collapse, Envisioning a Sustainable Future*. Post Mills, VT: Chelsea Green Publishing Co., 1992. Mihajlo Mesarovic and Eduard Pestel, *Mankind at the Turning Point*. New York: Dutton, 1974.

9. Ernest Mandel, *Marxist Economic Theory: II*, pp. 726-727. London: Merlin Press, 1962.

> What the Soviet economic planners are trying to find is a system of automatic response, of self-regulating factors, which would enable optimum results independent of any conscious human intervention. It is less important to writers like Kantorovich, Novozhilov, Nemchinov, Malyshev, and so on, to discover the economic laws of the epoch of transition from capitalism to socialism than to find solutions to practical problems. Among the latter, the problem of rational fixing of prices is the most outstanding. The Soviets were led gradually (later, rapidly) to rehabilitate to an increasing degree the automatic functioning of the market.

10. Anthony Giddens, *A Contemporary Critique of Historical Materialism*. Berkeley: University of California Press, 1981.

11. Ferdinand de Saussure, *Course in General Linguistics* (edited by C. Bally and A. Sechehaye, translated by Wade Baskin). New York: McGraw-Hill, 1966. p. 79 (first published in Francaise, 1915). The quotation is my translation from Francaise, which differs slightly from Baskin's. See Ferdinand de Saussure, *Cours de Linguistique Generale*. Paris: Payot, 1971. pp. 114-115.

12. Lacan characterized paranoid psychosis as a disorder of the signifier in his doctoral dissertation. Jacques Lacan, *De la Psychose Paranoiaque dans ses Rapports Avec la Personnalite.* Paris: Seuil, 1980 (presented as a doctoral dissertation in 1932)

13. Part 1, *General Principles* chapter 1, *The Nature of the Linguistic Sign*, in Saussure, op. cit. n. 11 above.

14. G. E. M. Anscombe, *op. cit.* note 2 to the introduction to Section IV above.

15. Jean Baudrillard, *Symbolic Exchange and Death: Selected Writings* (edited by Mark Poster) Stanford: Stanford University Press, 1988. pp. 124-125 (first published in Francaise in 1976)

16. See Elizabeth O'Conner, *The New Community*. New York: Harper and Row, 1976, and other books by the same author.

17. Solzhenitsyn, The Gulag Archipelago: an Experiment in Literary Investigation. New York: Harper and Row, 1974-78.

18. Joanna Macy, *Dharma and Development*. West Hartford, CT: Kumarian Press, 1973. Although I recognize that the Sarvodaya movement has suffered setbacks, I still believe that the success Macy describes illustrates the proposition that positive alternatives depart from and transform the secular metaphysical framework of economic society.

19. St. Ignatious Loyola, *The Spiritual Exercises of St. Ignatius of Loyola.* (translation by Elder Mullan, S. J.). New York: P. J. Kennedy

and Sons, 1914. p. 3.

> As strolling, walking, and running exercise the body, so every way of preparing and disposing the soul to rid itself of all the disordered tendencies; and after it is rid, to find the Divine Will as to the management of one's life for the salvation of the soul, is called a Spiritual Exercise.

19.5 After the Transformative Learning Center in Toronto, which is my new paradigm think-tank

20. Howard Richards, *The Evaluation of Cultural Action*. London: Macmillan, 1985.

21. Charles Kleymeyer, *Cultural Expression and Grassroots Development*. Boulder, CO. London: Lynne Riener Publishers, 1994.

22. "Render Unto the State What Belongs to the State," article published in *Die Zeit*, November 21, 1957, translated and reprinted in Ludwig Erhard, *The Economics of Success*. London: Thames and Hudson, 1963. p. 213.

> We run a grave risk of becoming bogged down in a morass of ultra-individualism. The reason is simply that we misconstrue the idea of freedom and would like to believe, out of sheer egoism, against our better judgment, and indeed against our own conscience, that freedom implies the right to do or not do whatever pleases the individual or the group, without regard to the community and the state. This I call misconstruing freedom.

23. Sir Stafford Cripps, *Towards Christian Democracy*. New York: Philosophical Library, 1946.

24. Jacques Maritain, *Christianity and Democracy*. New York: Philosophical Library, 1946. See also other works by this prolific and influential author. On Ruskin, see *Edward Alexander, Matthew Arnold, John Ruskin, and the Modern Temper*. Columbus, OH: Ohio State University Press, 1973.

25. Wittgenstein, Ludwig, *Philosophical Investigations*. Oxford: Blackwell, 1956 pr. 21

26. Wittgenstein, *op. cit.* paragraph 216. Wittgenstein's idea of language-game has been used by Jean-Francois Lyotard to support a postmodern view defined as —incredulity toward meta-narratives. Jean-Francois Lyotard, *The Postmodern Condition: a Report on Knowledge*. Minneapolis: University of Minnesota Press, 1993. p. xxiv, pp. 9-11. Using the method of language-games to deconstruct grand and overarching theories of all kinds, Lyotard said:

> Science possesses no general *meta-language* in which all other languages can be transcribed and evaluated. This is what prevents its identification with the system and, all things considered, with terror.

Id. p. 64. Somewhat contrary to the spirit of Lyotard's work, I suggest that the widespread global practice of exchange for money has the qualities of a language-game.

27. Keynes was quite aware that money could be created by fiat and devalued by deliberate policies. Hence, his views support the concept that the entire existence of the signifiers that organize the global economy depends on moral custom, or convention: cultural structures.

> Money is simply that which the State declares from time to time to be a good legal discharge of money contracts. The power of taxation by currency devaluation is one that has been inherent in the state since Rome discovered it. The creation of legal tender has been and is a government's ultimate bankruptcy or its own downfall, so long as this instrument still lies at hand unused. The tendency of money to depreciate has been in past times a weighty counterpoise against the cumulative effects of compound interest and the inheritance of fortunes.

Keynes, *A Tract on Monetary Reform* reprinted in *Collected Writings*. London: Macmillan, 1972. :IV, pp. 8-9.

> Lenin is said to have declared that the best way to destroy the capitalist system was to debauch the currency. As the inflation proceeds and the real value of the currency fluctuates much from month to month, all permanent relations between debtors and creditors, which form the ultimate foundation or capitalism, become so disordered as to be almost meaningless. And the process of wealth acquisition degenerates into gamble and a lottery.

Keynes, The Economic Consequences of the Peace, Collected Writings: II, pp. 148-149.

28. Paulo Freire, *The Pedagogy of the Oppressed*. New York: Continuum, 1982 (translated from Portuguese by Myra Ramos)

29. H. L. A. Hart, *The Concept of Law*. Oxford, Clarendon Press, 1961.

30. John Searle, *The Construction of Social Reality*. New York: Free Press, 1995. p. 28, 44

31. Searle, *op. cit*. p. 44.

32. Searle, *op. cit*. p. 45.

33. The people on my short list are renowned for what I call positive alternatives, and psychologists call *post-conventional moral judgment*. As I see it, research in moral development supports my belief that the conduct of millions of people represents a shift away from the norms of economic society. However, Aristotle observed long ago that:

> Most men wish what is noble, (*kalos*) though they choose what is profitable.

Nichomachean Ethics: VIII, xiii, 8)

Judgment and action are, nevertheless, quite related. Lawrence Kohlberg's well-known studies of the development of moral judgment places homo economicus (individualism, instrumental purpose, exchange) at stage two of moral development. Most adults act at stages three and four (which Kohlberg, after Piaget, regards conventional). They conform to the conventional norms of society, which happen to be, at this stage of human moral evolution, largely the norms of market capitalist societies. Their conformity to conventional morality, however, is not due to reflective judgment on the comparative merits of contemporary institutions and possible alternatives; rather it is due to:

- mutual interpersonal expectations
- wanting to be a good person in relationships
- interpersonal conformity (stage 3)
- conscientious support of the social system (stage 4). See Thomas Lickona (ed.) *Moral Development and Behavior: Theory, Research, and Social Issues*. New York: Holt, Rinehart and Winston, 1973; see pp. 34-35 in Lawrence Kohlberg, *Moral Stages and Moralization: the Cognitive-developmental Approach.* Parallel to Kohlberg, though relying on other researchers, John Rawls argues that humans have a natural—morality of association (like Piaget and Kohlberg's conventional stages): morality improves and brings justice into social arrangements, such as those Rawls advocates:

> The social arrangements would [once they are the norm] be kept in place by moral sentiments that are a normal part of human life.

John Rawls, *A Theory of Justice*. Cambridge: Harvard University Press, 1971. p. 489. Kohlberg identifies Rawls along with Socrates, Gandhi, and King as examples of post-conventional moral judgment characterized by a philosophical stance that analyzes social norms in the light of broad principles. Carol Gilligan is among those who have criticized Kohlberg for overemphasizing the justice principles and under-emphasizing the care ethic. Carol Gilligan, *In a Different Voice: Psychological Theory and Women's Development.* Cambridge: Harvard University Press, 1982. Gilligan views the forecast for a metaphysical shift to a post economic perspective as even stronger because, in addition to complementing the justice ethics as moral theories, her care ethics perspective finds roots for the growth of cooperation and solidarity in common experience.

> The experiences of inequality and interconnection, in parent and child relationship then give rise to the ethics of justice and care, the ideals of

human relationship—the vision that society treats self and others as equal and worthy—that, despite differences in power, fairness prevails. The vision is the one in which society responds to and includes everyone leaving no one left alone or hurt.

Gilligan, *op. cit.* pp. 62-63.

Because the normal and natural tendency of human moral development appears to be toward post-conventional thinking, the ethic of care, or both, it seems probable that people like those on my short list are numerous, perhaps at a growing rate. The basis for this hope blends with inspired moral leadership, conventional conformity, and enlightened self-interest; it may be able to guide our species—imprisoned though we are within our cultural structures—toward the sustainable and happy adjustments to physical reality.

Review Questions

1. In Marx's analysis of the inherent tendency toward infinite expansion, what observation of Aristotle's about money does he use to support his premise? P 179

2. Lange and Sraffa have shown that a sustainable economy is doable without capitalism. What basic pre-agreed guidelines are necessary for this to happen? P 181

3. Why does Marx remain important to the understanding of political economy even though his theories did not solve the problem? P 178

4. The 18th century operated via a premise of incorrect ideals: nature as both savage and the source of true norms, and freedom as the source of the moral legitimacy of contracts. How did Saussure open the door to a new paradigm? P 190

b. How does Saussure's extended analogy set up the idea of socially constructed reality, P 187 which is also expressed in the phrase "curtains of meaning interposed between reality and us"? P 186

6. How might you see Saussure's system of dichotomy, which is his analysis of the aspects of human existence within time and outside time in relation to nonviolent transformation? P 192

7. "Use value functions as the horizon and finality of the system of exchange value." (Karl Marx) Consider the idea of *horizon* as an art literal and as an art metaphor, and then incorporate the idea of use value vis a' vis exchange value. What do you find? P 212

8. A basic flaw of economics is its link to the concepts framed by the mechanics of physics. It may thus be helpful to recall some common metaphors, which narrow the scope of the subject they describe because of their mechanical roots. Aside from the ones named in the book, are you aware of other mechanical metaphors that we use in everyday language related to economics, such as "gear up for"? Thus, human behavior is simplified in order to analyze it in terms of mechanical metaphors.

9. What new approach does Freire's work with consciousness-raising bring to the idea of nonviolent transformation? [P 203]

10. How does Wittgenstein's concept [P 11, 201] of language-game intersect with the Saussure system [P 192] and Freire's work [P 203] to support nonviolent transformation?

10

A Vision of a World Free of Poverty and Economic Insecurity

Recall the face of the poorest and weakest man you have seen and ask yourself if the step you contemplate is going to be of any use to him. Will he gain by it?[1]—M. K. Gandhi

The indictment of modern society that Martin Luther King Jr. made in April of 1968, in a sermon at the National Cathedral in Washington a few days before his assassination, remains valid. Reverend King said:

There is nothing new about poverty. What is new is that today we have the resources and the techniques to end poverty. The question is: "Do we have the will?"[2]

In Part 10, I elaborate on Dr. King's statement about poverty, which I know to be true and the heart of the issue. With it, I sketch a vision of a world without poverty and economic insecurity by way of asking what it would mean to have the will to end poverty. I do not advocate simple solutions; the simple solutions have not worked. I do not offer a blueprint, nor attempt to answer all the objections a skeptical reader might raise. Instead, I impart a kaleidoscopic vision of a world without poverty for readers whom I assume to be sympathetic: you likely care because, by choosing to read this book, you have some quality of what Aldous Huxley called the *perennial philosophy*: the nonsectarian religious and spiritual worldview.[3] For that reason, I expect that you will keep reading beyond my use of words like *spirit, love,* or *God*. I expect that you know from experience that what humanist and spiritual ethics have in common is more important than the points by which they civilly disagree; this is affirmed by the Marxists and Christians who were thrown together into the same dungeons by troops under Pinochet in Chile in 1973.

I broaden King's call to end poverty by calling for the end of the economic insecurity the middle classes now face. Even people who are not poor, as seen by their goods and services use at adequate levels, are now anxious because of their growing debt, or dependence on expensive life sustaining purchases such as prescriptions and other health-care. Their stream of income, which though here today may be gone tomorrow, is also their lifeline.

The goal Dr. King proposed at the National Cathedral was a goal for everyone, in addition to those in the direct line of fire: the poor and those threatened by poverty. The goal is even a logical one for the least generous among the most prosperous, because it is the goal conducive to building the culture of peace. In a less violent world, everyone will be safer.

Oft told is a tale about rich people, who make it their goal to keep the poor down. The rich fancy that by repression they serve their own upper class interests. A different tale is told by the wise affluent, aware that their interests and the interests of civility are the same.

Although in general, it is not true that the rich and the non-poor want poverty for the poor, Reverend King's indictment implies that the continued existence of poverty in our times is, in a sense, an intentional crime committed by society against the poor. Given that today's society has: 1) the techniques and resources to end poverty and 2) not ended poverty, it must be caused by either:

❑ an unintended consequence
❑ careless neglect
❑ the misunderstanding of what morality is
❑ a deliberate omission, or
❑ any combination of these, which cause most of the world's people to live in poverty.

Throughout most of history, an insidious, faulty assumption prevailed: it was natural and inevitable that the vast majority who toil would lead short lives in material deprivation. For example, in the early 19th century David Ricardo, the source of reason among the early economists, advocated free trade for Britain on the basis that free trade would lower wages, therefore, raise profits, and, thus, stimulate production. The logical analysis of market exchanges led Ricardo to conclude that competition among wage earners kept wages down to the minimum required to stay alive: food prices alone determined the minimum wage. Thus, cheap imported grains from France brought lower wages, which in turn gave a competitive advantage to British manufactures.

In 1798 Thomas Malthus, Ricardo's friend and the first to hold a chair of political economy at Cambridge, published a mathematical proof that any attempt to end poverty was futile: it would only result in augmenting the numbers of the laboring classes, which would increase the pressure of population on food supply; thus, it would reinforce poverty. Food supplies increased, Malthus believed, arithmetically, by adding to production. In contrast, due to human sexuality, our population increase is geometric: doubling, in this case, every twenty-five years, as it did in the British American colonies of his time, and whenever there is no famine to check it. Population increase is exponential, as in the series: 1, 2, 4, 8, 16, 32, 64, and 128. Malthus wrote:

> The power of population is superior to the power in the Earth to produce subsistence for man, so that premature death must in some shape or other visit the human race. The vices of humankind are the active and able ministers of depopulation. They are the precursors of the great army of destruction and often finish the dreadful work themselves. Should they fail, however, in this war of extermination, sickly seasons, epidemics, pestilence and plague, advance in terrific array, and sweep off their thousands and ten thousands. Should success be still incomplete, gigantic inevitable famine stalks in the rear and with one mighty blow levels the population with the food of the world.[4]

The mathematical argument of Malthus has proven wrong because the food supply grew faster than he expected. Today, Frances Moore Lappé, among others, has shown that the annual production of carbohydrates and proteins is more than sufficient to support the present global population. It is a population much larger than any Malthus thought possible.

Then again, the food supply would be more than sufficient if everyone ate from lower on the food chain.[5] Peter Singer, who holds similar views, does not oppose measures to limit population; instead, he holds that measures, such as strengthening women's reproductive rights and power to determine her sexual destiny are essential viable systems and resources to end poverty.[6]

In 1942, 1.5 centuries after Malthus, another economist, Joseph Schumpeter, made the mathematical argument that proved contrary to the Malthus theory. Schumpeter observed historical statistics that showed:

❑ the average growth of production to be above 2% per capita, which accrued from year to year as compound interest

❑ the distribution of income among the social classes was constant

He thus calculated that poverty would end in the US by 1978.[7] This mathematical argument proved also to be incorrect, though not for the reason Schumpeter half-expected: creeping socialism would stunt normal growth; instead, production did grow as much as he postulated, and the distribution of income among social classes did not hold constant. Disparity widened, inequality deepened, and the rising tide did not raise all ships.

Economic historian, Immanuel Wallerstein has estimated that, due to the economic and scientific progress of the last four hundred years, as much as 20% of the human population has escaped poverty, leaving by implication the vast majority, at least 80%, in poverty.[8] That high percentage corresponds to the World Bank numbers of 20% to 24% identifying the poorest of the poor.[9] The poorest lack food, adequate shelter, education, health care, drinking water, and sanitation.

The Federal Republic of Germany, one of the world's richest countries, is a 70-20-10 society.[10] It means that an estimated 70% are not poor, 20% move in and out of poverty during their lifetimes, while 10% are permanently poor. If Germany's pattern is typical of the rich countries, then at least half of that 70% have economic insecurity; this bears out in my experience serving middle class clients in my law practice in the US. Viviane Forrester's account of what she calls economic horror in another rich country, France, further supports the finding.[11]

Dr. King suggests that the answer to the decisive question depends on qualities of will: whether humanity has the will, at last, to end poverty, or whether inhumanity will continue to commit the crime against humanity, which is the exclusion of most people from the full grace of our resources. The answer (predictive outcome) does not depend on the logical analysis of market exchanges, on mathematical models, or on the statistical analysis of historical data. It depends on the choices that people make, which result from the principles we hold to be self-evident.

As a reverend, Dr. King was a member of a profession devoted to teaching the continuing relevance of ancient wisdom of which the qualities of will is a recurrent theme. In addition, King had training in philosophy and often cited Immanuel Kant who defined will as: the capacity to act from principle, which is that any given human action proceeds from a subjective principle, or maxim: the idea or guide which it exemplifies. Kant defined will this way to distinguish human action from things of nature. Speaking in a contemporary idiom, the sociologist Anthony Giddens describes human action as: *reflexively self-regulated*. In a manner similar to a number of other recent social theorists, Giddens thinks of society as: a process of structures-formation, rather than as a set of given structures.

Identifying will as:

1) the guidance of human action by social rules and
2) the processes of:
- ❒ interpreting
- ❒ monitoring
- ❒ restructuring and
- ❒ renegotiating meanings and relationships is one way to think about will. The cluster of dimensions, however, within that simple yet polysemous word, *will* is crucial to ending poverty.

The means to that ultimate end is a kaleidoscopic vision with the flowing creativity vital to finding ways to overcome the epidemic; it is a creativity, which needs to mirror a world ever recreating itself through social structures formation. Yet, when we struggle to end poverty, we do meet resistance from the habits of the mind that conceives modern institutions not as evolving structures with fresh, dynamic, emerging human interaction, but as unalterable, static, will-less things. Nevertheless, even alongside modern business and government, older institutions continue as potential grassroots portals:
- ❒ families and extended families
- ❒ churches
- ❒ voluntary associations remind us: they operate via different principles: alternatives are nearby.

To clarify this, and what I think Reverend King meant by—the will to end poverty—I link to the ideas of five leading critical observers of today's global economy with comments upon their analysis. Like the sifting patterns in a kaleidoscope, which yet reflect the systematic nature of the structure formation process, this vision is one among millions of people worldwide committed to doing whatever works to end poverty.

Before my comments on the current analysis, I will further scrutinize some ideas of Adam Smith. In 1776, he established some basic rules of the economic game, which most people have followed most of the time since. Thus, we rotate the 'scope to see the world in another colors pattern. Smith wrote:

> In almost every other animal species, each individual when full-grown is independent and in its natural state has occasion for the assistance of no other living creature. Yet, man has almost constant occasion for the help of his brethren; and it is in vain for him to expect it from their benevolence only. He will more likely prevail if he can interest their self-love in his favor and show them that it is to their advantage to do for him what he requires of them. Whoever offers to another a bargain of any kind, proposes to do this. —Give me that which I want, and you

> shall have this, which you want—is the meaning of every such offer. In this manner we obtain from one another the far greater part of those good offices of which we stand in need. It is not from the benevolence of the butcher, the brewer, or the baker that we expect our dinner, but instead from their regard to their own interest. We address ourselves not to their humanity but to their self-love, and never talk to them of our needs but of their advantages. No one but a beggar chooses to depend chiefly on the benevolence of his fellow-citizens.[12]

Juxtapose what Smith wrote with the reality that the principal teachings of the world's religions and traditional cultures condense into an appeal of three words—please be good. The religions and traditional cultures still believe that we are here to love and help one another. Many have identified the good with God and have identified the aim of life as serving it.

At the beginning of the modern age, however, Smith and a number of others asserted that far greater benefits to society as a whole flow from orderly selfishness than from goodness. Europe was becoming in their time a center of worldwide market exchange. Societies built on market relationships needed principles different than those provided by the moral codes of supportive local communities.

Smith rested most of his case on the enormous increase in wealth made possible by the division of labor, which, in turn, he attributed to the human tendency to barter and to exchange commodities for sale in markets. Larger markets called for more specialization, which meant that each worker, confined to a very limited task, would develop greater skill, dexterity, and judgment. Smith also attributed the blessings of machinery mainly to market exchange because it was the specialized worker who was most likely to invent machines to ease tasks; moreover, the capitalist was most likely to pay for new inventions and install them into service.

Smith recognized that in earlier and ruder ages all people had useful employment. In his time, the produce of society languished because a considerable portion of the population remained idle either as members of a leisure class living via rents and profits, or as unemployed workers. Even so, the net result was that even the poorest worker in England at that time was elevated from the savage because the increased production caused by the greater division of labor, which was spurred by larger markets, far exceeded the losses due to idleness.

Smith was not anti-benevolent, though he did not think that benevolence could be the mainspring of human progress, while he thought that self-interest channeled through exchange in free markets, could be. Even so, as he clarified in his book *Theory of the Moral Sentiments,*[13] he thought that the good will, which humans naturally offer to one another was indispensable. In a perfect Smith world, the magic of the market would drive the accumulated wealth of society ever higher through ever:

❐ greater advancements in manufacture and agriculture
❐ finer divisions of labor
❐ larger markets.

At the same time, the natural sentiments of sympathy would guarantee the maintenance of civilized manners and morals. They would assure in perpetuity a social safety net for beggars, orphans, and others unable to live by barter. Although he bases his theory of ethics on natural sympathy and not on revealed religion, in his chapter about education in the *Wealth of Nations,* he proposed that the laboring masses should continue to be instructed from the pulpit on Sundays in the same Judeo-Christian virtues of love thy neighbor preached for centuries in Europe. The upper classes, however, were to study, as well, the newer disciplines of political economy and natural philosophy.

Smith held that the sole purpose and point of economic activity was to produce the wants and conveniences of life, what he called *values in use*. In a system based wholly on organized benevolence, such as Plato's *Republic*, people would produce use values directly, as other people needed them. It would be their conscious aim to input socially by producing what other people needed. Smith found it much more effective to produce goods to take to market to sell, to devote one's energies to produce what he called *value in exchange*. The direct result was profit for the producer; the indirect result was value in use: the satisfaction of people's needs and desires. Value in use answers the question Gandhi posed as quoted at the beginning of this chapter. It provides some concrete benefit to someone. The invisible hand of the market would lead people to deliver more value in use by approaching the goal indirectly, seeking direct value in exchange.

From Smith's distinction between value in use and value in exchange I derive the principle of the vision: **benevolence produces use value, self-interest produces exchange value**. Benevolence is weak, while self-interest is strong (those are the initial qualities, arguably the most significant, though not the lasting ones). The constant will to end poverty is the commitment to reshape modern institutions until they accomplish what benevolence would accomplish if it were strong enough. It is what Dr. King called love in action.[14] This is the invisible active principle behind the shifting kaleidoscope of diverse antipoverty programs.

The high-level ancient wisdoms teach the unity of all life; modern society teaches the infinite worth of every individual; both propose the welfare of all as the goal of social cooperation; both teach and propose, in a word: benevolence, which in three words is: value in use. For 230 years, Adam Smith and followers have persuaded most of the world, most of the time, that market economies are the realistic way to put ideals as generally accepted into practice. Meanwhile, poverty and economic insecurity have not gone away. Modern society has broken its pledge to respect the intrinsic worth of each person and it has rejected far too many. Because each person is of infinite worth, the unemployed, homeless, and alcoholic should not be forced to live in the streets; no middle class professional women should suffer chronic high blood pressure because she cannot pay taxes.

The early advocates of modern ideals, including Adam Smith, supposed that they would preserve the best of ancient wisdom, while liberating humanity from ancient shackles. In practice, at least five problems inherent in the Smith model—meet human needs by the commodities exchange—have formed a chasm that separates what ought to be from what is. The first inherent structural problem is that, contrary to what Smith hoped for, self-interest and benevolence often interfere with one another. For example, if, for whatever reason, a country's commercial agriculture does not meet all of its people's need for food, benevolence becomes engaged to provide free or subsidized food. It matters not whether benevolence is from a government program, a church, or other NGO that donates the food. Commercial agriculture, however, then loses incentives, because the farmers cannot sell food to people who are getting free food. The system of meeting needs via commodity exchange, thus, becomes less effective. Farmers may be forced to leave their farms for urban streets—destitute and homeless. The example illustrates a fundamental problem: if we do not want, via negligence, to kill people by starving them, something has to give way: either dependence on benevolence, or dependence on markets.

I propose that, in the final analysis, dependence on markets must be modified. Love is the basic law, the supreme law of the human species; though sometimes the tough love of commodity exchange prevails in free markets because, at times, that works better than any alternative. The test of policy is what Gandhi surmised, "If it does not work for the weakest and poorest then it does not work"; thus, it is time to try something else. Dr. King defined the ultimate ideal, which describes the framework within which institutions should be evaluated, restructured, and modeled upon the beloved community.[15]

To conclude discussion of Adam Smith, I pose a methodological point: did Smith care to know how it was that his butcher, brewer, and baker brought him his dinner? He did not know when he was a child, nor in his dotage; in a sense, he did not know even when he was a middle-aged professor at Glasgow University. The honest answer to the question, "Why do people do what they do?" is always "I have some ideas and opinions, nevertheless, I do not and, in fact, can not know." Nor do we know, as we organize diverse projects to fight poverty, what motivates people to stop:

❒ apathy and, thus, improve their situations

❒ alienation, so to partake in a social cause. As a practical principle for community organizing, we should not assume that self-interest or benevolence or any other concept names the spirit that moves people. The best methodology is to begin as a *radical empiricist* without preconceptions, though sensitive to the spirit leading as we encounter it, joining in what God is doing, as we find it in the thinking and feeling of people on the ground.

The will to end poverty is to act on principles that begin, sustain, and complete the healing process that will end poverty. The principles include:

❒ patience

❒ persistence

❒ sensitivity to diverse contexts

❒ the openness to search for and apply tactics that might work.

It does not help to say that, "All problems would be solved if people were more caring," or "People never will be caring; thus, we must accept a world of selfishness and violence." A will to end poverty cultivates Dr. King's—a tough mind and a tender heart. [16]

We now have an outline of the basic needs as met by the exchange of commodities model as pioneered by Smith. With it in mind, I will confirm the vision of how to overcome the problems inherent in it, by commenting on the analysis of current critics of the global economy.

Paul Volcker:

> The problem [the recent collapse of the Indonesian economy and several others] is not regional; it is, instead, an international issue. Every indication, thus, points to a systemic issue in the literal sense arising not from a *deux*

> *ex machina* but from within the ordinary workings of the international financial system. By emphasizing the systemic nature of the financial problems, I do not want to be misunderstood. I believe that in the long-term, *crony capitalism*, state ownership, and *official industrial policies* are less efficient than open competitive markets.[17]

Comment—The usual devices of our Smith world at the level of the international financial system follow the same code at the local level: give me this, which I want... the Smith quid pro quo. Such is the code of exchange in markets: buying and selling. The second inherent structural problem in such a system is that any economy may collapse at any time, because, for whatever or for no reason, enough people may at once decide not to buy. The exchange value of a thing is what people will pay for it; when nobody wants to buy it, the value of it shrinks; when the value of many things dissolves, economies collapse. An inherent problem of instability—meeting needs by commodity exchange—translates into opportunities for taking steps to end poverty.

Many schemes exist for modifying markets to benefit the poor, such as governments encouraging collective bargaining via the Keynesian economics in the 1930s; they make some economies more stable, though others become less stable. The "visible hand" of government, which stabilizes the "shaky invisible hand" of the free market, can rescue the poor from merciless labor markets paying starvation wages, while it wards off collapse, or rebuilds after a collapse. What I advocate here is the constant will to take advantage of the opportunities that history presents.

Volcker believes, nonetheless, that in spite of the inherent systemic tendency of open competitive market economies to collapse, they are still better than crony capitalism, state ownership, or official industrial policies. More than three or four alternatives are at hand, however; the number is quite large. The will to end poverty is the will that seeks and finds the alternatives that translate the abundant techniques and resources of our shared achievement of science and technology into the welfare of all the people. In a number of cases:

❒ state ownership, for example: utilities, public lands, education, transportation, and other infrastructure

❒ official industrial policies, such as: an array of vital protections.

Volcker disbelieves those two structures, even though they do insure the welfare of all people.

George Soros:

> The current campaign against moral hazard, e.g. government guarantees

> leading private banks to make unsound loans, is just an excuse for resisting any kind of interference with the market mechanism. This resistance is based on the false doctrine of our age: financial markets automatically tend towards equilibrium from which it follows that there is no need to interfere because markets correct their excesses.[18]

Comment—What holds humanity prisoner with the poor in the worst cells is not the Smith market conceived as barter in which people exchange surplus for surplus. Humanity's prison, therefore, is the third inherent structural problem: our addiction to the market. Progress has made humanity dependent, as an addict drugged, on the market mechanism. In modern times, poverty and insecurity threaten to arise whenever the market fails to move forward with stability to keep investments flowing, which would have created jobs, tax revenues, and goods and services. Thus, the market traps us because we will not escape it. Soros, therefore, is right to say, "The government must interfere with the market." The market is too important for us to allow it to govern itself. Soros further advocates:

> The IMF should be only a global lender of last resort lending cash at low interest into slow economies everywhere, as the Federal Reserve bank does in the US.

A *Tobin tax* has to be levied upon all international financial transactions to: 1) discourage speculation with no productive purpose and 2) raise revenue for worldwide antipoverty projects. The proposals by Soros can be regarded as a post-market correction measure designed to make the global market that we have all come to depend upon more stable, reliable, and credible.

A complementary way to cope with humanity's addiction to markets is the path we need to pursue so to enable the first means. We can think of it as pre-*market correction*, or *market-snafu prevention*: the legacy from which we humans lived civilized on Earth for several thousand years before becoming dependent on commodity exchange for our livelihood. Before the shift, market exchange was a mutually useful activity, which added comfort and ease to life, though not life's necessities.

A world without poverty would be more than a world in which governments corrected market failures. It would, as well, be a world in which the ancient pre-market institutions: families, service clubs, lodges neighborhoods, churches, small towns, cities, national governments, and the more recent United Nations would care for people and shelter them against the ultimate rejection the market can inflict upon the people: nobody wants to buy what they have to sell.

Jeff Faux and Larry Mishel:

> Many policy-makers, for a long time, denied the reality of the slowdown in *per-capita growth*, the stubborn persistence of rising poverty, or the mal-distribution of income. When the reality became impossible to deny, policy-makers still belittled its importance. In the wake of a crash of financial markets and the subsequent tumble into deep recession of about forty percent of the world's population, the question of inequality can no longer be shrugged off and ignored.[19]

Comment—An unacceptable level of inequality has mushroomed with the intensified globalization and neoliberalism in recent years; inequality flourishes in countries that have chosen to accept less equality in exchange for more liberty.[20] Gross inequality peaks where trade liberalization, with or without a veneer of political liberalization, brings no liberty at all to the people. Maria Mies cites examples from Asian factories wherein women:

❒ make the owners wealthy
❒ work long hours for low pay
❒ lack health benefits
❒ are denied:

• compensation when their eyesight fails due to the repetitive exacting work in poor light
• free speech and union solidarity
• breaks for toilet or even water. [21]

Inequality is a vital part of the Smith system, in which he acknowledges at least three reasons why a fourth inherent structural problem is the inequality inherent in the world that exchange value built. As he notes, wealth is capital, which is like the "seed saved for next year's planting" as in the early and simple society. The "seed consumed" will cause everyone to go hungry. Reducing social inequality by the more just distribution of wealth faces the objection that it gives more money to workers, who will *consumer spend* to increase their consumption and, thus, take capital away from the wealth-creating class. As Alfred Marshall wrote a century after Smith:

> The laborer, without the aid of his or someone else's capital, would not long be alive.[22]

Investors do so only when they expect profits; they only give when they expect to get more back. Thus, the inherent flaw in the logic of exchange is that growth and the accumulation of profit go together. Hence, no increase in the wealth of the owners will result in no growth and negative growth for the poor. Such circumstances, nevertheless, do not make it a mathematical certainty that inequality will widen; it likely will though, because one half of the inequality is that willpower that activates the economy, guided in the Smith world by the principle of self-interest that Smith immortalized: "Give me this of which I want," with its quid pro quo, "and I will give you that of which you want." As this cause became more entrenched through history, inequality widened. Contrary to Schumpeter's prediction, the poor remained poor while the rich got richer, because wages are low. Smith wrote:

> Seldom does the person who tills the ground have wherewithal to maintain himself until he reaps the harvest. His maintenance is advanced to him from the stock of a master, the farmer who employs him, though not unless he was to share in the produce of his labor or unless his stock was to be replaced to him with a profit. At what level the common wages of labor are set depends everywhere upon the contract made between those two parties, whose interests are by no means the same. Workers want to get as much as possible, the owner to give as little as possible. In such disputes, the owners hold out much longer. A landlord, a farmer, a master manufacturer, a merchant, though they did not employ a single worker, could live a year or two upon the stocks that they have acquired. Most workers could not subsist a week, few could subsist a month, and scarce any a year without employment.[23]

Rising inequality is an inherent structural trend in the Smith world, though now and then the trend reverses as it did in Smith's time, for the reasons that Smith noted, in the British colonies in New England. Rising inequality returned in the US after the 1940s war economy, managed by Roosevelt, had led to greater equality than the US had known. Most notably, Sweden reversed inequality, as did other West European social democracies in the decades after WW II.[24] Sweden succeeded because its:

❑ business, labor, and government worked together in a number of crucial ways

❑ retained corporate earnings were the main source of capital for investments (the same in most modern nations)

❑ corporations had carte blanche to keep their earnings tax exempt as a public working capital subsidy

❑ moderate executive salaries and profits shrank Sweden's former harsh income disparities. Business operations had finance, research and development had finance; however, private enrichment, had no finance. Thus, the great Swedish corporations—Volvo, SAAB, Weyerhauser, Electrolux, and Erickson—prospered in world markets, better overall than did their competitors from free market economies. Meanwhile:

- ❑ wages were raised
- ❑ *paid retraining* prevented worker's fear of job loss
- ❑ women's wages were set equal to men's wages.

The postwar model that Sweden achieved was not perfect; it has survived only in a modified form; nevertheless, it did, and still does show the world how to solve one crucial problem: how to capitalize business well enough while keeping inequality in check.[25] Sweden's achievement adds renewed poignancy to the words of Dr. King.

> We now have, not only the resources and techniques to end poverty, we have the knowledge that capital, like seeds for the next harvest, can be preserved without the rot of gross inequality. Now we know that a modern economy can at once reduce inequality and compete in world markets.

Vandana Shiva:

> On 3 March 1998, the USDA and Delta Pine Land Inc., the world's largest cottonseed company and a holding of Monsanto, announced that they had jointly developed and received a patent for a new agricultural biotechnology. With the benign title, Control of Plant Gene Expression the new patent permits its owners and licensees to create sterile seeds by the selective programming of a plant's DNA to kill its own embryos. The patent applies to plants and seeds of all species. What is the result? Farmers saving, for example, pods of peppers, heads of wheat, and the like will stockpile "seed morgues." The system will force farmers to buy seed from companies each year. It is dubbed the "terminator" technology by NGOs such as Rural Advancement Foundation International; which proclaim that the biotechnology threatens farmers' independence and the food security of more than a billion poor farmers in the third world.
>
> The right of free trade on a global scale is being established as the highest right. The World Trade Organization and its smaller bodies now consider the people's right to safe and adequate food as—a non-tariff trade barrier to be dismantled and destroyed. At the heart of this conflict is the right of citizens to safety versus the right of corporations to profit.[26]

Comment—The fifth structural problem inherent in meeting needs through commodity exchange is the profit imperative, a close relative of the fourth problem. Smith did not anticipate it; he advocated a system based on voluntary exchange between willing buyers and sellers; he did not expect that the system would generate an imperative that would override human choice and humane ethics. The consequence is a social structure such that, at times, many buyers choose not to buy, or many sellers choose not to sell, which is intolerable. Exchange has become the lifeblood of society, so that if commerce stops, all else stops; thus, commerce goes forward with an exchange only if it bears enough profit. Hence, government at every level, from city councils to the UN, must focus first on creating a favorable climate for business. If government cannot establish an environment in which businesses make profits, it cannot do anything else; profits are the imperative priority.

We can accept a few setbacks to profit here and there without shutting down the system. In the end however, anything that obstructs the "humvie of commerce" must step aside while the world works as it does. Therefore, if:

- ❑ the safe disposal of toxic wastes takes too much away from profit then: safety must go
- ❑ halting global warming conflicts with profits then: abnormal climate change will continue
- ❑ genetic diversity conflicts with profits then: biodiversity must go
- ❑ human rights conflict with profits then: rights must go
- ❑ indigenous cultures and the ecosystems that support them conflict with profits then: nature must go
- ❑ international law conflicts with profits then: law must go
- ❑ farmers saving seed for the next crop conflicts with profit then: the bio-continuity of civilization must go
- ❑ the socially responsible use of public or private property conflicts with profits then: the ethical use of land must go

Those values that must be sacrificed if they pose a threat to profit making may contrast with your experience and appear as *deterministic*. Victories for the environment and human rights, even where profits must be sacrificed, do show that the world's decision-making processes do not always maximize profits at the expense of all else. My assertion, however, is that profit can be reduced only to a limited extent without bringing the system to a halt. Hence, whatever threatens this imperative must go. The practical implication is that to stabilize the system we should rely more on meeting needs through non-profits such as:

- ❒ co-op housing
- ❒ groups of parents who share childcare
- ❒ co-op gardens
- ❒ public bus and rail passenger services, which have budget deficits, which are paid by other revenues
- ❒ the nonprofit hospital or school that calls in volunteers to help.

Any number of non-mainstream gambits will help turn the tide. The main strategy is: mobilize resources to meet needs.

Sweden had once solved two parts of the problem by: 1) making it institutionally possible to run industry with only moderate rates of profit and, thus, 2) freeing the pursuit of other values from the profit imperative. What, however, happens to profits after they are made? A major part of ending poverty consists of apportioning profits, rents, and moving them toward worthwhile uses. The social reclamation of the accumulated surplus can happen in many ways, which includes: private foundations devoted to charity, fund raising, organizing, taxation, and socially responsible action by owners. The basic strategy remains: mobilize resources to meet needs. The vision I sketched takes the principles that humans act upon to be the main causes of historical events. The set of principles I endorse calls for the will to:

❑ take advantage of historical opportunities
❑ use creative other means to make power listen
❑ persist with patience by acknowledging and respecting the value of diversity and the freedom of ideas
❑ be the radical empiricist who:
- does not assume the answers in advance of proof
- discards what does not work
- finds what does work so that revised modern institutions with vigorous ancient institutions end poverty.

The value in exchange principle from Smith needs revision and addendum by shifting the kaleidoscope toward his value in use principle. Value in use is more basic than value in exchange. It states the point and purpose of human cooperation.

Notes

1. M. K. Gandhi quoted in the Introduction to "Kuruvilla Pandikattu," in *The Meaning of the Mahatma for the Millennium*. New Delhi: Maadhyam Book Services, 2000. p. 1.

2. Martin Luther King, Jr. recorded in the video documentary *Eyes on the Prize*.

3. Aldous Huxley, *The Perennial Philosophy*. New York: Harper, 1945.

4. Thomas Robert Malthus, *On Population*. New York: The Modern Library, 1960. (first published 1798) pp. 51-52.

5. Frances Moore Lappe, *Diet for a Small Planet*. New York: Ballantine Books, 1971.

6. Frances Moore Lappe and Joseph Collins, *Food First*. Boston: Houghton-Mifflin, 1977; Peter Singer, *One World: the Ethics of Globalization*. New Haven: Yale University Press, 2002.

7. Joseph Schumpeter, *Capitalism, Socialism, and Democracy*. New York: Harper and Brothers, 1946. pp. 64-67. (first pub. 1942)

8. Immanuel Wallerstein, *Unthinking Social Science*. Philadelphia: Temple University Press, 2001. pp. 107, 113, 167.

9. Shaohua Chen and Martin Ravaillon, *How Did the World's Poorest Fare in the 1990s*? Washington DC: The World Bank, 2000. Policy Research Working Paper # 2409.

10. Lutz Leisering and Stephan Leibfried, *Time and Poverty in Western Welfare States: United Germany in Perspective*. Cambridge UK: Cambridge University Press, 1999. p. 242. (first published in Deutsch 1995)

11. Viviane Forrester, *L'horreur Economique*. Paris: Fayard, 1996.

12. Adam Smith, *The Wealth of Nations*. London: J.M. Dent, 1954 (first published 1776). p. 13.

13. Adam Smith, *The Theory of Moral Sentiments*. Oxford: Clarendon Press, 1976. (first published 1759)

14. Martin Luther King, Jr. *Strength to Love*. Philadelphia: Fortress Press, 1963. pp. 36-46.

15. John J. Ansbro, *Martin Luther King, Jr.: the Making of a Mind*. Maryknoll, New York: Orbis Books, 1982. pp. 187-97.

16. Martin Luther King, Jr. *Strength to Love*. Philadelphia: Fortress Press, 1963. pp. 9-16.

17. Paul A. Volcker, (past US Federal Reserve Chairman): "The Sea of Global Finance" in Will Hutton and Anthony Giddens (Eds) *Global Capitalism*. New York: The New Press, 2000. p. 77.

18. George Soros, "The New Global Financial Architecture" in Will Hutton and Anthony Giddens (Eds.) *Global Capitalism*. New York: The New Press, 2000. p. 91.

19. Jeff Faux and Larry Mishel, "Inequality and the Global Economy" in Will Hutton and Anthony Giddens (Eds.) *Global Capitalism*. New York: The New Press, 2000. pp. 106-07.

20. Rational arguments proposing criteria for deciding how much inequality is ethically acceptable are in John Rawls, *A Theory of Justice*. Cambridge: Harvard University Press, 1971. As is the case with most of the books cited herein, a large pool of literature exists that comments on Rawls' arguments.

21. Maria Mies, *Patriarchy and Accumulation on a World Scale: Women in The International Division of Labor*. London: Zed Books, 1986. p. 136.

22. Alfred Marshall, *Principles of Economics*. New York: Macmillan, 1948. p. 544 (first edition published in 1890)

23. Adam Smith, *The Wealth of Nations*. London: J. M. Dent, 1954 (first published 1776). pp. 58-59.

24. Amartya Sen, *On Economic Inequality*. New Delhi: Oxford University Press, 1973.

25. See the chapters about Sweden in Howard Richards and Joanna Swanger, *The Dilemmas of Social Democracies*, available, as well via http://global-economy.info

26. Vandana Shiva, "The World on the Edge," in Will Hutton and Anthony Giddens (Eds.) *Global Capitalism*. New York: The New Press, 2000. pp. 119-120, 122, 124.

Review Questions

1. What is the central theme in Part 10 as realized by the Reverend Dr. King? P 209

2. What is the reality that supports the awareness that the interests of affluence and civility are the same? P 210

b. Is it more of an idealistic sentiment or a realistic principle?

c. What is the direct link that economic injustice and poverty have with incivility?

d. Compare and contrast the incivility of the affluent with that of the poor.

e. Do the incivilities of one class cause the incivilities of the other or can this be determined?

f. Is the incivility of the poor a reflection of the affluent incivility?

g. What happens to the incivility of the affluent when the incivility of the poor transforms into a caritas activism?

3. Kant defined will as the capacity to act from principle. Anthony Giddens views: 1) human action as being reflexively self-regulated and 2) society as a constant process of structures formation. Synthesizing Kant's definition and Gidden's current analysis, what does this fact of our human potential and our "built-in tools" mean when you consider the fact that we have not ended poverty? P 212

4. Erroneous notions about poverty held in the past, likely help poverty persist; what are some of the main features, which are obvious, in the development of the poverty propaganda? P 210 – 212

5. Adam Smith asserted that *orderly selfishness* was more beneficial to society than benevolence Smith's rationale, which has not passed the test of time, is mainly that increased production brought about greater division of labor, which in turn spurred larger markets; thus, the *magic of the market* would drive the accumulated wealth of society ever higher. Which of the author's five structural problems, thus,

directly speaks to that basic dichotomy? p 214
b. What does Smith mean by the idea of orderly selfishness?
c. Does that modifier place limits on the ethic of freedom?
d. What are the five structural problems, as defined in Part 10, which frame the larger problem? p 244 - 252
6. What fact of mass production—key to the industrial revolution—did Smith observe and praise that remains as a driving mechanism in the global economy? p 214
b. How do you see the long-term consequence of such a defining shift in the metaphysic of Homo sapiens?
7. The goal of ending poverty is, as well, the goal of creating a culture of peace. What, therefore, is the common survival mechanism, which 1) the poor feel compelled to use and 2) authority exploits as the reason, isolated from any other factor—to institutionalize it as a problem—made worse and exaggerated by authority on behalf of power: the owners of production? p 210
b. How would you describe the relationship between the feminization of labor and—the feminization of poverty—with the institutionalization of poverty?p 220
8. Capitalism has created an industry by exploiting the consequences—poverty and, thus, street crime—of their profit driven economy. What is the other major exploitation by capitalism of a more obvious human suffering and pathos? Hint: this exploitation receives much more press and public attention than the prison industrial complex.
b. Which general groups of citizens, do you suppose, largely pay for such inverted justice and draconian ethic?
c. Why, might you suppose, do these large groups (masses) of citizens who pay act against this injustice for all?
9. George Soros contends that the resistance of any interference with the market is based on the false doctrine—financial markets automatically tend towards equilibrium. The author agrees and, thus, devised a pre-market correction or snafu prevention as one fix. What plan or approach would you advocate as the most effective? p 219
10. Paul Volcker claims that in spite of the inherent systemic tendency of open competitive market economies to collapse they are still better than crony capitalism, state ownership, or official industrial policies. The author counters that more than three or four alternatives exist, adding that the will to end poverty seeks and finds alternatives.

Beyond the advantages of public ownership of basic needs production and delivery mentioned on page 218, what are the other potential perquisites and the overall benefit of civic custody of basic services and commodities to the public? P 218

11. What Dr. King called—Love in action—is benevolence with an agenda: the will to end poverty. What is the action commitment necessary to bring the ideal of benevolence and love to reality? [Hint: one verb and a noun with its adjective, both of which seem to be remote from love and benevolence] P 215

11

A Logical Plan for Peace

Let us not tire of preaching love; it is the force, which will overcome the world. Let us not tire of preaching love, though we see that waves of violence succeed in drowning its fire. Love must prevail, as only it can.
—Oscar Romero, 25 September 1977 [1]

Peace

A logical plan for peace is tucked away in the next-to-last chapter of Heikki Patomaki's excellent recent book, *After International Relations: Critical Realism and the Construction of World Politics*.[1] Most of the book deals with the technical issues in the methodology of social science research. I start my commentary on Patomaki's book at the next-to-last chapter because violence threatens everybody, thus peace is a topic in everyone's best interest. The book as a whole, asks the question, How can social science best contribute to the building of peace? It answers the question by advocating research methods grounded in the philosophy of *critical realism*.

The next-to-last chapter builds upon the peace research done by Karl Deutsch and his collaborators [4] (henceforth, Deutsch) in the 1950s. Their logical method was the study of peace via observing places where peace prevailed. Next, they studied the peacemaking process by noting times when peace did not prevail in those same places; they then examined the historical transition from violence to peace. It should be possible to derive a logical plan toward peace from the findings of such research. The plan would prescribe nurturing and strengthening the causes that produced peace in historical cases where a transition from violence to peace has been achieved.

Deutsch identified a number of cases to study, all of which were in the North Atlantic region, including peace between the US and then British territory of Canada, peace between Sweden and Norway, and others. Although the initial focus was on wars between nation-states, their findings have wider applications. I believe, as I sense Patomaki does too, that some of the ideas they advance, such as the idea that peace results from integration, suggest ways to diminish violence at any level.

Deutsch published his results in his book: *Political Community and the North Atlantic Area*. In it, the formation of *political community* refers to: 1) the amalgamation of formerly independent political units under a common sovereign and 2) the process of integration of independent states into what the authors call a *pluralist security community*. In the latter, war between two nations becomes so unthinkable that neither side prepares for it, using the relationships of Canada to the USA and Norway to Sweden. Much of the Deutsch study applies, as well, to the prevention of civil war because the conditions that favor peaceful cooperation between nations are largely the same as those that make civil war within nations unlikely; the study applies secondarily to civil war as a defined object of study.

The conclusions of *Political Community and the North Atlantic Area* are numerous, complex, and hedged by methodological caveats. They cast doubt on some theories and common sense notions about how peace might be achieved, while they tend to confirm others:

❑ the theory—peace can be achieved by maintaining a balance of power among likely combatants—is not confirmed.

❑ the neo-Hobbes theory—an alleged war of all against all will only cease by granting a monopoly of the legitimate use of force to a single sovereign—is not confirmed.

❑ the idea that people will unite when they are forced to unite by the threat of a common enemy is only partly true because the unions, thus, produced are temporary.

❑ issues regarding armaments and military budgets, commonly known as *peace issues*, and concerns about which peace movements take the lead, turn out to be of relatively minor importance in the peace-building processes, however

❑ the related peace movement idea—wars will cease when cultures cease to glorify war, and war becomes seen as reprehensible—turns out to be significant.

❑ creative negotiations by leaders, which today might be classified as skill in *conflict resolution* or *conflict transformation* have also proven significant.

The great weight of the evidence accumulated and analyzed by Deutsch, however, serves to support the principal conclusion for which Patomaki cites in *After International Relations*. A security community (peace) is established when the general expectation prevails that institutions, which provide means for peaceful change, will function reliably and effectively. This main conclusion is consistent with that reached more than a decade earlier by Quincy Wright who found in his massive study of the history of war that the principal cause of war (if indeed *cause* is the right word here) is the difficulty of organizing the institutions of peace.[2]

It would be misleading to say that Patomaki rests his case solely on the Deutsch evidence. The proposition—providing reliable institutions for effecting peaceful change is the single most important key to establishing a security community—is one Patomaki tended to believe regardless, for several reasons. He found corroboration in *Political Community and the North Atlantic Area*.

The meaning of *institutionalizing peaceful change* takes form within the chapters wherein Deutsch studies the prospects of the North Atlantic area becoming a stronger multinational security community than it was in the 1950s. The decisive factors are: 1) compatibility of major values and 2) what the authors call in several contexts: *responsiveness*.

In the North Atlantic area, the core values of a largely common way of life are those of democracy and constitutional government under the *rule of law*. The authors cite as an example the experience of US military personnel stationed in Western Europe who were tried for offenses committed there in European courts. The commitment to the rule of law was so similar in the US and in Western Europe that no case existed in which the US objected that its citizens were not given a fair trial. Deutsch also points out that the US was (in the 1950s) committed to a modified free enterprise economy, while the UK and other European nations tended toward democratic forms of socialism. The compatibility of values at the level of democracy and rule of law favored peace among the North Atlantic nations, even when their electorates supported different philosophies regarding the proper role of the government in the economy.

Democratic constitutionalism provided the core compatible values in the North Atlantic case, which was the only case thence studied. For those reasons, the book does not determine whether peace is built by sharing any core values, some core values but not others, or, specifically, by sharing the values of democracy and the rule of law.

A second major factor often mentioned by Deutsch is what they call responsiveness. Deutsch was influenced by the cybernetic theories of society in vogue at the time.[3] He tended to see government as a feedback loop, which processed messages in which ever-changing groups expressed their ever-changing demands and then adjusted the system to better satisfy their demands. Where the outcome was peaceful amalgamation or integration, it was usually in large part because the system responded by providing for citizens what they wanted. Usually they wanted more rights and liberties, more equality, and more prosperity. International peace and social peace tended to overlap and to be enhanced by government action, which was *mutually responsive* to the needs of other countries (as in the Marshall Plan) and responsive to its own citizens. In the multinational security community of the North Atlantic there was:

> ...an acceptance by the government of each country of substantial responsibility for:
> - ❐ high and stable levels of employment
> - ❐ rising standards of living
> - ❐ security for most individuals against one or more hazards such as:
>   - old age
>   - workmen's accidents
>   - illness
>   - unemployment
>   - high rents
>   - cost of housing
>   - excessive fluctuations in the prices of agricultural products.
>
> In the US, these trends have been associated with such legislation as the:
> - ❑ Social Security Act of 1935 and its subsequent extensions:
> - ❑ Employment Act of 1946
> - ❑ various items of housing legislation
> - ❑ succession of farm price support bills.
>
> Broadly similar legislation, with similar social effects, has been enacted in all countries belonging to the first and second of our income groups in the North Atlantic area. The particular items covered have varied, of course from country to country and so has the manner in which each particular problem was dealt with in each case. In their cumulative effect, however, these changes have been astonishingly similar—not the less so for being accepted in their essentials by conservative as well as liberal and labor parties in most of the countries concerned.[4]

The authors quote from an earlier study by P. E. Corbett:

> The welfare of the individual in society should be recognized as an end in itself and the purpose of all organization at the national or international level. The direct effort to promote it may also prove to be the speediest road to general and lasting peace.[5]

Although the institutions of the *Political Community* and the *North Atlantic Area* were formed nearly fifty years ago, Patomaki's references to it in *After International Relations*, published in December of 2001, are apt to the present times. At present, nine of ten wars are civil wars;[6] globalization is quickly eroding national sovereignty; thus, it is ever more evident that Deutsch is right to reject the so-called *realist position* (not to be confused with Patomaki's critical realism) in which war could be understood as the product of anarchy among sovereign states. Today we need merely see the Palestinian experience to know that the failure of the legitimate processes calling for peaceful change will likely to lead to violence.

Patomaki uses the following diagram, simplified here, to illustrate his account of how peaceful change and, therefore, peace can be facilitated by the work of social scientists:

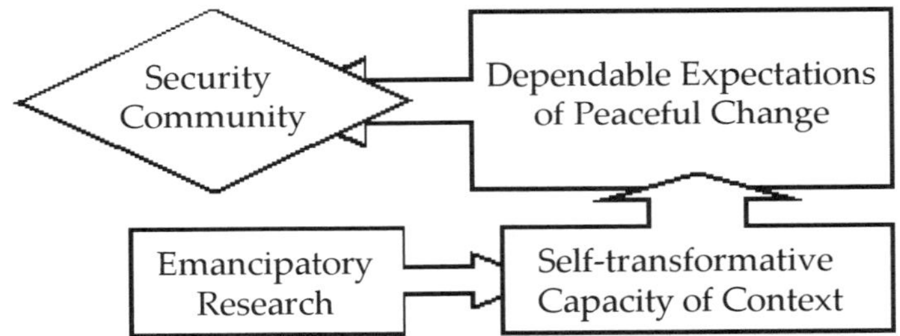

Starting from the lower left corner of the diagram is *emancipatory research*, which Patomaki advocates. It contributes to the *self-transformative capacity of context*: the ability of a society to change, which leads to *dependable expectations for peaceful change*, which leads to a *security community*: the assurance of peace.

Perhaps the most important and controversial point underlying Patomaki's diagram is that social science research can contribute to peaceful change by a systematic critique of current beliefs. That is what science does.[7] Beliefs and the institutions, which rest upon them, change, in part, because science demonstrates that the beliefs are false. Social contexts grow in self-transformative capacity as they grow in the ability to reconsider and revise currently held beliefs and as they better understand the causes of the unintended consequences of actions, which are based upon them. Patomaki advocates a scientific form of nonviolence: *satyagraha*: the force of truth. Thus, his logical plan for peace sets us in the middle of contemporary controversies concerning technical questions in the methodology of social science research.

My discussion of the technical questions will have three stages. First, the focus will be on claims to know what is true. The questions about truth will result mainly in questions about 2) *structures*, which will prove to be best understood in social science as 3) *rules*, relationships, and practices.

Truth

The work of authors associated with critical realism such as: Roy Bhaskar, Rom Harre, Elizabeth Anscombe, Mario Bunge, Karin Knorr Cetina (in important respects), and Patomaki rescue words like: • *truth* • *reality* • *cause and effect.* Truth (and the others) needs rescue from its current pariah status resulting from its association with such intrinsically pejorative concepts as:

- ❑ totalizing
- ❑ metaphysics of presence
- ❑ essentialism
- ❑ onto-theology
- ❑ logo-centrism
- ❑ normalizing
- ❑ compulsory heterosexuality

Moreover, some of the older notions used pejoratively to attack truth, are:

- ❑ meaningless metaphysics
- ❑ ideology
- ❑ closed society
- ❑ inquisition.
- ❑ dogma

For the Patomaki scientific nonviolence to work, peacemakers must be able to speak of the truth, or a truth, or a *rational truth claim*, or something of the sort, and contrast it with a belief, which may be: widely held, even widely taken for granted, nevertheless, false. Speaking more generally, a number of intellectuals consider it important to *reclaim reality*, in Roy Bhaskar's phrase, as a necessary step in the process of emancipating humanity from dysfunctional and oppressive institutions.[8]

I will discuss one of the reasons why, in the 20th century, scholars of the democratic left have seen a political need to make a case against certain prominent forms of non-realism: 1) the reigning empiricism in the social sciences and 2) one important view of what it means to understand a text in the humanities. This brief discussion will set the stage for introducing Patomaki's attempt to stake out *critical realist principles*, which at once: 1) rescue truth from its pariah status and 2) orient social science toward the critique of social structures.

Let us suppose with Patomaki that: 1) a main contribution of social science toward peace is to increase the effectiveness of the institutions organizing peaceful change and 2) the way research makes institutions more effective is by finding truth, or something like truth, so that the rules and practices comprising the institutions become based on beliefs more accurate to reality. This second supposition may require more willing suspension of disbelief than a conscientious lover of wisdom would be willing to grant because, after all, social reality is ever-changing, infinitely varied and complex. Yet, the successes of the natural sciences demonstrate that human minds do not shrink or quake in the face of reality. When it comes to building a better mousetrap, or a guided missile pinpointed to destroy its target, human minds seem able to produce technologies, which work because the principles they apply are true. As a result, the second supposition, in as much, says that a science of society is viable; this has been more than entertained in the past two centuries as the social sciences have flourished: millions of people now have social science degrees and careers, and billions of dollars have been spent on social science research. Thus, the idea that humans might learn peace via learning truth has, at least, some plausibility.

Let us put forth a third supposition, which clarifies a point Patomaki presupposes: in a wise traditional formulation, human beings are a union of soul and body perpetually attracted both by the inspirations of love and by the temptations of self-interest. Consequently, social scientists, like all human beings are subject to not one but two golden rules; the other is: those who have the gold make the rules. In this third supposition, it is likely that some sort of self-interest would become entrenched in methodological rules followed by mainstream social science research, because self-interest is entrenched everywhere else. One way this could happen would be to create a standard methodology, which explains and predicts social phenomena without calling into question the basic structures of society through which those who have the gold acquire the gold. It would look like science, though not do what science does: systematically analyze existing beliefs in the name of truth.

Given that human nature is not entirely self-interested, it is not surprising to find an endless tug of war within social science faculties (each mind and heart, too). The tension is between: 1) the technical research procedures that do not criticize social structures, though are conducive to successful fund-raising and 2) the intellectual consciences, which recognize that war, poverty, and the destruction of the biosphere will not end without calling into question the basic structures of society, through which—those who have the gold acquire the gold. What one would suspect from a basic knowledge of human nature, in fact, happens in social science as illustrated here.

In *Macroeconomics in the Global Economy,* a textbook by Jeffrey Sachs and Felipe Larrain, the syllabus includes the factors that cause high or low unemployment. [9] The book, nevertheless, has not a word about the historical evolution of the moral and legal structures that make unemployment a chronic problem in all modern societies. Instead—census data, national accounts data, national and international labor statistics, prices, debts, and quantities of money—dominate the textbook. The given information, which is the basis for learning to make calculations, is pre-interpreted in categories defined by existing institutions. Thus, the text teaches the causes of unemployment only in the sense that the student explains and predicts unemployment by writing equations in which the substitution of constants for the independent variables yields a value for the *dependent variable*.

Other examples are provided by Patomaki's discussion of the research tradition associated with J. David Singer's *Correlates of War Project*. The most recent fruit is *Triangulating Peace* by Bruce Russett and John Oneal, which comments informally on a number of theories of peace, mainly *Realpolitik* and *liberal-Kantian* theories. The serious side of the book, however, lies not in its comments on theories, but in its scientific testing of theories. The authors operationally define variables, which *Realpolitik* and liberal-Kantian theories hypothesize as conducive to peace. They define peace (and war). They draw on datasets that count all known instances of peace and war from 1885 to 1992. They call their method *epidemiological*, by analogy to *probabilistic research* in medicine, which tests the effects of drugs, or treatments, or nutrients, by correlating the independent variable tested with dependent measures of health, calculating the probability, given X, that Y will also be found.

Studies like *Triangulating Peace* feature exercises in retrodiction. Whatever the theory explaining peace might be, the empirical analyses testing the theory are statistical calculations. That is to say, given that one knows by assigning a number to a set of events in the past, equations can be derived and statistical tests can be run, which connect those events to whether there was war or peace. Peace is predicted, though it is not really predicted because it has happened. Thus, a hypothetical peace could have been predicted based on what went before it. The good news shows that Russett and Oneal's results prove that the liberal-Kantian variables of—democracy, trade, and international organization—predict peace to a level of statistical confidence equal to that found when using *Realpolitik* variables to predict peace. As found in the method used by Sachs and Larrain, explanation and prediction are achieved by analyzing datasets. The authors feel that they can confidently predict events by projecting such analyses into the future: They proclaim, "Peace will prevail throughout a region when all the states therein are democratic." [10]

From Patomaki's point of view, Russett and Oneal's confident prediction of future events is too confident. Critical realism maintains that in open systems, predictions are, strictly speaking, impossible, although this does not mean that nothing can be anticipated. Patomaki points out that, even judged in terms of their own methodological standards, the statistical demonstrations of the democratic peace theory require massaging of the data. They require, for example, defining *war* in a way that does not include: the US covert operations to overthrow democratically elected regimes. More importantly, Patomaki holds that such studies should not be judged by their own methodological standards, thus, instead by the higher standards of a critical realist methodology.

In the philosophy of social science, methodologies for social science research such as those used by Sachs, Larrain, Singer, Russett, Oneal, and others are justified in books like Ernest Nagel's *The Structure of Science*[11] and Karl Popper's *The Poverty of Historicism*.[12] They argue for the unity of science, claiming that there is no important methodological difference between natural science and social science. There is, certainly, something called *understanding*, (G *Verstehen*), which contrasts *explanation* (G *Erklaren*). Understanding, as a research method requires, as the etymology of its German equivalent implies: trying to stand in other peoples' shoes to see how the world looks to them. From understanding, one learns the meanings for which: acts, signs, symbols, and relationships have for the actors and the people using the signs and symbols within the relationships. Nagel, Popper, and other stalwarts of orthodoxy, however, view Verstehen not as a science. It may be a source of hypotheses for scientists to test; nevertheless, it is not science. If you want to specialize in Verstehen for its own sake, then you must walk across the campus to the humanities building, where you will learn to interpret texts. Treating everything that is not science as *hermeneutics* and everything that is not Erklaren as Verstehen, excludes a study of human action, which would have made structures visible by examining their construction in practice and in discourse.

The explanation and understanding dichotomy—Erklaren vs. Verstehen—leaves the democratic left out in the cold. Mainstream explanation proceeds with no reference to any critique of the basic moral and legal structures of society. Its mainstream other: the humanistic study of the meanings found in life and in texts is an art form, which may be a fertile source of hypotheses to test; nevertheless, it is never, of itself, dynamic. Meaning, therefore, never is an influence as a variable, a force, or a factor.

To summarize this discussion of the epistemological plight of scholars on the democratic left, four assumptions appear:
1) social science builds peace through the constructive criticism of institutions 2) some sort of legitimate claim to scientific truth or accuracy is an essential part of constructive criticism 3) human nature being what it is, powerful claims to monopolize scientific truth and accuracy have been asserted on behalf of social science research methodologies, which systematically refrain from examining the basic moral and legal structures of society 4) as shown through this hypothetical: suppose you are Habermas, Ricoeur, Giddens, Marcuse, Patomaki, or some other conscientious left-leaning scholar. You are convinced that the institutionalization of peaceful change will not become a worldwide achievement until the basic structures of the modern world-system are substantially modified. From your view of this assumption, Sachs, Larrain, Singer, Russett, Oneal, Nagel, Popper, and others—writing equations or doing statistical tests relating some socially constructed entities to others—are skating over the surface of reality; they never come to grips with the processes by which socially constructed entities become constructed. The structures they skate over are just the ones that need reconstruction to achieve peace and justice. It would then be politically important to you to take stands on technical issues in the methodology of social science research, which reject the Erklaren/Verstehen dichotomy. You might write *Knowledge and Human Interests,*[13] or *Freud and Philosophy,*[14] or *New Rules of Sociological Method,*[15] or *One Dimensional Man*[16] partly because you are looking for a way to assign causal powers to meanings. This consideration helps to explain why Patomaki in *After International Relations* repeats often and emphatically that meanings are causes. Seeing meanings as causes brings structures into view.

Establishing that meanings are causes is, however, more the background than the foreground of *After International Relations*. A more central concern of the book is: coming to terms with contemporary anti-realists who are convinced that claims by social scientists to know the truth or even a truth are specious in theory and likely to lead to oppression in practice. To that end, Patomaki outlines three principles of critical realism:
1). *Ontological realism*: some things exist as they are in the natural world and in society: the basis of scientific truth claims
2). *Epistemological relativism*: every claim to know the truth is fallible and subject to correction; truth is relative to the prejudices, chance circumstances, theoretical framework, and the position in society of

the person or group making the claim.

3). *Judgmental rationalism*: some claims about truth are more rational than others; it is often possible to tell, with reasonable accuracy, which ones they are.

Principle 2) attempts to give contemporary antirealism its due, while 3) seeks to give it no more than its due. The first principle, the most fundamental of the three, represents a break with empiricism, insofar as empiricism takes the discovery of scientific laws as a matter of finding constant conjunctions among phenomena. For critical realists, the underlying structure is the object of study (what science is about) not the surface appearance or the phenomenon. The meaning of the title *After International Relations* is that mainstream IR as an academic discipline was ill conceived: 1) it took relations among nation-states as its object of study, and 2) it adopted David Hume's empiricism, which surfaced near the same time as the nation-state, as the main philosophy behind its research methods. The datasets of Singer, Russett, and Oneal are an updated, mathematically and statistically sophisticated version of Hume's phenomena. (More precisely: Hume's *impressions* and Kant's *intuitions*)

Structure

How, then are people to talk about those actual existing objects of scientific inquiry, which are not simple apparent phenomena, which one can see, name, rank order, scale, correlate, and test for significance? Patomaki introduces an elaborate technical vocabulary, which is designed to be the terminology of the science of world politics, which is meant to supersede IR. Most of the vocabulary is drawn from the realist philosophies of science of Roy Bhaskar and Rom Harre; some is adapted from ideas of Anthony Giddens and other social scientists. Among the key, interrelated, terms in Patomaki's technical vocabulary some of the most central include:

- ❑ causality
- ❑ causal complex
- ❑ relations
- ❑ structure.

My focus will be upon this last conceptual terminology: structure. Roy Bhaskar writes:

> The objects of scientific investigation are structures, not events; the structures exist and act independently of the conditions of their identification and, in particular, in open and closed systems alike. These structures are:
>
> ❒ non-empirical though empirically identifiable
>
> ❒ trans-factually efficacious though only contingently manifest in particular outcomes
>
> ❒ they form the real ground for causal laws.[17]

The question about *truth*, thus, becomes a question about structure if structure is the preferred: 1) point of entry into Patomaki's complex of interrelated critical realist terms and 2) bridge leading to understanding how critical realism relates to other major approaches to social science. How is this highly controversial word to be used in the social sciences? What effect does structure have on peacemaking and peace-building, which is conceived as—achieving effective and reliable means for dealing with conflict and social change nonviolently?

Before discussing Patomaki's views concerning how to think about structure, I will stroll on for a number of pages continuing to use the word *structure* as if everyone knew what it meant. I postpone the question about what structure means in order to respond to a more important question: "Why quibble?" (Or, "Why engage in arguments that may seem like quibbling?") If several theories converge in concluding that democracy leads to peace as Russett and Oneal point out, "Does it really matter whether this conclusion is reached using their methodology or using Patomaki's?" Russett and Oneal even agree with Patomaki and Bhaskar: peace is the product of a laborious process of institution building; Russell and Oneal quote Quincy Wright: Peace is artificial; war is natural.[18] They quote Deutsch:

> In a security community, nations give up military violence and replace it with *dependable expectations of peaceful change*. [19]

Given that Sachs and Larrain never pretended to do the work of an Immanuel Wallerstein or a Karl Polanyi, is anything gained by calling attention to their disregard of the transformation through time of the normative structures whose present workings they study? Given that critical realists and postmodernists alike hold that human institutions need to be invented because natural institutions are absent, does the realist claim that structures have causal powers make a difference?

The questions just raised about quibbling have, I think, good answers: Patomaki does not go out of his way to quibble. Critical realism is not an exclusive philosophy: it does acknowledge the findings of scientists who do not identify with it, or who do not employ the methods it recommends.

Furthermore, critical realism, which began as a philosophy of natural science, is not an exotic proposal for the use of untried methods; it claims to be a superior account of the history and practice of science; its aim is to give an account of why science succeeds. One of its main theses is: if no ontologically real structures with causal powers existed, the success of science would be inexplicable.[20] Unlike the philosophies loosely called *positivist*, however, it does not advocate a *nomological-deductive* method for the social sciences in putative imitation of the natural sciences, far from it.

I think it will help to discuss some issue areas where differences in methodology have clear practical consequences. With respect to the issue of the relationship of peace to democracy, Russett and Oneal's disagreements with Patomaki are, to a considerable extent, more academic than practical. Patomaki and Russett disagree about the merits and limitations of the statistical analysis of datasets; they differ about how best to keep improving research methods with the aim of finding methods that are, in general, increasingly reliable. About the appeal of fostering democracy as a step toward peace, however, they propose concepts and methods for research that lead to similar policy proposals.

I will discuss four other issue areas, which regard the difference between the research for and about structures as causes and the research that disregards structures as causes, which is of great practical, as well as academic, significance. Using these four examples, I shall cast doubt on the adequacy of certain *Humean* (David Hume) social science procedures, often loosely called *empiricist* or positivist.[21] I will assert that in these four areas, the research examining the basic structure of the modern world system has much to offer with important practical possibilities.

It should be added that neither Russett and Oneal nor Patomaki want their research to be used to promote simpleminded attempts to further liberal democracy everywhere. Narrowly conceived, the promotion of democracy can be a way to:

- impose the norms of a neoliberal capitalist economy
- constitute the—nondemocratic other—as the enemy
- fan the flames of ethnic conflict.

Granting, however, that the authors under review are of one mind in resisting the drawing of simplistic conclusions from democratic peace theories, I would assert that in the light of the considerations discussed below, Patomaki's critical realist approach is superior via giving persuasive reasons why such simplistic conclusions should be avoided.

Capital Flight

In the preface to the most recent edition of *Managing World Economic Change*, Robert Isaak notes that capital flight is a peril every nation fears and is forced to take deterrence measures to as best it can.[22] A subtext, however, is that given certain economic conditions that drive investors away, capital flight is as natural as windstorms and earthquakes. Thus, capital flight is studied as a phenomenon that occurs under certain conditions and not others. Social scientists do empirical research to determine the conditions under which much of it happens.[23] Capital flight: owners move their capital, generally from a place where they fear they will lose it or where earnings are low and into a place where risk is lower and/or earnings are higher.

A strict empiricist methodology that skates over the surface of socially constructed realities can:

❒ name capital flight
❒ rank-order it • scale it • correlate it with other phenomena
❒ test relationships among variables relevant to capital flight for significance.

Other types of methodology, which may interpret more and calculate less, might be classified (using Anthony Giddens' concept of the *double hermeneutic*) as ones that accept the presupposed meanings to the phenomena of capital flight by non-social-scientists. These include:

❑ *earnings* in the language of accountants
❑ *ownership* as defined by the law and by ordinary language
❑ *risk* as defined by insurers and by common sense. This class of methodologies then processes units of analysis defined by presupposed lay (non-scientific) meanings: operationally defined measurements, models, charts, graphs, metaphors, theories, hypotheses, and the like. A theory illustrated with a graph, for example, might show a relationship between a measure of *perceived risk* and a measure of *capital flight*.

I suggest that some appropriate occasions exist for saying that a scientific discourse is about structure and that it ascribes causal powers to structure. The occasions are those where the lay meanings underlying capital flight are examined. One might first examine people who own capital and move it, which, more specifically, is the freedom to move what one owns as one sees fit. The times when basic norms concerning property and free markets are rescued from the invisible background of social life and placed in the visible foreground are good times for saying the inquiry is structural. Thus, a social science, which examines structures as causes, has more to say about capital flight than the Humean, which thinks of causes (or what would be causes if, in fact, cause exists) as constant conjunctions among phenomena.

The Race to the Bottom

In *Globalization from Below,* Jeremy Brecher, Tim Costello, and Brendan Smith define the race to the bottom:

> A destructive competition exists in which workers, communities, and entire countries are forced to cut labor, social, and environmental costs to attract mobile capital.[24]

Capital flight is capital leaving. The race to the bottom sacrifices social objectives to entice capital to come.

What actually happens in the race to the bottom is that governments (and other) structures compete to attract investors. Often (though not always) they compete by lowering the costs of doing business: wages, taxes, environmental cleanup, and so forth. Investors then will usually give in to the lure of profitable deals, even when they have doubts about the ethics, morality, and legality of the deals.

Although I use only the word *government* in what follows, I added parenthetically—and other—in the preceding paragraph because governments often do not have effective power. Sometimes a nation's competitive bids to attract investors are orchestrated more by military and or financial elites than governments; also luring investors are the international orgs such as the IMF, World Bank, and aid consortia alone or in collusion with one or both of the military and financial elites.

The reason I parenthetically added the phrase—though not always—is that sometimes governments will compete to attract investment by raising certain costs of business. They might raise taxes to provide better police protection or schools, or take stronger measures to provide a clean environment. Governments may also do nothing to lower wages, but just sell investors on their country by pointing to the low wage levels they already have.

Jeffrey Winters studied the government's efforts to attract investment to Indonesia from 1965 to 1995, using a method like the one John Stuart Mill, in his *Logic,* called: the method of concomitant variation.[25] (Indonesia is one of the countries where it is hard to tell what combination of government, military, wealthy elites, and foreign advisors makes policy.) Thus, the so-called government consciously:
1) saw itself in competition with other countries to attract investors
2) knew that Indonesia was vulnerable to competition from other third world states with wages even lower

3) used low wages as a selling point for foreign investors
4) kept wages low by suppressing unions, and not enforcing the guarantees of labor rights within Indonesia's constitution
5) had well planned environmental and conservation objectives, which it often had to weigh against its need to attract investors and
6) taxes could be attuned to favor investors, though overall, taxes were not a big factor: Indonesia did not collect much in taxes: oil royalties and foreign aid mainly funded its budgets.

Winters showed that Indonesian eagerness to attract investment went up or down (concomitantly varied) according to the extent of capital mobility and how critically Indonesia needed money. *Mobile capital,* which was able to bring investments in quickly or able to take investments out quickly, garnered the most favors. Investors whose assets were tied up in heavy fixed capital equipment, which was hard to move, caught fewer favors. When oil revenues rose, Indonesia's need for foreign investment fell: its willingness to accept foreign investment through onerous terms decreased; thus, its negotiating stance stiffened. When oil revenues decreased so did barriers to foreign investment, while incentives designed to attract investors increased.

The competition among governments to attract investments, as Winters studied it, is a quasi-natural process, which displays certain constant conjunctions of phenomena. One might even speak figuratively of *investment flows* and of *wage levels* as if they were —water flows and water levels; and, thus, one might literally report that the former tends to—go where the latter is low.

In addition, one can study the race to the bottom as an effect caused by structures. One can think of it as a game played within the normative framework provided by certain basic moral and legal structures of the modern world-system. Perhaps the most basic of the structures, like those discussed above, validates capital flight: people, including artificial persons such as corporations, are (with limited exceptions) free to do with their money and other property what they wish to do, for whatever reason.

Adding this banal structural observation, at once, implies two corollaries of great practical and theoretical importance. There is no reason to expect that: 1) everyone who wants a job will have one. People without independent incomes in business or professions can normally be expected to want a job; nevertheless, no one is obligated to give them a job. If X decides to hire Y, X will. X, however, could have done otherwise. If X, for whatever reason, chooses to decline to hire Y, X will decline. Despite many volumes of economic theory to the contrary, there is no reason to expect full employment. There is no reason to think that lack of full employment needs to be explained by government interference with market forces or by any policy error or unusual circumstance. Someone choosing to hire someone sometimes happens and 2) investors will invest to create enough jobs and produce enough goods to make the entire world prosperous. Investors invest when they please: the money is theirs to do with as they please.

The two consequences of a *basic structural norm* (which correlates to Giddens' *structure set*) suggest some additions to the analysis of the race to the bottom. It takes place in a world where it is expected that:

- ❒ workers will always outnumber jobs
- ❒ a government's practice of providing incentives to attract investors will never bring about full employment at equitable wages worldwide
- ❒ the race will not lead to the utopia of an entire world developed.

Human needs, therefore, will always outnumber needs met via the agency of investors who put up capital to produce goods and services in the expectation of making profits from making sales.

How might the race to the bottom turn around to become a march to the top in which nations cooperate to achieve social and environmental objectives? The question clarifies that thinking of structures as causes makes a practical as well as a theoretical difference. Much of the empirical research like that of Winters, however, contributes to understanding the problem, the additional insight provided by paying attention to structures is almost essential: structural change is needed to solve the problem.

The Growth Imperative

In his General Theory John Maynard Keynes wrote:

> The psychology of the community is such that when aggregate real income is increased aggregate consumption is increased, but not by so much as income. Hence, employers would make a loss if the whole of the increased employment were devoted to satisfying the increased demand for immediate consumption. Thus, to justify any given amount of employment there must be an amount of current investment sufficient to absorb the excess of total output over what the community chooses to consume when employment is at the given level.[26]

Keynes calls this a *psychological fact*, the term *structural fact* is, however, better: psychology implies that the economy's need for growth (enough current investment to absorb the excess of current output over current consumption) could by abolished by psychotherapy. It makes it seem as though there would be no need for growth if some attitude-change moved people to spend every dollar they took in. Calling it the *psychology of the community* makes it sound as though there could be a different community with a different psychology, such that growth would be unnecessary to make up for the shortfall in consumption. Actually, any community with a similar social structure has the same problem: it is unreasonable to expect people to spend every dollar they receive; people will either spend or save.

Keynes' argument shows that the growth imperative is not just a matter of ill will. It is not just that greedy global corporations and people have unbridled appetites to keep reinvesting profits in order to accumulate profits endlessly. Nor is it just a matter of good will. It is not just that the private and public sectors both work to promote growth because their leaders love the poor and wish to enlarge the economic pie so that there will always be bigger slices for the poorest: growth is a matter of keeping the system going; therefore, it is an imperative built into the structure of the system. The alternative to growth is that, as Keynes points out, "Employers would make a loss," which means layoffs, bankruptcies, and a downward spiral. A structural growth imperative exists to command growth regardless of whether it comes from good or bad intentions and regardless of whether the consequences are good or bad.

Making a virtue of a necessity, the path of steady economic growth is often equated with the path to success. The concept of *growth* solves Keynes' problem because it plows back much money into the economy as investments every year so that, overall, no lack of aggregate demand persists: merchants can sell their products and thus, can pay their employees.

Furthermore, vital growing industries can sometimes—as in the heyday of the growth of the social democratic economies of Western Europe in the 1960s—bring in profits large enough to make it possible to pay high wages. *Productivity growth* can be translated into increases in employee compensation. Moreover, growth expands the tax base, which enables the government to expand public services.

Solving society's principal problems through unlimited and continuous economic growth extending into the indefinite future sounds too good to be true and it is. Making growth compatible with ecological concerns requires restricting it to green growth, which is not easy to do. Maintaining islands of high wages in a world sea of low wages requires maintaining growth year after year, which entails the endless development of new products. It involves the battle to: 1) keep technological leads and 2) entice investors to keep investing, which in tandem with raising wages is even harder. Thus, in practice, it is impossible to keep ahead in technology while:

- ❑ keeping investment flowing enough to match aggregate demand with aggregate supply
- ❑ sopping up unemployment with new jobs
- ❑ keeping the economy growing fast enough to reduce poverty,
- ❑ subject to the constraint: only green growth counts as true growth.

The growth imperative has the effect of putting even the rich parts of the world: those nations, which have succeeded in growing economically, on a treadmill where they must run faster and faster just to stay in place. No amount of these is enough:

- ❒ consumption
- ❒ new products invention
- ❒ new marketing strategies.

No amount of sacrifice of other values to do whatever it takes to keep growth going is enough. As Keynes wrote:

> For at least another hundred years, we must pretend to ourselves and to everyone else that foul is fair and fair is foul, for foul is useful and fair is not. Avarice, usury, and precaution must be our goals for a little longer still. Only they can lead us from the tunnel of economic necessity into daylight. [27]

These lines from Keynes, however, are misleading insofar as they promise light at the end of the tunnel because, by Keynes' own reasoning, there is no reason to expect the growth imperative to ever stop, as long as the structures, which give rise to it, are in place. Every caring and aware human being must ask the questions: How did we get on this growth treadmill? How can we get off it? Research that examines the basic systemic structure of the modern world offers much toward answering these questions.

The Holocaust

I want to use the holocaust to sort, at least in part, what might appear ambiguous in Patomaki's argument. Then again, he finds support for his views in the empirical evidence supplied by the Deutsch careful historical case studies. They support the conclusion that peace can be established by creating reliable and effective institutions for achieving peaceful change in the directions most people want: more rights and liberties, equality, and prosperity. Then again, Patomaki finds much to criticize in the methodologies, which use the statistical analysis of datasets to confirm theories (most notably Kant's), which lead the authors to predict that, "Peace will prevail throughout a region when all the states there are democratic."[28] Patomaki might appear to be agreeing with Deutsch, not with Singer, when using the similar Deutsch methods to arrive at similar conclusions. A short discussion about how one might understand the holocaust may clarify this ambiguity; it may provide another example of why attention to basic structures has both methodological and practical importance.

My uncle Jack, a second lieutenant in the United States Army, was among the many who gave their lives to prevent tragedies like the holocaust from recurring. Tragedies like the holocaust have, nevertheless, happened again in: Argentina, Biafra, Cambodia, Chile, Indonesia, Rwanda, and elsewhere. Through peace research, many scholars have furthered the cause Uncle Jack accepted by volunteering to fight Hitler. They have learned how to prevent holocaust-like tragedies by understanding the causes.

A Humean scholar seeking to discover the causes of events like the holocaust is faced with the initial difficulty of deciding what to count as like the holocaust. Using a Humean methodology, one would have to identify a class of phenomena as *holocausts* and then seek to determine what other classes of phenomena are constantly conjoined with it or frequently conjoined with it at a high level of statistical significance. What a scholar chooses to regard as a tragedy like the holocaust would reveal the scholar's ethical orientation and make known the sorts of policy recommendations likely to emerge from the research. If the choice is to focus on anti-Semitism, then the class of similar phenomena to be studied will include the pogroms in Russia, Poland, and other places. If the choice is to focus on the systematic killing of the members of an ethnic group, then other holocaust-like events will be defined as *genocides*. If the choice is to focus on the systematic killing of any group of people, who are considered unworthy of life and deserving of death by other people who have the power as well as the will to destroy them, then Indonesia in 1965 and all of the aforementioned states where tragedies would count too. If the choice is to focus on:

❒ rage out of control
❒ the intelligent and systematic implementation of cruelty or
❒ the ideological construction of the other as evil: then still different datasets will be defined.

Then again, one can take the view that there was only one holocaust: in Germany and in German-occupied areas in the early 1940s. Its victims were Jews, Communists, Socialists, labor leaders, gypsies, homosexuals, and some others condemned to die for various reasons. In this last view, one might give up trying to understand the holocaust with the methods of social science, understood as methods that measure the impacts of variables on variables. The *holocaust-like event* would not be a variable because there was no more than one; thus, there would be no class of such events to count, rank, or scale, in order to give a variable a numerical value. One might then revert to trying to understand the holocaust with the methods of history, conceived as methods for studying unique events.

Unless one studies the holocaust as a unique phenomenon, defining the class of holocaust-like-phenomena excludes information. Any member of the class of such tragedies will have characteristics additional to and different than other tragedies lumped together with it in the same class. Furthermore, no reason exists to suppose that the boundaries marked by assigning a name to a class of events correspond to any fault lines along which causal powers move. Assigning a name to a class of phenomena and, thus, defining a variable operationally, is no guarantee that one has grasped forces at work in reality. As Knorr Cetina reminds us: "A stable name is not an expression and indicator of stable thing." [29]

Whatever does not count for defining the class to be studied operationally will not be regarded at all, insofar as the class, though not its individual members, then becomes the object of study. The class, so defined as an object of study, may and may not have some real relationship to causal powers.

Such considerations lead to a reason why Patomaki can repose more confidence in the Deutsch studies than in those conceived in the Singer *Correlates of War* tradition. Patomaki emphasizes that classes are never causes. To calculate the impact of X on Y where X and Y are variables (classes) is never to give a causal explanation. Causes must be sought among things, not among the names of the classes used to put things in categories. Further, the very process that puts a number of historical phenomena into the same category in order to define a variable is a process that loses information about things. The Deutsch group lose comparatively little information in his extensive case studies of particular transitions from *armed mutual suspicion* to the peaceful security community, with their:

- ❑ complex and qualified conclusions

❑ methodological caution
❑ use of elementary mathematics. They are less prone to covertly treat classes as causes, or to treat measurements of quantitative relationships among classes as tests of causal hypotheses.

Patomaki does go further than Deutsch by proposing a critical realist methodology for peace studies. Patomaki recommends an approach that is explicitly not Humean. On the other hand, Patomaki's critical realist approach is not restricted by the doctrine that because world political events are unique no causes producing them can be identified.

This does not mean though, that in place of 1) the *positivist* notion: once the values of the independent variables are known, then the value of the dependent variable can be predicted and 2) that in place of the notion found in some versions of Marxism: the laws of the accumulation of capital decree one inevitable result: a third, realist notion now exists authorizing social scientists to predict the future. No, meanings are causes because they explain human action. A characteristic of human action, however, is that the actor could have done otherwise. Critical realism and idealism merge in the human actors who are able to transform the meaningful contexts of their actions. It is realistic to say that the ecological niche of the human species is the cultural animal, and that cultural animals create social structures. As Roy Bhaskar writes,

> If there are social explanations for social phenomena (if a social science of social forms is possible), then what is designated in such explanations —the social mechanisms and structures generating social phenomena— must be social products themselves; so, like any other social object, they must be given to and reproduced in human agency. Society is a social product.[30] At once, it is the ever present condition and the continually reproduced outcome of human agency, which is the duality of structure.[31]

It may well be the case, as the neo-realists maintain, that in the past it has been hard to change the rules and principles of global order except by military means. Nothing in the nature of things, however, makes this necessarily the case. Peaceful change is, in principle, doable.

For critical realism, the route to preventing the recurrence of holocaust-like events is more than one of gauging causal factors that are linked to violence. It is more the course of learning how to bring forth positive structural change, which facilitates creating cultures of peace where ethnic hostility is in remission. In Patomaki's somewhat esoteric terminology, the question is about the self-transformative capacities of contexts. It is less about the crimes of

Hitler and more about how to move beyond the fallible and ineffectual Weimar Republic. It is less about the immediate conditions that triggered the outbreak of WW II and more about the failure of the Treaty of Versailles to establish a viable international peace after WW I. It is less about the crimes of Suharto and more about the weakness of the fledgling social democracy proclaimed in Indonesia when the Dutch departed in 1955. Such is the thrust of Patomaki's last chapter, "Beyond Nordic Nostalgia." The chapter discusses reversing the decline of Scandinavian social democracy. Apart from the fact that it is natural for Patomaki, a Finn, to be concerned with his own part of the world, the concerns of the last chapter are a logical outcome of the argument of the book. The entire world needs models of reliable and effective peaceful change: the kind the Scandinavian social democracies once provided.

Transforming Rules, Relationships, and Practices

The word *structure* occurs frequently in talk about issues such as those discussed above and, more generally, whenever it is a matter of unacceptable dilemmas (such as severe unemployment or environmental destruction), intractable social and economic contradictions, or persistent poverty or whenever it is a matter of imagining a juggernaut unstoppable by human wills. The structure is said to override human desire and ethics, and to alone produce, irreversible changes in society with names like: • *globalization* • *commodification* • *alienation*. The structure stymies peaceful change. Better conceptual tools for thinking about structure would make peace and justice easier to achieve. Some part of the problems alleged to be structural problems, might more easily resolve with the aid of better ways of thinking about social structure.

Jean Piaget and Anthony Giddens are among those who have published extensive discussions of the use of the term *structure* in science, particularly in social science during the 19th and 20th centuries. I refer the reader to them, instead of summarizing them.[32] Giddens reviews how the term has been used by the French writers known as *structuralists* and *post-structuralists* and by the US sociologists known as *structural-functionalists*. I will limit my comments to how Patomaki defines the term in 2001. Patomaki's definition is the outcome of a constructive critique of the definitions of structure as provided by Giddens and Bhaskar; the critiques are outcomes of the constructive critique of two centuries of thought concerning the best way to consider structure.

One standard use of the term can be disregarded at the outset. Structural problems are sometimes assumed to be about social inequality, which can be defined by classifying people into groups in ways relying on a definition of structure as *composition*. Social scientists speak, for example, of the *age structure* of a human population, meaning the age composition of the population: how many are under five years old, over ninety years old, and how many are in each age class as defined. Similarly, one can speak of an *income structure* by saying that the top ten percent take fifty percent of the income, while the bottom fifty percent get a mere ten percent of the income; or, one can speak of a world *wealth structure,* such that the richest one percent own more than the next sixty percent own. Nonetheless, classes are not causes; thus, it is more important to know why, though knowing how much inequality exists helps as well. For present purposes, it is better to reserve the designation *structural problems* for use in discovering the causes that produce inequality and the traps that frustrate efforts to reduce inequality.

Structure defined as composition or *classification* can therefore be disregarded for present purposes. Such compositional structures are, Patomaki says, "Causally and therefore ontologically secondary to the conceptually much richer *relational structures*." [33]

Patomaki begins a discussion of structure by considering the conclusions of Anthony Giddens' extensive work on the concept, which features the ideas of *rules* and *resources*. Giddens' careful and complex views suggest that to learn what comprises the structure of a society one asks: a) What are the rules? b) Who controls the resources?

The idea that social structures are rules is plausible: the structural problems discussed above are about property rights, in one way or another; property rights are legal rules. Ludwig Wittgenstein examines rules in his *Philosophical Investigations* showing rules to be a theme worth tracing to shed light on aspects of social life often placed under such headings as norms, roles, games, discourse, practice, *habitus*, meaning, and custom.[34] Wittgenstein's work serves to reassure those who share Michel Foucault's fear that to give rules a central role in social analysis would be to succumb to the naive illusion that a ruler who makes the rules governs society. Furthermore, within a post-Wittgenstein (and post-Heideger) account of rules, to choose to say that institutional structures are made of rules is not to deny that they are made of practices. On the contrary, it affirms that structures are made of practices.

To place rules as a central theme of social science has the advantage of building a land bridge between social science and jurisprudence; it keeps jurisprudence from detaching as a separate intellectual continent. It facilitates dialogue toward world peace through world law by framing it in the common vocabulary of dialogue about rules. Giddens notes that an image the word *structure* evokes is that of the girders of a building. Thus, the girders of a society are its guiding principles: the rules.

Giddens stops short of defining social structure entirely as a matter of rules because he finds that the idea of rules does not lend itself to an adequate account of the role of power in structuring human relationships. He adds *resources* to his definition because he believes that to understand a social structure one must know not only what the rules are, but also who has power to command resources. The trouble with this addition is that it can be called redundant because it is the rules of society which decide who has power to command resources. Then again, making allowance for *power* as a concept independent of rules seems intuitively plausible, partly because at times it seems that naked power overrides the rules. Mainstream political science generally favors making power, rather than rules, the central organizing theme for research.

Giddens' concession to the thesis that power trumps rules may seem correct from the viewpoint of mainstream political science. Though it may seem correct, and no doubt is partly correct, I will argue that it is less correct than it may seem. Political scientists often distinguish authority and/or legitimacy from the concept of *power*. Social rules (norms), they say, prescribe who is supposed to rule and make the laws, though in a showdown (simplifying theory for clarity) military force, economic force, or both might overpower the legitimate government. After the holders of real power seize control of the government in disregard of the norms of the rule of law, they can then make up rules to suit their ends. They can expound an ideology to provide legitimacy for their rules and then compel the children in all schools to study it as Suharto did with the *pancasila* ideology in Indonesia, as Stalin did with dialectical materialism in Russia, and as Salazar did with a corporatist version of Roman Catholic social doctrine in Portugal.

The thesis that power trumps rules withstands scrutiny better in the case of military power than in the case of economic power. Even in the case of military power, the thesis has its limitations; the studies by Hannah Arendt [35] and Gene Sharp[36] show that even military power depends upon consent and consensus. The over-generalized notion that people who have military power can afford to ignore social rules is also shown by cases wherein the possessors of moral legitimacy nonviolently defeated the possessors of military hardware. That occurred several times in the history of the twentieth century.

Economic power, however, is the linchpin of the modern world-system. In the case of economic power, the thesis that power overrides the rules appears in a different light when it is recognized that the economic power of property owners consists entirely of rights created and maintained by legal rules. Although, certainly, the rule of law in a modern state implies that the police may use physical force, this does not mean that the rules have no customary, conventional, and moral force. It means, instead, that the physical power of the sovereign democratic state is committed to supporting the rules through law-enforcement.

Economic power's dependence on the legal rules that define property rights was made clear by John R. Commons in *Legal Foundations of Capitalism*, first published in 1924. Commons wrote:

> Economic power is simply power to withhold from others what they need. In short, the change in the concept of property from physical things to the exchange-value of things is a change from the concept of holding things for one's own use to withholding things from others' use, protected, in either case by the physical power of the sovereign.
>
> The transition from the notion of holding things for one's own use and enjoyment to the notion of economic power over others evidently accompanies the historical evolution of property from slavery, feudalism, colonialism and a sparse population, to marketing, business, and the pressure of population on limited resources. Where production was isolated, or the owner held under his control all of the material things as well as the laborers necessary to the support of himself and dependents, the concept of exclusive holding for self was a workable definition of property. When, however—markets expanded, laborers were emancipated, people began to live by bargain and sale, population increased and all resources became private property—then the power to withhold from others emerged gradually from that of exclusive holding for self as an economic attribute of property. The one is implied in the other, though it does not unfold until new conditions bring it to the fore. Just as the scales of the reptile become the feathers of the bird when the environment moves from land to air, so, exclusive holding for self becomes withholding from others when the environment moves from production to marketing.
>
> The transition was noticeable as long as the merchant, the master, the laborer, were combined under small units of ownership; it becomes distinct, however, when all opportunities are occupied and business is conducted by corporations on a credit system which consolidates property

> under the control of absentee owners. Then the power of property per se, distinguished from the power residing in personal faculties or special grants of sovereignty comes into prominence. It becomes a power to extract things in exchange from other persons, in the absence of and wholly separate from individual human faculties a power of property per se, silently operating though clearly seen and distinguishable from the manual, mental, and managerial abilities of its owners.
>
> This power of property in itself: the power to withhold, seen in these extreme cases, is a mere enlargement of that power existing in all property as the source of value in exchange and perhaps distinguished as waiting-power: the power to hold back until the opposite party consents to the bargain. While as investors, they perform the indispensable service of waiting for compensation, yet as bargainers they determine through their power to wait what shall be the terms on which that compensation shall be made...
>
> This enlargement of property from economy to economic power also separates, or at least distinguishes, management from ownership. For the activity of management is mainly that of proportioning the factors so as to get the largest net result from all; however, the function of ownership is that of determining the conditions, terms, prices or values, at which the factors shall be obtained from others or the product sold to others. [37]

Commons' analysis shows that the command over resources—*economic power*—is inseparable from legal rules and the privileges conferred by legal rules. Thus, in this important respect, rules constitute power. Although it is undoubtedly largely true, that those who have the gold make the rules, it is also largely true, that the rules determine who has the gold.

Thus, insofar as structural problems, such as capital flight and others discussed above, are problems about economic power, they are also problems about rules. They are ones that define what property owners can do to exclude others from their property in:

- ❐ bargaining
- ❐ moving their property from place to place
- ❐ using or not using their property and, as Commons' emphasizes,
- ❐ withholding permission for others to use their property until their terms are met.

For a reason different than mine, Patomaki, as well, thinks that Giddens' account of social science does not understand the complex interplay between rules and power quite right. Patomaki sees that Giddens' account of structure does not amply incorporate Foucault's widening of the concept of *power* to include *productive power.* Patomaki writes:

> Productive power is the idea that power also produces elements of the social world—discursive knowledge, techniques, practical knowledge and skills, which constitute internal social relations. Many of the consequent effects may be unintended.[38]

Patomaki's critique of Giddens ala Foucault blends into a broader critique, which draws on the idea that power constitutes social relationships. Patomaki frames his critique initially in terms of compositions (classes) and relations:

> Giddens's definition of structure as rules and resources does not sound plausible because the term 'structure' is normally used in connection with compositions and/or relations.[39]

Disregarding compositions (classifications such as: *the income structure of the population*) for the reason given above, the proper use of the word *structure,* thus, comes to depend, for Patomaki, upon relations. This brings us back to Karl Marx who does not write about structure, though he does write everywhere about *social relationships* (G *Verhaltnisse*). Marx's constant theme is that political economy is a pseudo-science: a quack imitation of engineering, which charades as natural that which are, in fact, historically contingent social relationships. The most important of the relations is that between the owner of the means of production and the worker who has nothing to sell but labor-power.

Giddens, however, does not neglect relations in his account of structure. In particular, he does not neglect the relations that were central to Marx's critique of political economy. Instead, he interprets them within a framework of rules and resources. Giddens begins a long discussion of structures by defining them as: rule-resource sets that are involved in the institutional articulation of social systems. He does this by considering the role of private property relationships in Marx's analysis of modern capitalism. Giddens writes:

> Consider what is involved in the following structural set: private property⇨ money⇨ capital⇨ labor contract⇨ profit. The structural relations indicated here mark out one of the most fundamental transmutations involved in the emergence of capitalism and hence contribute in a significant way to the overall *structuration* of the system.[40]

Thus, the Giddens *rules and resources* account of social structure makes specific use of the *relations* that Marx analyzed, though using a terminology different than Marx's, and slightly different than Patomaki's. Therefore, Patomaki concludes with a relational definition of social structure, which owes much to Foucault's idea of *positioned practice*: productive power defines the positions occupied by the actors. It follows:

Definition 6: The term social structure refers to internal and external relations of positioned practice; these relations are implicated and/or generated by the components of the relevant causal complex.[41]

Rules are not exempt from the Patomaki definition. In each of the next three sentences of his text, he explains what internal and external relations are, he writes of rules and/or of constitutive rules. Like Giddens, Patomaki employs the idea of *rules* in explicating the meaning of *relations*.

It is easy to lose sight of the forest while looking at the trees. The broad intellectual canopy provided by rules may and may not be broad enough to house everything that needs saying to flesh out the concept of *social structure*. It may and may not be broad enough to house what needs saying about:

- power
- *productive power relations*
- practices, and
- economic power
- control of resources
- positions.

What remains clear, nevertheless, to vary the metaphors, when the dust settles and the fog lifts, is that we are no longer in Kansas, if Kansas is the flat Humean prairie of conjunctions among phenomena, where science is about finding out the degree of probability with which the value of an independent variable predicts the value of a dependent variable. We are, instead, living on the blue planet third from the Sun, upon which humans create social structures. Institutions have been constructed; they can be deconstructed and reconstructed; the forms can be transformed. Given these structural obstacles to institutionalizing peaceful change:

❑ capital flight
❑ the race to the bottom
❑ the growth imperative
❑ the ineffectiveness of social democracy (leading to exacerbated ethnic conflict), it becomes easier to see, once one leaves Kansas, that nothing is inevitable about them. Whatever else the Giddens and Patomaki analyses of social structure may imply, they do imply that structural obstacles are moveable.

Thus, let us move some. In Patomaki's terminology, let us advance the emancipatory project of enhancing the self-transformative capacities of contexts. To this end, I will draw some practical suggestions for peace building from the post-Wittgenstein discussion of *rules* in H. L. A. Hart's *The Concept of Law*.

Hart defines law as: the union of primary and secondary rules.[42] The secondary rules prescribe which of the primary rules become laws. For example, it may be a secondary rule that a constitution approved by *plebiscite* is law. It may be a secondary rule that whatever a duly elected parliament enacts is law, or that whatever a Supreme Court decides is the meaning of an ambiguous statute is law.

Hart's definition of *law* has implications of what it would take to achieve world peace through world law, some of which he described in a chapter devoted to international law. Hart's definition sheds light on the principle for peace as stated by J. L. Brierly in *The Law of Nations*:

> The existence of a police force does not make a system of law strong and respected; instead, the strength of the law makes it possible for a police force to be effectively organized. [43]

The idea of secondary rules as a framework for identifying and changing primary rules, also clarifies Patomaki's point: peace should not be conceived as the achievement of any kind of final order; instead, it forms the institution of a reliable processes for achieving constructive social change. The institution of the peaceful processes for change consists, largely, of accepting secondary rules that determine which putative primary rules are legitimate and valid rules. The secondary rules define what counts as a legitimate change in the primary rules.

Hart's account of rules in general, which are primary rules, sheds even more light on peacemaking. He finds that rules have three aspects: a) regularity, b) criticism c) an internal aspect.

a) *Regularity*. A rule is, first, an observable regularity in people's conduct: a pattern. A complex interplay occurs between the regularities prescribed by cultural norms and the regularities observed in practice. Nonetheless, there are regularities. It follows that if structures are rules (at least to some considerable extent), then structures will change via changing regularities in people's conduct. Gandhi took such a view of change when he strove to change his own conduct, as a first step toward changing society. Although Gandhi never used the word *structure*, his life stood for the proposition that structural change does begin when one voluntarily follows different rules in daily practice. For example, Gandhi wrote:

> Now let us consider how equal distribution can be brought about through nonviolence. The first step towards it is for him who has made this ideal part of his being to bring about the necessary changes in his personal life. He would reduce his wants to a minimum, bearing in mind the poverty of India. His earnings would be free of dishonesty; the desire for speculation would be renounced. His habitation would be in keeping with his new mode of life; self-restraint would be exercised in every sphere of life. When he has done all that is possible for his life, only then

> will he be in the position as an example to preach this ideal among his associates and neighbors. [44]

The present analysis clarifies that individuals and groups do change the regular patterns of their behavior; when they do, they are not simply working outside the system, leaving the existing social structures intact. Structures are largely, at least, regular patterns of behavior; to change the rules people live by is to change structure.

b) *Criticism*. A rule is, in Hart's analysis, an ideal of proper or correct conduct. Violating it authorizes other people to criticize the violator. Punishment may result; then again, social disapproval may be enough. If violation never has a consequence, then the rule does not exist; a past rule that is now a relic may, through habit, still garner status as a *rule*; nevertheless, it is now a former rule no longer followed. Because structures are (at least to a considerable extent) patterns of behavior whose violation leads to disapproval, it follows that the weight of a community's value judgments is a constituent part of social structure. Changing the moral, and ultimate legal, judgments of the citizens of a society is an essential part of changing social structure. If, for example, the weight of public opinion is that war is not a proper instrument of national policy, what Betty Reardon calls the *war system*,[45] to some extent ceases to exist. Normative criticism is an active ingredient of rules, which are that from which structures are made. The Deutsch study gives practical examples of this point by showing that the antiwar sentiment of the people in Sweden facilitated a peaceful outcome when Norway seceded from Sweden. Likewise, US citizens played a vital role preventing the US from invading Mexico when its nationalized US corporate petroleum interests. Generally, taking a stand for conscience, when done by shifting society's values constructively, is more than just wishing the social structure would change: it is changing it.

(c) *Rules have an internal aspect*: Obeying rules is internal to the minds of the people who follow them: they take guidance from rules. The race to the bottom, for example, attracts investors who take guidance from the rules of accounting. The corporate managers who make investment decisions follow the rules of sound management. They deliberately cut costs and choose to accept offers to invest in nations that offer favorable terms. They do not intend to produce a world of poverty and violence. They do intend to comply with their fiduciary duties as the managers of the funds that others have entrusted to them. Their deliberate acts contribute to the race to the bottom, with other causes, even though they do not intend its consequences.

When the causal links between rule following and its, at times, unknown and/or unintended consequences become better known, it will be easier to design institutions that work. Correctly following the socially approved rules should lead to socially desired results, though often it does not. Emancipatory research is then needed to increase the self-transformative capacity of the context. It is needed to mesh the inward and subjective aspect of rule following with the objective consequences of following the rules.

Evaluating the objective consequences using emancipation as the standard, gives privileges to freedom as a value. Patomaki's sympathies are generally with those who name the desired outcome of social change as emancipation, following the lead of Jurgen Habermas who, in *Knowledge and Human Interests* defined emancipatory science as: a science whose governing interest is to produce knowledge that liberates. Patomaki, however, broadens the scope of the dialogue about goals; freedom is not the only value.

> Social practices and systems can be evaluated from a number of normative standpoints, including economic efficiency and stability, as well as rights, justice, democracy, human flourishing, and ecological well-being. [46]

To Patomaki's open list, I add *stewardship* (Gandhi's *trusteeship*): a virtue that promises to transform economic power and, thus, overcome structural obstacles to peaceful change. As Gandhi points out, the need for trusteeship does not disappear with democratic or public control of resources. Public sector managers, as well as private sector and nonprofit sector managers, are called by stewardship to use property for the good of others. They too are tempted by self-interest to exercise economic power to withhold the use of property until a bargain is struck maximally favorable to them.

I will extend my discussion of Hart's internal aspect of rules in order to make the point that peace building requires attention to both the subjective and the objective sides of structural transformation. The internal aspect of rules represents the subjective side.

When *The Concept of Law* was published in 1961, Hart's insistence that rules have an internal aspect drove a wedge into the armor of positivism. The person who follows the rule does so deliberately in the privacy of her or his mind. Observers cannot see the internal aspect, which is contrary to: behaviorism, behaviorist interpretations of Wittgenstein, Hume's doctrine that science is about finding constant or probable conjunctions among the sense impressions of observers, certain versions of French structuralism, post-structuralism, and Marxism. Positivists were famous for denying that what they called *introspection* was a legitimate method for science. Science, for them, had to be based upon what could be observed. The unobservable might as well not exist. Hart's internal aspect of rules, in contrast, reflected the reversion of the post-Wittgenstein theories of human action to the Aristotelian principle that people act according to their characters and based on their beliefs, which may and may not coincide with the objective facts.

Today the genie is out of the bottle. Although statistical methods are still entrenched in the practice of social science, nobody now defends them by appealing to empiricist and positivists basis. "Positivism is a swear word that nobody swears by," as Bhaskar remarked. It is generally conceded that rules and, therefore, social structures consist, in part, of the subjective beliefs and attitudes of people. A rule exists, in part, because people subjectively look to it for guidance; thus, Aristotle won. If *structuralism* means that people do not continually renegotiate, choose, and reconstruct the patterns of social life, then structuralism is wrong. Something like the theories of structuration offered by Giddens, Patomaki, Pierre Bourdieu, Michel de Certeau, or Jacques Derrida, is right, or closer to right.

Although mistaken, it is tempting to conclude that the rules: 1) governing society are only the rules of daily life writ large and 2) of daily life are just the subjective *maxims of actions,* named by Kant as the principles individuals choose to guide their conduct. If these tempting conclusions were true, peace could be established by spiritual conversion. The following example shows why such a subjective approach to peace is incomplete. Suppose that a group of people change the rules they follow in daily life: • the bookkeeping rule: buy cheap and sell dear, which defines homo economicus and • love they neighbor as thyself, which is prescribed by religions. The *internal aspect* of the new rule is that each person in the group takes it as a guide. The group follows the new rule's guidance (or believing they are following it, which amounts to the same thing as long as it is the subjective side that is under consideration). The group members withdraw money from their savings accounts and use the money to buy food and shipment of the food given to hungry people in a third world country. A consequence of the free food for the third world country is that the local farmers cannot sell their products. The farmers must quit farming and migrate to the cities joining other ex-farmers who were forced to migrate to the city for a different reason: capital-intensive corporate agriculture displaced them. They join the homeless begging on the city streets. The subjective rule adopted by the donors of food, thus, proved to have disastrous objective consequences. The food donors encountered a structural problem, and just when we thought we had learned to solve structural problems by changing the internal aspects of rules and, therefore, the rules that constituted the structures.

The general point is the same as the one made by the previous example of the corporate managers who participate in the race to the bottom. They do intend to follow the rules of homo economicus, the rules prescribed by generally accepted accounting principles. They intend to manage their businesses properly. They aim to be faithful to the fiduciary duties they owe to their shareholders. Poverty and violence are the objective consequences not the subjective intentions of the maxims to which they look for guidance.

The general point is that changing the internal aspect of rules is necessary, although not sufficient to change social structures. The internal aspect of rules is not going away nor will it disappear as a *Paretian derivative* that can be disregarded by social science because it has no causal power.[47] People who follow rules, however, often do not know the causal powers of their compliance; social scientists often do not know them either. Patomaki argues that it is their job to discover them. They can know them, Patomaki claims, by using a critical realist methodology that seeks to link causes and effects, where rules are an essential part of the causes. The subjective rules people follow, the internal aspect of rules, is part, though only part, of the causal complex that leads to the consequences.[48]

Overemphasis on: 1) the causal efficacy of the subjective side leads to the illusion that structures will transform by spiritual conversion or 2) the objective side leads to the illusions that: a) structures will transform by public policy, without spiritual conversion or b) no structure transformation is needed. The objective illusion is the *Keynesian illusion*, after Keynes, who proposed to leave the subjective values of the masses of the people alone. Keynes proposed to correct the instability and, to some extent, the injustice of capitalism through *macroeconomic policies* guided by the new science of *macroeconomics*, of which he was one of the founders. Ordinary people would go on buying and selling as usual; business people would make their business plans as usual.

The *policy instruments* of the nation-state, however, managed the context in which they made their calculations expectantly by those instruments to be wielded by the international economic institutions, which Keynes envisaged. Government policy instruments would manage the system to make it work better, without requiring any improvement in the manners and morals of the general population. The instruments are:

- ❑ taxes
- ❑ interest rates
- ❑ public spending
- ❑ price supports
- ❑ price controls as needed
- ❑ publicdeficits surpluses calculated to offset the business cycle
- ❑ foreign money exchange controls
- ❑ bank reserve requirements
- ❑ government backing for collective bargaining, and other means for adjusting the money supply.

Swedish economist Gunnar Myrdal was another of the founders of macroeconomics. He was an architect of its successful application in the formation of public policy in post WW II Sweden. Myrdal believed, however, in the importance of the subjective side of social transformation. He believed that the success of social democracy depends mainly on the deliberate practices of the mass of the people working to mobilize resources to meet needs in cities, cooperatives, at every NGO level, and, thus, less on central government policy. Myrdal wanted social planning to be the framework for realizing the Jeffersonian ideal of grassroots democracy; he wanted a welfare culture, characterized by:

- ❒ solidarity
- ❒ participation and
- ❒ identification with the community.

Myrdal wrote:

> The reason why it is important to stress the deeper changes of people's attitudes—as a causal factor underlying the trend toward intervention and planning in the Western world—is that these psychological changes, related to the whole development of our modern society, make the process nonreversible.[49]

Ultimately, the *macro-managing* of the modern welfare state proved to have severe limitations. The gains of social democracy have proven more reversible than Myrdal thought they were. Social democracy in Sweden and elsewhere encountered *structural problems.*[50] Experience has shown that although macroeconomics may be a partial solution to structural problems, it is not the whole solution. Although Myrdal was mistaken to the extent that he thought that the forward progress of social democracy was nonreversible, the principle he enunciated might, nevertheless, be right. If there had been more emphasis upon the deeper changes of people's attitudes, then perhaps the progress of social democracy would have been permanent. It would have been lasting in the sense that its enhanced capacity for continual self-transformation would have been preserved.

Social democracies have declined, as did the influence of Keynesian economic theory (roughly the theory that led the post WW II West European social democracies). The decline suggests something wrong with the general concept of: improve society without improving people. I do not mean to oppose this suggestion in favor of the explanations of the decline of social democracy, which focus on the crises of regimes of accumulation. Neither do I mean replace it with the explanations of the decline of social democracy, which focus on the global liberalization of trade, production, and finance, which enhanced the exit options of capital. Instead, I propose to integrate this suggestion with them. A theory of social structure in which structures are rules, relationships, and practices suggests that if structures are to be transformed, it will require something more multifaceted than any combination of policy instruments wielded by well-informed civil servants. Therefore, if, as asserted: 1) structures are made partly by rules and 2) rules have an internal aspect, then it follows: structures will not change without a change in the beliefs and conscious behavior of the people who follow the rules.

Patomaki advocates research that is emancipatory in the sense that it increases freedom. Learning how systems and structures work is liberating because it facilitates transforming them so that they work better. The future is undetermined and, thus, enhanced by inspired human action. Emancipatory research can uplift human action and potential.

Peace research of the kind that Patomaki advocates contributes to a future in which doing what is subjectively considered right produces what is objectively good. It brings us closer to a future in which people who conscientiously follow the rules, which are regarded, as correct and proper in their social milieu do not fall into structural traps, which produce results they do not imagine or intend. Although emancipatory research does not prevent the oppression of the weak by the strong, it is likely to empower the weak and monitor the strong by making oppression visible. Although it does not prevent antisocial motives from overwhelming pro-social motives, it is likely to encourage moral education designed to strengthen pro-social motives. This is true because it shows that social structures are (in part) constituted by deliberate human action.

Summary

A logical plan for peace, which is implicit in *After International Relations,* starts with work in the social sciences that is devoted to freedom and other values. Patomaki advocates research guided by a critical realist methodology and philosophy. Critical realism attributes the success of the natural sciences to their ability to grasp the causal powers of the real structures, which produce the phenomena that scientific theories explain. Realistic social science seeks social causal explanations and for that reason it sees the future as open to improvement through deliberate choices. Emancipatory research as performed with the methods of critical realism improves self-transformative capacities, both within societies and between societies. It makes peaceful change easier to institutionalize. I have simplified Patomaki's multifaceted account by suggesting that peace-enhancing structural transformation must proceed both on the *subjective side* and on the *objective side.* Reliable expectations that needed changes can be achieved nonviolently lead to peace.

After International Relations considers many of the topics of which I do not mention a number of points concerning structural problems and transformation, which are in the spirit of the book, though are not in the book, and which its author may not agree with. These points summarize as follows:

⇨ because democracy facilitates peace, the success of democracy makes peace more likely

⇨ a successful democracy is a social democracy; it delivers the goods

⇨ to deliver them, it is necessary to cope with structural obstacles and ultimately to transform structures

⇨ because they are made of rules (etc.), structures do, with effort, transform

⇨ rules change because behavior changes.

Notes

* Because the word *love* occurs only three times in the paper that follows, these words taken from a homily by the martyred Salvadoran Archbishop Oscar Romero might appear as an irrelevant introduction. Instead of explaining their relevance to this paper's central themes, I propose the discernment of their relevance as an exercise for the reader. A group discussion about this paper might begin with the question: What does the rest of the paper have to do with the introductory quotation?

Peace

1. Heikki Patomaki, *After International Relations: Critical Realism*

and the (Re)construction of world politics. London: Routledge, 2001.

2. Quincy Wright, *A Study of War*. The analysis of this study suggests that the prevention of war involves simultaneous, general, and concerted attacks on educational, social, political and legal fronts." Id. at p. 1310 Chicago: University of Chicago Press, 1965.

3. Karl Deutsch, *The Nerves of Government*. New York: Free Press, 1966.

4. Karl W. Deutsch, Sidney A. Burrell, Robert A. Kann, Maurice Lee Jr., Martin Lichterman, Raymond E. Lindgren, Francis L. Loewenheim, Richard W. Van Wagenen, *Political Community in the North Atlantic Area*. Princeton New Jersey: Princeton University Press, 1957. pp. 135-36.

5. P. E. Corbett, *The Individual and World Society*, Center for Research on World Political Institutions, Princeton University, publication no. 2, 1953, p. 59. Cited by Deutsch and collaborators p. 164.

6. Peter Wallensteen and Margareta Sollenberg, "Armed Conflict 1989-1999," *Journal of Peace Research* September 2000, pp. 635-649. The authors count 110 armed conflicts during the period, defined as having at least 25 battle deaths. Counting each of these as a war, (although the authors limit the term *war* to conflicts with more than 1,000 battle deaths), the breakdown is 94 civil wars, 9 civil wars with foreign intervention, and 7 interstate wars.

Truth

7. Thus, Max Weber:

> What we must vigorously oppose is the view that one may be 'scientifically' contented with the conventional self-evidence of very widely accepted value judgments. The specific function of science, it seems to me, is just the opposite: namely, to ask questions about these things which convention makes self-evident.

Max Weber, *The Methodology of the Social Sciences* (a collection of his writings edited by Edward Shils and Henry Finch). New York: Free Press, 1949. p. 13.

8. Roy Bhaskar, *Reclaiming Reality, a Critical Interpretation of Contemporary Philosophy*. London: Verso (New Left Books), 1989.

9. Jeffrey Sachs and Felipe Larrain, *Macroeconomics in the Global Economy*. Englewood Cliffs NJ: Prentice-Hall, 1993. p. xvii.

10. Bruce Russett and John R. Oneal, *Triangulating Peace: Democracy, Interdependence, and International Organizations*. New York: W. W. Norton, 2001. p. 122.

11. Ernest Nagel, *The Structure of Science, Problems in the Logic of Scientific Explanation*. New York: Harcourt Brace and World, 1961.

Max Weber, cited above, is also one of the sources of the Verstehen/ Erklaren distinction.

12. Karl Popper, *The Poverty of Historicism*. Boston: Beacon Press, 1957.

13. Jurgen Habermas, *Knowledge and Human Interests*. Boston: Beacon Press, 1971. Habermas starts with a version of the Erklaren/ Verstehen distinction, conflating technical instrumental knowledge with Erklaren, and practical social understanding with Verstehen. He transcends this dichotomy by proposing a third kind of knowledge, emancipatory or liberating knowledge.

14. Paul Ricoeur, *Freud and Philosophy: an Essay on Interpretation*. New Haven: Yale University Press, 1970.

> ...a disjunction: either an explanation [Erklaren] in terms of energy, or an understanding [Verstehen] in terms of phenomenology. It must be recognized, however, that Freudianism exists only because of its refusal of that disjunction. p. 66.

15. Anthony Giddens, *New Rules of Sociological Method* (2nd edition). Stanford: Stanford University Press, 1993. Giddens brings sociology into dialogue with post-Wittgenstein philosophies of human action. The result is a social science of which the label neo-Aristotelian in the respect that deliberate human action plays key roles in explanation. Meanings are causes.

16. Herbert Marcuse, *One Dimensional Man*. Boston: Beacon Press, 1964. Marcuse criticizes behaviorism and empiricism generally. The transformation of society requires the work of the negative, which denies what is actual and enlarges the domain of what is possible.

Structure

17. Roy Bhaskar, p. 9 *Scientific Realism and Human Emancipation*. London: Verso (New Left Books), 1986. p. 106.

18. *Triangulating Peace*, p. 85.

19. *Triangulating Peace*, p. 75

20. The bedrock of the case for scientific realism, of which critical realism is a variant, is the argument from the success of science. Most versions of the argument have the following structure:

SS1: The enterprise of science is much more successful than can be accounted for by chance. SS2: The only explanation for this success is the truth, which is approximate truth, of scientific theories. SS3: We should, therefore, be scientific realists.

Andre Kukla, *Studies in Scientific Realism. New York: Oxford University Press, 1998. p. 12.* [explanation added]

21. I am not distinguishing the broadly empiricist tradition epitomized in traditions stemming from David Hume from an equally broad notion of *positivist*. Patomaki writes:

> By positivism I mean the set of abstract and closely interrelated ideas such that:
> ❑ causality is about constant conjunction (whenever A follows B follows)
> ❑ the properties of entities are independent
> ❑ their relations are external or non-necessary
> ❑ the basic things of the world are *atomist*, or at least constant in their inner structure
> ❑ being can be defined in terms of our perceptions or knowledge of it.

After International Relations, p. 3. Patomaki remarks:

> With Bhaskar (1986: p 226), however, I concede that: "Most of positivism is already contained and elegantly expounded in the writings of Hume".

After International Relations, p. 41.
Giddens characterizes the traditions that are loosely called *positivist* as follows:

> First, a conviction that all 'knowledge' is capable of being expressed in terms which refer in an immediate way to some reality, or aspects of reality that can be apprehended through the senses. Second, a faith that the methods and logical form of science, as epitomized in classical physics, can be applied to the study of social phenomena.

Anthony Giddens, *New Rules of Sociological Method*. Stanford: Stanford University Press, 1993. page. 136.

Capital Flight

22. Robert Isaak, *Managing World Economic Change*. Englewood Cliffs NJ: Prentice-Hall, 2000.

23. I use the phrase—*what actually happens*—to introduce a description in terms of a neo-Aristotelian theory of human action, rooted in categories drawn from ordinary language. It could be argued that all descriptions are equally theory-laden; and that no description has any more right than any other to claim the privilege of naming what actually happens. It could be argued that a description couched in operationally defined terms would be superior to my common sense naming of what actually happens because it would facilitate communication among scientists by specifying the procedures for measuring the phenomenon to be studied. It could be argued that there is no way to tell which of the infinite number of ways any given phenomenon could be described is a good description to start with until one finds out, after doing scientific research, which description leads to the most fruitful results. I do not agree with any of the three arguments that could be made.

Instead, I claim, agreeing in this respect with Peter Winch, that a description made of common basic words that function in social life, like—people who own capital move it—has a rightful priority over a description in a technical language devised for scientific purposes. It is *ground level* and a *place to begin* in a more justifiable sense than the *atomic facts* and *protocol sentences* of the positivists were. See Peter Winch, *The Idea of a Social Science* as it relates to philosophy. London: Routledge & Paul, 1958.

The Race to the Bottom

24. Jeremy Brecher, Tim Costello, and Brendan Smith, *Globalization from Below*. Cambridge MA: South End Press, 2000. page. 5.

25. Jeffrey Winters, *Power in Motion: Capital Mobility and the Indonesian State*. Ithaca NY: Cornell University Press, 1996.

The Growth Imperative

26. John Maynard Keynes, *General Theory of Employment, Interest, and Money*. New York: Harcourt Brace, 1936. p. 27

27. John Maynard Keynes, quoted by E. F. Schumacher, *Small is Beautiful*. New York: Harper & Row,
1973. p. 20.

The Holocaust

28. *Triangulating Peace*, p. 122.

29. Karin Knorr Cetina, "Objectual Practice," in Theodore Schatzki, Karin Knorr Cetina, and Eike von Savigny (eds.), *The Practice Turn in Contemporary Theory*. London: Routledge, 2001. p. 184.

30. Roy Bhaskar, *Scientific Realism and Human Emancipation*. London: Verso (New Left Books), 1986. p. 122-23.

31. Bhaskar, op. cit. p. 123.

Transforming Rules, Relationships, and Practices

32. Jean Piaget, *Structuralism*. New York: Basic Books, 1970. Piaget discusses the use of the term by Claude Levi-Strauss, Noam Chomsky, and many others. Anthony Giddens has discussed social structure thoroughly. The glossary at the end of his *The Constitution of Society* defines structuration, structural principles, structural properties, structure, and structures, as well as related terms such as *system*. Anthony Giddens, *The Constitution of Society*. Berkeley: University of California Press, 1984. pp. 376-377. See also the discussions of structure in his *New Rules of Sociological Method: A Positive Critique of Interpretive Sociologies*. New York: Harper & Row, 1976; and *Central Problems in Social Theory: Action, Structure, and Contradiction in Social Analysis*. Berkeley: University of California

Press, 1979. Almost all of his books say something about the concept of structure. For critical discussions see, besides Patomaki, C. G. A. Bryant and D. Jary (eds.) Giddens' *Theory of Structuration: A Critical Appreciation*. London: Routledge, 1990; Ira J. Cohen, *Structuration Theory: Anthony Giddens and the Constitution of Social Life*. London: Macmillan, 1989.

33. *After International Relations*, p. 117

34. Ludwig Wittgenstein, *Philosophical Investigations*. New York: Macmillan, 1953. Throughout, and especially paragraphs: 31, 54, 81-87, 100-103, 133, 146-155 (rule and principle), 200-202, 206-08, 227-238, 380.

35. Hannah Arendt, *On Violence*. New York: Harcourt Brace & World, 1970. Arendt's analysis provides a theoretical account of the ineffectiveness of military hardware where there is no capacity to act in concert. It can almost be said that she described the collapse of the Soviet Union two decades before it happened.

36. Gene Sharp, *The Politics of Nonviolent Action*. Boston: Porter Sargent, 1973.

37. John R. Commons, *Legal Foundations of Capitalism*. New York: The Macmillan Company, 1939 (first published 1924). pp. 52-55.

38. *After International Relations* p. 113.

39. *After International Relations* p. 116

40. Anthony Giddens, *The Constitution of Society: Outline of a Theory of Structuration*. Cambridge: Polity Press, 1984. pp. 185-86.

41. *After International Relations* p. 117

42. H. L. A. Hart, The Concept of Law. Oxford: Clarendon Press, 1961.

43. J. L. Brierly, *The Law of Nations: an introduction to the international law of peace*. Oxford: Clarendon Press, 1949. p. 73.

44. M. K. Gandhi, *My Socialism*. Ahmedabad, India: Navajivan Publishing House, 1959. p. 30.

45. Betty Reardon, *Sexism and the War System*. New York: Teachers College Press, 1985.

46. *After International Relations*, p. 158

47. See the critique of Pareto's (causally efficacious) residues and (ineffective) derivatives in Winch's *The Idea of a Social Science* p. 103 ff. In agreement with Patomaki and partially in agreement with Winch, I wage a never-ending struggle against a prejudice entrenched in the social sciences since, at least, Condorcet. Thus, it has been assumed that: what lends itself to mathematical treatment and/or analysis in terms of self-interest is deemed material, while what lends itself to discussion in natural languages and in the languages of the religious and ethical belief-systems that have guided human cultures is deemed idealistic. I argue that the opposite is, in fact, true: language-guided practice is our material reality; mathematical models are abstract ideas, at least, until they become incorporated into technology.

48. Although I have made the point that social structures and rules are centrally involved in Patomaki's account of social causality, I have not attempted to summarize it. He summarizes it as follows:

> The notions of context and complex form the core of CR methodology. According to def. 1, cause is an insufficient but necessary part of a condition that is itself unnecessary but sufficient for the production of a result, i.e. the INUS condition. There are five necessary social components in any causal complex (K) capable of producing events, episodes, tendencies and the like, namely: • actors (AR)• regulative and constitutive rules (RU) • resources as competencies and faculties (RE) • relational and positional practices (PRA) • and meaningful action (AN). Also, actors and their characteristic logics of action are historically constituted. These related and interdependent components along with the emergent powers and properties of consequent social systems together create the sufficient but unnecessary complex for the production of a result. Hence, there is never a single cause and always a causal complex exists: K = [AR, RU, RE, PRA, AN] perhaps including emergent properties and powers. *After International Relations* p. 119.

49. Gunnar Myrdal, *Beyond the Welfare State*. New Haven: Yale University Press, 1960. p. 36.

50. For accounts of the structural problems encountered by Swedish social democracy see my *The Revenge of the Iron Law of Wages*, Chapter 8 of *The Dilemmas of Social Democracies* available on my web site www.howardri.org, and the works cited there in the footnotes; Chapter 9 of *After International Relations* and the works there cited; and, generally, the Marxist literature on regimes of accumulation and their crises discussed and cited by David Harvey in *The Condition of Postmodernity*. Oxford: Blackwell, 1990.

Review Questions

Peace

1. "Deutsch is right in rejecting the so-called *realist position*: war understood as the product of anarchy among sovereign states…" P 231 What does that description mean to you?

b. Compare and contrast the Deutsch statement with the recent reality that nine of ten wars are civil wars. If you think Deutsch should amend his statement, how would you have him re-write it?

2. What would you think might be the ingredients for the recipe of a pluralist security community (p.s.c)? Use the US, Canada, Mexico, and Cuba as a test case.

b. What do you see as the need to be recognized by all four countries as the basis for a p.s.c?

c. What structure do you think the p.s.c. would consist of in its fully functional form? P 229

3. As a conceptual metaphor, what does the word *building* [as peace building] represent as a vital element for the peace process? A building might accommodate many of these—virtual structures—in this case peace structures. In its association with the concept of peace, the word *building,* thus is at once a verb and its resultant noun.

Truth

4. In your opinion, what role does truth and or Truth play in relation to peace building?

b. Are both truth and Truth always positive peace players?

c. What is your sense of why truth in peace building is vital, though maligned based on your sense of human nature? P 232-233

d. In your view, why might some scholars and leaders see truth as unimportant in the peace process?

d. Should the definitions of truth be modified for the purposes of peace building?

e. Who are the actors in the peace building who should be charged with bearing the truth to the process?

5. In the—prediction of peace for a nation, what are the liberal-Kantian variables that when present show that peace will, in fact, occur? P 235

6. What is your sense of the importance of the primary goals of the *critical realist principles:* 1) returning truth to its logical status as the standard and 2) reorienting the social sciences to engage in a critique of social structures? P 233

7. "Perhaps the most important and controversial point underlying Patomaki's logical plan is that social science research can contribute to peaceful change by a systematic critique of current beliefs." What do you think makes that a controversy? P 232

b. In what context and or from whose interests does the critique of belief become a problem?

Structure

8. How would you envisage the structure-based approach of the realist sociology contrasting with mainstream ideas especially as it comes to us through the news media? P 239

9. "Patomaki's critical realist approach is superior in giving persuasive reasons why such simplistic conclusions should be avoided." Describe the critical realist approach as it applies to building peace in the midst of tension and conflict. P 240

b. What effect does structure have on the processes of peacemaking and peace building?

c. Compare the structural flaws within the institutions allowing war with those allowing the global economy to proceed unaccountably.

d. Do you see the institutions involved with peacemaking and economics as largely the same? Do you associate economic institutions more with warmongering?

e. Which institutions do you think are involved with peacemaking?

f. In your opinion, rate (scale: 1 to 5), the following economic institutions in terms of peacemaking: • the CIA • trade orgs (WTO, NAFTA) • World Bank or IMF • NATO, an oil cartel • any global resource cartel • the UN Security Council • an economic development institution • World Court • a UN research institution • a UN aid institution • an NGO economic justice / peace research and action.

Capital Flight

10. What role do you see capital flight playing in the drama of peace, especially within the context of developing and third world economies? Capital flight is a child of the global economy and modernity.

b. Do you think that is because the world has become more compliant for the owners of capital? P 241

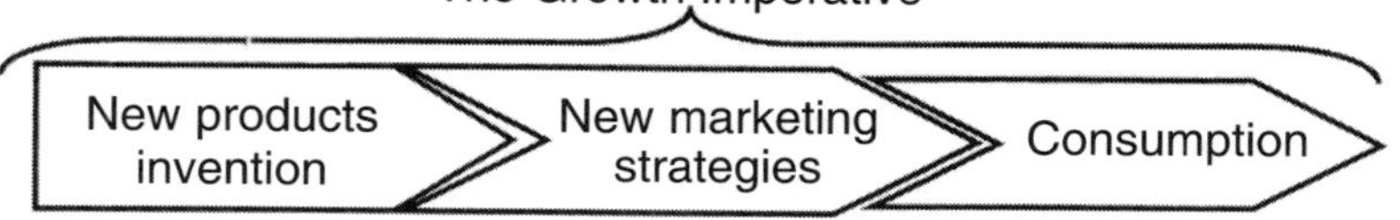

11. Describe how capital flight within a country would likely bring the tension necessary to cause civil unrest.
12. Support the idea that capital flight is the twin villain of—wealth to poverty disparity—and its oppression of workers and consumers. Can one exist without the other?
b. Can you cite examples (current, recent, or distant) of civil conflicts caused by the structures that authorize capital flight, wealth to poverty disparity, and violation of worker human rights?

The Race to the Bottom

13. Would you define capital flight and race to the bottom as two aspects of same fact, or do you see one occurring without the other?
14. What relationship do you see between capital flight and the race to the bottom?
15. What role does collusion between corporations and the government play in fostering the conditions for tension and conflict?
16. How much less likely would tension and conflict be if governments did not create conditions favorable for capital to roost?
17. Could the complicity of capital and government occur in a true democracy?
18. How might you envisage the race to the bottom turning around to become a march to the top in which nations cooperate to achieve social and environmental objectives?
b. What, in your view, is the single-most important approach or requisite to turning the race around?

The Growth Imperative

19. What is your sense of the growth imperative as the impetus for the race to the bottom?
20. To what degree do you think the growth imperative urges capital to flee?
21. What are the business panaceas for the growth imperative? Hint: two of the three panaceas are advertiser driven, which costs consumers and the environment dearly.
22. How might you argue against the growth imperative? Some

keywords might include: • counterproductive • deceptive • intangible goals • unsustainable • no objective • destructive ethics.

23. Maintaining islands of high wages in a world sea of low wages requires keeping growth going year after year, which requires the endless development of new products. What do you see as the growth or non-growth alternative(s) to growth via new product technologies? p 245

24. *Research and development* for new products requires keeping technological leads and enticing investors, which is not easy. What alternative do you think a nation and the world as a whole might use instead?

25. Consider so-called economic growth in the modern world. Describe how you see it in contrast to the growth of a skill or art for joy and beauty, or the economic growth of nature?

The Holocaust

For critical realism, the route to preventing the recurrence of holocaust-like events is more than one of gauging causal factors that are linked to violence.

26. In your judgment, what must be done first to prevent the genocides and holocausts of our so-called economy? p 246

b. What ways are you aware of or practice to make that happen?

c. Do you think reparations and apologies are a symbolic help? If not, how would your describe their effect upon society?

d. What is your sense of the current global economic powers vis-à-vis genocide and holocaust?

Transforming Rules, Relationships, and Practices

27. What two questions would you ask to know the composition of the structure of a society, its design? p 250

28. What advantages do you see in placing rules as a central theme of a social science?

29. What is your opinion of "the thesis that power trumps rules, which seems to be correct from the viewpoint of mainstream political science?" What value is contained in the fact that military power trumps rules more easily than economic power? p 252 Can you site an example of temporal nature of that fact? What global trend in the 20th century is making this fact a moot one?

30. What bookkeeping rule defines homo economicus? p 260

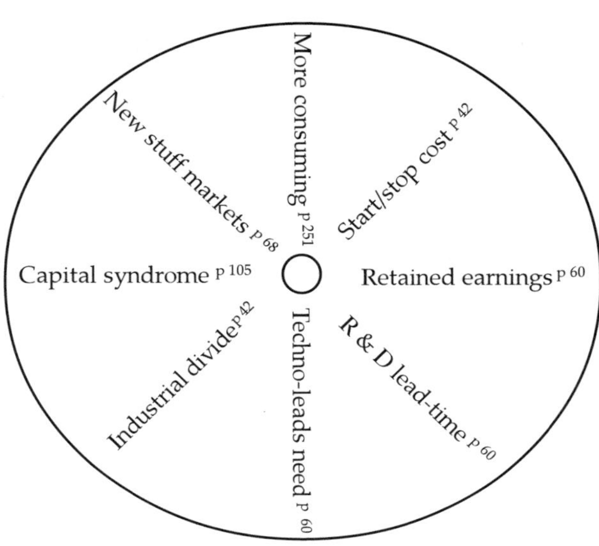

Treadmill of Growth

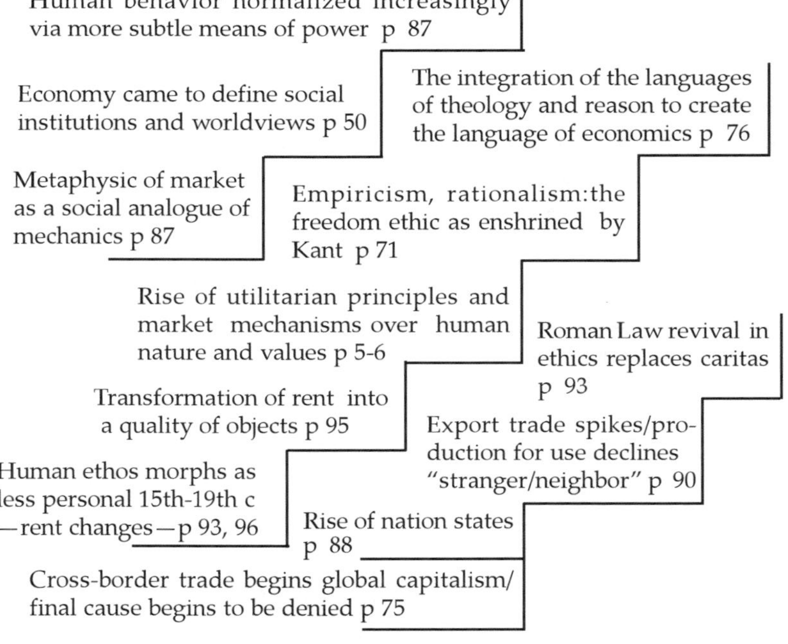

Global Trends through History (*basis of treadmill*)

To: Mr. Alfred Verrecchia Chief Executive Officer Hasbro, Inc. 1027 Newport Avenue, Pawtucket, RI 02862

Dear Mr. Verrecchia:

Hello, my name is Savannah Cooley; I am nine years old. My sister Claire, who is seven, owns six of the Hasbro *My Little Ponies* and has much fun playing with them. She wants five more of the ponies for her friends. My dad will help me now to say what I feel.

Our family is careful about what we buy because we consider each purchase a "vote." We spend money carefully, and want to vote with each purchase for a better world—not only for our kids, but also for the people who make the things we buy. We are writing to request information about the working conditions of the people in China who make the *My Little Ponies* toys. We would like Hasbro Inc. to assure us that the workers who make the ponies are:

- paid a living wage
- working adults age eighteen or older
- have break times
- have comfortable environments to work in.

Please let us know the facts of these matters, so that we may make our choice accordingly.

Our family feels inspired by the work of the youth in the group **Kids can Free the Children** http://freethechildren.com; we feel called to help their cause. In addition, four of our friends signed this letter because they, as well, need to know your response, or lack of it, to this inquiry. Please work in partnership with us for a better world.

Sincerely,

The Cooley family with Sanderson Beck, Jeannie Clark, David Faubion, and Charlotte Warren

Cc: Craig Kielburger/ founder: Kids Can Free the Children
Cc: Marc Kielburger/ cofounder of Leaders Today

See http://global-economy.info for the Hasbro response and follow

Index

A

A Contemporary Critique of Historical Materialism 187
Absent cause 124
Absolute wealth 183
Accounting causality 64
Accumulation 75, 100, 107–109, 112, 114, 125, 130, 132, 136, 140–145, 205, 224, 230
, progressive 105
Africa 108, 114, 134, 136, 138, 181
African cultures, destruction of 130
After International Relations 233, 234, 236, 242, 243, 268, 269
Agape 91
Agriculture 87, 136, 220
Alienation 111, 113, 119, 183, 255
Althusser, Louis 101, 122, 125–127, 147
Amin, Samir 136, 138
Ancient cultural cosmologies 50
Ancient Futures: Learning from the Ladaka 40
Ancient Greece 49, 73, 123, 178
ideals 100, 104
pre-market institutions 223
Anomie 8, 9
Anthropology 51
Anti-essentialism 122–125, 149, 189
Anti-Keynesian trend 66
Anunciar 162
Aquinas, St. Thomas 69, 114, 127, 202
patriarchal/naive way 148
Arbeitskraft 181
Archai 148
Argentina 24
Aristotle 13, 29, 32, 37, 45, 69, 71, 73, 74, 78, 101, 103, 112, 114, 116, 122, 123, 127, 138–140, 147, 150, 183, 211
patriarchal/naive way 148
Asia 85
Atomist 271
Augustine, St. 116, 202
patriarchal/naive way 148
Australian coalmines 141
Auto-centric accumulation 136
Autonomy 136, 154
Ayer, Sir Alfred 31
Ayni ruway 178

B

Ballot box 21
Barter 86, 91, 202, 223
Bateson, Mary 46
Baudrillard, Jean 191
Bauer, P. T. 167
Baumol, William 28
Behavioral economics 103
Bentham, Jeremy 7, 15, 35
Benevolence 219, 220, 230
Bioneer 40
Bionetwork 192
Bionomics 160
Biotechnology 226
Bluestone, Barry 21
Bourgeois 103, 104, 120
Brazil 24, 28, 78
Britain 61, 63, 89, 110, 114, 193, 214
Buddhism 46
Bund 178
Burke, Edmund 76
Burma 110

C

Cambodia 200
Cambridge 214
Canclini, Garcia 135
Canon law 92, 102

Capital 14, 106
Capital accumulation, global logic 108
Capital and Communities 21, 34
Capital, by Marx 36–38, 78, 101, 104, 149, 181, 183, 207
Capital flight 245–248, 259, 261, 272
Capital investment 60, 136, 193
mobility 20, 22, 30, 31
outlays 105
personified 109
syndrome 105
Capital-intensive 1, 61
Capitalism 6, 27, 65, 68, 103, 106, 108, 109, 112, 123, 140, 141, 149, 183, 185, 222
, constitutive rules of 205
, global expansion of 105
, instability of 159
Capitalist economic categories 204
economy 141, 185
global economy 140, 143, 150
market economy 112, 185
production 105, 181
society 103, 112, 202
world economy 20, 90, 97, 150
Capra, Fritjof 183
Care ethic vii, 45, 55, 211
Caritas 74, 91, 97, 102, 117
Carnap, Rudolf 31
Causal explanation 59
factors xiv
mechanism 22, 145
models 125, 145, 148
powers 13, 33, 124, 149, 152
Causality, linear concept of 41
Cause 23, 31, 41, 58, 63, 73, 84 – 86, 88, 125
and effect 89, 123, 124
and effect mechanisms 131
archai 147
Chavez, Cesar 165
Childcare 111, 141, 165, 228
China xiii, 49, 181
Choice 8
code 8
Chrematistics 78
Christian Democrat 200
Chronic excess capacity 42
Church of the Savior 194
Circular and cumulative causation 59, 61, 70
Circulation 104, 113, 149
of commodities 36, 183
of money 183
Civilizations 10, 49, 72, 103
Classical economics 7, 77, 103, 109
market theory 103
Clothing 12
Collective bargaining 44, 48, 166, 222
Colombia 129
programs 128
Colonial rule 26, 92, 107, 110, 153
Command structure 49, 75
Commerce, laws of 76
Commodity 64, 96, 103, 111, 115, 149
exchange 220, 222-3, 226
form 149
law of value 190
Commodity-Money-Commodity 78–81, 202
Common law of commerce 92
Communism 132, 133
Comparative advantage xv, 1–4, 6 –9, 12, 14, 22, 38, 43, 47, 59, 129, 175, 205
Competition of capitals 103
Competitive markets 6
Comprehensive conceptual system 112
Concept of Law, The 261
Concordia 91
Conflict resolution 234
transformation 234

Conscience 169, 200, 209
Consciousness-raising 202
Constitutive 140
rules 11, 202, 205, 260
Constitutivity 147
Consumer choice 9, 46, 48, 185
goods, low-wage 58
power 43
Contradiction and Over-determination 125, 126
Contradictions 103, 104, 124, 181-185, 204
Contributing factor 85
Corn Laws 129, 185
Corporate-welfare state 81
Correlates of War 253
Correlates of War Project 240
Cosmology 37, 69, 133
Cost of production 105
Counter-cyclical budgets 65
Counter-cyclical spending 66, 159
Course in General Linguistics 187
Cripps, Sir Stafford 200
Critical mass 165, 166
realism 233, 236, 237, 240, 242, 244, 254, 268, 275
Cuba 181
Cultural anthropology 187
Cultural Expression and Grassroots Development 199
Cultural structures 83, 84, 113, 130, 134, 162, 171–173, 185, 193, 194, 209
Culture 12, 51, 72, 83, 160, 170, 171
of solidarity 166
Currency devaluations 159
Curtains of meaning 191

D

Dani, of Indonesia 12
Dante's hell: modern cities 40
David Ricardo 2
Day, Dorothy 205
De-alienation 111
Debs, Eugene 205
Decentralized 69
Deconstruction 138
of development 128
Deficit spending 159
Deflation 63
Deindustrialization 205
Deleuze, Eugene 135
Deliberate action 109, 148
Demand 42, 43
Democracy 51, 141, 154, 177, 178
Denmark 185
Denunciar 162
Deontic ethics 9
Derrida, Jacques 31, 124, 152
Desarrollo Rural Integral (DRI) 130
Descartes, Rene 73, 86
Design revolution 45, 49, 50
Deutsch, Karl 233–236, 251, 253
Deutschmarks 65
Development discourse 128, 130–132, 134, 136–138
economics 133
planning 132
Dharma and Development, a Study of Sarvodaya Shram 199
Diachronic 187, 189, 191, 195
linguistics 187
Diachrony 138
Dualisms 113
Dumont, Louis 10
Dutch 12
Dutch Oost Indische Companie, The 89
Dynamis 75

E

Earth ethic vii
Eastern civilization 193
Ecclesia 178
Eco-friendly technologies 40, 51
Ecological Design 40
Ecological design 52, 53, 205
niche 12, 160
norms 68

Ecology 29, 38, 160, 193
Economic activity 66, 72, 112, 193, 219
actors 13, 48
factors 1, 12
fundamentalism 160, 175
growth 2, 65–68, 132
ideology 10, 17, 199
metaphysic 31, 127, 199
policies 44, 47, 142
Economic power 41, 162, 173
revolutions 181
society 10, 50
society, worldview of 199
stability 80, 142
theory 4, 14, 16, 47, 64, 70, 73, 92, 159, 187, 207
Effective demand 13, 62, 68, 131, 168
Efficiency 1, 28, 60, 168
Efficient cause 70, 74–76
Egoism 162, 209
Egypt 86, 138
Ehrenreich, Barbara 107
Eisler, Riane 158, 177
Ekins, Paul 52
El Salvador 13
Elizabeth Anscombes terminology 191
Emancipatory research 237, 263, 268
science 263
Empirical generalization 199
Empiricist 50, 71, 245-6, 264, 271
Employees 21
Employers 62
Employment 60, 62- 64, 68
Enabling condition 22
Enclosure movement 87, 130
Encountering Development 122, 135
Energy budget 47
Energy-intensive 84
England 7, 70, 83, 86, 92, 93, 130, 218
Enlargement of markets 90
Enlarging markets 85
Enlightenment 114, 125
humanism 100
metaphysic 127
Epidemiological method 240
Episteme: craft knowledge 49
Epistemological relativism 242
Epistemology 13, 69, 91, 124, 129
, realist 137
Equality 28, 36, 100, 104, 225
, gender 135
Equivalence, law of 191
Erhard, Ludwig 200
Escobar, Arturo 122, 128, 131, 132, 134, 136, 137
Essentialism 123, 144
Essentialist 122, 124, 131, 134, 140, 143, 145, 147
Ethic of autonomy 136
Ethical global economy 158
philosophy 10, 26
principles 5, 27, 52
skepticism 29, 47
structure 36, 130
Ethics 5, 9, 11, 13, 16, 27, 29, 35, 36, 46, 48, 50, 53, 55, 69, 75, 83, 90–92, 101, 116, 119, 128, 129, 135, 153, 154, 211, 219, 227, 229
Ethics of virtue, 193
Ethnology 110
Etymology of *economy* 50
Europe 2, 5, 63, 73, 85, 87, 88, 92, 165, 181, 218, 219
Europe, medieval 83, 90
European culture 170
Evaluation of Cultural Action, The 199
Exchange 222, 227
process 62, 104, 183, 195
value 105, 111, 113, 191, 192, 205, 219, 222
value of work 191, 192
Expanding markets 92
Expansion of markets 70
of US industry 24
Expansionist prescriptions 65
Explain 123
Explanan 2, 3, 41, 59, 86, 89,

104, 107, 108, 132
Explananda 2
Explanandum 3, 5, 14, 21–23, 41, 85, 89, 104, 107, 132
Explanation 23, 240, 241, 270
, paradigmatic Enlightenment notion of 125
scientific 3, 26, 73-4, 107
Explanatory principle 5, 101, 109, 149
Exploitation 104, 107, 140, 205
Export lead 70
Export-led growth 2, 67
Extension of markets 84
External aid 132

F

Factors 3, 109, 125, 185, 207
of production 1, 2
Faux, Jeff 224
Feminism 100, 162
Feminization of poverty 130
Final cause 74, 75, 147
causes 70
Findhorn 40
First principles 138
Flexible accumulation 106
Ford Inc. 29
Foreign markets 70
Foucault, Michel 87, 100, 122, 125, 132, 135–137
France 61, 83
Frank, Andre 130
Free choices 54
Free competitive markets 167, 168
enterprise system 132
Free market economic theory 158
market ideology 177
markets 7, 52, 66, 220
trade 7, 9, 27, 28, 59, 61, 214, 226
Free-floating exchange rates 44
Freedom 6, 9, 26, 64, 104, 135, 193, 209
Freire, Paulo 203
French revolution 90
Friedman, Milton 102, 103
Fuller, R. Buckminster 29, 40, 45, 48, 51, 52, 134, 205

G

Galileo 23
Gandhi 46, 60, 158, 172, 179, 213, 220, 262, 264
Gaudium 91
Geertz, Clifford 49
Gemeinschaft 10, 92
General Motors 43
Germany 2, 61, 108, 216
Gesellschaft 10, 92
Giddens, Anthony 83, 216, 255, 256, 259, 260, 273
Gilligan, Carol 149, 158, 211
Global capital mobility 31
capitalism 106, 138, 139, 177, 187
economic regime 106
economy xiii, xiv, xv, 1, 27, 30–33, 41, 55, 60, 64, 72, 75, 78, 85, 90–93, 100, 101, 105, 107, 109, 110, 113, 114, 128, 139, 140–143, 145, 150, 158, 165, 170, 172, 174, 175, 183, 185, 187, 195, 199, 202, 205, 217
Global factory 20, 33
forces 131, 173
institution 27
labor 26
Global market 1, 20, 60, 150, 176
market economy 173
mobility 20
nature of economic power 173
network 132
patterns of trade 20
quasi-machine 33
trade in labor 26
transformation movement 199

village 26
Globalization 24, 29, 255
Globalization from Below 246
Globalization of production 20, 24, 27–32, 43, 58, 73, 185, 195, 205
God 221
Gold 65, 79, 176
Government intervention 6, 64
Grammatology, a Metaphysic of Presence 124
Greed 6, 162
as a value 75
Green growth 67, 68
technology 41, 48
Gross domestic product 8, 47
inequality 224, 226
Growth 10, 15, 26, 60, 63, 67, 78–80, 83, 86, 87, 133, 153, 160, 185, 207, 211, 215, 224, *250*
ideal 67

H

Habermas, Jurgen 66, 242, 263, 270
Hampshire, Stuart 101, 116
Harre, Rom 33, 101, 124, 149
Harrison, Bennett 21
Hart, H. L. A. 203
Harvey, David 105
Hecksher, Ely 59
Hegemony 128, 138, 140, 178
Henderson, Hazel 8, 29, 141, 205
Hermeneutics 241, 246
Hill, Christopher 74
Historical discontinuity 83–85, 88, 89, 91, 92
explanations 43
Hobbes, Thomas 73, 86, 234
Holland 88, 185
Holocaust 251–253, 273
Holocaust-like event 252
Homo economicus 77, 102, 103, 117, 164, 183, 185, 211
sapiens 47, 49, 67, 191
Howe, Candace 58
Human action 11, 73, 103, 116, 148, 149, 194, 202, 205, 216
Human Action: a Treatise on Economics 16
Human choice 227
economic systems 47
habitats 51
nature 6, 123, 162
planning of socialism 185
rights 45, 166, 200, 227
species 48, 111, 134, 195
suffering 134
welfare 6, 96
Human-friendly technology 51
Humanism 100
Humanitarian values 169
Humanity 7
Hume, David 73, 75, 243, 245
Huntington, Samuel 12

I

Iberian Peninsula 89
Idealism 113, 127
Ideals 114
Ideological distortion of reality 125
justification 86
Ideology 5, 10, 73, 75, 103, 108
ILO 163
India 49, 167
Indigenous cultures 227
Individualism xiv, 10
Indonesia 12, 13, 221
Industrial divide 42
economies 44
policy 42, 44, 61, 66, 222
revolution 83, 86
Industrialization 61, 132, 136
, deliberate 132
Inequality 224–226
Inflation 12, 65
Instability 8, 43, 183, 222
Institutional structure of modern society 11

Institutionalizing peaceful change 235
Instrumental rationality 70, 72
Insurance 21
Integral development 133
Integrated Rural Development 128
International division of labor 22, 25, 106, 185
division of labor theory, the new 58
market xiv, 129
Monetary Fund (IMF) 172, 176, 194, 195, 223
trade vi, 10, 16, 25, 30, 40, 59, 61, 70, 88, 100, 101, 125, 187, 205
International trade theory viii, 14, 92
Internationalism 145
Interpretation and the Sciences of Man, 11
Investors 24
Invisible hand of the market 219
Isolationist 136
Italy 61

J

James, Thomas 74
Jameson, Fredric 124, 144
Japan 2, 4, 12, 28, 30, 42, 61, 70, 79, 108
Japanese trade surplus 12, 13
Job security 21, 106
Jubilee, ancient biblical principle 177
Judeo-Christian 219
Judgmental rationalism 242
Jung, Carl 124, 135, 151
Jusgentium, law of all nations 92
Just price 71, 76, 86, 91, 97
Justice 36, 68, 73, 104, 116, 119, 158, 174, 175, 211, 229

K

Kaldor, Nicholas xv, 59, 60, 63 - 68, 76, 102
Kalos 211
Kant, Immanuel 26, 32, 35, 69, 71, 114, 136, 216
Kantian ethics 5
Kerala, India 53
Keynes, John Maynard 59
Keynesian 222
economics 43, 45, 64
King Jr., Martin Luther 171, 205, 213, 214, 216, 217, 221, 226
Kleymeyer, Charles 199
Koinonia 178

L

Labor 1
control, system of 108
costs 3, 20, 21, 25, 129
force 60, 108
Labor force, feminization of the 129
, global division of 107
market 181, 183
movement 165
Party 200
power 36, 104, 105, 181, 183
theory of value, the 100, 104, 183
unions 6, 30, 48, 165, 178, 187
unions voting 21
Labor-intensive 2, 58, 61
goods 1
Lacan, Jacques 124, 127, 189
Landlords 94
Lange, Oskar 185
Language as a market, a xv
games 33, 202, 209
Language-game 103
Lappé, Frances Moore 215
Latin America 58, 153, 162, 199
Law of commerce, Roman 92
of Nations, The 261
Laws of profit 143
Left ideologies 142
Legal Foundations of Capitalism 258
Legitimation Crisis, The 66

Liberal-Kantian theories 240
Liberalism 169
Liberation theology 162
Lilly Drugs Inc. 60
Lindblom, Charles 83
Linguistics 187, 189
Living wage 2, 22, 83, 281
Loans 6, 92, 102, 223
Local economies xiv, 53
Locke, John 70, 86
Longue Duree 83
Lovins, Amory 46
Low wage areas 58
Loyola, St. Ignatius 199

M

MacDonaldized world 24
Machinelike 128, 138
MacIntyre, Alasdair 148
Macpherson, C. B. 73
Macro-level 63, 128
Macro-management 66, 267
Macroeconomic policies 266
 principles 205
Macroeconomics in the Global Economy 239
Magic of the market *219*
Malaysia 26
Maldevelopment: Anatomy of a Global Failure 154
Malthus, Thomas 214
Managers 21, 25, 95, 185
Managing World Economic Change 245
Mansfield, Lord 89
Manufacturing trade deficit 58
Maquiladoras 27
Maritain, Jacques 200
Market as a language 187
 as a language, a xv
 behavior 71, 130
 demand 42, 48
 forces 23, 24, 26, 32, 33, 41, 43, 50, 73, 75, 163
 individualism 178
 mechanisms 6, 64, 185, 223
 model 167
 phenomena 74
 rationality 53, 167
 value 104
Market-leading/market-led 86
Market relationships 178, 218
Market-snafu prevention 223
Marketing 3, 20, 61, 68
Markets 6, 41, 85–87, 105, 167
Markusen, Ann 58
Marx 17, 36, 67, 78, 83, 96, 101–104, 107, 109, 110, 113, 118, 127, 130, 141, 143, 149–152, 169, 181, 183, 185, 187, 191, 194, 205
Marxian concept 111
Marxist 100
 metaphysic 113
 metaphysical bias 112, 113
 paradigms 147
 revolutionaries 113
 terminology 183
 theories 100
 tradition 114, 149
Mass production 42, 44, 45, 48
 production technology 41–44
Mater 178
Materialistic individualism xiv
Matrix 31
Mechanical metaphors 11
 root metaphors 125
Mechanism 48, 87, 107, 145, 191
 of accumulation 145
Mechanistic metaphysics 11
Meiji restoration 42
Merchant, Carolyn 107
Merck 2
Mesoamerica 49
Meta-economics 46, 73, 80
Meta-language 209
Meta-narrative 151, 209
Metaphysic 33
 of economic society 10, 69, 73, 199, 202, 203

of rent 93
(s) 37, 49
: defined 12
Metaphysical 32, 33
shift 10, 11, 55, 200, 202, 211
Metaphysic, replace extant 74
Metaphysic, surrogate 119
Metaphysics, economic justification for 31
Methodology of economic science 102
Mexico 27
Mies, Maria 100, 106, 108–111
Mill, John Stuart 7, 26, 32, 59
Minor inefficiency 32
Mishel, Larry 224
Mobile capital 247
Modern global economy 83-4, 107
ideals 100
Western civilization 193
Modernity 100, 149
Modernization 70
Mollison, Bill 46
Monetarist 63
Money 8, 12, 13, 27, 40, 43, 50, 62–65, 70, 72, 78, 86, 94, 101–105, 110, 118, 130, 140, 142, 150, 163, 168, 172, 176, 181, 183, 195, 205, 209
Money-Commodities- Money 183
Money, owners of 181, 203
Monolithic system 143, 150
Mother Teresa 205
Multicultural 28, 170
Multinational corporations 25
Myrdal, Gunnar 59, 70

N

Natural framework 192
Natural resources 1
worth 112, 113
Nature 29, 80, 97, 115, 117, 138, 193, 208, 227
Naylor, Larry 12, 13
Negative growth 225
Neo-Keynesian xv, 59
Neoclassical economic theory 10
economics 1, 5, 6, 8, 10, 13, 59, 61, 64
economists 59, 65
opponents 69
trade theory 1
Neoliberal 66, 172, 175
economic fundamentalism 160
economics 163
global corporate 163
philosophy 176
trend 177
Neoliberalism 47, 65, 106, 130, 224
Netherlands, The 83, 88-9, 97, 160
New products process 68
Newton, Sir Isaac 75, 86
Noddings, Nel 149, 164
Non-Western cultures 134
Nonaction 165
Noncausal 205
Nonexistence 32, 139
Nonprofit 30, 103, 141, 161, 228
Nonviolent transformation 194
Norberg-Hodge, Helena 205
North Korea 181
North Sea oil 63
Nussbaum, Martha 148

O

Official industrial policies 222
Of Grammatology 124
Ohlin, Bertil 59
Oiko-nomos 78
On Violence 193
Ontological realism 242
OPEC oil cartel 44, 12, 13
Opportunity cost 183, 185, 207
Optimism, plausible 159
Orderly selfishness 218
Ousia 123
Outlay 62, 71, 105

Over-determination 123, 125–127, 145, 147

P

PAN 130
Paradigm 74, 96, 107, 125, 148
Pareto optimality 9
Pareto, Vilfredo 69, 102
Pareto-optimize 168
Partnership relationships 177
Patomaki, Heikki 233–240, 242–245, 251, 255–256, 259–261, 263, 266, 268, 269
Patriarchal 27, 107, 123, 135, 141, 148
Patriarchy 108
Patriarchy and Accumulation on a World Scale 100, 106
Peace of Westphalia 88
Peking 67
Per-capita growth 224
Perceived risk 246
Perennial philosophy 213
Performative force 140, 147
performance 147
Permaculture 40, 177
Perot, Ross 65
Personal autonomy 28, 135
Pharmaceutical industry in the US 60
Philosophical Investigation 202, *256*
theories 83, 87
Philosophy 49, 69
of education 162
Physical reality 8
Physics 22
Pigou-optimize 168
Piore, Michael 41
Planet Neighborhood 40
Planning model 167
Plato 49, 219
Pluralist security community 234
Polarization 61
Policy instruments 266
Political Community and the North Atlantic Area 234 - 236
Political economy 7, 9, 74, 95, 102, 103, 120
Political Economy of Growth, The 114
Political theories 83
Portugal 2, 88
Positive alternatives 194, 208, 210
reinforcement 3
Positivist 254, 264, 271
Post-Marxism 145
Post-structuralism 122, 135, 137, 138
Post-structuralist anthropological approach 131
Potlatch 30
Poverty 133, 136, 137, 162, 183, 194, 205, 213, 214, 216, 217, 221–223, 226, 228
Poverty, de-politicize 137
Poverty of Historicism, The 241
Power 257, 261
, balance of 234
, economic 257 – 259, 261, 264
, productive 259, 260
Praxis 148
Pre-market correction 223
Preferred choices 8
Primitive accumulation *107*
Principia Mathematica 75, 80
Private property 11, 23, 41, 94, 178, 185, 199, 205, 227
Privatization 166
Product development for export 61
markets 1, 2
Production of Commodities by Means of Commodities 185
Productive efficiency 1
power relations 261
Productivity growth 250
Profit imperative 227
Profits 21, 29, 129, 132, 140, 142, 143, 153, 161, 163, 185, 199, 214, 224, 226
Proletariat 203
Property 22, 24, 26, 31, 32, 104
and contract, the laws of

203
rights 22, 26, 31, 32, 50, 66, 87, 195
Protections 222
Protective tariffs 61
Psychological fact 249
manipulation, methods of 108
Psychology 62, 94
of the community *249*
Purchasing power 62, 65, 131
Puritan ethic 136

Q

Quality of objects 96
Quasi-explanans 132
Quasi-machine 7, 32, 33, 126
Quasi-mechanism 22, 23, 27, 32, 49, 86, 87, 187, 193
Quasi-mechanisms 205
Quine, Willard van Orman 124

R

Race to the Bottom 246–249, 261, 263, 265, 272–273
Racism 123
Radical empiricist 221, 228
Radio 43
Rational 127, 191
Rationalism 71
Rationalist 127
theories 50
Realism 102, 125, 138, 151, 176
Realist position 236
Realpolitik 240
Reclaim reality 238
Regimes of accumulation 105, 267
Rent 93–95
Rent, Ricardo's theory of 95
Resource constraints 45
Resources 256, 258–260, 267, 274
, control of 261, 264
Responsive, mutually 236
Responsiveness 235
Retained earnings 60
Revealed choices 8, 29, 47, 50, 54
Revenues 29, 43, 62, 223
Ricardo, David 2, 14, 95, 98, 153, 185, 214
Rice 13
Right livelihood 46
Risk 246
Robinson, Joan 67
Romero, Oscar Archbishop 233
Rule of law 235, 252
Rules 238, 239, 242, 254, 256–260, 262–265, 268–270, 274
, primary 261, 262
, secondary 261
Ruskin, John 200
Russian revolution 126

S

Sabel, Charles 41
Sales 62, 202
Samizdat 174
Samuelson, Paul 59, 143
Saturation of goods markets 44
Satyagraha 237
Saussure, Ferdinand de xiv, 122, 187-189, 190-193
Saussure's terminology 191
Schumacher, E. F. 46, 70, 73
Schumpeter, Joseph 215
Script 147
Self-determination, ethical theory of 47, 48
Self-reliance 110
Shiva, Vandana 226
Signified 187
Signified/diachronic/work 195
Signifier 187
Signifier/Synchronic/Salary 193, 195
Silver 79, 88
Singer, Peter 215
Slaves 5
Small is Beautiful 46
Smith, Adam 22, 92, 94, 97, 101, 109, 112, 115, 163, 191, 217, 218, 220, 221, 224–226

Smith, Dorothy 135
Social accounting 59, 62, 67, 71
barriers 164
behavior 11
consensus 65, 67
constructions 124
democracy 177, 178
democratic welfare 205
effort 105
evolution 181
formation 139
homologues 76
instability 8
Social issues 51, 66, 75, 100, 163
justice 33, 53, 67
machine 203
market economy 199
movement 123, 199
norms 166, 171, 211
partners 65, 66
peace 66
phenomena 11, 73
physics 59
problems 162, 205
product 100, 113, 195
production 181
psychology 102
reality 10, 145, 193
relations 50, 55, 84, 181, 185
relationship 49, 178
roles 202
rules 203, 217
safety net 175, 177, 219
Social science 10, 11, 103, 123, 125, 126, 128, 148
structure 103
structures formation 217
transformation 159, 166, 169, 193
values 191, 193
wealth 105
world 143, 194, 205
Socialist 109, 111, 165, 169, 176
planning 185
Societas 177
Sociology 83, 187
Socrates 139
Solidarity 114, 159, 163-165, 171, 173, 178, 211, 224
, ethic of 91
Soros, George 222
South Africa 70
South Korea 24
Southeast Asia 31, 58
Sovereignty 50, 136, 236
Soviet Union 112, 174
Spanish Empire 88
Specialization 1, 83, 218
of labor 7
Specialized production 60
Sphere of production 113
Spirit 213, 221
Spiritual 29, 88, 175, 199, 213
needs 168
regeneration 7
study 171
teachings 46
Sraffa, Piero 185
Sri Lanka 134
St. Augustine 202
Stability 11, 223
Stabilize demand 43
Stagnation xiii, 63, 66
State ownership 222
Statistical methods 32
Steady-state economics 66, 183
Steel 42
Structural fact 249
problem 159, 220, 222 - 224, 226, 256, 267
Structure 243–244, 246, 248-251, 254- 256, 259-262, 265-267, 269, 271, 273
, age *255*
, income 255
Structure of Science, The 241
Structure set 249
, wealth 255
Structures formation, process of 217
, relational 256
Subsidies 6, 66

, public working capital 225
Supply 42, 89, 112, 193
and demand 207
and demand, law of 7, 76
equal demand 67
, food 131, 215
Surplus of value 103
value 104, 105, 109, 149
Sustainable 40, 46, 48, 67, 128, 133, 168, 183, 185, 211
technology 40, 44 - 46, 51, 52, 177
Sweatshops 27, 141
Sweden 185, 225
Swiss bank 30
Synchronic xiv, 187
linguistics 187

T

Taiwan 24, 26
Taussig, Michel 135
Tautology 2, 8, 12
Taxation, theory and practice of 67
Taxes 21, 64, 95, 161, 199
Technai 49
Techno-optimism 46
Technology, appropriate 46
choice 40, 41, 44, 46, 48, 51
lead 60, 61, 64, 70
theories 83
Technostructure 49, 50–51, 62, 75
Temporary fix 106
Thatcher 63, 205
The End of Capitalism : a Feminist Critique of Politics 122, 139
The Second Industrial Divide: Possibilities for Prosperity 41
Theology 76
Theory of the Moral Sentiments 219
Third world 20, 24, 107, 109, 115, 128, 131, 133, 134, 137, 141, 146, 176, 205, 226
Thomas, St. 91
Tobin, tax 35, 223
Todd, John 40, 45
Tonnies, Ferdinand 10, 17
Toulmin, Stephen 101, 116
Trade deficit 58
Trade unions 108
Trading Industries, Trading Regions 58
Traditional Asian cultures 55
cultures 8, 12, 218
metaphysics 50
value rationality 70
Transformation 165, 170, 185, 193, 199, 205
movement 169
Transformative 198
Treadmill of growth 68, 82, 83, 120, 251, 280
Triangulating Peace 240, 270
True growth 67
Truth 237–243
TV 13, 40, 43, 52, 174

U

UAW 43
UN 14, 163, 223, 227
Underdevelopment 130, 133, 153
Understanding 241, 244, 270
Unemployment xiii, 12, 63, 205
, structural 34, 106
UNESCO 153, 179
Unions 142, 165, 172, 178
Unitas 178
United Steelworkers of America 144
Universal health care 185
Unpayable debt 159, 205
Untested feasibility 146, 203
US 24, 132, 139
deficit spending. 65
Department of Justice 144
dollar 44
economic hegemony 106
family values breakdown theory of 4
Federal Reserve bank 223
imports xiv

US industrial expansion 24, 132
rising inequality 225
tax laws 24
USAID 133
Use value 104, 112, 191, 192, 219
USSR 167
Utilitarianism 7
Utopian socialists 111

V

Value 104, 105, 185, 189
, commodity law of 191
exchange process 195
in exchange 219, 228, 258
in use 219, 220
Variables 32
Vereinigung 178
Vietnam war 31
Viner, Jacob 14
Violence 27, 41, 107, 111, 126, 193, 203, 207
Volcker, Paul 221

W

Wage labor 8, 70
Wages 153, 165, 181, 225
cut 214
, high 21, 68, 159, 185
kept low 21
, low 22, 24, 34, 58, 60, 129, 225, 222
, Ricardo's theory of 23
, tactics to raise 21
Wallerstein, Immanuel 83, 84, 160, 216
War system *263*
Waren 149
Water metaphor 96, 163
Wealth 7
Wealth of Nations, The 73, 163, 219
Weber, Max 72, 83
Welfare, a myth about 8
economics 7, 168
of the whole 46
state 199, 205
:2 47
Well disciplined labor *20*
Western civilization, the categories and cosmologies 202
Europe 133, 185
European social democracies 159
European welfare states 187, 200
Europe's welfare states 133
philosophy 49, 71, 136
Wittgenstein, Ludwig 11, 31, 209
Wolff, Richard 123
Women's rights 133
Working capital subsidy 225
Works and Days 49
World Bank 128, 130, 131, 133, 172, 194, 195, 216
Trade Organization, WTO 226
World's great religions 46
Worldview 10, 32, 33, 35, 37, 49, 69, 73, 194, 203, 213
WW II 24, 43, 61, 65, 130, 132, 199, 225

Z

Zweckrationalitat 73